# The South Caucasus 2021:

## Oil, Democracy and Geopolitics

**Fariz Ismailzade and Glen E. Howard, Editors**

STRATEJİ
ARAŞDIRMALAR
MƏRKƏZİ

**Center for Strategic Studies**
**Baku, Azerbaijan**

**The Jamestown Foundation**
**Washington, DC**

D1277633

THE JAMESTOWN FOUNDATION

Published in the United States by
The Jamestown Foundation
1111 16<sup>th</sup> Street NW
Suite 320
Washington, DC 20036
http://www.jamestown.org

For more information on this book of the Jamestown Foundation, email pubs@jamestown.org

ISBN 978-0-9816905-8-2

Cover art provided by Peggy Archambault of Peggy Archambault Design

# Jamestown's Mission

The Jamestown Foundation's mission is to inform and educate policy makers and the broader policy community about events and trends in those societies which are strategically or tactically important to the United States and which frequently restrict access to such information. Utilizing indigenous and primary sources, Jamestown's material is delivered without political bias, filter or agenda. It is often the only source of information which should be, but is not always, available through official or intelligence channels, especially in regard to Eurasia and terrorism.

Origins

Launched in 1984 after Jamestown's late president and founder William Geimer's work with Arkady Shevchenko, the highest-ranking Soviet official ever to defect when he left his position as undersecretary general of the United Nations, The Jamestown Foundation rapidly became the leading source of information about the inner workings of closed totalitarian societies.

Over the past two decades, Jamestown has developed an extensive global network of experts – from the Black Sea to Siberia, from the Persian Gulf to the Pacific. This core of intellectual talent includes scientists, journalists, scholars and economists. Their insight contributes significantly to policy makers engaged in addressing today's new and emerging global threats, including that from international terrorists.

# The Center for Strategic Studies' Mission

As a research and policy recommending institution dedicated to innovative studies on national, regional and international issues, Center for Strategic Studies (CSS; known by the acronym SAM in the Azerbaijani language) provides an intellectual forum for international dialogue in order to bring different views together and thereby contributing towards the formation of a common ground. The mission of CSS is to promote collaborative research, enhance the strategic debate and provide decision-makers with high-quality analysis and innovative proposals for action.

# CONTENTS

# THE CAUCASUS REGION

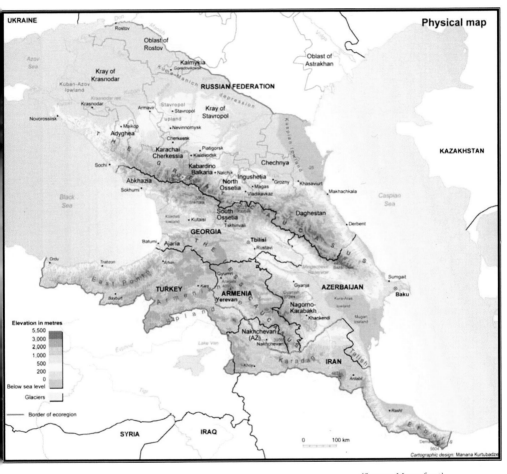

*(Source: Mapsof.net)*

# ABOUT THE BOOK

The socio-global processes, which occurred at the end of the 20$^{th}$ century – most notably the end of the Cold War, as well as the collapse of the totalitarian Soviet society and Warsaw Treaty Organization – resulted in a serious change in the political environment of international relations and in the emergence of a new geopolitical situation. After the collapse of the USSR, the new post-Soviet independent states immediately joined the international system and began a new foreign policy course that expressed their interests, thus resulting in the formation of a new order of global relations. Due to the collapse of the Soviet Union, the Caucasus has seen numerous crises since the region gained independence. Some of these crises have not yet been resolved.

The South Caucasus is a very important region where many powers such as neighboring countries Russia, Iran and Turkey, as well as superpowers, namely the US and the EU, are vying for political and economic influence. Today's energy issues play a significant role in a globalizing world. Therefore, many states are trying to strengthen their positions in the Caucasus and Caspian basin. The Caspian region plays a key role in the diversification of EU energy supplies, and it becomes increasingly obvious that the events in the Caucasus and Caspian region have the potential to impact European security. The EU and the US fully recognize that the Caspian Sea region influences European energy security.

Considering the aforementioned trends, the Center for Strategic Studies (CSS) decided to publish an edited volume entitled *The South Caucasus 2021: Oil, Democracy and Geopolitics*. CSS invited many outstanding local and foreign experts from the areas of international relations, political science, economics and sociology to participate in the book project. This publication, written between 2009 and 2010, aims to assemble the experts' views on specific regional issues such as economic, political and security prospects in the South Caucasus as well as evaluating the direction of future events in this critical part of the world.

*The South Caucasus 2021: Oil, Democracy and Geopolitics* addresses the most vital issues of the region, such as territorial conflicts, oil and natural gas resources, geopolitical complexities, pipeline politics, important analysis of the geopolitical risks for the next decades, geopolitics of the Caucasus-Caspian Basin, religion, demographic and migration prospects, and the policy course of the superpowers. Therefore, the book is essential reading for students and researchers of post-Soviet history and Caucasus studies, sociology, Caspian Sea politics, political science, international relations, as well as for experts in the areas of energy and economic issues.

# FOREWORD

**Ramiz Mehdiyev,**
*Doctor of Philosophy,*
*Professor, academician of the National*
*Academy of Sciences of Azerbaijan*

A retrospective of the 20 years of independence experienced by the countries of the South Caucasus clearly demonstrates the difficulties involved in building a state and restoring an economy after more than 70 years under a Soviet regime. Each one of the three post-Soviet republics of the South Caucasus – Azerbaijan, Georgia and Armenia – has chosen its own path of development; each is developing its own particular model of political, economic and socio-cultural transformation. The results are the subject of the research included in this book presented for the reader's judgment. Proceeding from the current financial and military-political positions of these states, an international group of foreign researchers has analysed the prospects for regional progress through the next decade. In 2021, Azerbaijan, Georgia and Armenia will celebrate 30 years as independent nations.

Forecasting future developments in situations, processes and tendencies is a thankless and complex task for any scientist or analyst; change in any region does not always occur at the same rate as transformations in the global alignment of forces. The South Caucasus is one of the few regions in the world that is consistently considered to be a priority on the daily international agenda. The geopolitical importance of this part of Eurasia keeps it on the table for discussions concerning global security, economic integration, the transit of hydrocarbons from the Caspian basin and new logistical arteries.

At the same time, the region exercises the minds of politicians and analysts as the venue for three ethno-territorial conflicts and a tangle of unresolved problems and offensives. These present daunting obstacles in the way of regional development which create additional problems for the realization of potential projects.

The region's conflicts began with the open occupation of 20 percent of Azerbaijani territory by Armenian forces between 1988 and 1994. Armenian aggression is the most serious threat to stability and safety in the South Caucasus, as the puppet regime generated by the self-proclaimed entity in Nagorno-Karabakh creates problems both for the further progressive development of Azerbaijan, the full realisation of its economic, political and human potential, and fulfilment for Armenia, which has become a mono-ethnic state serving as an advance post for Russia.

The continuation of these conflicts deprives the South Caucasus of its potential destiny as an effective and associated synergy of three republics in economic unity. Despite this, two of the region's states, Azerbaijan and Georgia, are participants in several large regional projects, such as the Baku-Tbilisi-Ceyhan oil pipeline, the Baku-Tbilisi-Erzurum main gas pipeline, and the historical transport corridor "the Great Silk Road," which connects Asia and Europe. Political stability, accomplished economic policies and the maturity of key sectors in the countries' economies generate conditions for the initiation of new geo-economic projects funded by the states. One such project is the Baku-Tbilisi-Akhalkalaki-Kars railway, financed by Azerbaijan and Turkey. The current project is an important segment of the "West-East" transport corridor and offers the prospect of connecting Beijing with Paris.

Significant opportunities open up for the South Caucasus in the development of transportation, information-communication technology, financial services, tourism, agriculture and other sectors. All these serve to enhance the well-being of the population and improve our citizens' standards of living.

Undoubtedly, the driver of economic development in the region is the Republic of Azerbaijan, which now represents two-thirds of the economy and demography of the South Caucasus. The country holds 30 billion dollars (2010) in currency reserves; more than Armenia and Georgia combined. The Azerbaijani economic model of development is already attracting the attention of international financial structures. Thus, intensive growth in the economy (9 percent growth in the national economy in 2009 in times of global financial crisis), the realization of large regional energy and transportation projects and economic diversification are the hallmarks of modern Azerbaijan. Investments by Azerbaijani companies into the Georgian economy have not only advanced Azerbaijan in regional leadership, but have also made an important contribution to the economic prosperity of the neighboring country, which in turn has brought the relationship between these two states and their peoples to a qualitatively different level.

The energy resources of the Caspian basin create a broad base for increased prosperity in the region. However, the irregular development of the states of the South Caucasus causes anxiety and concern. On the one hand, projects costing tens of billions of dollars are being realized in the region. On the other hand, Armenia is isolated and sits outside the joint economic projects because of the burden of aggression committed against its neighbour Azerbaijan and its unconstructive position adopted in the negotiating process within the OSCE's Minsk group since May 1994. By the end of 2010, Armenia's government debt had reached 50 percent of the country's real gross national product. Further, the region contains a number of semi-criminal regimes, internationally unrecognised, which are the results of open military actions. Armenia's unyielding position on the liberation of Azerbaijani lands and the use of those territories as transshipment points for drug trafficking and the creation of so-called "gray zones" raise obstacles to the fulfilment of intraregional integration.

It is absolutely clear that the road to effective and thorough development for the states hinges on peace and safety in the region. The South Caucasus is the common home of those who live there. I have no doubt that there will come a time when the South Caucasus will be a place of peace and dialogue, with mutual understanding between people and complementary cultures.

# Introduction:

# The Caucasus: Freed from Illusions, Freed to Seize Opportunities

**Dr. S. Frederick Starr**,
Chairman,
Central Asia-Caucasus Institute,
Paul H. Nitze School of Advanced International Studies (SAIS) of
Johns Hopkins University

Dear Reader:

You are about to read an important book on an urgent issue. The security of the Caucasus region is in a state of profound flux, as is the security of each of the three states that comprise the Central Caucasus. No one doubts that recent developments affecting each of the three countries separately and all three together are, with respect to security, "game changers." But which of these many developments are really the decisive ones, and just how do they alter the security situation on the ground? This is the first challenge that the editors set for the various participants in this effort.

Given the number and variety of recent shocks to the region, some kind of "geopolitical Richter Scale" is needed to measure their respective force. At least four major shocks must be evaluated. First, the lingering impact of Russia's 2008 war on Georgia, which did more to alter post-Soviet borders than any other event since 1991. Second, since 2008, Turkey, the US, and the countries of the EU have all changed the extent and nature of their engagement with the Caucasus, individually and together, and especially in the security sphere. To mention only one such shift, President Obama's ill-advised attempt to erase the legacy of the Armenian-Turkish tragedy of 1915 has now come and gone, but its own legacy in the Caucasus has yet to be evaluated. Third, the effects of the world economic crisis must be gauged for each of the three Caucasus economies, and for their status as participants or outsiders to the global economy. Fourth, sudden, transformative changes in both the supply and delivery of gas and oil are altering arrangements that have been in place for a decade, closing down some possibilities and opening up others. It is already clear that these shifts will redraw the world's energy map and alter the place of the Caucasus within it. Finally, less dramatic but inexorable and profound changes are taking place within the three societies and cultures of the Caucasus.

Clearly, the moment has arrived to take stock. True, each of these processes is still in progress, with none of them having run its course. Equally clear, their impact will be different on Azerbaijan, the country with by far the largest economy in the region and with three times the population of its Caucasus neighbors, Armenia and Georgia. But this, too, is part of the story. Bluntly, conceptions of security that have prevailed from the moment of independence are now in question. But it remains difficult, if not impossible, to discern the new paradigms that will replace them. This task, too, is part of the challenge that the editors set for the contributors.

How, then, should you, the reader, approach this book? Everyone will process the rich body of evidence – researched, written and compiled in 2009-2010, and presented here – in his or her own way. However, an approach that may enable you to discern the topography of the new geopolitical terrain is to focus first on the main drivers of change. Over several centuries, writers on the Caucasus have tended to focus their analysis on the role of external powers. This is natural, given the location of the region at the point of convergence of Iran, Russia, and Turkey. Further justification of this approach is the reality that the three Caucasus states are small, both in territory and population, ranking between 74th and 135th in the world on both indexes, and their immediate neighbors are far above them on both scales. The fact that the neighbors are all long-established sovereignties, with rich histories as imperial powers and facing difficult challenges in finding their own proper roles in a globalized world, further validates such an approach.

It is precisely the relations between the Caucasus states and neighboring countries, as well as with bigger powers, that further a field that is so problematic today. A decade ago it was fashionable to consider Russia and

Turkey mainly under the rubric of "pipeline politics" and Iran mainly as an ideological state. Now, each country's motives are more complex, combining elements of economics, geopolitics, and psychology. And while Europeans and Americans once focused on the sovereignty of the Caucasus states, today their concerns are both more diverse and more diluted.

Concerning the Americans, the recent record bespeaks a kind of "inadvertent disengagement." Verbal commitments to Georgia before and after the Russian war have not been matched by deeds. Washington had no ambassador in Baku for more than a year, blindly neglected to consult with President Aliyev when it was in the throes of negotiating with Turkey and Armenia, and then failed to include Azerbaijan in a meeting on nuclear arms while including both of the other two Caucasus states. A hastily arranged letter by President Obama to President Aliyev and visits from the US Secretaries of Defense and State acknowledged that relations had gone off the tracks, but were short on concrete steps to right them. Meanwhile, Yerevan also suffered from US policy, when the Obama initiative to open Armenia's border with Turkey failed.

Nor were relations between Turkey and the Caucasus any better. First, when the Russian army attacked Georgia, Turkey made minimal objections. Then, the Erdogan government showed a disconcerting eagerness to ignore its commitment to link any opening to Armenia with a withdrawal of Armenian forces from occupied Karabakh. After playing along with the Obama initiative with Armenia, it suddenly reversed course and passively allowed the project to collapse in Parliament. All the while, Turkey was working with Moscow to organize a Caucasus Stabilization and Economic Cooperation Platform that excluded Europe and America. And to make matters worse, the Islamist AKP Party cast doubt on Turkey's continued commitment to the ideal of a secular state, which is a bulwark of all Turkic governments in Azerbaijan and Central Asia.

Russia's use of arms to detach two Georgian territories sent a clear message to both Azerbaijan and Armenia, namely, that it is prepared to resort to military action to impose a "zone of privileged interest" throughout the region. The three Caucasus countries did not fail to notice that Putin was exploiting his improved relations with both Ankara and Washington to further this end. As for Iran, it proved to be either unwilling or unable to provide its partner, Armenia, with easy access to the outside world when Russian action closed Armenia's access through Georgia. In Azerbaijan, Teheran continued its low-level support for those Azerbaijani Shiites who favored Khomeini's formula for relations between religion and the state. Finally, the EU under President Sarkozy should receive some credit for bringing the Georgian war to an end, but it quickly forgot the aid commitments it announced at its September 1, 2008 summit. Indecisiveness regarding energy exports through the Caucasus and lack of a serious response when Russia brushed aside both EU and OSCE observer missions after the Georgian war seemed to further marginalize Europe's role. The EU subsequently announced its intention of forging a new policy with the Caucasus, but to date this remains, like the Obama administration's analogous statements, without practical results.

Are there common elements in these various recent maneuvers by external powers regarding the Caucasus? Each reader will have to decide for him or herself. However, it appears that all of them have shown an unseemly willingness to make deals affecting the Caucasus over the heads of the Caucasus states.

How have the Caucasus states dealt with these unwelcome developments? Since the dawn of their independence, all three have tried to meet their security needs through a close alignment with a single external power, either the US or Russia. An important question posed by the authors of this book is whether events have invalidated this tactic. If so, then what alternatives are left to Yerevan, Tblisi and Baku? The obvious alternative was pioneered by Kazakhstan in 2007 under its Foreign Minister, Kassym-Jomart Tokayev: a strategy based on balancing positive relations with all the major external players. Resembling the 19th century concept of a "concert," this "multi-vectored" approach allows a relatively weak state to deftly manipulate good relations with external actors in such a way as to maintain the highest possible degree of sovereignty and independence. Is this the future for the three states of the Central Caucasus? The following essays provide rich material in order to evaluate this hypothesis.

One thing is certain: a strategy based on alignment or one based on balance enables external powers to play the three Caucasus states against each other. This can only be harmful to the long-term interests and viability of the

Central Caucasus states themselves, and of the region. Is there a solution to this "Rubik's Cube?"

The answer lies in the ability of Armenia, Azerbaijan and Georgia to identify and act upon their common interests. The history of the past two decades is not encouraging in this respect. True, Azerbaijan and Georgia have often found a common language, and Armenia has at times been able to act in consort with Georgia. But like post-colonial countries elsewhere, all three have been so single-mindedly focused on buttressing their individual sovereignties that collaborative initiatives have been rare or nonexistent. Is this changing? Several chapters of this book provide intriguing insights on this issue. Professor Gerard Libaridian wisely reminds us of parallel developments in the recent history of the three new states, and even moments when common concerns briefly dominated. Other authors suggest commonalities in areas as diverse as the transport of goods and energy, economic reform, and rural development. Freer trade with Europe, parallel efforts to make their militaries NATO-compatible and WTO membership are collective interests of those sharing a "common home in the Caucasus." Yet the asymmetries remain, and in some areas are widening. Suffice it to note that Azerbaijan's population is expanding and growing younger while Georgia's is shrinking and Armenia's is ageing.

Looming over all these issues and hampering the recognition and embrace of common concerns is the unresolved issue of Karabakh. The pages that follow offer no solution to this complex and stubborn problem but they do enable the reader to approach it with fresh eyes. Reading this volume, one cannot help but ask the naïve but crucial question: "Why have the positive incentives to finding a solution to the Karabakh problem fallen so far short of the need?" Each reader will want to answer this for him or herself, drawing on the insights from diverse fields and disciplines. In the end, the "dismal science" of economics may provide the most useful way of framing the question: "Why have none of the participants or their well-wishers abroad, paused to calculate the opportunity cost of allowing the Karabakh question to remain unresolved?"

Cynics are quick to point out that some or all members of the OSCE's Minsk Group may have had a practical interest in allowing the issue to fester indefinitely. But, to the extent this is true, those opposing or delaying a solution have never been confronted with a serious estimate of the opportunity cost of inaction. This volume can be seen as a source book for anyone seeking to estimate the nature and scale of these foregone benefits. Some are purely national, denying to each country valuable opportunities and rich resources. Others are regional, preventing the three states from taking common action in areas that vitally affect their interests. And still others are global, creating hazards for the entire international community and retarding the development of a Caucasus security regime from which all would benefit. If this volume contributes to a deeper and more realistic understanding of the opportunity cost of the continuing conflict over Karabakh, its editors and authors can have the satisfaction of knowing that their arduous effort has not been in vain.

# PART ONE:

## INTERNAL DEVELOPMENTS AND PROSPECTIVE CHANGES

# RELIGION IN THE CENTRAL CAUCASUS: CURRENT STATE AND FUTURE TRENDS

Elmir Guliyev,
Senior Research Fellow,
Institute of Strategic Studies of the Caucasus

## Introduction

Sandwiched between Europe and Asia and linking the Eastern-Christian civilization with the Islamic world, the Central Caucasus (CC)[1] unites dozens of peoples who speak various languages and profess different religions. Simultaneously similar and disparate, Armenia, Georgia and Azerbaijan have learned to co-exist while each is on an ever-lasting quest for self-determination and supremacy. To reach this goal, they strive to obtain political stability and foster military-political and trade-economic links with the powerful neighboring states. This situation mirrors ancient times when Caucasian Albania tried to form alliances with Persia and the Byzantine Empire, particularly during the Middle Ages, leaving the destiny of the Caucasus dependent on mighty neighbors.

The same circumstances occured in the 18th-19th centuries, when Georgian Tsars and several Azerbaijani khans aimed to gain the protection of Tsarist Russia. Presently, the political establishments of Azerbaijan, Georgia and Armenia have actively sought a reliable ally such as the US and have tried to tear down Russia's geopolitical firewall. Forging relationships with Europe

---

[1] According to the structure of the Caucasian region proposed by Eldar Ismailov, Azerbaijani scholar and Director of the Institute of Strategic Studies of the Caucasus, it is expedient to consider Azerbaijan, Georgia and Armenia as parts of the Central Caucasus and not the South Caucasus. Accordingly, the regions of Turkey adjacent to these three states or the North-Western *ostans* of Iran form the South-Eastern Caucasus. Such an approach substantiates the model of political and economic integration of the Caucasus in the format of "three plus one" including three countries of the Central Caucasus as well as neighboring regional powers such as Russia, Turkey and Iran. See for details: Исмаилов Э. Новый регионализм на Кавказе: концептуальный подход // Кавказ и глобализация. Том 1 (1), 2006, p. 7-26.

define all three states' external policies. However, the resolution of this task is marred by the political rivalry between them and the interests of many countries interconnected with the Caucasus, which is located at different civilizations' "junctures." Russia badly needs to remain influential in the Central Caucasus to maintain its territorial integrity and substantiate its claims to being a global power. The United States and its Western European partners consider the Central Caucasus as a transport corridor linking Europe with Central Asia, thus providing an alternative to the transit monopoly of Russia. As far as Iran and Turkey are concerned, the fight for influence in the region is not only a continuation of the competition to be a leader in the Muslim Ummah, but a way to increase their role in global projects.

The battle for the Eurasian Balkans (as wisely put by geopolitical scholar and former US National Security Advisor Zbigniew Brzezinski) becomes fiercer due to the potential reshaping of the political map into a "New" Middle East. The source of inner tension in the Caucasus derives from interrelated ethnic contradictions and historic offences due to territorial claims. Differences between various factions bring particular color to these situations and influence the order of geopolitical forces.

Religion has traditionally influenced the political processes of the Caucasus while its importance has transcended the ethnic and economic factors during various time frames. Following the accession of Vachagan III the Noble, Tsar of Albania to the throne (487-510), the bloody and uncompromised struggle against fire worshippers and pagans was used to unite all people around the Albanian Church.[2] During the 15th-16th centuries, religion played a special role in the destiny of Azerbaijan's Turkic tribes mobilized under the Shia banner by favoring the Safavis in power. Christianity left its imprint on the political preferences of Georgian rulers who leaned toward any alliance with Byzantium and later, Russia in their fight against Muslim neighbors. Armenian settlers in the Caucasus used their spiritual proximity with the Russians to infiltrate administrative

---

[2] Father Alexy (Nikonorov). История христианства в Кавказской Албании <http://baku.eparhia.ru/history/albania/christianity/vachagan_iii/>.

mechanisms and use Imperial resources in line with their ethnic and cultural ideas[3].

In the modern period, the religious factor is used to lobby national interests within regional and international organizations, while its impact on the foreign policies of the states in the Central Caucasus is less visible. Ethnic conflicts in the region have no religious grounds in spite of efforts by external forces. At the same time, the element of religion has undergone serious changes within the last twenty years by becoming increasingly prominent in internal political processes. Furthermore, it is used by external forces to promote political and cultural agendas. In brief, the importance of religion for the future of the region should not be underestimated. In this article, we will attempt to track religious development in the Central Caucasus and estimate its impact on important regional and global projects.

## Relations Between State and Confessions: Twenty Years of Religious Freedom

After gaining sovereignty, the states of the Central Caucasus embarked on their secular, democratic way of development. However, guidelines on this pathway still remained unclear at the beginning of the 1990s. Intensive transformation of public ideals has led to social and cultural uncertainty and freethinking with no limits. "The Soviet" man has plunged deep into an identity crisis: the number of social categories used to define the Soviet era man and his place inside society seemed to lose their boundaries and values[4]. The diffusion of religious and quasi-religious studies caused the rejection of the Communist idea which used to replace the religious ethics with "natural" norms of behavior. The public blame on atheism has become so visible that politicians and public figures have started to respect religious traditions that ironically contradict their atheistic convictions. The liberalization of social and economic relationships has uncovered "the loneliness" of contemporary man, while moral nihilism has challenged the religion as a way to perceive the world. The inability of the elite to unite citizens around common cultural and political ideas has led to the

---

[3] Лурье С.В. Историческая этнология
<http://www.gumer.info/bibliotek_Buks/History/Lyrie/67.php>.
[4] Андреева Г. М. Психология социального познания. М.: Аспент Пресс, 2000, p. 187.

atomization of society. The formation of larger ethnic and cultural communities has also been marred by the processes of global exchanges, which involved the Central Caucasus at the crossroads of the 20th and 21st centuries. To summarize, post-Soviet societies have started a phase of social disintegration where the attitude toward religion is not the least one in the process. Traditional religious institutions now have a chance to bring back their lost influence and take part in nation building processes. However, the prospect of an "open society" and free competition with other confessions has been perceived by the clergy as a danger to their own social position and identity. Fearing changes and not prepared to open up a dialogue, the clergy has preferred to play the role of legitimate support to national traditions by gaining the confidence of the larger masses.

Meanwhile, the social playground of post-Soviet states has been and continues to be an attractive one for the syncretic and universalistic sects as well as the psychotherapeutic and neo-pagan cults. Taking advantage of some parts of the population who distrust the official clergy, non-traditional movements shape their propagation using social and religious protests. Quite contrasting in their ideas and social settings, they differ in their high level of theological and social activities from dominating religions and their attitude toward the social and political order. Making an intensive impact on people, they allow their supporters to feel the influx of positive emotions. As people feel an increased sense of self-confidence, they cut off all links with "the past." The multifaceted content of tasks and methods used by the cults makes them preferable to the dominant traditions, which ask for patience and compassion to maintain the existing order. In this case, one can note the particular attractiveness of liberal protestant churches adapting easily to ever-changing conditions, tolerating relativity in relation to many ethical norms and combining the religious service with the elements of mass culture.

At the turn of the century, clashes between traditional and non-traditional religions engendered discussions about the importance of spiritual traditions, boundaries of freedom of faith and challenges of cultural globalization. Leaders of the Central Caucasian states attempt to appease confrontations between the official clergy and non-traditional movements at the expense of the legitimization of hegemony on one side and the reduction of protests on the other. In this regard, attitudes toward non-traditional religions remain a specific indicator of democratic transformations while the analysis of general trends in interactions between confessions can be useful in foreseeing the political, social and cultural development of the region.

## Azerbaijan: Secularity Against "Political Islam"

In Azerbaijan, the authorities evenly distance themselves from all types of confessional groups and religious organizations. The Law on the Freedom of Faith does not envisage the interference of public agencies into the internal affairs of communities and the delegation of functions from some branches of power. According to R. Mehdiyev, the principal commitment to the secular model of statehood suggests the realization of the freedom of faith taking into account the diversity of religious forms and ensures favorable conditions "for positive and non-confrontational development of religious life in the country and a fostering of stability in Azerbaijani society."[5]

In the 1990s, the liberal character of legislation and non-interference of the State has favored various types of missionary organizations infiltrating Azerbaijan. Steered from foreign centers and often supported at the diplomatic level, some communities used to advocate convictions and ideas that disintegrated the social structure of society. While dealing with problems caused by the collapse of Soviet economy and Armenian occupation, the State has tolerated all social conflicts with a religious background and prevented only the attempts of abuses of freedom of faith by political forces, totalitarian sects and extremist groups. The wait-and-see position taken by authorities has allowed religious movements to use their masked potential and demonstrate its compatibility (or lack of compatibility) with the social and cultural environment.

In the course of recent years, the situation has changed inside the country by defining the main priorities in the State-confession relationship: the creation of conditions to meet religious needs; ensuring an understanding between confessions; and the prevention of destructive influences. Some

---

[5] Мехтиев Р. На пути к демократии: размышляя о наследии. Баку: «Şərq-Qərb», 2007, p. 585.

efforts are made to organize religious awareness campaigns and competitive professional theological courses. Though the results obtained are far from satisfactory, the State tries to add a constructive color to the religious processes. For this reason, changes have been inserted into the Law on the Freedom of Faith. According to these changes, Muslim religious rites and ceremonies can only be led by the citizens of Azerbaijan who have had a religious education in the country. This progressive step is seen in the recent issuing of a license to the Baku Islam University to run educational activities in higher education. Since then, the admission of students and PhDs is done on the basis of a common test organized by the State Students Admission Commission. Graduates of this institution obtain their state diplomas upon completion of their studies.

Underlining the historic importance of tolerance, the authorities demonstrated their readiness to co-operate with all traditional confessions. This is also reflected in the statements from the head of state related to religious communities inside the country on the occasions of Muslim, Christian and Jewish holidays, as well as budgetary support for projects that reconstruct and restore religious monuments, thus creating conditions for supporting the cultural and religious identity of ethnic minorities. At the same time, the specific patterns of confessional composition require the authorities to pay closer attention to the problems of Muslims, who constitute almost 96 percent of population.

The Muslim communities that passed the state registration are united under the Caucasus Muslim Board (CMB). According to the Law on the Freedom of Faith, the mentioned structure enjoys the status of being the historical center of Muslims in the country and the registration of Muslim communities is done only with its written notification (Article 12). The attitude of the society toward the CMB is not quite ambiguous and some public figures deem this structure as the remnant of an Imperial system that does not meet modern requirements.[6] Nevertheless, the CMB coordinates the activities of Muslim organizations in the country and favors inter-religious dialogue. The Sheikh-Ul-Islam Allahshukur Pashazadeh, the Chairman of the CMB, used the means of popular diplomacy for the

---

[6] Интервью председателя Центра по защите свободы совести и вероисповедания DEVAMM И. Ибрагимоглу агентству «Новости-Азербайджан», 9 September 2008 <http://www.newsazerbaijan.ru/exclusive/20080909/42476974.html>.

settlement of the Armenian-Azerbaijani Nagorno Karabakh conflict and supports the idea of the participation of religious leaders in the peace process. In April 2008, he created the initiative with the late Patriarch of Moscow and All Russia Alexy II to establish the Consultative Council of Religions under the United Nations, which would ensure the effective interaction of religious organizations and peacekeeping structures.

However, the popularity of Sheikh-Ul-Islam Pashazadeh at the global level does not compensate for the low activity of his structure inside the country. Executive authorities and judiciary institutions do not always heed the appeals of the CMB when making decisions related to the interests of Muslims. This is also seen in recent decisions taken by the courts upon the demolition of two half-constructed mosques in the Surakhany and Yasamal regions of Baku. This act was criticized at the XII[th] Congress of the CMB held in August 2009.[7] Multifaceted religious processes inside Azerbaijani society and the world require the more active participation of the CMB in religious education. A more effective human resources policy can be managed by attracting young theologian specialists and refreshing confidence among believers.

The opposition to official Islam is felt among the Shia communities of pro-Iranian orientation; Sunnis-Salafis of orthodox affiliation; Nursists, followers of Said Nursi, the Kurdish-Turkish specialist of theology; and some Sufi tarekats. Among the latter, followers of Nakshbandy Sheikh Osman Nuri Topbash (Turkey) are active particularly in the capital and various regions of the country. Meanwhile, supporters of Avar Sheikh Said-efendi Chirkeevsky (Dagestan) are seen mainly in northern and northwestern parts. Some members of the Jamaat Tablig movement, who actively practiced during the mid-'90s, are practically idle today and do not impact the current religious situation in the country.

Among non-traditional movements of the non-Islamic affiliation, the most active ones are the Protestant Churches (Baptists, Adventists, Pentecostals, and Jehovah's Witnesses), the Roman Catholic Church, the Krishna Consciousness Movement, and the Baha'ist community followers.[8] Their

---

[7] Зеркало, 13 August 2009.
[8] It is thought that the following religions are traditional in Azerbaijan: Shia *Mazhab* (*Jafarit*) and Sunni *Mazhab* (*the Shafiites* and *the Hanifis*); Orthodoxy and Judaism. In recent years, the

converts are not subjected to public ostracism. Nevertheless, their missionary activities cause societal concerns because they do not accept national traditions, which can serve sometimes as a reason for social conflicts. Antagonism of some protestant groups with a dominating social and cultural paradigm is seen more clearly in their specific attitude toward the armed conflict with Armenia.[9]

During the last two decades, non-traditional and independent religious communities have succeeded in significantly increasing the number of social supporters. While the official clergy does not make an effort to help develop the spiritual upbringing of the population, there are independent missionaries and a considerable number of Azerbaijani citizens who received their religious education abroad. These people proselytize enthusiastically without having any support from the state; they face legal and organizational difficulties, which increase their popularity among the discontented.

The contradictory nature of the current situation is explained by the fact that independent missionaries using freedom of faith are not responsible for the social consequences of their activities. In the mid-1990s, there were few familial or economic conflicts with a religious impetus; however, in recent years, religious convictions are often used for organizing criminal activities. On the 17th of August 2008, a bloody terrorist act was perpetrated at the Juma Mosque in the Narimanov region of Baku (it is known among the local people as Abu Bakr Mosque). This event resulted in the death of two Azerbaijani citizens. The reaction of the authorities was immediate when the activities of the Abu Bakr Mosque were stopped by the court. This

---

Roman Catholic Church has been added to these mazhabs. Nevertheless, there are some protestant churches, which aspire to be traditional faiths (such as Baptists, Lutherans), who started to come to Azerbaijan as Catholics in the 19th century. Besides that, followers of the Albanian Apostolic Church have been living historically in the territory of Azerbaijan. Currently, their religious traditions are revived by *Udins*. The community of *Molokans* – Spiritual Christians – has been living in Azerbaijan for almost two centuries. They have been settled in Transcaucasia at the basis of the Decree signed by the Emperor Nicholas I. The Baha'i faith is being advocated in Azerbaijan practically since the year of 1863 when Mirza Hussain Ali (*Bahaulla*) declared himself as the "Promised." In this article, we treat these religious groups as non-traditional ones due to their specific form of religion differing from the dominant contemporary religions.

[9] See: Quluzadə M. Dinimizi qorumaq hamımızın borcudur // Dövlət və din. İctimai fikir toplusu, № 1 (5), 2008, p. 54.

Mosque had been the place of ideological clashes between the moderate Salafis and the radical Kharijites. In order to prevent religious intolerance, the authorities decided to undertake decisive measures to stop any law violations in the field of freedom of faith. Tougher control resulted in the destruction of two "illegally built" mosques which caused a huge public outcry. In May and June of 2009, Azerbaijan's parliament, the Milli Majlis, adopted other amendments to the Law on the Freedom of Faith. It was aimed at minimizing external influence and toughening countermeasures against illegal religious activities.

Despite these steps, the general attitude of the state toward independent and non-traditional communities remains restrained and less than adequate. The authorities demonstrate their readiness to communicate with all religious organizations, which are loyal to the secular principles and respect the religious-spiritual traditions of the Azerbaijani people. The country's leadership has a clear understanding that the state policy on freedom of faith and expansion of links with leading confessions should not infringe on the rights of citizens for freedom of faith and religion. However, the format of a future relationship between the state and confessions in Azerbaijan is not clear at present. It is evident that the return of the permissiveness that reigned at the end of the past century in Azerbaijan is not expected. The liberalization of the religious sphere led to the activation of independent Muslim communities, which formed several radical groups. In addition, this could mobilize Muslim organizations into a common religious and political community and increase their role in political life. In its turn, it will increase the influence of Iran and Turkey and weaken the position of Russia; the West and Israel, on the other hand, will not be content with the role of external observers. This substantiates well-founded concerns about the politicization of Islam in Azerbaijan, which could lead to political destabilization throughout the whole region.

Conversely, it is unlikely that the leadership of Azerbaijan will opt for the limitation of religious freedom, since it could negatively impact democratic changes as a whole and undermine the confidence of democratic institutions. The prevention of a natural transition from atheistic ideology to traditional religion will increase corruption, devalue morals and undermine the national idea. Besides that, the marginalization of opposition groups could make them an easy target for religious extremism.

In this author's opinion, increasing control over the religious sphere through supporting traditional confessions, developing inter-religious dialogue and creating conditions to run religious and educational activities would be most constructive. However, while paying particular attention to traditional religion, it is important to note its degree of compatibility with the general course of public development. Traditional studies favor the protection of civil solidarity particularly in a period of social hardship. But, it is not so suitable for fast developing societies oriented to absorb and perceive progressive ideas and technology. Many religious leaders and theologians understand the necessity of critical revision of well-rooted religious traditions (while there is a wide spectrum of different opinions related to the acceptable limits of reforms). The prospect of Islamic modernization is also being discussed by influential Azerbaijani politicians[10]. Nevertheless, for the time being, the reformist approach remains a very unpopular one among Muslims. Therefore, the role of religion in the public life of Azerbaijan depends on the ability of religious leaders to modernize Muslim traditions by turning the religious institutions into bearers of progressive ideas and moderators of public conscience.

**Georgia: Between a Liberal Project and Orthodox Nationalism**

In contrast with Azerbaijan, where the religious communities have a marginal position, in Georgia the Orthodox Church plays a significant role in public and political life. In the second half of the 1990s, when there was a deep political, social and economic crisis, the Orthodox Church of Georgia (OCG) used significant resources to maintain the country's religious and political solidarity. Though Church popularity never fully recovered after the Soviet era, Georgian politicians and public figures demonstrated publicly their commitment to the Church traditions. On the 30th of March 2001, the Parliament of Georgia adopted a Constitutional law, which underlined the exclusive role of the OCG in the history of the country and voiced the possibility of establishing a concordat between Church and State. On October 14, 2002, the Constitutional Agreement was signed between the State of Georgia and the Georgian Apostolic Autocephalous Orthodox Church. It was ratified practically unanimously. Thus, Georgia became the

---

[10] See, for example: Mehdiyev R. Qloballaşma dövründə dövlət və cəmiyyət. *Azərbaycan* newspaper, 25 September 2007.

first state in the post-Soviet territory where the relations between the state and religious organization were regulated by a Constitutional agreement.

According to the concordat, the state recognized the OCG as the agent of public power acting in the interest of the whole Georgian society with Orthodox monks enjoying specific rights. In particular, the Catholicos-Patriarch has immunity. Furthermore, Church monks were neither drafted to the army nor forced to divulge information acquired from confessions. Also, the State recognized Church marriages and ensured the creation of pastors in military bases, prisons and penitentiary places. OCG was given a larger role in the sphere of education and the elective course of religion was organized at secondary schools.

At the same time, the State recognized all Orthodox churches, monasteries, ruins, relevant land plots and the Church treasury in the country as the property of the Church (excluding those under private property) under state protection. The Church property was exempted from land and property taxes and could not be confiscated from the Church. Additionally, the State promised to partially compensate the damage done to the Church during the period of independence in the 19th-20th centuries.[11]

The Constitutional agreement ensured a great privilege to the OCG ahead of other institutions, which could not even establish legal relations with the state until recently. The Civil Code of Georgia (1997) defined these organizations as the juridical person of public law, while the Law on the Juridical Persons of Public Law (1999) did not envisage any procedure for the registration of religious organizations. The situation changed after the adoption of amendments to the Civil Code in April 2005, when religious organizations received the right to be registered under the non-commercial juridical law of public law. However, this situation is not satisfactory to many religious organizations. Thus, the Armenian Apostolic Church (AAC), the Roman Catholic Church, the Evangelist-Lutheran Church and the Baptist Church of Georgia refused the state registration and demanded either the adoption of a special Law on religious organizations (currently, there is no such law in Georgia) or the establishment of simple contractual

---

[11] Non-official translation of the Constitutional agreement between Georgia and the Orthodox Church of Georgia is available in Russian at the portal Православие.ru: <http://www.pravoslavie.ru/cgi-bin/sykon/client/display.pl?sid=364&did=825>.

relations (not the constitutional agreements) between the State and all religious organizations[12].

The intensive "collaboration" between the authorities and the Orthodox Church created concern for Georgian liberals. The concordat relations were established when the political leadership of the country had been strongly discredited in public. The then head of state Eduard Shevardnadze favored the Patriarchate trying to convince the Orthodox believers and religious nationalists. However, after the Rose Revolution, the priorities of the authorities changed, and the corporate interests of the OCG did not coincide with the political policy aimed at strengthening democratic institutions and liberalizing the religious sphere. The result was the Catholics-Patriarch Iliya II's proposal, on the eve of the parliamentary and presidential elections of 2007, to restore the Monarchy Rule of the Bagrationi Dynasty.[13] Prince David Ghiorghievich, the head of the dynasty, has Georgian citizenship and serves the sub deacon of the Catholics-Patriarch.

The biggest resistance to Georgian liberals is from the Orthodox nationalists who have significant influence in the Synod. In 1997, the OCG left the World Church Council and the Conference of European Churches under their pressure. On the 18th of August 2003, the Synod announced that the anti-church activities of pro-Western liberals "could become a reason for serious confrontation in society." It is noted in the protocol of the meeting of the Synod that political, economic and cultural integration with the West, any form of dialogue with non-Orthodox confessions, as well as the neglect of Church traditions under the pretext of democracy and freedom of expression are unacceptable for Orthodox believers.[14]

Following the August 2008 Russian-Georgian War, the relations between the Georgian authorities and the Patriarchate were strained further. The entourage of the head of state was concerned that the efforts of the OCG to foster religious ties between the people of Russia and Georgia serve Russian

---

[12] Независимая газета, 14 April 2001.
[13] <http://www.religare.ru/article46333.htm>.
[14] Белякова Н.А. Очерк религиозной ситуации в Грузии <http://www.ia-centr.ru/archive/public_details084d.html?id=46>.

interests.[15] It appeared that the OCG was obliged to reject publicly the accusations of favoring the interests of foreign states. "As neutral as the Church of Georgia is in its relations with internal political forces, it is more actively involved as the guarantor of solidarity between the Georgian nation and territorial integrity of Georgia in foreign policy processes," says the statement of the Patriarchate.[16]

The relationship of the OCG and other confessions is not simple inside the country. The missionary activities of non-traditional groups, particularly in Georgian ethnic environments, are perceived very negatively. Annual reports of the People's Protector of Georgia, the US State Department and international organizations note attacks on the representatives of minorities by different public figures and politicians.[17] Religious discrimination is observed also at secondary schools where those schoolchildren not professing the Orthodox faith or refusing to attend the religion history courses are subjected to pressure from teachers or schoolmates.[18]

In 1999-2004, followers of the excommunicated monk Basil Mkalavishvili committed acts of violence in the country. This monk was sentenced to six years of imprisonment for organizing many crimes against the representatives of minorities. In July 2008, on the eve of the war in South Ossetia, he was freed early and resumed his religious activities in the church where he served before. Another religious figure called Paata Bluashvili, the head of the Djvari organization was accused of being involved in many religious violent attacks. He has been on the run since 2007. In May 2007, the European Court for Human Rights in Strasbourg acknowledged numerous violations of the European Human Rights Convention against 97

---

[15] Колодин К. Саакашвили записался в антиклерикалы
<http://www.izvestia.ru/georgia1/article3132814/>.
[16] Statement of the Georgian Patriarchate from 5 September 2009
<http://www.patriarchate.ge/_en/?action=news_show&mode=news&id=98>.
[17] See, for example: European Commission against Racism and Intolerance. Second Report on Georgia (June 2006)
<http://hudoc.ecri.coe.int/XMLEcri/ENGLISH/Cycle_03/03_CbC_eng/GEO-CbC-III-2007-2-ENG.pdf>.
[18] Human Rights Centre. State of freedom of religion in Georgia since the adoption of Constitutional Agreement between Government and the Orthodox Church of Georgia. Religious freedom report (April 2008)
<http://www.humanrights.ge/admin/editor/uploads/pdf/ReligionReport.pdf>.

members of the Gldan congregation of Jehovah's Witnesses and recommended that Georgia pay compensation to the victims.[19]

According to the Department for Human Rights under the General Attorney's Office of Georgia and the Apparatus of the People's Protector of Georgia monitoring the religious situation in the country, during the last three years, there has been a tendency to downplay religious discrimination. In January 2008, President Mikheil Saakashvili in his second inaugural address underlined the necessity of maintaining tolerance. Representatives of several religious minorities were invited to the inauguration ceremony.[20] Nevertheless, law enforcement bodies do not make the necessary efforts to reveal violations of religious freedom and do not always undertake the relevant measures against people involved in such legal violations.

We can assume that the tense political situation in Georgia and the uncertain geopolitical prospects do not allow the current authorities to be in open confrontation with the OCG. Possibly, the situation will change and the Saakashvili administration will obtain real achievements in talks about NATO membership or resolving ethnic and political conflicts. But, we cannot forget that the Georgian identity is closely linked to Orthodoxy, and the Church effectively uses the political situation to strengthen its position. Currently, the anti-Russian mood of the authorities are in contradiction with the anti-West rhetoric of the OCG, and the future of State-Church relations in the country depends on how the political and religious elite will be able to synchronize these contradictory trends.

**Armenia: No Hint at Refusal of Great Power Aspirations**

The specific format of Armenia's State-Church relationship is that the ethnic self-consciousness is identified fully with the religious one. Therefore, the Armenian Apostolic Church traditionally fulfills not only the function of a spiritual mentor, but protects the political interests of the Armenian elite. The Constitution of the country recognizes "the exclusive mission of the AAC as the national church in the religious life of the

---

[19] <http://www.kavkaz-uzel.ru/newstext/news/id/1185797.html>.
[20] See: Bureau of Democracy, Human Rights, and Labor, US Department of State. International Religious Freedom Report 2008: Georgia (2008) <http://www.state.gov/g/drl/rls/irf/2008/108447.htm>.

Armenian people and the development of its culture and protection of national identity" and admits the legislative regulation of relations between State and Church (Article 8.1). The importance of the Church in establishing and protecting the Armenian nation is also underlined in the preamble of the Law on the Freedom of Faith and Religious Organizations. At the same time, a concordat between the State and AAC has not been established yet.

On the March 17, 2000, the Memorandum on Mutual Understanding was signed between the Government of the Republic of Armenia and the Armenian Apostolic Church, envisaging the establishment of such relations. The document reflects the intentions of both sides to solve problems related to the property of the AAC, defines tax privileges, allocates a priority place to the Church in the state run media and cultural-educational programs, creates conditions to expand Apostolic studies in military bases, remand prisons, prisons, etc. However, principal differences between the sides on various issues prevented a finalized document from being written. It was again impossible during the next nine month period.

The conformist position of the Armenian clergy does not always coincide with the political course of the authorities who are interested in expanding relations with the West. On the one hand, the AAC as "the national" Church tries to maintain the religious homogeneity of Armenians and use it for the political mobilization of the population. On the other hand, it is obliged to ensure the cultural background for the strategic partnership of Armenia with Russia and the Euro-Atlantic integration of Armenia. The last issue puts Echmiadzin in an embarrassing situation due to the fact that Protestant groups are actively proselytizing. Besides this, the rapprochement between the AAC and the Armenian Catholic Church could lead to the loss of Church identity by the AAC. Indeed, this identity helps it play an integrating function. Today, the doctrine about the Supremacy of the Pope is the only reason which impedes the fusion of the two churches[21].

---

[21] Фейган Дж., Шипков А. Армянский конкордат
<http://www.archipelag.ru/ru_mir/religio/gko/questions/armenian-concordat/>.

At the same time, Echmiadzin is gradually expanding its sphere of activities. There are 30 chaplains acting as the basis of Field Spiritual Service Regulations in the Armed Forces. In August 2009, the government of Armenia granted graduates of religious schools the option to defer military service. Starting in 2005, the obligatory course of the History of the Armenian Church was inserted into the curricula of secondary schools. The Ministry of Education and Science jointly with the Center for Religious Educations of the AAC participate in the preparation of relevant educational materials. As a result, the European Commission against Racism and Intolerance has recommended several times to the government of Armenia to exclude from educational materials any data supporting fixed stereotypes against the followers of other religions and insulting the feelings of children of other religious minorities[22].

The situation with other confessions acting in Armenia and the attitude of the State and society toward these organizations are not homogenous. According to various data, the Armenian Catholic community has between 100 thousand and 180 thousand members,[23] and supports friendly relations with Echmiadzin, but experiences huge organizational difficulties. The Catholics have neither a religious school, nor their own temple. They organize their religious rites in Chapel. The Russian Orthodox Church is represented by four registered organizations. Two more Orthodox parishes are facing registration problems.[24] In general, the Armenian authorities value highly their relations with the Moscow Patriarchate (MP) and extend support to the Orthodox churches. A nunnery attached to the Orthodox Church is being built in Yerevan. The authorities also create conditions to maintain the religious traditions of Assyrians (followers of the Assyrian Church of the East) and Yezidi Kurds (Sun worshippers). However, their religious leaders voice concern over the missionary activities of Protestants. It is important to note that Armenian monks practically do not proselytize

---

[22] European Commission against Racism and Intolerance. Second Report on Armenia (June 2006)
<http://hudoc.ecri.coe.int/XMLEcri/ENGLISH/Cycle_03/03_CbC_eng/ARM-CbC-III-2007-1-ENG.pdf>.

[23] See: Interview of P.Yasayan, Monk of Armenian-Catholic parish in Yerevan, 7 March 2008 <http://www.wwjd.ru/news/catholic/Kard-Bertone-v-Armenii-na>.

[24] See: Interview of D.Abrahamian, Monk of the Orthodox Church of Intercession of the Mother of God in Yerevan given to the human rights organization Forum-18 on 9 February 2009 <http://www.forum18.org/Archive.php?article_id=1251>.

at all among other ethnic groups, which make up 5.3 percent of the population of the country.[25] A few communities of Kurds, Russians, Assyrians, Greeks and Ukrainians who identify themselves with other religions do not cause any concern for the authorities and official clergy.

Meanwhile, the consequences of State protectionism in relation to the Armenian Apostolic Church are felt fully by non-traditional confessions. First of all, this can be said about Jehovah's Witnesses and other Protestant groups.[26] The community of Jehovah's Witnesses passed the state registration in October 2004 thanks to international support. Since that moment, the pressure on members of this organization has increased. Particular concern is caused by the refusal of the Jehovah's Witnesses to be drafted to the army, which is seen as "a treachery of national interests" due to the aggressive external policy of Armenia.[27] An Amnesty International report cites that 82 Jehovah's Witnesses were jailed for refusing to join the army in Armenia on the 26th of September, 2007.[28]

The public opinion of the country understands the division of confessional groups into traditional and non-traditional. As written by Hranush Kharatyan, the Chairman of the Armenian Center for Ethnologic Studies, the transition to non-traditional movements in Armenia is perceived not as the realization of the freedom of faith, but the loss of the important element of ethnic identity. Therefore, the prevention of proselytism is not considered a limitation of human rights, but rather as "the right of groups to maintain their specific ethnic culture."[29]

---

[25] CIA World Factbook (September 2009) <https://www.cia.gov/library/publications/the-world-factbook/geos/am.html>.

[26] 13 February 2009, the Institute for War and Peace Reporting has published a series of complaints given by representatives of the religious minorities about discriminating actions of Armenian authorities and the Armenian Apostolic Church). See: <http://www.unhcr.org/refworld/docid/499a6f200.html>.

[27] <http://old.kavkaz-uzel.ru/digesttext/digest/id/722661.html>.

[28] Amnesty International. Armenia: Fear of the Freedom of Conscience and Religion: violations of the rights of Jehovah's Witnesses (16 January 2008). Russian version of Press Release is available at: <http://amnesty.org.ru/node/260>.

[29] Харатян Г. Армения: Религия // Центральная Евразия — 2008. Аналитический ежегодник. Швеция, 2009, p. 82.

As we can see, each of the CC states has its own variety of relations between authorities and religious organizations defined by specific features of ethnic and confessional structure and foreign policy priorities. In Azerbaijan, Muslim organizations do not have any privileges ahead of non-Islamic ones. At the same time, the authorities attempt to support tolerance. In Georgia, the Orthodox Church is vested with considerable privileges, but internal ecclesiastical contradictions and geopolitical realities oblige the Georgian Patriarchate to look to the political leadership of the country. In Armenia, the Apostolic Church has the possibility not just to influence public opinion, but also the political decisions of the authorities. Furthermore, we will see in detail the most important external and internal factors impacting on the relations between the State and confessions in the region.

**Religion and Ethnic Issues in the Central Caucasus**

For two decades, there have been two dominant trends in the CC: integration into the international community and resolution of ethno-territorial collisions. The ethnic division, with its "tectonic" activity that was present even during Soviet times, soon created hot spots of separatism and armed conflict. The ethnic identity of Caucasian people is linked traditionally with religion. In spite of this, the confessional thinking does not define the social and political environments of two opposing sides. Neither the Nagorno Karabakh nor Abkhazia clashes became "the fight for faith." Though, religious differences in both cases have been the source of additional motivation.

Since its outset in 1988, the separatist movement in Nagorno Karabakh has relied upon the religious moods of Armenians. Leaders of the separatists appealed to restore churches and demanded the party leadership of the USSR to transfer Christian temples to the area. In the early 1990s, the Council for Religious Affairs under the Soviet of Ministers of the USSR sanctioned the transfer of six temples, including the Albanian monasteries Amaras and Gandzasar, to the Armenians of Karabakh. Later, the Council for Religious Affairs repealed its decision on the transfer of two Albanian monasteries to the Armenians on the 21st of November, 1990. This decision caused indignation amongst Armenians. Rumors of excommunication of Armenians from "the monument of their religious heritage" spread out across all of the Soviet Union, and this event was considered "a psychological war against Christianity."[30]

The Catholicos of all Armenians, Vazghen I, has not stayed out of these processes. Since the beginning of the conflict, he encouraged the Armenians of Karabakh in their struggle for self-determination and appealed for "the just" resolution of this issue. On the February 25, 1988, Vazghen I sent an open letter to Mikhail Gorbachev demanding that Nagorno Karabakh be attached to Armenia.[31] On September 14, 1990, he forwarded a telegram to Gorbachev that appealed for "the force of law" to help the Armenians of Nagorno Karabakh realize their right to self-determination.[32]

Meanwhile, the Sheikh-Ul-Islam, Allahshukur Pashazadeh, the Chairman of the Caucasus Muslim Board (CMB), has maintained his wait-and-see position and used his influence to prevent bloodshed. On May 5, 1988, he met with Vazghen I. Following this meeting, such encounters became regular. On November 17, 1993, religious leaders of both countries met at the Saint Daniel Monastery under the mediation of Alexy II, the Patriarch of Moscow and All Russia. The participants of this meeting made an appeal to stop the bloodshed without preliminary conditions and not to internationalize the conflict. Another meeting of religious leaders in the same format took place in Moscow on the 15th of April, 1994. During the meeting, the wish was expressed to organize a meeting between the presidents of Azerbaijan and Armenia.[33]

In this way, the religious antagonism between Armenians and Azerbaijanis during the Nagorno Karabakh conflict retreated back and did not influence further events. Armenians like speculating about their geographical location in the European and Muslim world by talking about their specific mission

---

[30] This has been said by the Catholic monk Iozef Guncag, Assistant of the Provost of the Kostel of Saint Louis in Moscow. See: Мелик-Шахназаров А. Нагорный Карабах: факты против лжи <http://www.sumgait.info/caucasus-conflicts/nagorno-karabakh-facts/nagorno-karabakh-facts-4.htm>.

[31] <http://www.armeniaforeignministry.com/fr/nk/nk_file/article/61.html>.

[32] <http://www.sumgait.info/caucasus-conflicts/nagorno-karabakh-facts/nagorno-karabakh-facts-4.htm>.

[33] See: Силантьев Р. Религиозный фактор во внешнеполитических конфликтах на Кавказе / Религия и конфликт / Под ред. А. Малашенко и С. Филатова. М.: Российская политическая энциклопедия, 2007, p. 134.

of "the custodian of Christian values and human rights as well as the strategic security border of Europe."[34] However, the prospect of expanding ties with the Arab world and the opinion of the international community keep Armenian politicians from characterizing the conflict with Azerbaijan as a Christian-Muslim confrontation.[35]

The Georgian-Abkhaz conflict follows a religious pattern due to the fact that the groups of the Confederation of Caucasian peoples, including the very active Chechens under the leadership of Shamil Basayev, have fought on the side of the Abkhazians. However, this confrontation did not fit the inter-religious pattern. Firstly, Christian Cossacks, Ossetians and Russians were among the foreign mercenaries fighting on the side of the Abkhazians. Secondly, even after the exodus of ethnic Georgians, Christians currently constitute more than half of the population. As far as the Abkhazian Muslims are concerned, the level of their religious knowledge remains quite low, and there is still no mosque in Abkhazia.[36]

On the other hand, the conflict in Abkhazia provoked clashes inside the Orthodox Church of Georgia. In 1993, there were only four monks remaining in Abkhazia. In 1998, they established the new Eparchial Council of Sukhumi-Abkhazia. Formally remaining the canonical territory of the Orthodox Church of Georgia, it had been in fact under the management of the Moscow Patriarchate (MP). In October 2008, the Synod of the Russian Orthodox Church refused to accept the Sukhumi-Abkhazia Eparchy into the Russian Church.[37] Thus, the leadership of the Eparchy felt obligated to undertake radical measures, and during the extraordinary meeting of the Eparchial Council held on the 15th of September, 2009, it was decided to end

---

[34] Sahakyan V., Atanesyan A. Democratization in Armenia: Some Trends of Political Culture and Behavior // Demokratizatsiya: The Journal of Post-Soviet Democratization. Vol. 14, No. 3 / Summer 2006 <http://findarticles.com/p/articles/mi_qa3996/is_200607/ai_n17182658/>.

[35] In November 2007, on the eve of the presidential elections, Serzh Sarkisyan, the then Prime Minister of Armenia, had to account in front of journalists for his awkward statement about the strong religious element in Nagorno Karabakh conflict, which he made during an interview to the American newspaper *Los Angeles Times*. See: Агентство Новости-Армения, 10 November 2007. <http://www.newsarmenia.ru/karabah/20071110/41768503.html>.

[36] According to the sociological poll results (2003), 60 percent of respondents have recognized themselves as Christians and only 16 percent as Muslims. See: newspaper НГ-Религии, 17 March 2004.

[37] Kommersant, 07 October 2008.

the activities of the Sukhumi-Abkhazia Eparchy of the OCG in the territory of Abkhazia and restore the Abkhaz Orthodox Church which had not existed since 1795.[38]

The situation in South Ossetia is equally difficult. Following the halt of military operations, A. Pukhayev, the head of the South Ossetian Orthodox community, arrived in Moscow to ask the Russian Orthodox Church to take Orthodox Christians of the self-declared Republic under its omophorion. However, the MP did not wish to be involved in the territorial dispute with other Churches. In this case, Pukhayev established contacts with the Russian Orthodox Church Abroad (ROCA), and the Alan Deanery of ROCA was created in 1992, covering three Orthodox parishes. Another five parishes have remained under the supervision of "legal" monks from the Nikozsky and Tskhinvali Eparchies of the Orthodox Church of Georgia[39]. After having noticed the rapprochement between the ROCA and the MP in 2003, the head of Deanery stopped its relations with the previous partner. In November 2005, he joined one of non-canonical Orthodox (Starostil) Churches of Greece – the Synod of Opposites. Since that moment, the Alan Eparchy attempted again to become a part of the Russian Orthodox Church after the Five Days War. But, it received official rejection in October 2008 (jointly with the Sukhumi-Abkhazia Eparchy).

In spite of the political support that Moscow extended to the separatist regimes in Georgia, the MP cannot declare unilaterally the revision of canonical borders with the Orthodox Church of Georgia. In current conditions, it serves the interests of supporters of alienation of the Ukrainian Orthodox Church from the MP. Therefore, it recognizes its wrongful position in conflicting with the Constantinople Patriarchate due to the transition of the Estonian Orthodox churches to the jurisdiction of latter. The same can be said about the Romanian Orthodox Church due to the fact that the latter recognizes the Bessarabia Metropolitanate existing parallel to the canonical Moldova-Kishinev Metropolitanate. In this context, in spite of Russia's recognition of South Ossetia and Abkhazia, the

---

[38] Interfax, 18 September 2009. <http://www.interfax-religion.ru/?act=documents&div=942>.
[39] Силантьев Р. Указ. соч, p. 142.

officials of the ROC declared their recognition of the canonical territory of the Georgian Church[40].

In this way, the consequences do not allow the Georgian Patriarchate to control the Orthodox churches in Abkhazia and South Ossetia, which are de-jure subordinated to the OCG. The diplomatic efforts of the Georgian clergy did not bring the expected results. Understanding it, the Orthodox nationalists attempted to restore the image of Church by strengthening its influence in places of compact Azerbaijani and Armenian settlements.

In Kvemo-Kartli, the discontent of the local Azerbaijani population is caused by the installation of large crosses in Muslim villages and near graveyards.[41] Besides that, Azerbaijanis attempting to build mosques face strong resistance from the authorities. According to Elbrus Mamedov, the representative of the People's Protector of Georgia in the region of Kvemo-Kartli, it has been very difficult to build a mosque in the Muganly village of the Gardabani region even without a minaret.[42] The group of Orthodox monks in the Fakhraly village of the Bolnisi region has protested against the restoration of a mosque built in 1905.[43] Similar problems are also faced by the Muslims in Adjara.

This acute tension characterizes the relations between the Georgian Patriarchate and the Eparchy of the Armenian Church. Since Soviet times, the Armenian Apostolic Church has carried out its liturgy at only two temples in Tbilisi. But, the Armenians also claim five other churches in the capital, which are idle now. The most problematic issues are the Norashen Church in Tbilisi and the Surb Nshan Church in Akhaltsikhe. Meanwhile, the Christian-Democratic Movement of Georgia demands the return of several idle churches in the north of Armenia to the Orthodox Church of Georgia. Officially, the Patriarchate does not raise a question about these

---

[40] This has been said in particular in the statement of Archbishop Illarion Volokolamsky, the head of the Department for External Ecclesiastical Relations of the Moscow Patriarchate. See: RIA Novosti Agency, 13 September 2009.
<http://www.rian.ru/society/20090913/184808697.html>.
[41] Agency Novosti-Azerbaijan, 23 February 2009.
<http://www.newsazerbaijan.ru/exclusive/20090223/42743450.html>.
[42] Agency Novosti-Azerbaijan, 1 April 2009.
<http://www.newsazerbaijan.ru/obsh/20090401/42795016.html>.
[43] Agency APA, 15 September 2009.<http://ru.apa.az/news.php?id=142704>.

Georgian Churches in Armenia. Though, in February 2006, the Synod took the decision to restore the historical Eparchy of Agarak-Tashir in the territory of Armenia with the cathedra in Dmanisi (a frontier city in Georgia).[44] The reaction of the Armenian side has been restrained but responsive because the supporters of the OCG in Armenia are practically non-existant.

The reason for tense relations between the two confessions is explained by interethnic contradictions in the region of Samtskhe-Javakheti, which is populated mainly by Armenians. The mass resettlement of Armenians from Turkey to Samtskhe-Javakheti started after the Russian-Turkish war of 1828-29.[45] The geographical location and specific landscape features have favored the economic and cultural alienation of the region from the rest of Georgia and increased its dependence on neighboring Armenia. This is a matter of concern for the authorities because Armenians consider these lands to be a historical part of Armenia.[46] Therefore, alongside infrastructure projects, the authorities are actively trying to change the demographic balance in favor of the Georgians. In the religious sphere, it is observed through the strengthening of Orthodox influence and widening of land properties of the Georgian Orthodox Church.

As we can see, the ethnic factor brings serious corrections to inter-confessional and State-confession relations in the Central Caucasus. Based on such conditions, it is quite understandable that the authorities tend to cooperate with dominant religions. The latter remains loyal to the political course of the authorities and participates in national processes while new religious movements deepen disintegration between select ethnic groups and minorities as well as inside these movements. Traditional spiritual leaders of the ethnic minorities have opportunities to meet the religious needs of their followers though some friction between them and the dominating confessions (particularly in Georgia) still remains.

---

[44] <http://www.pravoslavie.ru/cgi-bin/sykon/client/display.pl?sid=363&did=1806>.
[45] See: Вачнадзе М., Гурули В., Бахтадзе М. История Грузии
<http://www.gumer.info/bibliotek_Buks/History/Vachn/16.php>.
[46] Лом X. Джавахети после Революции роз: Прогресс и регресс в поисках национального единства в Грузии. Рабочий доклад Европейского центра по делам меньшинств №38 (апрель 2006). <http://www.ecmi.de/download/working_paper_38_rus.pdf>.

Modern researchers of religious life in the Central Caucasus sometimes ask the following question: "How can relations between the State and the Church ensure the realization of individual rights for freedom of religion and faith?" Incontestably, this problem is important for the formation of a civil society in the region. However, geopolitical realities bring other issues to the forefront. For instance, there are the following questions: Can secularization ensure the strengthening of statehood in Azerbaijan without damaging national, spiritual and ethical values? How will the strengthening of the Orthodox element of national identity in Georgia impact the integrity of Georgian society? Is the Armenian national idea possible with the aggressive narration, which also includes the territorial claims of the Armenian Apostolic Church? To put it briefly, the religious factor holds tremendous importance for the future of the Central Caucasus, and it is watchfully perceived by all geopolitical actors.

**Religion in the Central Caucasus in Its Geopolitical Dimension**

During the last fifteen years, the geopolitical importance of the states located in the Central Caucasus has changed significantly. On the one hand, the transportation potential of the region increased greatly, and it became possible to bypass Russian to deliver energy resources of the Caspian basin to world markets. On the other hand, unresolved conflicts near hot spots in the south of Russia transformed from a factor of regional instability to potential global clashes involving superpowers. In this context, the geopolitical and economic interests of the big powers and military-political alliances dominate the interests of the states in the region by turning them into the subjects of a new Caucasian policy. In their turn, the religious factor and the speculations with freedom of faith become tools of political influence within the internal situation of independent countries as well as interstate relations in the whole region.

Much greater attention to the religious factor is paid by the United States – the main beneficiary of transnational projects in the region. The US State Department attentively watches the religious situation in the region and brings corrections to the policies of the states via diplomatic relations with various religious organizations. The main principles of US influence in this sphere are liberalization of religious policy and the fight against international terrorism. Traditionally being favorable to Evangelist

Protestantism, the US supports the globalization of Anglo-Saxon culture with its values: promotion of self-expression, equality and the ability to establish voluntary organizations.[47] Different protestant groups obtain political support from many European states and human rights organizations. Perceived as non-traditional organizations by local society and sometimes deemed as destructive sects,[48] the Protestant Churches consider themselves to be the carriers of historical missions and challengers of the traditional culture. They do not engage in ecumenical dialogue, and they associate themselves directly with the West by not hiding their geopolitical orientation.[49] At the same time, the achievements of Protestants in the Central Caucasus are not tangible. Therefore, it is still premature to speak about the Protestant card in the Caucasian policy of the US or EU.

The religious situation in the region has been hugely influenced by the global war on international terrorism initiated by the US. Immediately after the 9/11 tragedy, Azerbaijan stopped the activities of the Kuwaiti Fund-Revival of Islamic Heritage, which used to actively support the Salafi movement. In total, six charity funds suspected of links with terrorist organizations have been closed in Azerbaijan.[50] Anti-terror measures have destroyed the infrastructure of the Salafi organizations. It has not been restored in past years and has weakened the position of Sunni Islam. Strengthening of the Sunni factor in Azerbaijan is not in the interests of the West because the religious contradictions between the Turkish Sunnis and Azerbaijani Shias are almost the only civilian obstacle to fostering Turkish influence in the Caucasus. In addition, overseas strategists are interested in strengthening the Shia corridor from Lebanon to Azerbaijan; historically formed contradictions between the Sunni and pro-Persian Shia circles dismember the Islamic Ummah in a geopolitical context.

---

[47] Бергер П. Л. Культурная динамика глобализации / Многоликая глобализация / Под ред. П. Бергера и С. Хантингтона; пер. с англ. М.: Аспект Пресс, 2004. p. 16.

[48] For instance, according to Alexander Amaryan, the head of the Center for Assistance and Rehabilitation of Persons Who Suffered from Destructive Sects (Armenia), over half of registered religious organizations in the countries are the destructive sects. See: Новости-Армения, 19 April 2006. http://www.newsarmenia.ru/arm1/20060419/41552277.html

[49] Лункин Р. Протестантизм и глобализация на просторах Евразии / Религия и глобализация на просторах Евразии / Под ред. А. Малашенко и С. Филатова; Моск. Центр Карнеги. М.: Неостром, 2005. pp. 104-105.

[50] See: Interview with the then Minister of National Security of Azerbaijan Namiq Abbasov for the newspaper Эхо from 9 August 2003.

The religious element is traditionally present in the external policy of the Islamic Republic of Iran. Aspiring to play the role of the political leader in the Muslim world, Iran is interested in maintaining its influence in the Caucasus and preventing a Turkish breakthrough into Central Eurasia. Keeping the status of a regional power allows Iran to participate in transnational projects and breaks down external economic isolation. On the other hand, the strengthening of an independent Azerbaijan may lead to a rise in nationalism among Iranian Azerbaijanis, who would represent a potential threat to the territorial integrity of the state.[51] The leadership of the Islamic Republic of Iran reacts angrily to co-operation between Azerbaijan and the United States in the economic and military fields as well as the political rapprochement of its northern neighbor with Israel. Tehran is unhappy with the strategic partnership of the regime of Mikheil Saakashvili with the Americans. Attempts to prevent these processes using the Tehran-Yerevan-Moscow axis produce only temporary results. Tehran is not paying attention to the promises of the Kremlin.[52] Though lacking strategic allies, Iran is desperately using its economic, cultural and demographic potential to foster a presence in the region. However, the leverage of influence is not enough. In such a situation, the rise of political tension in the Caucasus serves the interests of the Mullahs' regime.

Where and how can Tehran use its religious trump card? Incontestably, first of all, it can be used in Azerbaijan with the mainly Shia population. During the first half of the 1990s, the war in Nagorno Karabakh and the hard economic situation were used by Iranian missionaries openly promoting revolutionary rhetoric. However, following the strengthening of centralized power in Azerbaijan (which coincided with the corrected foreign policy course in Iran, implemented particularly after Mohammad Khatami came to power), the idea of starting an Islamic revolution in Azerbaijan was put aside. Following the arrest of leaders of the Islamic Party of Azerbaijan in 1995, the activities of religious activists in the political arena have been practically invisible until the presidential elections

---

[51] According to CIA World Factbook, the number of Azerbaijanis in Iran is almost 16 million <https://www.cia.gov/library/publications/the-world-factbook/geos/ir.html>. Experts of UNPO put the number at up to 30 million people
<http://www.unpo.org/content/view/7884/144>.
[52] Russo-Iranian Relations from Iran's Perspective, by Ahmad Majidyar, 20 May 2009 <http://www.irantracker.org/analysis/russo-iranian-relations-irans-perspective>.

of 2003 when one of the activists of the Shia community, Haji Ilgar Ibrahimoglu, openly supported Isa Gambar, the opposition leader. This moment uncovered processes taking place inside the Shia community and demonstrated the fact that today Iran is not able to influence the political situation in Azerbaijan. At the same time, supporters of "Iranian Islam" dispose the wider network of religious communities in almost all regions of the country and actively run their public and religious activities. A significant financial contribution to organize the Azerbaijani Shia movement is given by the Iranian Cultural Center and the Imam Khomeini Assistance Fund. On the 19th of August, 2008, following the terrorist act in the Juma mosque in the Narimanov region, a group of Shia activists issued a statement deploring this crime as contrary to Muslim identity. This statement published in the news portal *Day.az* was signed by forty leaders from religious communities and public organizations.

In this way, Tehran does not leave any room to create a dynamic Islamic opposition in Azerbaijan, which could prevent the diffusion of nationalistic ideas while envisaging a rapprochement with Turkey and secular pro-Western ideologies. At the same time, the open clerical rhetoric of Iranian missionaries have transformed into appeals for cross-cultural dialogue in the last decade. Numerous cultural and educational programs implemented by the Iranian Cultural Center and private funds favor the promotion of the Persian language, student exchange between the institutes of Iran and the Central Caucasian states as well as the creation of a positive image of the Islamic Republic of Iran and its political structure[53]. It is notable that the Blue Mosque in Yerevan has been restored with the political and financial support of Iran.

In the geopolitical strategy of Turkey, the religious context is overwhelmed by the idea of a revival of the common Turkic identity. Nevertheless, Turkish Islamic movements (the international religious network of the followers of Said Nursi and Sufi Tarekats with its centers in Turkey) bring a considerable contribution to the strengthening of the international image of Ankara and contain the rise of Iranian influence. The moderate character of these movements and the clear respectful attitude to the secular principles

---

[53] Касымов Р. А. Политика Ирана в закавказских государствах
<http://www.iimes.ru/rus/stat/2005/15-05-05a.htm>.

of statehood has ensured the tolerant position of the authorities in Azerbaijan and other post-Soviet states. The situation started to change following the landslide victory of the Party of Justice and Development in the parliamentary elections held in Turkey in November 2002. Appealing for liberalization of the religious sphere and the limitation of the role of the army in the political life of the country, members of this party have created an image of moderate Muslims oriented toward rapprochement with the West. Fears related to the internationalization of the Erdogan phenomenon, which envisages a secular politician with a Muslim vision, have become the main reason for prosecuting Turkish missionaries and closing pro-Turkish religious organizations in post-Soviet territories. According to Nikolai Patrushev, ex-director of the Russian FSB, the activities of more than 50 members of the Nursi movement alone were prevented in Russia in 2002.[54] In May 2007, the Koptev Regional Court of Moscow declared a series of Said Nursi's books as extremist literature, while the Supreme Court of the Russian Federation ruled on the April 10, 2008 that Nursi's international organization is an extremist organization.

In Azerbaijan, tougher control has been applied to the activities of pro-Turkish religious groups suspected of planning to infiltrate the ruling structures. In November 2007, the Sheikh-Ul-Islam, Allahshukur Pashazadeh, declared Nursi members as radical Wahhabis by noting that their activities were damaging the interests of Islam[55]. In October 2007, law enforcement bodies of Azerbaijan detained Mehmet Harun Kayaci, the Chairman of the Independent Party of Turkey, who was subsequently sentenced to correctional labor for illegal religious propaganda.[56] In April 2009, the activities of Shehidler mosque and the Religious Center of Tarekat Nakshbandiya were closed under the pretense of repair.

The Turkish authorities are still reluctant to comment on the actions of Azerbaijani colleagues and distance themselves from linking the religious propaganda with the policy of Ankara. The unshakeable tranquility of the Turkish lobby in Azerbaijan, which is not so indifferent to the ongoing events, also has other reasons. First of all, limitation measures have been

---

[54] Кавказский узел, 11 April 2008 <http://www.kavkaz-uzel.ru/newstext/news/id/1211850.html>.
[55] Trend Agency, 16 November 2007 <http://az.trend.az/news/society/religion/1077128.html>.
[56] ANS PRESS Agency, 23 May 2008.

adopted exclusively in relation to persons and structures that violated the national legislation in the sphere of freedom of faith; secondly, the large network of pro-Turkish communities has not done any visible damage.

Among all geopolitical actors in the region, the Russian Federation is the least interested in altering the balance of religious forces. Without the possibility of offering economic assistance comparative to Western investments, the Kremlin is ready to take any measures to retain the Central Caucasus in its sphere of influence. Russia does not wish to see the military of the US and NATO next to its borders because the security of new transmission projects linking the Caspian basin with the Mediterranean endanger its interests in the energy markets of Europe. The protracted conflicts in Nagorno Karabakh, Abkhazia and South Ossetia can always become active ones, and it obliges the international community to watch the actions of Russia, which has demonstrated its readiness to protect "the offended party." It is in the interest of Russia to maintain uncertainty in the Central Caucasus until the Kremlin finds a way to implement its own geopolitical project. Therefore, it is absolutely unacceptable for Russian strategists to bring additional religious context to the political processes in these three neighboring states. To put it briefly, the position of Russia related to the religious trends in the region considerably compensates for the influence of other external forces.

Cooperating actively with the Russian Orthodox Church inside the country, the Russian authorities promote the strengthening of dialogue between Russia and the traditional spiritual leaders of the post-Soviet states. The Orthodox Churches in the region do not proselytize and favor maintaining cultural links between the local clergy and the Russian Orthodox Church. In such conditions, strengthening of non-traditional confessions is an indicator of the shifting axis of public development toward a non-Russian scenario. However, of all the non-traditional movements, the biggest concern for Russian analysts is the Salafists in the Central Caucasus. It is evident that the supporters of a puritan Islam constitute the core of radical Islamic resistance in the Northern Caucasus.

To our understanding, Azerbaijani authorities have less concern related to the radicalization of Muslims in the Northern Caucasus. In the first half of the 1990s, the Salafi movement in Azerbaijan was developing independently from the Northern Caucasian one. But, the second Chechen war served as an impetus to radicalize part of the Salafis inside the country. Nowadays, thoughts of Azerbaijani radicals are defined mainly by the achievements of their followers in the Northern Caucasus, and not vice versa. Unfortunately, declaring war against religious extremism, the Kremlin controls the processes in the region, but fails to eradicate the true reasons of the radicalization of Muslims. According to Alexei Malashenko, analyst at the Carnegie Endowment for International Peace, full disorder now rules in Chechnya, Dagestan and Kabardino-Balkaria, where terrorism is considered as revenge and the only way to express oppositional moods. This expert says that the current situation serves the interests of authorities who do not know how to solve their problems and content themselves by using force.[57]

## Conclusion

Distancing themselves from the euphoria of the religious revival of the early 1990s, the states in the Central Caucasus have started to differentiate their relations with traditional and non-traditional confessions taking into account national statehood building and the objective needs of society. Authorities are quite jealous of the attempts of international organizations to protect the interests of various confessions. During the contemporary stage, the trends of state policy applied to religious and ethnic minorities in Azerbaijan, Georgia and Armenia differ because each of the three states confronts global and regional challenges in its own specific way. In Azerbaijan, special attention is paid to the de-sacralization of public relations. All attempts to bring religious doctrine to relations between the state and social sphere are prevented. In Georgia, Orthodoxy is not considered as an obstacle for Euro-Atlantic integration. All conditions are being created for expanding the material and social basis for the Orthodox Church of Georgia. In Armenia, the Apostolic Church enjoys exclusive privileges and remains the guarantor of "the Armenian idea" independently from the political course of the authorities. Maintaining these trends in the next decade is the most probable scenario of the development of the

---

[57] This has been said by the Russian specialist in Islamic studies at the seminar – Events in Caucasus: propaganda or impartiality? – held at the Moscow Carnegie Center on 14 September 2009. <http://www.polit.ru/news/2009/09/15/malashenko.html>.

religious situation (if the region will not be involved in a new divide of the Middle East).

The alternative way of development envisages the political, economic and civilian integration of the Central Caucasus. The participation in transnational projects, the experience of political integration among European states and opportunities offered in front of the common Caucasian house stimulate the rapprochement of the Central Caucasian countries. The necessity of turning the Caucasus into a common organism, currently understood in Azerbaijan and Georgia, is underlined at the highest level. But for the time being, cosmopolitan values are accepted by only a few elite groups benefiting from globalization. However, in order to solve inter-ethnic contradictions, it is necessary to be prepared for deep changes in the role played by ethnic and confessional stereotypes in national self-consciousnesses. Can competing people overcome the "self-determination syndrome?" Is stable supranational identity possible in Caucasus? How will the conflict of interests between the clergy and the state influence the primacy of common Caucasian interests over national ones? These matters of discussion remain open. Important ethnic conflicts in the region are far from being resolved, while contradictions between other ethnic groups can easily become new conflicts.

In the conditions of contemporary geopolitical realities, a third scenario is also possible. The aspirations of the United States to secure total economic and technological domination over its competitors clearly endanger the possibility of peace in the Middle East. Military actions against Iran – the central state in the Axis of Evil – promise to give new impetus to the technological development of the US and, more importantly, create energy problems for its competitors. War in Iran could become a humanitarian crisis for the Central Caucasian states, which will lead to a rise of nationalistic and fundamentalist ideas. In such conditions, the authorities will have to contain external dangers, while the prospect of regional integration will be more damaging. It is difficult to evaluate the political, social and cultural consequences of the influx of Iranian refugees into Azerbaijan. Presumably, the wave of Islamic solidarity will drastically increase the popularity of independent Shia leaders by making attempts to secularize public opinion less popular. In neighboring Georgia and Armenia, aggravation of contradictions between religions is expected.

Clearly, the future of the religious situation in the Central Caucasus in the middle term is quite uncertain. Although the regional political regimes aspire to independently define secularity, priorities of state and confession relations, the states of the Central Caucasus are very vulnerable to external factors. While maintaining peace in the region, these countries have a chance for political integration and full participation in global projects. However, time will show whether they are able to overcome contradictions and become full-fledged members of global politics.

# DEMOGRAPHIC AND MIGRATION PROSPECTS IN THE SOUTH CAUCASUS COUNTRIES

Rauf Garagozov,
Senior Research Fellow,
Institute of Strategic Studies of the Caucasus

To better understand the current situation unfolding in the South Caucasus, it is necessary to study and analyze trends in the migration and demographic processes taking place in the three countries of the region – Azerbaijan, Armenia and Georgia.

It should be noted that in spite of some common social, cultural and historical developments, these countries have had distinctive characteristics even during the Soviet era. These states differ in population, territory, religious background, ethnic composition and several other demographic and migration specifications. We will study these features in detail.

*Figure 1* shows data about the absolute population in these countries, including expected figures.[1] As seen in the graph, the largest population among the three South Caucasian countries is in Azerbaijan. It also clearly illustrates that the difference in population between Azerbaijan and the other two countries of the region is increasing at a constant rate.

---

[1] All calculations for the present article, excluding specially prepared ones, are done on the basis of the average version of the UN global demographic forecast of 2008.

*Figure 1:*
*Total Population, by Countries and Years (in thousands)*

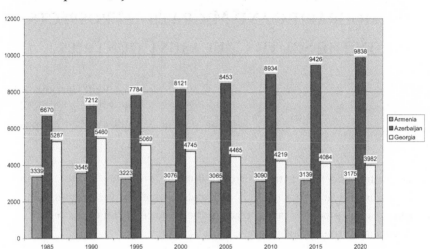

Source: Population Division of the Department of Economic and Social Affairs of the United
Nations Secretariat, World Population Prospects: The 2008 Revision,
<http://esa.un.org/unpp>, May 03, 2009.

The main factors of this trend are differences in birth rate, mortality,
demographic aging and migration. We will study each of these.

**Birth Rate**

Birth rate is the positive population reproduction characterized by the
appearance of new members of the population. In order to measure the
birth rate, the system of indicators is used in a specific way. It involves
determining the overall level, dynamics, intensiveness and figures in various
sub groups of the population (social, economic and demographic groups).
The predominant and simplest indicator of birth rate is the crude birth
rate.[2]

*Figure 2* reflects data on the birth rate in the countries of the South
Caucasus by years based on calculations of the crude birth rate.

---

[2] Number of births over a given period divided by the person-years lived by the population
over that period. It is expressed as number of births per 1,000 in a population.

*Figure 2:*
*Crude Birth Rate (births per 1,000 population), by Country and by Years*
*(%)*

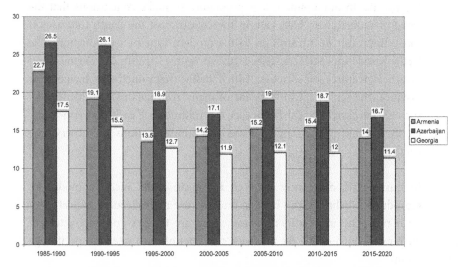

Source: Population Division of the Department of Economic and Social Affairs of the United
Nations Secretariat, World Population Prospects: The 2008 Revision,
<http://esa.un.org/unpp>, May 03, 2009.

As seen from *Figure 2* above, the highest birth rate among the South
Caucasus countries is in Azerbaijan. However, there is a common trend of
reduction in birth rate in all three states of the South Caucasus. This trend
coincides with global demographic processes resulting from many societies'
transition to modern reproduction. This type of reproduction, observed
mainly in Western European countries, is one of the consequences of the
so-called demographic revolution started in these societies at the end of the
18th century.

Experts indicate factors explaining "the reduction of demand" for children.
Advanced education and increased employment among women are prime
examples. At the same time, the appearance of absolute anti-contraception
drugs helps regulate family planning.[3] As a result, Western European

---

[3] Chikava, L. Demographic development in the South Caucasian countries: current trends and
future prospects. *The Caucasus & Globalization*. 1 (2), 2007, pp. 31-37.

countries have a reduced birth rate. The data for those countries shows 11 children per 1,000 people on average in 2002.[4]

Meanwhile, in our opinion, it is premature to make conclusions that the trend of reduction in birth rate in the countries of the South Caucasus is solely the result of a transition to the modern type of reproduction. The factor-based approach described above ignores cultural, religious and historical features of societies, which define reproductive behavior. For instance, the reproductive behavior of many Azerbaijanis is influenced by such social-psychological factors as the tradition of early marriages, the family cult and the patriarchal attitude in family relations still observed in rural areas.

In this regard, differences between European and Caucasian models of reproductive behavior can be seen once we use more detailed indicators of birth rate. The most important indicators are the sex and age factors of birth rate, which define the intensive character of birth rate of a specific age group.

For instance, if we compare the sex and age factors of birth rate in the countries of the South Caucasus with the respective average factors in Western Europe, we will see that the highest birth rate in the societies of the South Caucasus exists among women of 20-24 years, while the same factor in Western European states is noticed among women of 34 years and older.

In this context, only Georgian data shifts the peak of birth rate to the women of 25-29 years (See *Figures 3, 4, 5* and *6*). This is closer to the European norms to some extent.

---

[4]Population Reference Bureau. <http://www.prb.org>.

*Figure 3:*
*Age-Specific Fertility Rates, Armenia, 1995-2020*

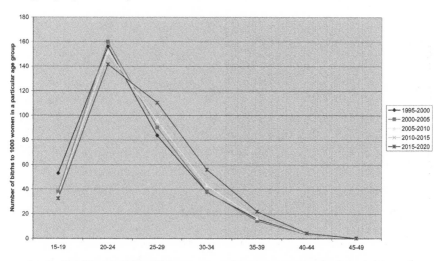

Source: Population Division of the Department of Economic and Social Affairs of the United Nations Secretariat, World Population Prospects: The 2008 Revision, <http://esa.un.org/unpp>, May 03, 2009.

*Figure 4:*
*Age-Specific Fertility Rates, Azerbaijan, 1995-2020*

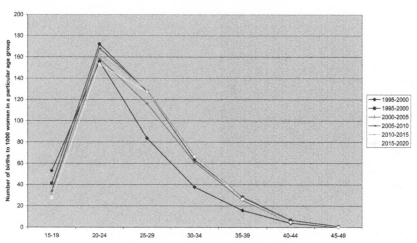

Source: Population Division of the Department of Economic and Social Affairs of the United Nations Secretariat, World Population Prospects: The 2008 Revision, <http://esa.un.org/unpp>, May 03, 2009.

*Figure 5:*
## Age-Specific Fertility Rates, Georgia, 1995-2020

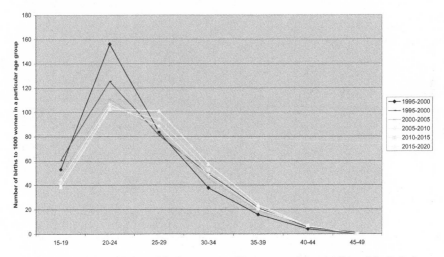

Source: Population Division of the Department of Economic and Social Affairs of the United Nations Secretariat, World Population Prospects: The 2008 Revision, <http://esa.un.org/unpp>, May 03, 2009.

*Figure 6:*
## Age-Specific Fertility Rates, Western Europe, 1995-2020

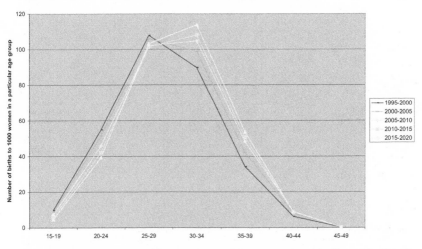

Source: Population Division of the Department of Economic and Social Affairs of the United Nations Secretariat, World Population Prospects: The 2008 Revision, <http://esa.un.org/unpp>, May 03, 2009.

Thus, the trend of a reducing birth rate in the countries of the South Caucasus cannot be considered as only the result of a demographic development process that is specific to Western European countries. In any case, the reduction of the birth rate in Azerbaijan is caused not by the particular change of social settings in the structure of reproductive birth rate, but by the common social and economic difficulties of a transition period. The period is complicated by a large influx of refugees and internally displaced persons (IDPs) due to the military aggression and occupation of part of Azerbaijan by neighboring Armenia. Special studies of factors and reasons for this trend in birth rate reduction in Azerbaijan during the 1990s have uncovered the material difficulties faced by families, which obliged them to postpone the birth of a second, third and even first child.[5]

Another important indicator used to analyze the level and dynamics of birth rate is the number of children per woman during the entire period of fertility.[6] *Figure 7* shows the common indicators of birth rate in the countries of the South Caucasus, different regions, Europe and the world.

---

[5]Мурадов Ш.М., Гезалова А.К., Эфендиев Р. Дж. Глобализация, демографическое развитие и трудовая активность населения в Азербайджане. Баку: Элм, 2007.

[6]The average number of children a hypothetical cohort of women would have at the end of their reproductive period if they were subject during their whole lives to the fertility rates of a given period and if they were not subject to mortality. It is expressed as children per woman. Aggregate indicator which is higher than 4.0 is deemed high while if it is lower than 2.15, this indicator is inferior.

*Figure 7:*
*Dynamics of Total Ferility Rate in the World, States of the South Caucasus, Regions and Europe in 1985-2020*

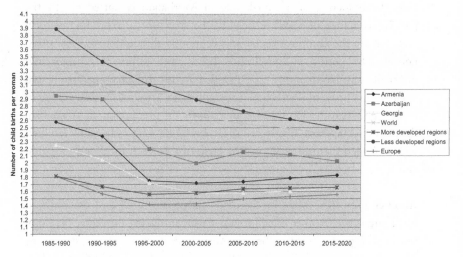

Source: Population Division of the Department of Economic and Social Affairs of the United Nations Secretariat, World Population Prospects: The 2008 Revision, <http://esa.un.org/unpp>, May 03, 2009.

The data in *Figure 7* reflects that the best indicators of birth rate among the three South Caucasian states are in Azerbaijan. According to the UN forecast, the number of births per 100 women for the period of 2010-2015 is: 212 – Azerbaijan; 179 – Armenia; 161 – Georgia. Taking into account that for even at the lowest rate of population reproduction of 2.1 (an average of 210 children per 100 women), all of the South Caucasian countries are able to ensure comprehensive population reproduction for the near future. At the same time, Azerbaijan will maintain the highest rate of reproduction in the years to come.

*Figure 7* demonstrates quite clearly the trend of reduction of the common indicator both for the region of the South Caucasus and the world as a whole. In this respect, the countries of the South Caucasus are not exceptions from the global trend of radical reduction of the crude birth rate that began in 1970. For instance, if during the first half of the '70s, the world average indicator of the crude birth rate had been equal to 4.99 births per woman of reproductive age, with a minimal rate of 1.6 and a maximum of

8.3, then starting from the second half of the '90s, these rates would have been 3.49, 1.1 and 8.0 births per woman of reproductive age, respectively. In this case, if during the first half of the '70s, the crude birth rate, which is inferior to the simple reproduction of the population, had been observed in 12 percent of countries worldwide, then by the end of the past century, the share of such countries would have increased to one third.[7] At the beginning of the new millennium, the group of countries with a low birth rate had gained another two countries from the South Caucasus – Armenia and Georgia.

**Death Rate**

The trends of population fluctuation are determined not only by birth rate, but also by the death rate. To measure the death rate, a fixed set of indicators is used by researchers. One of them is the crude death rate.[8]

The following *Table 1* reflects on average the indicator of this rate in countries of the South Caucasus, different regions, Europe and the world by 5 year intervals.

*Table 1:*
*Crude Death Rate in the Countries of the South Caucasus, Regions and the World (%)*

|  | 1995-2000 | 2000-2005 | 2005-2010 | 2010-2015 | 2015-2020 |
|---|---|---|---|---|---|
| **Armenia** | 8.6 | 8.4 | 8.7 | 9 | 9.2 |
| **Azerbaijan** | 7.2 | 6.7 | 6.8 | 6.9 | 7.1 |
| **Georgia** | 10 | 10.7 | 11.9 | 12.5 | 12.7 |
| **World** | 8.9 | 8.6 | 8.5 | 8.3 | 8.3 |
| **More developed regions** | 10.1 | 10.2 | 10.1 | 10.2 | 10.4 |
| **Less developed regions** | 8.6 | 8.3 | 8.1 | 7.9 | 7.8 |
| **Europe** | 11.6 | 11.7 | 11.4 | 11.6 | 11.7 |

---

[7] Human Development Report 2001. United Nations. N.Y., 2001.
[8] Number of deaths over a given period divided by the person-years lived by the population over that period. It is expressed as number of deaths per 1,000 people.

As seen from *Table 1*, the population increase in Azerbaijan is characterized not only by a relatively high birth rate in the region, but also by a relatively low death rate. This can be explained by the fact that among all other factors, this indicator is influenced also by the sex-age structure of the population. It means that in ageing societies such Armenia's and Georgia's, the death rate is higher than in younger countries such as Azerbaijan. This demographic aspect will be studied in detail below.

Particular emphasis is placed on infant mortality based on sex-age indicators. This is the indicator, which measures the infant mortality among children one year of age.[9] It is the most important indictor of social development as a whole. The level of infant mortality is determined not only by the level of public health, but also by the culture of the population, respect for hygienic requirements, ecological conditions, families' financial status, life and labor conditions, and other factors. Therefore, this indicator helps to evaluate the degree of development of a society and of public health. As seen in *Figure 8*, the countries of the South Caucasus are seriously lagging behind the developed regions of the world and Europe. For example, there were 26 cases of infant mortality in Armenia in 2006 (among 1,000 newly born children whose age is between zero and one year); 42 in Azerbaijan and 35 in Georgia, while the average in the developed regions of the world and Europe is eight.

---

[9] Probability of dying between birth and exact age one. It is expressed as deaths per 1,000 births.

*Figure 8:*
*Dynamics of Infant Mortality, by Country, Region and Years*

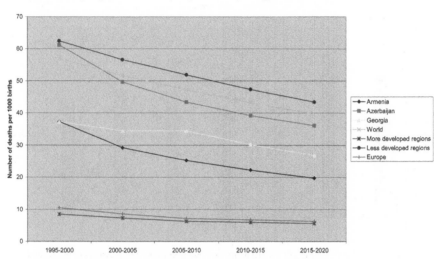

Source: Population Division of the Department of Economic and Social Affairs of the United Nations Secretariat, World Population Prospects: The 2008 Revision, <http://esa.un.org/unpp>, May 03, 2009.

This means that the countries of the South Caucasus have to undertake wider measures to improve various social systems and, more importantly, increase the growth capacity of their populations, upgrade their public health systems and ensure healthier environments.

**Natural Population Increase**

Population increase is the dynamic summary of the influx and outflow of people. The number of the population of a country is increased by births, but decreased by deaths. The difference between births and deaths for a certain amount of time is called the natural population increase.[10] *Figure 9* reflects data related to the natural population increase in the countries of the South Caucasus for the years 1985-2020.

---

[10] Crude birth rate minus the crude death rate. Represents the portion of population growth (or decline) determined exclusively by births and deaths.

**Figure 9:**

*Rate of Natural Increase in the Countries of the South Caucasus,*
*1985-2020*

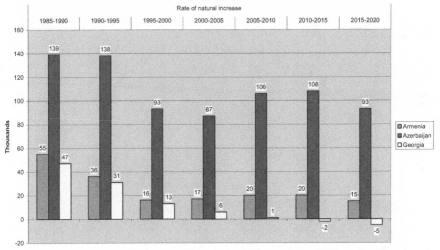

Source: Population Division of the Department of Economic and Social Affairs of the United
Nations Secretariat, World Population Prospects: The 2008 Revision,
<http://esa.un.org/unpp>, May 03, 2009.

As seen from *Figure 9*, there is a negative population increase in Georgia.
The population increases but at a decreased rate in Armenia, and there are
fluctuations in natural increase in Azerbaijan. These data proves that
Georgia has entered a phase of de-population. Armenia is close to this
stage, while it is not expected in Azerbaijan.

**Migration**

The population of a country is changing not only at the expense of the
natural increase, but also by the migration increase or net migration rate,
which measures the balance between immigration and emigration for a
certain period of time.[11] *Figure 10* shows data about net migration in the
countries of the South Caucasus for the years 1985- 2020.

---

[11] Net number of migrants, that is, the number of immigrants minus the number of emigrants.
It is expressed as thousands of people. "Migration balance," "net migration" and "migration
increase of population" all signify the difference between the number of incomers into a
certain territory and the number of outgoing people from the same territory for the same
period of time (ДЭС, p 385).

46

*Figure 10:*
*Net Migration, by Countries and by Years (in thousands)*

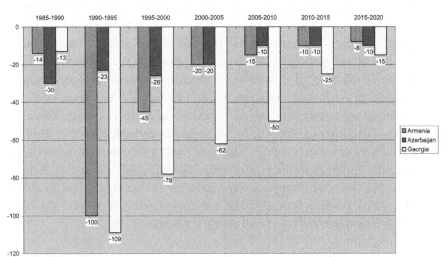

Source: Population Division of the Department of Economic and Social Affairs of the United Nations Secretariat, World Population Prospects: The 2008 Revision, <http://esa.un.org/unpp>, May 03, 2009.

As seen from *Figure 10*, though migration processes in the region had occurred during the Soviet period, they became especially intensive after the collapse of the USSR. The political breakdown caused "the great migration of peoples." The disappearance of the USSR not only intensified migration processes, but also influenced their nature and the main reasons of migration.

The factors, which influenced migration in the South Caucasus during the final years of the USSR and the post-collapse period, included inter-ethnic conflicts and wars started in the region. The most devastating conflict was the Armenia-Azerbaijan Nagorno Karabakh conflict. Therefore, during the years of the post-collapse period and the emergence of independent national states in post-Soviet territory, ethnic migration, sometimes called the Migration of Diasporas,[12] occured. The migrations resulted in Armenia becoming similar to a pure mono-ethnic state.[13]

All the countries of the South Caucasus have faced a significant influx of inter-country and intra-country migrations as well as the formation of the largest groups of refugees and internally displaced persons. The largest number of refugees and IDPs exist in Azerbaijan. For instance, in the beginning of 1990, the number of officially registered refugees from Armenia in Azerbaijan was equal to 207.5 thousand.[14] As a result of the Armenian military aggression and occupation of another seven regions of Azerbaijan adjacent to the territory of Nagorno Karabakh from 1991-1994, the number of refugees and IDPs has increased to 800 thousand according to UNHCR data from the year of 1997. The same data shows that there were 200 thousand refugees from Azerbaijan in Armenia.[15] Due to the inter-ethnic conflicts with Abkhazia and South Ossetia, there were almost 290 thousand internally displaced people in Georgia in 1997.[16]

Gradually, as ethnic divisions within populations have continued, the ethnic migration started to decrease by 1994. Then, it was replaced by economic migration. As noted by the World Bank, starting from the mid-1990s, migration movements in CIS territories became the result of weakened labor markets, lack of productive capacities of capital, low quality of life and increasing demand for unskilled labor.[17]

We will study the specific moments of migration in each country. It should be noted that migration data presented by official statistical agencies of all three states of the South Caucasus, which form the reports of the UN, are

---

[12] Mansoor A., Quillin B/ Migration and Remittances: Eastern Europe and the Former Soviet Union/ World Bank. Europe and Central Asia Region, 2006, p. 79.

[13] Reznikova O. Migration prospects in the post-Soviet expanse. *The Caucasus & Globalization*. 2 (4), 2008, pp. 71-85.

[14] Госкомстат Азербайджана, Баку, 1990.

[15] Refugees and Others of Concern to UNHCR.1997. Statistical Overview. Geneva, July, 1998, p 27.

[16] Бадурашвили И.Н., Гугушвили Т. Вынужденная миграция в Грузии.. В сб.: Миграционная ситуация в странах СНГ. М.: Комплекс-Прогресс, 1999, с. 113-117.

[17] Ibid.

often inaccurate. Therefore, we are obliged to mainly rely upon the estimations of experts when analyzing each phenomenon.[18]

## Armenia

According to expert estimates, during the period of 1991-2000, the population of Armenia decreased by almost 1.27 million people due to official and illegal leave cases.[19] Experts say that in the 1990s, net migration from these countries increased from 21 percent to 38 percent since 1989.[20] According to estimates from Armenian experts, the emigration level in Armenia will remain at 50 thousand people per year over the next 15 to 20 years.[21] The following factors keep emigration active among Armenians: difficult living conditions for the Armenian population; the maintaining of a tense situation in labor markets in Armenia; inability of the agricultural sector to ensure a decent lifestyle for a simple rural family; an invitation to migrate sent from the Armenian migrants who have already left the country.

## Azerbaijan

According to expert estimates, during the period of 1987-1994, net migration in Azerbaijan has totaled minus 350 thousand people.[22] Currently, the number of Azerbaijani laborers in Russia is up to 1.3 million people. In 2006, Russia adopted new migration rules facilitating the process of legalization of many labor migrants from Azerbaijan. Due to these changes, 600-700 thousand people from this group of guest workers are recognized as citizens of the Russian Federation. Besides in Russia, approximately 200 thousand Azerbaijanis work in Turkey and the UAE.

---

[18] Reznikova O. Op.cit.

[19] Погосян А.,Хоецян А., Манасян М. Особенности миграции населения Республики Армения. Центр миграционных исследований проблемы миграции и опыт ее регулирования в полиэтничном Кавказском регионе. Тезисы международной научной конференции. / Под общей редакцией Ж. Зайончковской и В. Белозерова. Ставропольский госуниверситет. Центр изучения проблем вынужденной миграции в СНГ. М., 2001.

[20] Reznikova O. Op. Cit.

[21] Арутюнян Л.А. Новые тенденции миграции в Армении. В сб.: Миграционная ситуация в странах СНГ. М.: Комплекс-Прогресс, 1999, с. 71-76.

[22] Yunusov A. Migration processes in Azerbaijan. Baku: Adiloglu, 2009.

Forecasts related to the migration influx from Azerbaijan to Russia have a contradictory character. Some experts think labor migration from Azerbaijan will increase mainly to Russia, where more labor resources are in demand,[23] while others hypothesize that the decrease in migration is due to the rise of xenophobia, nationalistic moods, the decline of economic conditions in Russia and the rising economy in Azerbaijan.[24]

**Georgia**

For a long time, Georgia has been a country of emigrants. Starting in the 1970s, the annual negative balance of migration has been equal to 20-25 thousand people. In the 1990s, emigration reached an unprecedented pace due to the unstable political situation after the collapse of the USSR, internal armed conflicts in South Ossetia and Abkhazia, as well as the drastically worsening living conditions and massive unemployment.[25] During recent years, economic reasons have become the main factor behind the native population leaving Georgia. The overall number of labor migrants is almost 400 thousand people per year. According to expert estimations, during the period of 1990-1997, net migration totaled minus 1.0766 million people – almost 20 percent of the whole population in the country.[26] According to the opinion of one expert,[27] due to de-population in Georgia and the influx of labor migrants from Georgia to Russia and other countries, the outward migration trend is practically exhausted. Others are of a different opinion, saying that the migration from Georgia to Russia and other countries will continue for some period of time.[28]

**Population Change in the States of the South Caucasus for the Period of 1985-2020**

Azerbaijan has not only the highest population among the countries of the South Caucasus, but also the highest increasing rate of population growth.

---

[23] Reznikova O. Op.cit
[24] Yunusov A. Op.cit.
[25]Бадурашвили И.Н., Гугушвили Т. Op.cit.
[26] Ibidem
[27] Reznikova O. Op.cit.
[28] Сванидзе Г., Кокоев К. Эмиграция из Грузии и ее причины. Центральная Азия и Кавказ, 4 (22), 2002, pp. 131-136.

*Figure 10* reflects absolute indicators of changes in the populations in all three countries of the South Caucasus.[29]

**Figure 10:**
**Population Change, by Countries and by Years**

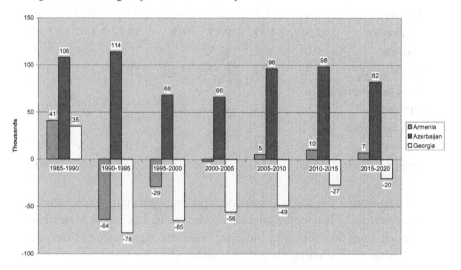

Source: Population Division of the Department of Economic and Social Affairs of the United Nations Secretariat, World Population Prospects: The 2008 Revision, <http://esa.un.org/unpp>, May 03, 2009.

Besides this indicator, which is the simplest one in characterizing the dynamics of population increase, another is used for a certain period of time to give a more exact forecast of changes in the population.[30]

*Table 2*, given below, reflects the population increase rates in the countries of the South Caucasus, different regions, Europe and the world.

---

[29] Population increment over a period, that is, the difference between the population at the end of the period and that at the beginning of the period. Refers to five-year periods running from July 1 to June 30 of the initial and final years. Data are presented in thousands.

[30] Population growth rate. Average exponential rate of growth of the population over a given period. It is calculated as ln $(P_t/P_0)/t$ where t is the length of the period. It is expressed as a percentage.

51

*Table 2:*

*Population Increase Rates by Countries and Regions, 1985-2020 (%)*

|  | 1985-1990 | 1990-1995 | 1995-2000 | 2000-2005 | 2005-2010 | 2010-2015 | 2015-2020 |
|---|---|---|---|---|---|---|---|
| **Armenia** | 1.2 | -1.9 | -0.94 | -0.07 | 0.17 | 0.32 | 0.23 |
| **Azerbaijan** | 1.56 | 1.53 | 0.85 | 0.8 | 1.11 | 1.07 | 0.86 |
| **Georgia** | 0.64 | -1.49 | -1.32 | -1.22 | -1.13 | -0.65 | -0.5 |
| **World** | 1.75 | 1.54 | 0.34 | 1.26 | 1.18 | 1.11 | 1 |
| **More developed regions** | 0.6 | 0.47 | 0.34 | 0.36 | 0.34 | 0.28 | 0.21 |
| **Less developed regions** | 2.09 | 1.82 | 1.62 | 1.47 | 1.37 | 1.28 | 1.15 |
| **Europe** | 0.39 | 0.18 | -0.02 | 0.08 | 0.09 | 0.03 | -0.03 |

As seen from *Table 2* given above, the highest population increase among the countries of the South Caucasus is observed in Azerbaijan. Meanwhile, starting from the 1990s, this indicator became a negative one in Georgia, reflecting the continuing decrease in population.

**Demographic Ageing**

Among demographic trends, particular attention should be paid to the ageing of populations, or the increase of the elderly in the population structure. UN experts have proposed the following scale: if the share of persons aged 65 and older is less than 4 percent, the country is considered to have a young population. The population is nearing ageing if this share is between 4 percent and 7 percent, and an aged population has a share that is higher than 7 percent.[31]

According to current UN data, Azerbaijan is nearing the ageing stage while Armenia and Georgia are countries with a demographically aged population. *Figure 11* reflects the dynamics of ageing in the world, countries of the South Caucasus and the regions. *Figure 11* shows how this will change the share of persons aged 65 and over in the population structure.

---

[31] Демографический энциклопедический словарь. М., Советская Энциклопедия, 1985, p. 117.

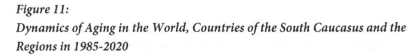

*Figure 11:*
*Dynamics of Aging in the World, Countries of the South Caucasus and the Regions in 1985-2020*

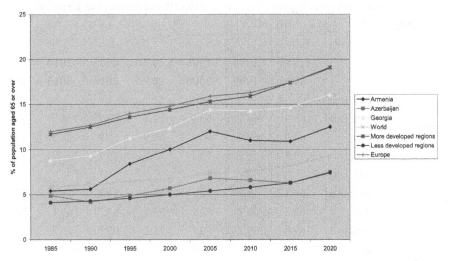

Source: Population Division of the Department of Economic and Social Affairs of the United Nations Secretariat, World Population Prospects: The 2008 Revision, <http://esa.un.org/unpp>, May 03, 2009.

The ageing process is taking place under the influence of two factors: decrease in birth indicator values (ageing from below) and increase in the average life expectancy (ageing from above). In the past, the low birth rate had already been observed in Georgia and Armenia, while it was relatively higher in Azerbaijan. According to the UN, the average life expectancy for countries of the South Caucasus during 2005-2010 is as follows: Azerbaijan – 70; Georgia – 73; and Armenia – 74. For comparison, the average is not exceeding 65 years in less developed regions of the world (see *Table 3*, below). Indeed, due to this reason, these populations are considered young with a high birth rate. In contrast, ageing in Europe is explained by a significantly increased level of life expectancy caused by ageing from above.

*Figure 3:*
*Life Expectancy in Births Observed in the Countries of the South*
*Caucasus, Different Regions, Europe and the World During the Years of*
*1985-2020*

| | | 1985-1990 | 1990-1995 | 1995-2000 | 2000-2005 | 2005-2010 | 2010-2015 | 2015-2020 |
|---|---|---|---|---|---|---|---|---|
| Armenia | Both sexes combined | 68.4 | 68 | 69.9 | 72.4 | 73.7 | 74.7 | 75.7 |
| | Male | 65.9 | 64.5 | 66.6 | 68.9 | 70.2 | 71.3 | 72.3 |
| | Female | 70.7 | 71.5 | 73.1 | 75.6 | 76.7 | 77.7 | 78.5 |
| Azerbaijan | Both sexes combined | 66.1 | 65.2 | 66 | 68.4 | 70.2 | 71.4 | 72.3 |
| | Male | 62.2 | 60.7 | 62.2 | 65.6 | 67.7 | 69.1 | 70 |
| | Female | 69.8 | 69.7 | 69.7 | 71.2 | 72.5 | 73.5 | 74.5 |
| Georgia | Both sexes combined | 70.5 | 70.5 | 71.1 | 71.6 | 71.6 | 72.6 | 73.5 |
| | Male | 66.5 | 66.5 | 67.3 | 68 | 68 | 69.1 | 70.1 |
| | Female | 74 | 74.3 | 74.7 | 75 | 75 | 75.9 | 76.6 |
| World | Both sexes combined | 63.2 | 64 | 65.2 | 66.4 | 67.6 | 68.9 | 70.1 |
| | Male | 61.2 | 61.9 | 63 | 64.2 | 65.4 | 66.7 | 67.9 |
| | Female | 65.2 | 66.2 | 67.4 | 68.6 | 69.8 | 71.1 | 72.3 |
| More developed regions | Both sexes combined | 74 | 74.1 | 75 | 75.8 | 77.1 | 78 | 78.9 |
| | Male | 70.3 | 70.3 | 71.3 | 72.2 | 73.6 | 74.7 | 75.7 |
| | Female | 77.4 | 77.9 | 78.6 | 79.5 | 80.5 | 81.3 | 82 |
| Less developed regions | Both sexes combined | 60.6 | 61.7 | 63.1 | 64.4 | 65.6 | 67 | 68.3 |
| | Male | 59.2 | 60.2 | 61.5 | 62.8 | 63.9 | 65.2 | 66.5 |
| | Female | 62 | 63.3 | 64.8 | 66.1 | 67.4 | 68.8 | 70.2 |
| Europe | Both sexes combined | 72.8 | 72.6 | 73.1 | 73.8 | 75.1 | 76.1 | 77.1 |
| | Male | 69 | 68.3 | 68.9 | 69.6 | 71.1 | 72.3 | 73.5 |
| | Female | 76.5 | 76.8 | 77.3 | 78 | 79.1 | 79.9 | 80.7 |

It should be noted that the average life expectancy of a newly born child is one of the best indicators of not only mortality, but also the level of social and economic development overall. Therefore, this indicator is used to define the so-called index of human development, a combined indicator reflecting the overall nature of social and economic development of a country.[32] According to these indicators, Armenia, which avoided a war in its own territory, is getting slightly ahead of Azerbaijan and Georgia, who have suffered full scale military assaults in their territories.

The countries of the South Caucasus differ by their populations' percentages of youth. The following graphs reflect changes in the share of population for the age group of 0-14 years (*Figure 12*) and 15-24 years (*Figure 13*).

*Figure 12:*
*Dynamics of Population Change in the Countries of the South Caucasus, World, Regions and Europe in 1985-2020*

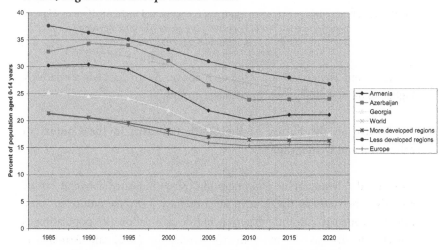

Source: Population Division of the Department of Economic and Social Affairs of the United Nations Secretariat, World Population Prospects: The 2008 Revision, <http://esa.un.org/unpp,> May 03, 2009.

---

[32] Besides average life expectancy of a newly born child, the following indicators are used also while calculating the indicator of human development: level of literacy among the adult population; share of people studying in educational institutions at the first, second and third level; average GDP in purchasing power parity (PPP in USD). See: Human Development Report 2008. NY, 2008.

*Figure 13:*
*Demographic Changes in the World, Countries of the South Caucasus,*
*Regions and Europe in 1985-2020*

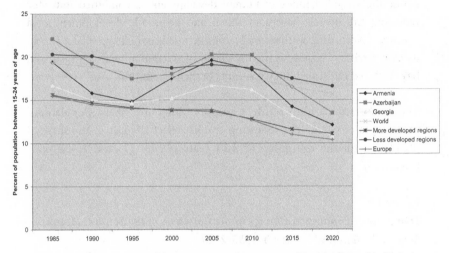

Source: Population Division of the Department of Economic and Social Affairs of the United
Nations Secretariat, World Population Prospects: The 2008 Revision,
<http://esa.un.org/unpp>, May 03, 2009.

As seen from *Figures 12* and *13* shown above, Azerbaijan has a relatively higher share of young people in both age groups.

**Perspective on the Future of the South Caucasus in the Context of Migration and Demography**

Based on the demographic and migration trends indicated above, it can be seen that the states of the South Caucasus have a diverse nature to some extent. Georgia is currently experiencing de-population (its population is expected to decrease by more than 4 percent by 2020) and Armenia is transition toward de-population. Azerbaijan, on the other hand, has higher figures in population and a higher population increase as well as a larger share of a young, labor-able population. Thus, dissimilar demographic trends create different priorities for each state.

For instance, the ageing of the populations in Georgia and Armenia sets new requirements for social insurance and the healthcare of elderly people.

The increase in population share of the elderly combined with a decreasing number of economically active people creates a demographic burden. Therefore, particular importance is attached to economic indicators of public welfare, or the ability of a society to ensure a decent ageing of its population.

Considering the relatively poor indications of social and economic wellbeing of the Armenian and Georgian populations,[33] there is a drastic increase in social and demographic burdens on the employed, able citizens. This explains the clashes and tension in relations between generations. Specifically designed economic and migration policies aimed at increasing the attractiveness of their societies would decrease the demographic burden and stop Georgian and Armenian emigration flows to neighboring countries.

Conversely, the higher share of youth in the population of Azerbaijan "pressurizes" political, economic and educational systems. Youth are usually the main agitators in society.[34] Adolescence is the period of highest interest and activity in public ideals, a driving force for social changes and the basis for different ideological movements. This is explained not only by the expanding physical abilities of youngsters, but also the particular needs of people at this age to seek their identity and place in the world.[35] In this regard, high quality education is the most important condition to convert the youth into valuable human capital because education can help young people find a well paid job and protect them from the influence of various extremist ideas and religious fundamentalism.

If Azerbaijan does set up a high quality educational system in the years to come, this will allow a drastic increase in the level of human capital and significantly decrease the risk of various emerging fundamentalist movements. Besides this, it is necessary to implement political and

---

[33] For comparison, we should note that according to UN data, the gross domestic product in USD per capita in 2007 has been the following: Armenia – 5 317; Georgia – 4 388; and Azerbaijan – 8 581. See: United Nations Economic commission for Europe URL: <http://w3.unece.org/pxweb/Dialog/Saveshow.asp>.

[34] Moeller H. Youth as a Force in the Modern World. Comparative Studies in Society and History. 10, 1968, pp. 161-188.

[35] Erikson E. Identity: Youth and Crisis. N.Y.: Norton & Company, 1968.

economic reforms in order to overcome the rising social inequality that manifests in protests and indignation. At the same time, this will hugely decrease the number of dynamic and labor able people who leave Azerbaijan.

Finally, we should pay particular attention to the resolution of frozen conflicts in the South Caucasus. The rapid settlement of inter-ethnic conflicts in the South Caucasus is the fundamental condition that can create the necessary environment for the integration of the states into the global market and secure a better economic status for their populations. At the same time, the events in Georgia during August 2008 demonstrated that unresolved conflicts in the South Caucasus can become a serious threat to the security of all three South Caucasian states. In this case, it is important to take into account the demographic factor while monitoring security issues.

Serious demographic disproportions observed in the countries of the South Caucasus – the population increase in Azerbaijan and the signs of de-population in Armenia as well as full scale de-population in Georgia – are not considered sources of inter-state conflict. However, the existing tension in the relations between states and, most importantly, the war between Armenia and Azerbaijan, causes the demographic factor to be particularly important for the security of the region. Suffice it to say that, according to 2008 CIA data, the number of men ages 16 to 49 and ready to serve in the army has been the following: Armenia – 642,734; Azerbaijan (three times bigger) – 1,727,464.[36] This difference in figures will only increase, as expected.

For instance, when the peaceful resolution of the Nagorno Karabakh conflict is marred deliberately by the Armenian side, the demographic factor can become another important argument in favor of Azerbaijan to use the military option in order to liberate its occupied territories taken by the Armenian armed forces.

In this regard, we can conclude that the delays in resolving the conflicts in the South Caucasus and, most importantly, the Nagorno Karabakh problem

---

[36] CIA- The World Factbook. <http://www.cia.gov/CIA-2009\factbook\geos\aj.html>.

can turn the demographic factor from being the issue of settlement into the issue of regional security by considering the particular role of the region in energy projects and other global issues.

# QUALITATIVE ECONOMIC FEATURES OF THE SOUTH CAUCASIAN COUNTRIES: PAST, PRESENT AND FUTURE IN THE EUROPEAN CONTEXT

**Vladimer Papava,**
Senior Research Fellow,
Georgian Foundation for Strategic and International Studies

Immediately after the restoration of their national independence in 1991, the three countries of the South Caucasus – Armenia, Azerbaijan and Georgia[1] – came to meet the challenge of a transition to a market economy. Nearly twenty years later, it is quite natural to ask where these countries are now on their way toward a market-oriented transformation.

All of the post-Communist states, including the countries of the South Caucasus, are facing some new challenges within this period of a global financial crisis.

These countries' future includes a strategic choice to move toward the Western style market economy. Pursuing this option may lead the South Caucasian states, if not to a complete integration into the European Union (EU), at least to getting much closer to it and to its standards.

---

[1] Generally, I am a proponent of defining the Caucasus as made up of the Central Caucasus, consisting of Armenia, Azerbaijan and Georgia; the South Caucasus, consisting of the northern provinces of Turkey and Iran, inhabited by Caucasian ethnic groups; and the North Caucasus, which is located in the south of Russia and is also populated by Caucasian ethnic groups (Ismailov, E., and Z. Kengerli. 'The Caucasus in the Globalizing World: A New Integration Model', *Central Asia and the Caucasus*, 2/20, pp. 135-144, 2003; Ismailov, E., and V. Papava. 'A New Concept for the Caucasus', *Southeast European and Black Sea Studies*, 8/3, pp. 283-298, 2008; Ismailov, E., and V. Papava. *The Central Caucasus: Problems of Geopolitical Economy.* New York: Nova Science Publishers, 2008). Nevertheless, in this chapter, in order not to deviate from the entire context of this book, I will adhere to the traditional division of the Caucasus into the Northern and the Southern parts only.

The key goal of this chapter is to inquire into the qualitative aspects of the economic development of Armenia, Azerbaijan and Georgia.

Before embarking upon an analysis of the economic problems of the three South Caucasian countries, we will first consider some general tendencies, challenges and dangers that may be observed in practically all of the post-Communist countries. Each of them is exposed to the same general threats, including those of the South Caucasus.

**Difficulties of the Market Transformations: "Leaders" and "Outsiders"**

Almost two decades have passed since the beginning of this historic process of transitioning to the market economy. Generalizing upon the accumulated experience[2] renders it is possible to draw a number of very important conclusions about the path already traversed in transforming a Communist economy into a market economy.

Notwithstanding the plethora of scholarly publications on the subject of the transition period, there are no generally accepted criteria for determining its completion. But the simplest formal (and indeed external) resolution of this question seemingly suggests itself: if the European Union recognises this or that country with a transition economy as one that is ready to enter its ranks, then in all probability one should concede that the transition period in this country has been completed and that its functioning economic system for all practical purposes has become European and market-based.

As is well known, the acceptance of the majority of countries in Eastern Europe and the Baltics (Estonia, Latvia, and Lithuania) into the EU has in essence already been decided. On the whole, one can interpret this to mean the completion of the transition period; that is, the period of transition to the European type of market economy. In other words, these countries are "leaders" in passing through the transition period with success. Henceforth, the discussion herein will use the term "leaders" to designate these countries. What about the South Caucasian countries of Armenia,

---

[2] For example, Åslund, A. *How Capitalism Was Built: The Transformation of Central and Eastern Europe, Russia, and Central Asia.* New York: Cambridge University Press, 2007.

Azerbaijan, and Georgia or other post-Soviet countries like Moldova, Russia, and Ukraine – those who are "outsiders?" Are they still in the transitional period?

It is obvious that these countries, which were "outsiders," are still far from developing European-style capitalism.

Capitalism by its nature is not homogenous.[3] The transitional period in "outsider" post-Communist countries has ended but, unfortunately, the economic (and not only economic) system of some of them is far from a European style of capitalism. It is better to qualify such a system as "Post-Communist Capitalism,"[4] that is, a society, which cannot be squeezed into the classic understanding of the word "capitalism" or within any other theoretically generalised model of capitalism.[5] The logic of this problem appears to be rather simple: if the collapse of the Communist system was essentially simultaneous in the countries of Eastern Europe and the former USSR, it follows that initially all were basically in the same situation and, consequently, the dragging out of the transition period to European capitalism is an artificial delay in making reforms in the economy (and in society, more broadly). This all-inclusive answer in itself contains many questions about the causes of the artificial slowdown in the process of reform which has resulted in Post-Communist Capitalism.

As the key to understanding the principal problems of post-Communist transformation in the "outsider" countries, it is expedient to conduct a comparative analysis of these countries with the "leaders" described above.

From the very incipience of the transition period, one special circumstance of great importance was not taken into account: the presence of the institutions of statehood. In particular, the states that were formed as a result of the collapse of the federal formations (above all, the Soviet Union

---

[3] For example, Dahms, H.F., ed. *Transformations of Capitalism: Economy, Society and the State in Modern Times*. Hampshire, UK: MACMILLAN PRESS, 2000; Gwynne, R.N., T. Klak and D.J.B. Shaw. *Alternative Capitalisms. Geographies of Emerging Regions*. London, UK: ARNOLD, 2003.

[4] Papava, V. *Necroeconomics: The Political Economy of Post-Communist Capitalism*. New York: iUniverse, 2005.

[5] For example, Coates, D. *Models of Capitalism: Growth and Stagnation in the Modern Era*. Cambridge, UK: Polity Press, 2000.

and the Socialist Federal Republic of Yugoslavia) and that were not the direct legal successors of these federal states lacked the institutions of statehood. As a result, their process of transition was compounded by the need to construct these institutions from the very beginning.[6] Under these conditions, the implementation of economic reforms according to schemas that had counted upon the utilisation of the corresponding institutions of the state (which were lacking in these countries) was foreordained to failure.

The advantage of the majority of the "leader" countries, compared with the "outsider" countries, was the presence of institutions of statehood, which significantly simplified and, thereby, accelerated the resolution of tasks associated with the transition to a market. Nevertheless, this factor cannot be deemed decisive in delaying the transition to a market in all "outsider" countries, for there are the examples of Slovakia, Slovenia and the Baltic countries, as EU member states, or Croatia, as an EU membership candidate country, all of which had to build state structures from scratch upon independence. Their example refutes the thesis about the fundamental impossibility of a rapid transition to a market amidst the process of creating these state institutions. As for the success of these countries in the matter of reforming their economies and, simultaneously, constructing the institutions of statehood, this is above all explained by the targeted thrust of measures adopted by the reformist governments in these countries. This, in turn, is explained by the human factor.

The human factor, as a rule, has decisive significance in practically any economic process. The character and possible success of economic reform in countries with a transition economy depend, to a large degree, upon the behavior of the person who finds himself in a transition process from *Homo Sovieticus* (i.e., someone who was formed under the conditions of a command economy and hence someone who was suppressed by the state and totally dependent upon it) to the type of person characteristic of a market economy, *Homo Economicus* (i.e., someone whose driving motivation is to receive the maximum utility in his household and the maximum profit in his firm). The type of person who carries out the process of post-Communist transformation is characterised herein by the

---

[6] Balcerowicz, L. *Socialism, Capitalism, Transformation*. Budapest: CEU, 1995, p. 146.

term, *Homo Transformaticus* – someone who cannot completely emancipate himself from fear of the state and from the habit of living at the latter's expense; such is the case even though he is gradually beginning to act upon the basis of his own private interests in order to achieve maximum utility and profit.[7] Because of the fact that the Communist regimes in "leader" countries ruled almost half as long as in the "outsider" countries, the type of person called *Homo Sovieticus* did not have time to develop fully. At the same time, *Homo Economicus* was not totally eradicated as happened in the "outsider" countries at the end of the 1930s. Consequently, in the "outsider" countries *Homo Transformaticus* was dominated by the characteristic features of *Homo Sovieticus*; by contrast, in the "leader" countries, the features of *Homo Economicus* prevailed. It is precisely this difference, which explains the greater readiness of *Homo Transformaticus* in the "leader" countries to undertake the transition to a market, in contrast to the situation in the "outsider" countries.

**Heritage of the Command Economy and the Threats from the Global Financial Crisis**

The absence of competition in command economies quashed the only effective stimulus for economic development. After the collapse of the Communist regimes and their command economies, the countries of the former Soviet Union found themselves with only a very small amount of goods to supply to the global market. With few exceptions, such as some hydro energy outputs, oil and gas extraction, and the primary processing of raw materials, the goods they manufactured failed to meet the high international standards as a result of their overall low quality and or high prices. In fact, no markets existed for these particular products. Moreover, in principle, there was no way that they could have existed; an economy of this type is nothing more than a corpse or a so-called "necroeconomy."[8]

---

[7] Papava, V. "The Georgian Economy: From 'Shock Therapy' to 'Social Promotion,'" *Communist Economies & Economic Transformation*, 8/8, pp. 251-267, 1996.
[8] Papava, V. "Necroeconomics—the Theory of Post-Communist Transformation of an Economy," *International Journal of Social Economics*, 29/9/10, pp. 796-805, 2002; Papava, V. *Necroeconomics: The Political Economy of Post-Communist Capitalism.*

Specifically, in the post-Communist countries, a necroeconomy has grown on top of the roots of the command economy's technical bases. The carrier of the necroeconomy's routine[9] is a *Homo Transformaticus*.

The majority of the necroeconomy in the public sector, as a rule, consists of large- and medium-sized processing industry enterprises that depend upon the types of goods they produce. When privatised, they move to the privatized necroeconomy.

The privatized necroeconomy indicates that a change in ownership by itself does not automatically entail the restarting of formerly idle enterprises. In other words, a "corpse's" status does not depend upon whether it is owned by the government or a private firm.

The contemporary global financial crisis has created complex problems for the world, including the economic development of the South Caucasian countries. It is precisely within the context of the current crisis that the subject of the attack of zombie-firms upon the global economy has become so topical.[10] The insolvent and, in fact, bankrupt firms that continue to operate despite their "mortality" are commonly referred to as "zombie-firms."[11]

A system of continued lending is the key source of the sustainability of these zombie-firms[12] with their loans granted by so-called "zombie-banks," which extend beneficial credits to the firms (in particular, interest rates for such loans are lower than average rates at the market level).[13]

---

[9] Nelson, R.., and S. G. Winter. *An Evolutionary Theory of Economic Change*. Cambridge: The Belknap Press of Harvard University Press, 1982.

[10] For example, Krugman, P. 'The Big Dither', *The New York Times*, March 05, 2009. Available from: <http://www.nytimes.com/2009/03/06/opinion/06krugman.html>; Krugman, P. "Wall Street Voodoo," *The New York Times*, January 18, 2009. Available from: <http://www.nytimes.com/2009/01/19/opinion/19krugman.html?_r=2&partner=rssnyt&emc=rss>.

[11] For example, Hoshi, T. "Economics of the Living Dead," *The Japanese Economic Review*, 57/1, pp. 30-49, 2006.

[12] Caballero, R.J., T. Hoshi, and A.K. Kashyap. "Zombie Lending and Depressed Restructuring in Japan," *American Economic Review*, 98/5, pp. 1943–1977, 2008; Smith, D.C. "Loans to Japanese Borrowers," *Japanese International Economies*, 17/3, pp. 283-304, 2003.

[13] Smith, D.C., ibid.

It is an established fact that many developed and post-Communist countries have resorted to certain special governmental bailout programmes in support of their financial institutions and real estate businesses, thus threatening to develop a zombie-economy. This threat may become quite real if the financial crisis continues long enough to enable the zombie-firms to take solid root.

It is precisely the financial crisis, which creates the favorable conditions for the establishment of zombie-economy foundations – that is, the zombie-ing of an economy. The zombie-ing of a necroeconomy is what happens in the post-Communist countries[14] which, in fact, is even worse than the simple economic zombie-ing that takes place in developed economies.

Consequently, the most important challenge for the South Caucasian countries and their economic development is to avoid their economy's zombie-ing.

It is important to note that in Russia, for example, the first symptoms of necroeconomic zombie-ing emerged in the immediate aftermath of the August 1998 crisis in the country, which gave rise to the phenomenon of the post-Communist zombie-economy.[15]

Theoretically, it must be made clear that the effective elimination of a necroeconomy and zombie-economy is unthinkable without an effective bankruptcy law. As the experience of many post-Communist countries has shown, most of the past attempts at formally adopting bankruptcy laws have unfortunately produced only "stillborn babies."[16]

---

[14] Papava, V. "Problema zombirovania postkommunisticheskoï' nekroekonomiki' (Zombification of the Post-Communist Necroeconomy)," *Vestnik instituta Kennana d Rossii* (Kennan Institute Bulletin in Russia), 15, pp. 37-48, 2009; Papava, V. "Post-Communist Capitalism and the Modern World of Dead Economy," *Bulletin of the Georgian National Academy of Sciences*, 3/2, pp. 198-203, 2009.

[15] Lindsey, B. *Against the Dead Hand: The Uncertain Struggle for Global Capitalism.* New York: John Wiley & Sons, 2002, pp. 210-211.

[16] Sánchez-Andrés, A., and J.M. March-Poquet. "The Construction of Market Institutions in Russia: A View from the Institutionalism of Polanyi," *Journal of Economic Issues*, XXXVI/3, pp. 1-16, 2002.

## On the Economy of the Soviet South Caucasus and the First Steps of its Transition to the Market

The South Caucasus is distinguished by its extremely diverse landscape and natural-geographical conditions. This, as well as the interests of territorial distribution of production in the former USSR, helped to form the special features of economic development in the South Caucasian countries.[17]

The economy of Soviet Armenia was characterized by the chemical industry, the production of ferrous metals, machine-tools, precision tools, textiles, clothing, leather footwear, and so on. Particular mention should be made of electric power generation and of the atomic power station, which was and still is the only one in the entire South Caucasus. Cognac production in the food industry still occupies a special place in the Armenian economy.

The economy of Soviet Azerbaijan was characterized by a sufficiently developed industrial base. This primarily applies to oil production and oil refinery, while metallurgy and the production of mineral fertilizers, fuels, lubricants, herbicides and synthetic rubber were also of great importance. Cotton-, wool- and footwear-manufacturing plants should be singled out among the enterprises of the light industry. As for agriculture, its produce was consumed not only in Azerbaijan, but also in other regions of the former USSR.

A sufficiently developed industrial base was also characteristic of the economy of Soviet Georgia – metallurgy, the production of ferrous alloys, machine-building (agricultural machinery industry, aeronautical engineering, shipbuilding) and the machine-tool industry, and the chemical industry. Agricultural produce and foodstuffs (primarily wine, mineral water, tea and citrus fruit) were mainly exported beyond Georgia and were in demand essentially throughout the former USSR.

---

[17] Adamescu, A. A., and E. D. Silaev, eds. Zakavkazskiy ekonomicheskiy raion. Ekonomiko-geograficheskiy ocherk (The Transcaucasian Economic Region. Economic and Geographical Essay). Moscow: Nauka Publishers, 1973; Gachechiladze, R. G., M. A. Nadzhafaliyev, and A. D. Rondeli. "The Regional Development Problems of Transcaucasia," *Geoforum*, 15/1, pp. 65-73, 1984; Herzig, E. *The New Caucasus. Armenia, Azerbaijan and Georgia.* London, UK: Royal Institute of International Affairs, 1999.

The collapse of the Communist system, Soviet society and the disintegration of the USSR led to a breakdown in cooperative relations among the enterprises of the former Soviet Union and the disappearance of the system for supporting the consumption of these enterprises' products. The question of reorienting foreign trade became urgent. Most industrial enterprises of the South Caucasian countries (as of the whole of the former USSR) were incapable of meeting the demands of international competition, as they formed the network of the necroeconomy. The economy of each of these countries could not avoid the trend toward de-industrialization.

The Caucasus as a whole, and the South Caucasus in particular, was always and is still today a conglomerate of contradictions.[18] In recent years, this was manifested in the political processes and the ethnic conflicts going on in the region.[19] In addition, the Russian-Georgian war in August 2008[20] has made the situation in the region more complicated.

As a result of these political, economic, and other factors, essentially all the South Caucasian states have found themselves, to one extent or another, in a profound crisis encompassing all spheres of their vital activity and is leading to an abrupt slump in production, a high level of inflation and a decline in the standard of living.[21] The conflicts have had an especially negative effect on the economy of the South Caucasian countries, as a result of which they have lost their potential for economic development.[22]

---

[18] For example, Nuriyev, E. *The South Caucasus at the Crossroads: Conflicts, Caspian Oil and Great Power Politics.* Berlin: LIT, 2007.

[19] For example, Cornell, S. E. *Small Nations and Great Powers: A Study of Ethnopolitical Conflict in the Caucasus.* Surrey: Curzon Press, 2001; Herzig, E., ibid, pp. 44-83.

[20] For example, Cornell, S. E., and S. F. Starr, eds. *The Guns of August 2008: Russia's War in Georgia.* Armonk: M.E. Sharpe, 2009.

[21] Curtis, G.E., ed. *Armenia, Azerbaijan, and Georgia: Country Studies.* Washington, D.C.: Federal Research Division Library of Congress, 1995, pp. 41-57, 115-129, 190-206.

[22] Polyakov, E. *Changing Trade Patterns after Conflict Resolution in South Caucasus.* Washington, D.C.: The World Bank, 2000. Available from: <http://lnweb18.worldbank.org/eca/eca.nsf/d1e666886eb626e2852567d100165168/23ac8865ee 0dc520852568fc005ba956/$FILE/ATT00ZE9/Trade+flows3.pdf>.

In 1996, Azerbaijan's GDP amounted to 42 percent of the 1990 level;[23] the volume of production and industrial output significantly decreased – in 1995, it was 72 percent of the 1990 level.[24] Before 1994, the economy of Armenia was in a depressed state; in particular, economic potential decreased by almost 90 percent, the GDP dropped ten-fold and the volume of industrial production shrank by 80 percent.[25] In Georgia, the GDP for 1990-1994 dropped by 72 percent, and the volume of industrial production fell by 84 percent.[26]

Beginning in 1994-1995, thanks to actively carrying out a reform policy, trends toward stabilization and improvement of the economy were observed in the South Caucasian states,[27] but the consequences of the global financial crisis were so profound that it will take more than one year to overcome them. What is more, success will be contingent on a radical and constructive domestic economic policy, as well as on an optimal combination of the interests of all the states of this region and the active attraction of foreign investments.[28]

Taking into account that the economic reforms in the South Caucasian countries are being carried out with the direct participation of the International Monetary Fund (IMF) and the World Bank (WB), it is not surprising that these reforms themselves are by nature essentially of the

---

[23] Samedzade, Z. *Etapy bol'shogo puti. Ekonomika Azerbaidzhana za polveka, ee osnovnye realii i perspektivy* (Stages in a Long Journey. The Economy of Azerbaijan over Fifty Years, Its Main Realities and Prospects). Baku: Nurlar Publishers, 2004, p. 463.

[24] Gajiev, K. S. *Geopolitika Kavkaza* (Geopolitics of the Caucasus), Moscow: Mezhdunarodnye otnoshenia Publishers, 2003, p. 104.

[25] Gajiev, K. S., ibid, p. 125.

[26] Papava, V. G., and T. A. Beridze. *Ocherki politicheskoi ekonomii postkommunisticheskogo kapitalizma (opyt Gruzii)* (Essays on the Political Economy of Post-Communist Capitalism (the Georgian Experience)). Moscow: Delo i servis Publishers, 2005, p. 162.

[27] Herzig, E., ibid, pp. 119-146; Khachatrian, V. "Basic Trends in Armenia's Economic Development in 1991-2001," *Central Asia and the Caucasus*, 2/14, pp. 130-135, 2002; Papava, V. "The Georgian Economy: Problems of Reform," *Eurasian Studies*, 2/2, pp. 52-62, 1995; Rasulov, F. "The Social-Economic Situation and the Prospects for the Economic Development of Azerbaijan," in B. Rumer, and Lau S. Y., eds., Central Asia and South Caucasus Affairs: 2003. Tokyo: The Sasakawa Peace Foundation, 2003, pp. 325-338.

[28] For example, Nuriyev, E., ibid; Starr, S.F. "The Investment Climate in Central Asia and the Caucasus," in J. H. Kalicki, and E. K. Lawson, eds., Russian-Eurasian Renaissance? US Trade and Investment in Russia and Eurasia. Washington, D.C.: Woodrow Wilson Center Press, 2003, pp. 73-91.

same type. Here it should be noted that Azerbaijan, with significant hydrocarbon supplies, did not hurry to actively cooperate with the international financial institutions. As a result, it was a little later with its market reforms than Armenia and Georgia.

## The Global Financial Crisis and the Anti-Crisis Measures of the South Caucasian Governments

Although financial markets are not well-developed in the countries of the South Caucasus it was expected that even these countries could not escape any negative implications of the global financial crisis. According to the IMF, whilst the economic growth rate across the countries of the South Caucasus and the Central Asia amounted to 12 percent a year in 2007, up from six percent in 2006, this indicator was expected to drop to less than two percent in 2009.[29] In fact the real GDP growth rate was 3.9 percent in 2009, and compared to other nations of the region, this economic decline was particularly drastic in Armenia and Georgia.[30] Unsurprisingly, the IMF has closely cooperated with countries of the South Caucasus.[31]

The impact of the global economic crisis upon the countries of the South Caucasus is not homogeneous at all. There is much in common between Armenia and Georgia, both of which are open economies[32] with no significant deposits of hydrocarbon resources. The key differences between

---

[29] For example, Jardaneh, D. "Crisis Brings Reversal of Fortune to Caucasus and Central Asia," *IMF Survey Magazine: Countries & Regions*, March 10, 2009. Available from: <http://www.imf.org/external/pubs/ft/survey/so/2009/car030909c.htm>.
[30] Regional Economic Outlook: Middle East and Central Asia. Washington, D.C.: International Monetary Fund, 2010, p. 53. Available from: <http://www.imf.org/external/pubs/ft/reo/2010/mcd/eng/10/mreo1024.pdf>.
[31] Burke, M. "IMF Lends Armenia $540 Million to Counter Crisis Impact," *IMF Survey Magazine: Countries & Regions*, March, 10, 2009. Available from: <http://www.imf.org/external/pubs/ft/survey/so/2009/CAR030909B.htm>; "Azerbaijan—Aide Mémoire for the 2008 IMF Staff Visit Discussions, December 10-17, 2008, Baku," *IMF External Relations Department*, December 16, 2008. Available from: <http://www.imf.org/external/np/ms/2008/121608b.htm>; "Current IMF-Supported Program," *Program Note: Georgia*, August 17, 2009. Available from: <http://www.imf.org/external/np/country/notes/pdf/georgia.pdf>.
[32] Georgia and Armenia have been members of the World Trade Organisation (WTO) since June 14, 2000 and February 5, 2003, respectively. Azerbaijan has been negotiating its WTO membership.

the two are associated with the Russian-Georgian War of August 2008, which had some specific consequences for Georgia's economy.[33] As for Azerbaijan, its revenues from oil and gas exports make for a rather different economic picture of this Caucasian country. Further, some similar approaches have been observed in the anti-crisis measures of the governments of all of the three countries of the Central Caucasus.[34]

In the absence of any serious deposits of natural resources, the global financial crisis had a very serious impact upon Armenia. This country was also gravely affected by the Russian-Georgian War. In particular, according to official sources, the direct and indirect damage caused to Armenia by the war is estimated to amount at USD 700 million.[35] For the first eight months of 2009, the GDP accounted for just 81.6 percent of its amount for the same period of 2008.[36] In fact, the real GDP in 2009 accounted for only 85.9 percent of Armenia's real GDP from 2008.[37]

As was expected, the crisis primarily hit the country's industrial sector wherein the enterprises of necroeconomy are concentrated. In 2008, the production rate in metallurgical and chemical industries fell to 9.6 and 14.8 percent, respectively, as compared to 2007.[38] In this regard, it must be noted that only 98.7 percent of the total industrial production volume was sold in 2008 and, more remarkably, some 70 percent of those sales took place in the

---

[33] Papava, V. "Post-War Georgia's Economic Challenges," *Central Asia-Caucasus Analyst*, 10/23, November 26, 2008. Available from: <http://www.cacianalyst.org/?q=node/4991>; Papava, V. "Georgia's Economy: Post-revolutionary Development and Post-War Difficulties," *Central Asian Survey*, 28/2, pp. 199-213, 2009.

[34] For example, "Government Offers New Plan to Boost Economy," *Civil.Ge, Daily News Online*, June 30, 2009. Available from: <http://www.civil.ge/eng/article.php?id=21180>; Khachatrian, H. "Armenia: How a Small Country Counters the Global Crisis," *Caucasus Analytical Digest: The Caucasus in the Global Financial Crisis*, No. 6, May 21, pp. 5-7, 2009. Available from: <http://www.res.ethz.ch/analysis/cad/details.cfm?lng=en&id=100521>, p. 6; Masimli, A. "Azerbaijan and the World Financial Crisis," *The Caucasus & Globalization*, 3/1, pp. 68-83, 2009, pp. 81-83.

[35] Khachatrian, H. "Republic of Armenia: Economy," in *Central Eurasia 2008*. Luleå: CA&CC Press, pp. 48-54, 2009, p. 48.

[36] "Main Statisical Data," *National Statistical Service of the Republic of Armenia*, 2009. Available from: <http://www.armstat.am/en/>.

[37] "Time series," *National Statistical Service of the Republic of Armenia*. Available from: <http://www.armstat.am/en/?nid=126&id=01001>.

[38] Khachatrian, H. "Republic of Armenia: Economy," p. 51.

domestic market,[39] which is a clear indication of the necroeconomic nature of some key sectors of the Armenian economy. So, the main problems in the Armenian economy are concentrated in the real sector.[40]

In November 2008, the Armenian Government came up with an anti-crisis programme that, inter alia, provides for the support of local industries by means of subsidising or issuing governmental guarantees to companies experiencing certain difficulties and even taking a stake in some of them.[41] Under the framework of this approach, more than 20 companies have already received governmental assistance in the aggregate amount of USD 67 million.[42] Obviously, the Armenian economy is exposed to a critical danger of zombie-ing under the conditions of the global financial crisis.

Presently, there is broad consensus over the fact that Azerbaijan has suffered the least damage from the global financial crisis as compared to the other countries of the post-Soviet world.[43]

An effective factor, which weakens the impact of the global crisis upon Azerbaijan's economy, is the country's foreign currency reserves that have been accumulated by means of oil and gas exports and that have created a so-called "safety cushion" for the country's economy.[44]

As was to be expected, particular hardships have been suffered by necroeconomic enterprises – specifically, the steel, aluminium and chemical industries.[45] Pursuant to official statistics, while the growth of the gross volume of industrial products in Azerbaijan reached 103.9 percent during the first eight months of 2009 as compared to the same period in 2008, the

---

[39] Ibid.

[40] Aris, B. "Armenian Banks Suffer at Hands of Real Economy," *bne – businessneweurope*, September, pp. 49-50, 2009, p. 50.

[41] Khachatrian, H. "Armenia: How a Small Country Counters the Global Crisis," p. 6.

[42] Ibid, p.7.

[43] For example, Hübner, G., and M. Jainzik. "Splendid Isolation? Azerbaijan's Economy Between Crisis Resistance and Debased Performance," *Caucasus Analytical Digest: The Caucasus in the Global Financial Crisis*, No. 6, May 21, pp. 12-15, 2009. Available from: <http://www.res.ethz.ch/analysis/cad/details.cfm?lng=en&id=100521>, p. 12.

[44] Hasanov, R. "Azerbaijan Republic: Economy," in *Central Eurasia 2008*. Luleå: CA&CC Press, pp. 83-91, 2009, p. 91.

[45] Hübner, G., and M. Jainzik, ibid, p. 13.

non-oil sector has demonstrated some decline; that is, the production rate for the same period of 2009 comprised only 94.3 percent of the similar indicator for the same period in 2008.[46] The City of Sumgayit, which is Azerbaijan's third largest city by population and was famous in the Soviet period for its military-industrial complex, presently represents a classic example of a necroeconomic center. Almost all of its enterprises – namely the state-owned chemical company Azerkimya plants, the state-owned Azerboru pipe factory and Azeraluminum – remain either completely idle or work at extremely low capacities.[47]

Also inoperative (or close to that status) are all steel and metal-rolling factories, which were created in the years of Azerbaijan's independence – namely, the Baku Steel Company, Baki Poladtekme JSC and DHT Metal JSC.[48]

One has to bear in mind the fact that the system of Azerbaijan's economic management still retains some old-fashioned institutional schemes. These include the independent disposition by almost all state-owned large industrial and infrastructure companies of their material and financial resources, the availability for many of those companies of some large budget assignations and their privilege of enjoying some "tax holidays."[49]

In early 2009, the Government of Azerbaijan came up with a package of anti-crisis measures. It includes some preventive steps against the artificial growth of prices on the consumer market as well as those aimed at strengthening the anti-monopoly regulation of the economy; the prevention of the government's illegal interference in the economy; the

---

[46] "Macroeconomic Indicators," *The State Statistical Committee of the Republic of Azerbaijan*, September 14, 2009. Available from: <http://www.azstat.org/macroeconomy/indexen.php?estat=archive&topic=30>. The fact is that after August of 2009, the data of the non-oil sector's growth volume of industrial products, unfortunately, was not published.

[47] Abbasov, S. "Beyond Energy Exports, the Global Downturn is Battering Local Industry," *Eurasia Insight*, April 27, 2009. Available from: <http://www.eurasianet.org/departments/insightb/articles/eav042709.shtml>.

[48] Abbasov, S. "Azerbaijan: Global Crisis Hits Baku Banks and Real Estate Sector," *Eurasia Insight*, December 01, 2008. Available from: <http://www.eurasianet.org/departments/insightb/articles/eav120108a.shtml>.

[49] Hasanov, R. "Management in Transition Economies: An Azerbaijan Republic Case Study," *The Caucasus & Globalization*, 3/1, pp. 84-91, 2009, pp. 89-91.

depositing of foreign currency reserves, which are kept abroad in the most reliable of local banks, and ensuring reliable governmental control over the investing of these resources in the real sector of economy; improving the government's investing policy; strengthening its control over the spending of budgetary funds; enhancing assistance to export-oriented enterprises; increasing the volume of privileged loans to businessmen; and intensifying the government's support of agriculture.[50]

The existence of the large necroeconomic sector, as well as the practice of financing businesses from public resources as one of the methods of combating the crisis, is a clear indication of exposure of the economy of Azerbaijan (including the necroeconomy) to the danger of zombie-ing, which was discussed above in the general context of post-Communist countries.

After the five-day Russian-Georgian War in August 2008,[51] and due to the global financial crisis, Georgia has come to face some new economic challenges.[52] The negative effects of the Georgian economic crisis might have been far more distressing had the international community not extended a helping hand in response to Russia's military aggression. At the conference held in Brussels under the aegis of the World Bank in October 2008, it was decided to allocate USD 4.55 billion in financial aid for post-war Georgia, of which USD 2 billion is a grant and the remainder a loan.[53] Georgia will receive these funds during 2008-2010 and a major part of it will be spent for the liquidation of economic damage caused to Georgia by the Russian military aggression.

2009 has hitherto been marked with an apparent decline in the Georgian economy. In the first half of the year, Georgia's GDP rate accounted for

---

[50] Masimli, A., ibid, p. 81.
[51] Cornell, S. E., and S. F. Starr, eds., ibid.
[52] Corso, M. "Georgia's Expansion Halts," *Caucasus Analytical Digest: The Caucasus in the Global Financial Crisis*, No. 6, May 21, pp. 5-7, 2009. Available from: <http://www.res.ethz.ch/analysis/cad/details.cfm?lng=en&id=100521>; Papava, V. "Post-War Georgia's Economic Challenges."
[53] *Georgia: Summary of Joint Needs Assessment. Prepared for the Donors' Conference of October 22, 2008 in Brussels.* The United Nations, The World Bank, 2008. Available from: <http://www.mof.ge/common/get_doc.aspx?doc_id=5994>.

only 89.3 percent of its own level in 2008, and finally the real GDP in 2009 accounted only 96.2 percent of that from 2008.[54]

The main problem in Georgia's economy is that, with the government's lesser control of the developments in the construction sector, the industry became dominated by "financial pyramids."

Under such circumstances, the ten largest companies of Georgia significantly reduced their production capacities and some stopped operating entirely[55] creating thereby favourable conditions for the succession of a necroeconomy.[56] Although the government periodically buys large amounts of fertilizer from Georgia's largest chemical factory, Azot, even this enterprise has had to stop its production.[57] Most surprisingly, however, these enterprises continued producing their products for the first months of 2009, in the "best" tradition of a necroeconomy and despite the obvious crisis in the Georgian economy, even though there was no demand for their output. They simply stopped their activities in April and May when the warehouses were completely filled with unwanted products.[58]

To help the country overcome the economic crisis, the Government of Georgia developed a so-called "new financial package," basically targeted to strengthen the banking and construction sectors.[59] Specifically, the government is planning to issue some treasury bills, which will be invested in infrastructure projects. The government, thereby, aims to provide some assistance to commercial banks that are going to be the key recipients of those treasury bills. In times of economic crisis, the treasury bills will enable the banks to raise some assured incomes from the national budget funds. In addition, the package provides for the weakening of the governmental regulation of banks. As a result, the government hopes that the banks will

---

[54] "Gross Domestic Product," *National Statistics Service of Georgia*. Available from: <http://www.geostat.ge/index.php?action=page&p_id=119&lang=eng>.

[55] Aris, B. "Donor Money Keeps Georgia Afloat," *bne – businessneweurope*, August, pp. 59-61, 2009, p. 61.

[56] Papava, V., and M. Tokmazishvili. "Necroeconomic Foundations and the Development of Business in Post-Revolution Georgia," *Caucasus and Globalization*, 1/4, pp. 84-95, 2007.

[57] Aris, B. "Donor Money Keeps Georgia Afloat," p. 61.

[58] Ibid.

[59] "Government Offers New Plan to Boost Economy."

be able to attract some additional lending resources. Further, the package envisages the issuance by the Tbilisi City Hall of some financial guarantees to construction companies as a means of encouraging banks to lend money to the construction companies, which will then be spent for the renovation of the old sections of the capital.

As one can see, although the problem of necroeconomy in times of an economic crisis is still a very timely one, fortunately, the government's anti-crisis plans have hitherto not given any indication that the government is going to finance necroeconomic facilities. On the other hand, it must be remembered that no official bankruptcy proceedings have been initiated to this point with respect to any of the necroeconomic enterprises of Georgia. Furthermore, as was noted above, the Government of Georgia is going to provide financial assistance to the construction companies, many of which represent "financial pyramids." This is nothing else but a step toward the zombie-ing of those construction companies and also of those banks, which will be extending loans to such construction companies owing to the financial guarantees from Tbilisi's City Hall.

Under the conditions of the global financial crisis, the South Caucasian countries need to combine their efforts in developing and adopting effective bankruptcy legislation in order to avoid the threat of economic zombie-ing.

### On the Economic Rapprochement with the EU

The key challenge for the South Caucasian countries is to achieve some level of general European economic standards and in this way to promote their economic development.[60] Thus, in the South Caucasian countries, the promotion their economic development must be a result of the rightly planned and implemented market-oriented reforms.

For the South Caucasian countries, transition to the free trade regime with the EU may become both a strong incentive and an effective mechanism to

---

[60] For example, Sekarev, A. "European Integration Process of Georgia, the Republic of Armenia and the Republic of Azerbaijan: Achievements, Shortcomings, Challenges," in *Moving Closer to Europe? Economic and Social Policies in Georgia, Armenia and Azerbaijan.* Tbilisi: Centre for Economic Problems Research. Available from:
<http://cepr.ge/images/doc/CEPR%20FES%20Book%20ENG.pdf>.

address their major challenge of achieving a general level of European economic standards. It will force these nations to carry out rather effective measures to implement consistent economic reforms. At the same time, the transition to the free trade regime will encourage and attract some new foreign investments which, in the long run, will result in the relative acceleration of economic growth rates.

Since 2004, all of the three South Caucasian countries have cooperated closely with the EU within the framework of the European Neighborhood Policy (ENP). In 2007, they joined the EU's Black Sea Synergy (BSS) initiative. In 2009, they also became involved in a brand new EU initiative called the Eastern Partnership (EaP).[61]

Despite Armenia's deep-rooted and somewhat controversial strategic partnership with Russia,[62] the European orientation is a clear foreign policy priority for Yerevan.[63] Furthermore, the Government of Armenia considers a free trade regime with the EU to be one of the key objectives of its foreign policy.[64]

Azerbaijan is interested in expanding its economic and trade cooperation with the EU even though EU membership will not be the country's priority in the foreseeable future. This may be explained, first of all, by a greater level of economic independence as compared to its South Caucasian neighbours, enjoyed by Azerbaijan due to its significant revenues raised from oil and gas.[65] Azerbaijan will need to join the WTO in order to obtain a free trade regime with the EU. The achievement of this goal will be contingent upon Azerbaijan's ability to carry out some significant reforms aimed at a greater liberalisation of its economy. It is important to note that

---

[61] For example, Mkrtchyan, T., T. Huseynov, and K. Gogolashvili. *The European Union and the South Caucasus. Three Perspectives on the Future of the European Project from the Caucasus.* *Europe in Dialogue 2009/01.* Gütersloh: Bertelsmann Stiftung, 2009.

[62] For example, Minassian, G. "Armenia, a Russian Outpost in the Caucasus?" *Russie.Nei.Visions*, No. 27, February 15, 2008. Available from: <http://www.ifri.org/files/Russie/ifri_RNV_minassian_Armenie_Russie_ANG_fevr2008.pdf>.

[63] Mkrtchyan, T., T. Huseynov, and K. Gogolashvili, ibid, p. 14.

[64] Khachatrian, H. "New Partnership with European Union Prompts Hopes in Armenia," *Eurasia Insight, Eurasianet*, November 30, 2006. Available from: <http://www.eurasianet.org/departments/insight/articles/eav113006a.shtml>.

[65] Mkrtchyan, T., T. Huseynov, and K. Gogolashvili, ibid, pp. 7, 83.

the EU has expressed its readiness to be Azerbaijan's partner in Baku's efforts to reach this goal. It is believed that Armenia and Azerbaijan are primarily interested in the EU as a counterweight to Russia.[66]

After the Russian-Georgian war of August 2008, the EU's role with respect to Georgia has significantly expanded.[67] The transition to the free trade regime was decided by the Extraordinary European Council, which met in Brussels on September 1, 2008.[68] The free trade regime is dependent upon Georgia's meeting those conditions, which Brussels has requested to be observed within the format of the ENP. These include the adoption of a new labor code, which would secure the same employee protections as found in the EU itself, and the enactment of European-style anti-monopoly and consumer rights protection legislation.

Although the Georgian government has generally welcomed the EU's initiative regarding the free trade regime, the EU's free trade regime preconditions to Georgia regrettably have hitherto been disregarded by Tbilisi. Neither the Letter of Intent sent by the Georgian Government to the IMF on September 9, 2008, for example, nor the Memorandum of Economic and Financial Policies for 2008-2009[69] make any impression that in the observable future the Georgian Government plans to amend the Labor Code and to adopt new European-standard anti-monopoly and consumer rights protection legislation. To put it in other words, the Georgian Government is by no means hurrying to implement a transition to the free trade regime with the EU.[70]

---

[66] For example, Lobjakas, A. "EU Goes Back to Drawing Board in South Caucasus," *Radio Free Europe/Radio Liberty*, September 10, 2009. Available from:
<http://www.rferl.org/content/EU_Goes_Back_To_Drawing_Board_In_South_Caucasus/1819518.html>.

[67] Mkrtchyan, T., T. Huseynov, and K. Gogolashvili, ibid, pp. 104-105.

[68] *Extraordinary European Council, Brussels, 1 September, 2008, 12594/08*. Presidency Conclusions. Brussels: Council of the European Union, 2008. Available from:
<http://www.consilium.europa.eu/ueDocs/cms_Data/docs/pressData/en/ec/102545.pdf>.

[69] *Georgia: Letter of Intent, Memorandum of Economic and Financial Policies, and Technical Memorandum of Understanding, September 9*. Washigton: The International Monetary Fund, 2008. Available from: <http://www.imf.org/External/NP/LOI/2008/geo/090908.pdf>, p. 10.

[70] Papava, V. "Is Georgians' European Dream Any Part of Government Policy?" *The Georgian Times*, December 15, 2008. Available from:
<http://www.geotimes.ge/index.php?m=home&newsid=14166>.

## Conclusions

The transitional period in "outsider" post-Communist countries has ended but, unfortunately, the economic (and not only economic) system of some of them is far from a European style of capitalism. The phenomenon of the "outsider" post-Communist countries can be explained by the human factor.

The dead enterprises, which the "outsider" countries received as their legacy of the command economy, have proven to be quite "tenacious of life." As a consequence, the market economies of "outsider" countries have been loaded by the burden of a necroeconomy.

The occurrence of financial crises has encouraged the emergence of a kind of routine that guarantees the stability of a government's bailout programs implemented through the banking sector in support of de-facto bankrupt firms. As a result, a network of zombie-banks and zombie-firms develops, upon which the entire system of a zombie-economy rests.

This threat of an economy's zombie-ing is even greater in the "outsider" countries given that this zombie-ing also has a great deal to do with a necroeconomy, which is a factor that will make it rather difficult to improve an economy's health after the end of the financial crisis.

The only effective mechanism to get rid of both a necroeconomy and a zombie-economy is to adopt a sound bankruptcy law which, in turn, requires the strong political will of the ruling elite.

In the absence of any serious deposits of natural resources, the global financial crisis had a very serious impact upon Armenia. As was to be expected, the crisis primarily hit the country's industrial sector and, particularly, metallurgical and chemical industries wherein the enterprises of a necroeconomy are concentrated. The Armenian Government came up with an anti-crisis programme that, inter alia, provides for the support of local industries by means of subsidising or issuing governmental guarantees to companies experiencing certain difficulties and even taking a stake in some of them. Obviously, the Armenian economy is exposed to a critical danger of zombie-ing under the conditions of the global financial crisis.

Azerbaijan's ability to cope with the global financial crisis – greater than that of any other post-Soviet country – is fueled by the following two factors: the underdevelopment of the financial sector and the domination of the oil and gas sector within the national economy. As was to be expected, particular hardships have been suffered by necroeconomic enterprises such as, specifically, the steel, aluminium and chemical industries. The existence of a necroeconomic sector, as well as the practice of financing businesses from public resources as one of the methods of combating the crisis, is a clear indication of the exposure of the economy of Azerbaijan (including the necroeconomy) to the danger of zombie-ing.

The summary economic indicators for 2008 clearly reflect the implications of both the global financial crisis and the Russian military aggression against Georgia. In Georgia, the economic crisis also has its own domestic roots. Under such circumstances, the ten largest companies in Georgia have significantly reduced their production capacities, with some of them having stopped operating entirely and, therefore, creating favorable conditions for the succession of a necroeconomy. Although the problem of a necroeconomy in times of an economic crisis is still very timely, fortunately, the government's anti-crisis plans have hitherto not given any indication that the government is going to finance necroeconomic facilities. On the other hand, no official bankruptcy proceedings have been initiated to this point with respect to any of the necroeconomic enterprises of Georgia. Furthermore, the Government of Georgia is going to provide financial assistance to construction companies, many of which represent "financial pyramids." This is nothing else but a step towards the zombie-ing of those construction companies and also of those banks, which will be extending loans to such construction companies.

For the South Caucasian countries, transition to a free trade regime with the EU may become both a strong incentive and an effective mechanism to address their major challenge, which consists of achieving a general level of European economic standards. Doing so will be vital to Armenia's, Azerbaijan's and Georgia's ability to further promote their economic development.

# PART TWO:

# TOWARD AN ENHANCED ENERGY POLICY DIALOGUE – GLOBAL AND REGIONAL INITIATIVES

# CASPIAN PIPELINE POLITICS AND EUROPEAN ENERGY SECURITY

John Roberts,
Energy Security Specialist,
Platts, London

The relationship between the Caspian and the European Union is both strategic and commercial. The European Union and the Caspian have a mutual interest in developing their energy relations and in further developing the existing energy corridor through the Caucasus. The region already supplies considerable volumes of oil to the European market. At a time when the European Union is seeking to diversify its sources of gas imports, the Caspian shows promise as it includes Turkmenistan, which is totally dependent on gas exports, and Azerbaijan, which is eager to develop gas for export.

The EU and the Caspian states, together with the companies that handle so much of the export flows from the Caspian to European, Mediterranean and Atlantic markets, have a shared interest in what is commonly called the Southern Energy Corridor. Broadly speaking, this term is usually used to describe a mélange of routes that serve to connect oil and gas producers in the Caspian, along with a range of Middle Eastern energy suppliers, including Iran, Iraq and even Egypt, to a variety of major international markets. This paper focuses on one core element of a broader Southern Energy Corridor – the route through which existing and planned oil and gas pipelines transit Azerbaijan and Georgia to reach either Turkey or Georgia's own Black Sea ports, thus giving Caspian producers (Kazakhstan and Turkmenistan as well as Azerbaijan) access to European, Mediterranean and Atlantic markets.

European governments and European companies have an extraordinarily strong incentive to help develop robust ties between the two regions. The European Union would like to see the Southern Energy Corridor become a core section of its planned "Fourth Gas Corridor" – a new pipeline route to Europe to add to those that already carry gas from Russia, Norway and North Africa. EU officials have spoken of prospective purchases of as much as 60 billion cubic meters per year (bcm/y) of gas from Turkmenistan, Kazakhstan and Azerbaijan.

For companies, the Corridor has served as a major transport artery for the provision of supplies and equipment for energy projects in the region for more than 15 years. This is crucially important for all major companies doing business in Azerbaijan and for a considerable number engaged in developing the oil and gas resources of Kazakhstan and even Turkmenistan, not least since the Caspian is one of the few regions prepared to offer international energy companies the opportunity to develop hydrocarbon resources on a production-sharing basis.

In addition, while stressing the way in which the importance of the Southern Corridor is likely to grow as oil and gas traffic expands, it also fulfills several other key functions. These include its role as a road and rail artery bringing in basic foodstuffs, machinery and white goods. In addition, of course, the air above this land corridor constitutes a major supply route for NATO forces in Afghanistan.

**Core Elements in the Caspian-EU Energy Relationship**

For the European Union, its concern with the Caspian has largely been shaped by its view of energy security as a whole. EU policy is commonly described, not least by senior officials of the European Commission, as resting on three pillars: competitiveness, environmental sustainability and security of supply. During the five-year term of the first Barroso Commission (2005-2010), the emphasis was very strongly placed on the first two pillars; under the Second Barroso Commission, which began in early 2010, Commission officials say the stress will be very much on security of supply. In specific terms, there is a determination to secure access to new sources of supply as well as to diversify Europe's energy balance, not least because of the need to combat climate change by promoting the use of renewables.

What remains unclear is how this will impact gas. One of the key factors in both EU thinking with regard to Caspian energy and in the minds of Caspian governments is the degree of reliance they should place on gas exports to the European market. In this context, the question is whether the EU will accept the view that gas is a natural complement to both nuclear and wind power, since nuclear power stations essentially need to be run all the time, whereas gas stations can be run intermittently with their output switched on as needed. Wind power is only available intermittently, and therefore needs backup from more flexible sources when (as happens much of the time), output is minimal or non-existent.

In March 2006, the European Council, which comprises the heads of government of the EU members, stated the importance it attached to the Caspian when it approved an action plan that stated clearly "new gas supply routes should be opened up in particular from the Caspian region and North Africa" (Presidency Conclusions: Energy Policy for Europe (EPE); Indicative List of Actions; Clause 4). This remains EU policy. But, four years later, the focus will be on a new energy security of supply directive that the EU is expected to approve in the first half of 2010 to see how much substance it provides to the declaration. The new directive is expected to give a major boost to various specific aspects of current EU policy, notably support for the principal of interconnectors in Europe (to help overcome the consequences of such crises as the Russia-Ukraine gas disputes of January 2006 and January 2009); and promotion of new pipelines – such as Nabucco, the Interconnector Turkey-Greece-Italy (ITGI) and White Stream – designed to carry gas from Caspian (and, in some cases, Middle East) suppliers to European markets. The European Commission has already officially designated these three projects as priority projects for Europe, and EU funding has been granted for detailed studies for both Nabucco and ITGI and for an initial feasibility study for White Stream. The directive may also elaborate on the role the EU intends its proposed Caspian Development Corporation (CDC) to perform. The issues of how these pipelines are likely to develop, and the role that the CDC may play, are considered later.

In terms of energy, three main elements traditionally underpin Caspian-European relations – the consumers' need for energy, which means that all energy supply sources are important; the producers' need for access to markets; and the role that international companies play in developing Caspian energy resources. All three elements remain important for oil; in the case of gas, the possibility that Europe may no longer face a gas squeeze – or at least not for the next four or five years – potentially reduces the importance of the first point, but the second and third elements remain as important as ever.

Overall, the European Union is worried about its energy security in general and gas supplies in particular; while the countries of the Caspian have a vital interest in expanding or developing new export routes for both oil and gas. This puts a premium on the Southern Energy Corridor, defined here as the route through the countries of the southern Caucasus from Azerbaijan to Georgia and thence to Europe and the Mediterranean by way of Turkey or the Black Sea.

In energy security terms, the importance of the Southern Corridor can scarcely be understated. Current hydrocarbon traffic is already significant in global terms, but the key to its future is whether it will grow, as both producers and consumers hope that it will, so that it becomes one of the pre-eminent routes in the world for the transit of both oil and gas. The Corridor's importance for producer states, particularly for Azerbaijan at present and for Kazakhstan in the future, is self-evident. So is its importance for the international companies with stakes in the various upstream ventures that are so dependent on energy transit through the Corridor. They obviously have a vested interest in ensuring that it flourishes.

But in energy security terms, the calculus for the European Union as a whole is somewhat different – a difference that relates to the fact that, for Europe, the energy issue primarily concerns gas, not oil. This is because oil is an essentially fungible commodity; if one supply source – or several – is cut off, then other sources can fill the gap or, if the cutoff comes at a time when there is little or no spare capacity elsewhere, the impact can be shared and rationing instituted amongst consumers, either by price or by regulation. That is because the transportation system for oil is essentially global. Massive pipelines or tanker lines may routinely carry large volumes of oil from one specific supplier to one specific customer, but in extremis oil produced pretty much anywhere can be delivered to pretty much anywhere else.

But gas, particularly pipeline gas, is still largely a bi-lateral issue in which long-term agreements and non-interruptability of supply are crucial. By and large – although liquefied natural gas (LNG) is making substantial inroads into this model – it is an industry in which specific dedicated suppliers serve specific dedicated markets, based on long-term contracts that may commonly reflect the seller's requirement for assurances that the high cost of investment will be covered by long-term sales and the purchaser's interest in securing long-term supply guarantees. In general, there is far less flexibility; if gas cannot be shipped through a pipeline, whole new industries, such as the liquefied natural gas industry, have to be developed as an alternative means of transportation. In sum, gas is an issue that concerns both the terms and conditions of actual supply arrangements as well as the terms and conditions of third country transit.

### Current Oil and Gas Traffic in the Southern Corridor

As of early 2010, the Corridor was routinely carrying around 1.1 to 1.2 million barrels of oil a day (mb/d), and has the capacity, using existing infrastructure, to carry an additional 400,000 b/d. Some 900,000 b/d passed through the 1,768 km Baku-Tbilisi-Ceyhan (BTC) pipeline from Azerbaijan to Turkey's Mediterranean port at Ceyhan, while the rest was carried by rail to ports in Georgia or transported via the Baku-Supsa line to the Georgian Black Sea port of Supsa. Current traffic represents around 2.5 percent of the world's cross-border trade in oil, but close to 50 percent of all oil exports from the Caspian countries of Azerbaijan, Kazakhstan and Turkmenistan.

In gas, the only major line currently in operation, the South Caucasus Pipeline, carries some eight billion cubic metres of gas a year (bcm/y) to Georgia and Turkey. In 2009, this represented just one per cent of the world's cross-border trade in gas, but it still accounted for around 15 percent of the gas exports from Azerbaijan, Kazakhstan, Turkmenistan and Uzbekistan.

For both Azerbaijan and, somewhat unexpectedly, for Kazakhstan as well, the creation of the 1.2 mb/d capacity BTC proved to be the principal mechanism whereby the two major Caspian producers were able to break the stranglehold on oil export routes held by Russia as a result of Moscow's inheritance of Soviet energy transport infrastructure. In gas, the South Caucasus Pipeline, also known as the Baku-Tbilisi-Erzurum pipeline because it connects into Turkey's main East-West trunkline at Erzurum, is already starting to play a similar role for Azerbaijan and may yet play a major role in diversification of delivery routes for Turkmenistan and Kazakhstan as well.

The twin BTC and SCP lines – both of which are operated by BP by virtue of its leading role in the consortia that developed the Azerbaijani oil and gas fields that feed the pipelines – constitute the current backbone of the corridor. There are plans for the expansion of both lines; but equally important, there is the prospect of the construction of wholly new lines specifically intended to carry Kazakh oil through Azerbaijan and Georgia to marine terminals on Georgia's Black Sea coast. At the same time, new gas pipelines would be required (if not immediately, then eventually) as and when a Trans-Caspian Gas Pipeline (TCGP) is built to carry Turkmen gas to European markets.

**Potential Oil and Gas Traffic in the Southern Corridor**

In terms of the Corridor's potential, and thus its strategic significance in terms of energy security, the following points remain salient. Firstly, Kazakhstan and Azerbaijan have joint plans for the shipment of an initial 500,000 b/d of oil across the Caspian and then via the corridor to the Black Sea and Ceyhan, and for subsequent growth of this system to anything between 750,000 b/d and 1.2 mb/d. This, coupled with planned increases in output from the existing Azeri-Chirag-Guneshli (ACG) oil field complex to a level of around 1.2 mb/d, means that it is quite reasonable to consider that in a relatively short time, perhaps in 2016 or 2017 or so, the Corridor will be carrying some 1.7 or 1.8 mb/d of crude, while eventually it could well carry upwards of two million barrels of oil a day.

In terms of gas, the corridor's role is likely to prove just as important. Azerbaijan already has one giant project whose start-up is intimately linked with the expansion of the Southern Corridor – the second phase of the giant Shah Deniz gas field project, commonly dubbed SD-2. The first phase of Shah Deniz, a giant field discovered in 2000, is the sole source for

Azerbaijan's current gas exports to Turkey and the bulk of its gas sales to Georgia (some gas produced by the State Oil Company of the Azerbaijan Republic, SOCAR, is also delivered to Georgia via older pipelines).

SD-2 has been ready for launching for more than two years, but as of February 2010, formal approval of the project was awaiting the necessary conclusion of a new agreement between Azerbaijan and Turkey. Inter alia, the new agreement will have to settle a number of contentious issues: notably, how much SD-2 gas would go to Turkey; the terms under which SD-2 gas would transit Turkey to European markets; the revision or replacement of a previous agreement under which gas from the first phase (SD-1) was sold to Turkey at a fixed price of $120 per thousand cubic metres ($/tcm); and Turkey's right to sell the SD-1 gas it did not consume domestically to customers further down the line at whatever price it could secure.

### Azerbaijani-Turkish Relations and Their Impact on Energy Issues

Turkey has yet to complete two specific processes that are key to the successful expansion of gas traffic through the Southern Corridor. The first is the ratification of the Nabucco Inter Governmental Agreement (IGA) of July 13, 2009, and the associated signing of a host government agreement, known as a PSA, setting out the specific duties and obligations of the Turkish side in developing and operating Nabucco facilities in Turkey. The second is a new gas agreement between Azerbaijan and Turkey, which will cover direct Azerbaijani sales to Turkey and the transit of gas through Turkey for projects such as ITGI or the Trans-Adriatic Pipeline (TAP).

To the Nabucco consortium, the question of a new Azerbaijan-Turkey gas agreement is ostensibly irrelevant: everything with which the Nabucco partners are concerned is covered by the IGA and the associated PSA. But there is a deeper problem that needs to be resolved. Azerbaijan's relations with Turkey are currently strained because of Baku's perception that Ankara is moving too fast toward a détente with Armenia without comparable progress being made toward a resolution of the Nagorno Karabakh conflict. To Baku, which has long regarded Turkey as a major diplomatic ally, the Turkish-Armenian détente is happening at a time when Armenian forces not only control the Azerbaijani exclave of Nagorno

Karabakh itself but also large swathes of Azerbaijan surrounding Nagorno Karabakh from which hundreds of thousands of Azerbaijani refugees have fled.

The question this raises is whether Turkish completion of the Nabucco IGA process, whilst undoubtedly necessary to get Nabucco off the ground, is sufficient to achieve this task. Once signed, the companies developing the Shah Deniz gasfield would have a clear set of arrangements that would enable them to sell their gas, and prospective customers to buy their gas, under fully commercial conditions.

But, would the Azerbaijani government go along with such action? In the absence of either a marked improvement in bi-lateral relations with Turkey, or an upturn in the atmosphere of the ongoing Nagorno Karabakh discussions under the auspices of the OSCE Minsk Group, it is reasonable to assume that a move by the companies developing Shah Deniz to take advantage of Nabucco to supply Azerbaijani gas to Europe might prompt tensions between the companies and the Azerbaijani government.

This is not set in stone. Relations between the companies and the Azerbaijani government are good; indeed the appointment of an Azerbaijani national to head BP's Azerbaijani operations has led company officials to describe relations as excellent, an important factor since BP is the most important foreign partner in all four of Azerbaijan's biggest energy projects: development of the Azeri-Chirag-Guneshli (ACG) oil field complex; development of the Shah Deniz gas field; and construction and operatorship of the giant twin BTC and SCP pipelines that serve to carry output from these fields to international markets.

In this context, the long-drawn out negotiations on a new gas agreement with Turkey assume increasing importance. It is not that they necessarily impact directly on Nabucco; it is because any failure to conclude such an agreement is likely to reflect a broader level of mistrust between Baku and Ankara and, quite possibly, a conviction in Baku that for Azerbaijan the bottom line is that resolving the Nagorno Karabakh dispute to Azerbaijan's satisfaction is more important than promoting gas exports. Until the Turkish détente with Armenia began, there seemed to be little connection between these two issues; as of early 2010, it may be quite difficult to separate them.

The official word from both Baku and Ankara is that they are confident that their disagreements on energy supply and transit will be overcome, and a new agreement will be signed in the near future. Moreover, both the European Union and the United States have urged both sides to complete these negotiations. But a modest word of caution is probably in order. As recently as the summer of 2009 it was generally thought in diplomatic circles that such an agreement would be signed in advance of the international treaty on Nabucco, which ended up being signed by the governments of the five original Nabucco partners in Ankara on July 13, 2009. When this did not happen, it was assumed that the Turkish-Azerbaijani agreement would follow within a few weeks. It has not and the delay in concluding such an agreement, exacerbated by Turkish-Azerbaijani tensions over the Nagorno Karabakh conflict and Turkish overtures to Armenia, has contributed to a marked deterioration in the formerly strong relations between Ankara and Baku.

**The Impact on SD-2**

Lack of a transit agreement has already delayed SD-2 by more than two years, and has even prompted some members of the consortium developing Shah Deniz – notably Norway's Statoil – to suggest it might be time to think of alternative export routes for SD-2 output, notably via Russia. As for the Azerbaijanis themselves, when the energy conference season got underway in September 2009, there was scarcely a gathering at which Azerbaijani officials and diplomats did not raise the question as to whether the White Stream project to construct a gas pipeline from Georgia under the Black Sea to a European terminal in either Ukraine or Romania might be developed before Nabucco. Previously, the overwhelming assumption in the energy community would have been that Nabucco's prospects were much brighter than those of White Stream, and that the latter's best hope of becoming reality was for Nabucco to pave the way for Caspian gas to reach Europe. White Stream – which would require substantially higher initial costs than Nabucco – would then follow on once the viability of Caspian exports to Europe had been demonstrated.

Concerns at the failure to secure a transit agreement have resulted in

Azerbaijan raising, at least verbally, a variety of alternative options. SOCAR officials have spoken of the possibility of sending their gas eastward, across the Caspian, to Turkmenistan from whence it would be transported via the Central Asian Gas Pipeline (CAGP), which opened in December 2009 and currently carries Turkmen gas to China.

This is not a particularly strong prospect; the option is almost certainly stressed simply to put pressure on Turkey. Of more immediate concern, however, is the fact that the delays in securing a Turkish transit agreement prompted both Russia's Gazprom and Iran to offer to purchase its entire output. For two years, Azerbaijan resisted such advances, agreeing only to arrange much smaller deals whereby gas produced by SOCAR itself, rather than by the BP-led consortium developing Shah Deniz, would be sold to its neighbors. Russia would receive 500,000 cm a year initially, rising to 1 bcm/y, while Iran would get limited volumes of gas, essentially in a swap deal to compensate it for the provision of gas to the Azerbaijani exclave of Nakhichevan, which lies on the other side of Armenia and has only aerial connections with the rest of Azerbaijan.

However, in January 2010, SOCAR announced an increase in planned deliveries to Russia, saying it would supply Gazprom with an initial 0.5 bcm of gas in 2010, but that it would raise this in a couple of years to 2 bcm/y. This is not a particularly large amount and, indeed, it can be viewed as an Azerbaijani contribution toward the stabilization of Russia's troubled North Caucasus regions by helping ensure that these comparatively remote regions do not face energy shortages. But the January agreement for some of the gas going to Russia to be drawn from Shah Deniz is significant. It represents the first time that the field's gas has been earmarked for any recipient other than the original three marketed destinations – Turkey, Georgia and Azerbaijan itself. The amounts are likely to be small, being essentially defined by the fact that from 2010 onwards SD-1 will produce between 0.5 and 1.0 bcm a year more than initially projected, thus enabling SOCAR to meet at least part of its planned sale to Gazprom through supply of SD-1 gas. But it is clearly a shot across Turkey's bow, a warning that Ankara cannot take for granted the supply of all or most of SD-2 gas to serve destinations in Turkey or requiring transit through Turkey.

## A $50 Billion Investment Dilemma

Despite current tensions, it seems almost inconceivable that Azerbaijan and Turkey will fail to conclude a transit agreement. There is simply too much riding on the issue. Although one major gas project, SD-1 is already in operation, as much as $50 billion in fresh energy sector production and infrastructure development is hanging on the successful conclusion of an Azerbaijani-Turkish transit agreement.

*Azerbaijan*

The second phase of Shah Deniz (SD-2) is crucial for several reasons. As of early 2010, it is expected to come on stream in or around 2016, with the precise date dependent on formal Azerbaijani government sanction for the project and with this in turn dependent on the successful conclusion of Turkey's Nabucco arrangements and/or the new Azerbaijani gas agreement with Turkey. The project's developers currently anticipate production will be around 14-16 bcm, but a slightly higher rate of production of around 17 bcm is not to be ruled out. All this would be additional to Phase One output, expected to reach a plateau level of around 9 bcm in 2010. Almost all of Shah Deniz output, from both Phase One and Phase Two, would be earmarked for export westward via the South Caucasus Pipeline (SCP), currently operating at an annual capacity of around an 8-9 bcm but, with additional pressure stations, capable of carrying some 20-21 bcm/y. While existing gas sales to Turkey would be maintained, and some SD-2 gas would also be supplied to Turkey as well, it is reasonable to suppose that at full capacity around half of Azerbaijani exports via the SCP would in fact be intended for destinations beyond Turkey, with most of it headed for the Austrian hub at Baumgarten via the Nabucco pipeline. SD-2 is officially estimated to cost $20 billion. However, as of early 2010, one leading industry official, Dr. Wolfgang Peters of Germany's RWE (which wants to bring Turkmen gas into Azerbaijan for onward shipment via Nabucco to Europe), was estimated SD-2 would cost $25bn.

In addition, Azerbaijan has a number of other major opportunities for gas development, notably the associated gas produced by ACG and, separately, a major layer of gas lying under the ACG field complex (which requires a wholly new agreement for development since it lies at a depth below that covered by the original 1994 production sharing agreement governing ACG field development). In addition, France's Total is at the exploration phase in the Absheron field, where gas was discovered at the start of the decade, but in quantities that at that time were not considered commercially viable. There is a "chicken-and-egg" argument as to whether it is field development or transport pipelines that need to be developed first. However, as and when it becomes clear that there will definitely be a direct pipeline connection from Azerbaijan to a major European hub – the role most closely associated with Nabucco – that will also likely signal Azerbaijan to commit itself to a new round of negotiations seeking to develop these substantial resources, as well as to launch the second phase of Shah Deniz.

*Iraq*

A number of international companies, including RWE, Austria's OMV, and Turkish and Middle Eastern companies are involved in developing the Pearls project in the Kurdish Autonomous Region of northern Iraq. This project, intended to produce between 8 and 10 bcm of oil from a string of gas fields in the KAR, will cost roughly $8 billion to develop. In addition, the Iraqi government is looking to Turkey and Nabucco as an outlet for gas from its yet-to-be developed giant field at Akkas, close to the Syrian border. The timing for Akkas, however, is more related to internal security conditions in Iraq than to any timetable for Nabucco's implementation.

*Turkmenistan and Kazakhstan*

Strictly speaking, development of specific gas projects in these countries is not necessarily determined by access to European networks via Turkey, since they both possess connecting lines to Russia while Turkmenistan has, and Kazakhstan will soon also possess, the ability to connect the bulk of its gas resources to pipelines flowing east to China. And, of course, Turkmenistan now also possesses two major pipelines delivering gas to Iran. The EU's Caspian Development Corporation proposal is specifically targeting Turkmenistan as a source of gas, but any development of a CDC-inspired gas flow to Europe is not particularly focused on early use of an export route via Turkey. A Turkish route is, of course an option but the CDC approach is best considered a follow-up to the current generation of projects.

However, the fate of one particular project in Turkmenistan, the 10 bcm/y offshore gas production facility currently under development by Malaysia's PETRONAS Carigali in the Caspian Sea, is closely linked to the prospects for westward export via the South Caucasus Corridor and Turkey. In November 2009, Turkmenistan specifically stated that European companies looking to develop a Trans-Caspian pipeline, which would then feed into Nabucco or other delivery systems to Europe passing through the South Caucasus, should specifically look to the PETRONAS operation as a source of gas. The statement was in marked contrast to previous general statements by the Turkmens that if importers were to build a pipeline to Turkmenistan, then Turkmenistan would undertake to fill it. Moreover, it contradicted agreements dating back to 2003 – epitomized by a tri-lateral agreement with Russia and Kazakhstan in May 2007, that Turkmenistan, Kazakhstan and Russia would jointly develop a Caspian Coastal Pipeline to carry gas from Turkmenistan's Caspian regions to markets in or beyond Russia. The CCP project was very much focused on using PETRONAS gas as a baseload. Kazakhstan does occasionally look at the issue of exporting gas westward to Europe via a Caspian crossing, but no specific projects are dependent on this. It is worth noting, however, that a US-funded study on a possible Kazakh gas pipeline to Azerbaijan is expected to be completed in mid-2010.

## Pipeline Dependency on Transit Through Turkey

At least four major pipeline projects – or concepts – are essentially predicated on Caspian and/or Middle Eastern gas reaching Turkey and then being successfully transmitted through Turkey for delivery to European markets. These are Nabucco, ITGI, a Trans-Balkan line and White Stream.

### Nabucco

This pipeline project was evaluated to cost €7.9 billion throughout 2009, but with its officials saying the sum would obviously vary, depending on such key factors as the price of steel and the degree of application of "green" technology in providing power supplies for the pipeline and associated facilities. This point self-evidently also holds true for other proposed projects that have yet to place firm contracts for steel pipe delivery. The completion of the IGA and PSA process should be followed very rapidly with the inauguration of an "open season" for the Nabucco pipeline, under which Nabucco's partners would solicit firm commitments for transport of gas through the planned Nabucco line from Turkey to the Austrian hub at Baumgarten. Since Nabucco is largely predicated on Azerbaijani gas (although it should be noted that it is also likely to carry gas from a variety of other sources, notably Iraq and perhaps Egypt in its early years, and Turkmenistan subsequently) confirmation of its construction and of the launching of SD-2 will require an expansion of the South Caucasus Pipeline from around 8-9 bcm/y capacity at present to its maximum design capacity of around 20 bcm/y. The SCP work alone could add as much as $2 billion to energy development work in the Southern Corridor.

*ITGI*

The project for an Interconnector Turkey-Greece-Italy (ITGI) is, in effect, a string of projects that would enable gas from the Caspian and Middle East to reach Italy. The first element, an interconnector between Turkey and Greece, was opened in late 2007 and is in active use; the next two elements, a section across the peninsula of Greece and a sub-sea crossing of the Adriatic to Otranto in Italy are currently at the advanced planning stage. The EU has designated Poseidon, the 12 bcm/y, 203 km maritime connector, a priority project and has awarded it €100 million in seed finance. Poseidon's cost is put at €600 million. The 15 bcm/y, 590 km connection across Greece from Komotini to Thesprotia, the jumping off point for Poseidon, is put at €900 million.

There are other major pipeline proposals that also need to be taken into account, notably the Trans-Adriatic Pipeline (TAP), significant because one of the major partners developing Shah Deniz, Norway's Statoil, has a 50 percent stake in this plan to construct a pipeline from Greece to Albania and then under the Adriatic to Italy. This offers a shorter route than Poseidon and has the potential to improve regional energy security by making use of played-out Albanian gas fields for regional gas storage.

*A Trans-Balkan line*

The EU is also backing the development of a South European Gas Ring, which would aim to carry gas to a number of countries, notably in the western Balkans, which have little or no access to gas, and to connect them up both to each other and to existing gas lines in the region. In this context, the construction of a West Balkans gas pipeline is under study, creating a line from Greece to Austria that would serve Macedonia, Serbia, Bosnia-Herzegovina and Croatia en route. With ITGI operational, such a line could be served with either (or both) Caspian gas transiting Turkey or North African gas supplied via Italy.

*White Stream*

In addition, there is one proposed project, which aims to carry Caspian gas to Europe but without first transiting Turkey. This is the White Stream project aimed at building a cluster of eight bcm/y-capacity lines across the Black Sea from Georgia to either Romania or Ukraine. This project has generally been considered a long shot, a possibility to be considered once Nabucco is up and running, once the South Caucasus Pipeline has been filled to its 20 bcm/y design capacity, and once it is clear that gas from Turkmenistan as well as Azerbaijan is also available to justify the cost of a wholly new line all the way from Baku to southeastern Europe. However, the possibility – and it is no more than a possibility – that Azerbaijan and Turkey may not be able to resolve their differences over the flow of gas through Turkey has certainly prompted increased Azerbaijani interest in the project. Unlike Nabucco and ITGI, however, the sources of financing for White Stream remain unclear and its proponents are still not ready to indicate what they believe the cost of their project might be.

## The EU's Emphasis on Nabucco and Connections to Greece, Italy and the Balkans

The European Union is no idle observer of this delicate balance between upstream field projects and the pipelines required to carry them to market. Its concern with seeking new sources of gas supply makes it keen to access Caspian energy and that has led the European Commission to give active support to such projects as ITGI, Nabucco and White stream. This support has included strong diplomatic backing for efforts to secure the Nabucco IGA, and a major commitment to back the ITGI, since it would also serve, in extremis, as a way of carrying North African gas from Italy to the Balkans, even though its normal role would be to carry Azerbaijani and/or

Middle Eastern gas west via Turkey to Greece and Italy.

The EU has also provided financial support and has contributed to the ability of at least one major project, Nabucco, to secure further financing. It has provided €200 million for Nabucco, which is currently helping to pay to get detailed engineering studies under way, and it has furnished €100 million for ITGI, for similar purposes. The EU's public backing for Nabucco also contributed to an environment in which the European Investment Bank has said it is prepared to provide up to a quarter of Nabucco's total financing – roughly €2 billion – and this in turn has encouraged various export credit agencies and the European Bank for Reconstruction and Development to consider how they might be of service. A detailed financing plan for Nabucco is due at end-2010.

A further aspect of EU energy security policy is also relevant in regard to both ITGI and Nabucco. The EU places a high premium on the development of interconnectors within its member states – lines that are capable of carrying gas in either direction. Nabucco is designed as an interconnector so that, in an emergency, it could carry North Sea or Norwegian gas down to Turkey, although its normal role would be to transport Caspian and Middle Eastern gas in the opposite direction.

It is highly significant in this regard that ITGI is currently finalizing plans for an interconnecting spur between Greece and Bulgaria. The vulnerability of Bulgaria, which receives 93 percent of its gas from a single source, Russia, to crises in which it is not involved was amply demonstrated in the Russia-Ukraine gas disputes of 2006 and 2009, when the country witnessed massive gas shortages. Indeed, The EU was an early backer of ITGI, precisely because it provides the ability to carry North African gas via Italy to the Balkans, even though it would normally be used to carry Caspian and Middle Eastern gas westward to Greece and Italy.

Ironically, although Moscow clearly dislikes Nabucco and would prefer to see Caspian gas carried to Europe by means of its own projected 63 bcm/y, €25 billion South Stream project, Nabucco might actually assist Russia in exporting more of its own gas to the EU. The Russia-Ukraine gas crises obviously unnerved a number of European customers of Russian gas, particularly those like Bulgaria and Slovakia who relied overwhelmingly on it. But once it is possible to deliver alternative supplies to these countries in an emergency, via Nabucco or smaller scale interconnectors, they no longer need to worry so much about their reliance on a single supplier. Likewise, this development of an effective gas supply insurance policy means that other countries can also feel more secure about purchasing Russian gas should they find it to be cheaper than gas coming from other suppliers, such as Norway, North Africa or even, in the future, the Caspian.

### The EU's Big Idea: The Caspian Development Corporation

The EU is often accused of being bureaucratic, but sometimes it does think big – really big. It has done so in the case of the Caspian Development Corporation (CDC). This is a concept that aims, in essence, to convince producer countries such as Azerbaijan, Turkmenistan – and perhaps even Kazakhstan and Uzbekistan as well – not only that the EU is serious about wishing to import gas from them but is prepared to set up a mechanism under which it would either itself purchase or guarantee the purchase by companies serving the EU market of truly massive volumes of Caspian gas.

The CDC has several main aims. These include aggregation of volumes, provision of cast iron financial guarantees, diversification of both currency and political risk, and prospective assistance in technology transfer.

In practice this means that the EU is prepared to create a structure through which it can go to a major producer and order – or underwrite – large volumes of gas for delivery to Europe by means of the Southern Corridor. In specific terms, EU officials say, this means they would be able to go to Turkmenistan and order as much as 60 bcm/y of gas on a long-term 20-30 year basis.

The EU is not dogmatic about purchasing the gas itself; it would be perfectly happy if the effort to develop the CDC were to be pre-empted by commercial agreements that would provide for Turkmen gas to flow westward to Europe in similar quantities. But the CDC is a proposal that aims to break the deadlock as to whether giant delivery contracts need to be preceded, followed or accompanied by infrastructure creation, not least because , as the EU has said, the CDC would be available, if necessary, to "provide transmission infrastructure in challenging environments." This is as close as the EU has come to stating it would be prepared to play a direct role in securing one of the most problematic elements of a Southern Corridor expansion, the development of a Trans-Caspian Gas Pipeline between Turkmenistan and Azerbaijan.

Significantly, EU presentations on the CDC include a direct statement that it would not involve actual production of gas – a key issue in that Turkmenistan, although prepared to award risk-and-reward production sharing agreements to companies working in its Caspian offshore prospects, remains reluctant to do the same onshore, where only China's CNPC has been able to secure such an agreement. In other words, the European Commission believes it is possible for Europe to secure gas from Turkmenistan without European companies seeking a stake in Turkmenistan's onshore gas resources and that, if necessary, the EU is in some as-yet-unspecified way prepared to help build the necessary pipelines to carry the gas from Turkmenistan to Europe.

As of early 2010, the EU is still trying to transform the CDC concept into a workable model. It has commissioned a study from the World Bank into how the CDC might operate and has been careful to consult extensively with its own Competition Directorate to ensure that any CDC aggregation of volume purchases could be achieved without falling foul of EU competition law. Whether the World Bank study will go along with the vision of massive throughput to include as much as 60 bcm of gas from Turkmenistan alone, or whether it will seek to persuade the Commission that it should adopt far more modest targets for total Southern Corridor throughput, remains a matter of considerable controversy.

**The Physical Security of the Southern Corridor**

As the EU grapples with the issue of how to fill the corridor and thus cement the energy relationship between the Caspian and Europe, it obviously has to address the issue of the Corridor's physical security, not least in the light of the Georgian War of August 2008.

This brings two core issues into focus in considering Southern Corridor security: the role of Russia, since it effectively constituted one side in the Georgian War, and the role of the European Union itself, since it was the

EU, then under the presidency of France, that took the lead in arranging the ceasefires that ended the actual fighting in Georgia and which now has direct security responsibilities in terms of ensuring Russian and Georgian compliance with the ceasefire terms. The EU faces a distinct credibility problem in its handling of the ceasefire agreements, since the prevailing view in both Georgia and a number of EU member states is that the EU is not responding effectively to the challenge posed by Russia. In particular, there is concern that within days of Russia signing the ceasefire terms, Moscow then broke them when it unilaterally declared that it was recognizing Georgia's breakaway territories of Abkhazia and South Ossetia as independent states and was therefore no longer bound to withdraw the bulk of its forces from these territories as it no longer regarded them as being integral parts of Georgia.

In addition, there is also a widespread perception that Russia remains opposed to development of the Southern Corridor, since its development further weakens its own former monopolistic control of Caspian export pipelines. This view, again found throughout the Caucasus and in many European government circles as well, also holds that Russia poses a security threat to the Corridor's development because it possesses the undoubted ability – if it should so choose – to destabilize the region and thus, potentially, to choke off oil and gas exports passing through the Corridor.

Tthere is also the distinct possibility of internally-generated unrest stemming from the not-so-frozen conflicts in the South Caucasus itself, notably the Nagorno Karabakh dispute and the questions of the future of South Ossetia and Abkhazia. In Turkey, the question of whether the government will be able to secure a peaceful resolution in its war with the rebel Kurdish PKK movement remains a significant issue in considering the safety of both current and existing oil and gas pipelines.

During the Georgian War, Russia went to great lengths to stress that the war was not about control of energy routes. In this, ironically, it was aided by a peculiar incident at Valve Station 30 on the BTC line in Turkey just before ground fighting started on August 7. At some point during the late evening of August 5 (the incident only being reported in the early hours of August 6), an explosion damaged BTC Valve Station 30 forcing an immediate cessation of oil flow through the line. Turkish officials said it was an accident; the PKK claimed it had launched an attack on the station. Oilmen familiar with the installation considered it an attack. Regardless of what – or who – caused the blast, the fact that a flow of some 800,000 b/d of oil was halted before the fighting broke out took a lot of pressure off the oil markets. By the time the Georgian crisis was really under way some 36 hours later, the market had already adapted to the loss of the biggest energy carrier in the region. Thus, when fighting did break out and there was concern about its impact on oil and gas pipelines, oil markets reacted with relative equanimity. It should be noted, however, that the origins of the explosion remain highly controversial, not least since the PKK had never previously mounted a successful attack on the BTC, either during its three-year construction period or during its first two years of operation.

During the actual fighting, Russia did not appear to target energy pipelines or installations to any significant extent. At the time, Georgian officials said Russian warplanes had targeted BTC and its twin, the South Caucasus gas pipeline, in their bombing runs. Yet, as the principal example given occurred where the pipelines pass close to the Georgian air base at Marneuli, and as the pipelines themselves were not damaged, this is perhaps best viewed as an uncertain and isolated incident.

What the war did show, however, was that Russia did not have to say it was seeking to exercise control over the pipelines or even to attack them directly; its actions demonstrated that Russian military power was a factor that both regional governments and international companies and governments involved in developing the Corridor would have to take into account.

Perceptions matter, but perceptions change. One of the curiosities of the war is that, quite naturally, once the fighting was over the Caspian investors in Georgia – essentially Azerbaijan and Kazakhstan – began to row back on their plans for expanded energy activities in the stricken republic. But by 2009, this view was succeeded by a longer-term perception that the Georgian War had not irretrievably damaged the security of the Southern Corridor. This led, in turn, to a return to active development of the Kazakh oil terminal at Batumi and the Azerbaijani terminal at Kulevi – the latter located just a few kilometers from the current Georgia-Russia stand-off line along the Black Sea coast by Abkhazia. It also led the Kazakh and

Azerbaijani governments to push ahead in 2009 with practical measures for implementing the KCTS transportation system under which Kazakh oil would cross the Caspian to Azerbaijan and then be transported to European markets by the BTC line and by prospective new pipelines to Georgia's Black Sea terminals, notably Batumi.

**Security Issues in the Corridor**

So long as all parties involved in – or affected by – Caspian production, consumption or transit are in agreement that energy affairs are essentially commercial, there is no problem in terms of provision of security. But the perception that there is a problem in such a sensitive area ensures that the problem needs to be addressed.

For Russia, and for at least part of the fragmented Georgian opposition, NATO is part of the problem. But at a time when the European Union has prime responsibility for hard security issues concerning Russia's military role in the Georgian territories that Russia has recognized as independent states, the failure of the EU to secure Russian military withdrawal from what it considers to be integral territories of the Georgian republic showcases the weakness of current hard security arrangements in the region. And this, in turn, prompts renewed discussion of a more direct role for NATO in the physical security of the South Caucasus. It should be noted that Azerbaijani diplomats have raised the issue of whether there is a role for NATO in securing the Southern Corridor but, particularly since the Georgian War, NATO has made it quite clear that it has no mandate to offer such protection. What it may be able to do, however, is to work in conjunction with the EU's military teams to help provide the transit countries of the South Caucasus with improved reconnaissance information and an enhanced advanced warning capability.

**Conclusion**

As of early 2010, the future of the Southern Corridor rests largely on the triangular relationship between Azerbaijan, Turkey and the European Union. If Azerbaijan and Turkey are able to resolve their differences, that will lead directly to the start-up of Caspian exports to major European markets in general and, almost certainly, in particular lead to the successful implementation of the Nabucco pipeline. The European Union has a vital interest in securing a rapprochement between Baku and Ankara; but whether this can be done without, at the same time, moving significantly toward a final settlement of the Nagorno Karabakh issue is becoming a question in its own right. Until late 2009, the development of the Southern Corridor for Azerbaijani gas exports and the settlement of the Nagorno Karabakh dispute – even though the twin BTC and SCP pipelines pass within 20 kilometers of the Azerbaijani-Armenian ceasefire line – were generally regarded as quite separate issues that would be resolved on quite separate timetables.

This may no longer be the case. Azerbaijan is beginning to examine the prospect of shipping gas from Georgia to Romania as compressed natural gas (CNG), thus cutting out Turkey altogether. At the same time, Russia would like to purchase as much SD-2 gas as possible; and Baku has at least raised the possibility that it might entertain such an idea. Illustratively, Azerbaijan agreed to a small volume of first phase Shah Deniz gas being supplied to Russia as part of its otherwise relatively modest 2 bcm/y accord with Gazprom.

The European Union has a cluster of highly experienced diplomats working on Caspian, Caucasus and Southern Corridor issues. But if the EU wants to ensure that the Southern Corridor does start to carry large volumes of Caspian gas to European markets by the most obvious route – Turkey – it now looks as if it will have to integrate its foreign, energy and security policies to a much greater degree than heretofore, while addressing the overall issue at the very highest level.

For the European Union, the key question clearly remains the flow of Caspian hydrocarbons to Europe. But to Azerbaijan it increasingly appears to be the need to ensure that Turkey does not desert it in the search for a peaceful resolution of the Nagorno Karabakh conflict. As for Turkey, the issue is increasingly becoming the totality of its relations with the European Union: as a provider of transit facilities, as a partner in European energy security and, of course, as a candidate nation for full membership of the European Union.

# AZERBAIJAN'S PLACE IN EURO-CASPIAN ENERGY SECURITY

**Robert M. Cutler,**
Senior Research Fellow,
Institute of European, Russian and Eurasian Studies,
Carleton University

The evolution of Caspian Sea basin energy transmission networks is entering a crucial phase. Azerbaijan is the crucible where questions concerning the future structure of geo-economic relations in Eurasia (and also therefore crucial aspects of the general geopolitical structure of world politics) are today being resolved. Azerbaijan's significance arises both from the volume of its natural energy resources and from its irreplaceable role as a bridge from Central Asia and the Caspian Sea basin to the Black Sea basin and Europe. Most recently, this significance has only been underlined by the implementation of a multi-vectored energy export strategy.

This chapter sketches a perspective of the medium-term future on the basis of the long-term, medium-term and short-term past. The first section summarizes three centuries of international politics in Greater Southwest Asia with a focus on Russian-Turkish relations, which historically and in the future constrain South Caucasus developments especially in present-day energy geo-economics. The second section examines more closely the evolution of the region's energy geo-economics over the past two decades, distinguishing between Greater Central Asian and Greater Southwest Asian geo-economic energy complexes.

On that basis, the third section focuses principally on the most recent events in Greater Southwest Asia, which affect prospects for the production and marketing of Azerbaijan's energy resources. The fourth section addresses one of the essential geo-economic links between Greater Central Asia and Greater Southwest Asia. It gives particular attention to the possibility of a Trans-Caspian Gas Pipeline from Turkmenistan to

107

Azerbaijan, including the obstacles to such a project and ways to overcome them. The fifth section looks into the near future, emphasizing projects for the transit of Caspian Sea basin energy resources to Europe across the Black Sea. The concluding section recapitulates the meaning of this survey of recent and near-future events, from the perspectives of the three-century and two-decade perspectives set out in the beginning.

## 1. The Long Perspective from Three Centuries

From a long-term historical perspective, the present international system in the Euro-Caspian meta-region is unprecedented. This is so, not only because of the emergence of the three South Caucasus countries as modern states. Just as fundamental is the fact that never since the Treaty of Utrecht, which created the "European State System [as] an indissoluble unity [where] all States, east and west, were involved in every contest between any of its members," have relations between Russia and Turkey been so close.[1]

Up until the First World War and creation of the Soviet Union, bi-lateral Russo-Turkish relations were almost uniformly unfriendly. During most of the eighteenth century, the Russian and Ottoman Empires were both strong states, and their mutual relations were conflictual. For roughly the first two-thirds of the nineteenth century, throughout the Concert of Europe, Turkey was a weak state; Russia, meanwhile, was strong up until the Crimean War and then weak afterwards. Their bi-lateral relations were characterized by mitigated antagonism up until the Crimean War, and by unmitigated antagonism afterwards. Then under the unipolarity of Bismarck's international system, at the end of the nineteenth and beginning of the twentieth century, Russia was a strong state and Turkey was weak; and their bi-lateral relations were antagonistic throughout.[2]

---

[1] Frederick L. Schuman, *International Politics: The Western State System in Transition* (New York: McGraw-Hill, 1941), p. 59.

[2] For a detailed historical survey, on which the material in this section is based, see Robert M. Cutler, "[Russian Imperial and] Soviet Policy toward Greece and Turkey: A [Comparative International] Systems Perspective," pp. 183-206 in *The Greek–Turkish Conflict in the 1990s*, edited by Dimitri C. Constas (London: Macmillan, 1991), available at <http://www.robertcutler.org/download/html/ch91dc.html>, accessed May 30, 2010.

The character of relations changed briefly in the early twentieth century. Following the end of the First World War, the Republic of Turkey and the Union of Soviet Socialist Republics – both newly created and weak states – shared an interest, up until the mid-1930s, in opposing the West in general and the United Kingdom in particular. Turkish-Soviet relations deteriorated after Hitler's rise to power, however, as Turkey became caught between Soviet and German imperatives. Until then, their common weakness led them to co-operate on a series of bi-lateral and multi-lateral issues.

Thus relations were conflictual when one or both of the states were strong relative to the international system and cooperative when both were weak. After the Second World War, up through the first period of nuclear superpower détente (early 1970s), both became stronger relative to the general international system than had previously been the case; however, the hierarchical bipolar Cold War system held potential conflicts between them in check. In the late Brezhnev period and up until Gorbachev (1975-85), Soviet diplomacy became less tolerant of Turkey's further increasing regional profile, and bi-lateral relations deteriorated as a result.

The record since the end of the post-Cold War transition (2001-present) is unique but is most closely analogous to the decade and a half following the end of the First World War. Russia and Turkey have both become revisionist states in the classical sense, in that they seek to alter the status quo established after the disintegration of the Soviet state led to a reorganization of the general international system. Their bi-lateral relations are so close that it is proper to refer to a Russo-Turkish entente, if not approaching an alliance, and, increasingly, in energy geo-economics in particular. In contrast to the situation after the First World War, however, neither is a weak state. This is the important sense in which the present-day situation is unprecedented.

## 2. The Closer Perspective from Two Decades

Hydrocarbon energy resource development in Central Asia and in the South Caucasus began autonomously of one another, but they were not intimately bound together. By circumstances, they share the same chronology. Three definite phases in the development of Caspian Sea region energy networks may be delineated since the Soviet "space" began to recover from the USSR's disintegration in the early 1990s. The first phase in this schema covers the years 1993-1998; the second, 1999-2004; and the third, 2005-2010.

Together these comprise the first meta-phase of a broader historical arc that I will address in the conclusion. These phases follow the established triadic progression of the evolution of complex systems. (A complex system is a system of which the behavior cannot be predicted from the study of the behavior of its constituent parts.)[3] These phases are emergence, goal-oriented self-definition (autopoiesis) and self-organized coherence. In ordinary language these three phases mentioned may be called "bubbling up," "settling down" and "running deep."

In the realm of Eurasian energy development, this means that the years 1993-1998 were marked principally by manifold proposals for new resource explorations and development, and pipeline construction. "Bubbling up" refers to how, after the Soviet state disestablished itself, new possibilities for new patterns of international relations began to percolate from events on the ground, relatively free from the hierarchical constraints that characterized the bipolar Cold War system. The phrase "settling down," referring to the period 1999-2004, identifies the fact that it was during those years that some of those projects acquired a life of their own and moved toward physical realization, while others died or perhaps entered a state of suspended animation. The phase of "running deep" designates the years (2005-2010) when those projects acquired life, were finally born and began to operate and thrive.

*Greater Central Asia*

In Greater Central Asia more broadly, the bi-lateral Kazakhstan-Russia and Turkmenistan-Russia relationships are so significant that the Kazakhstan-Russia-Turkmenistan triangle may be justifiably said to be the foundational basis for the evolution of Central Eurasian energy geo-economics overall, even though the relations between Kazakhstan and Turkmenistan are only

---

[3] Based on [Yaneer Bar-Yam], "NECSI Guide: About Complex Systems," <http://www.necsi.org/guide/study.html>, accessed May 30, 2010.

now beginning to manifest through cooperation over the gas pipeline to China.

In the Central Asian theater, a different strategic player – a "fourth vertex" – adds itself as the principal motor of developments in each of the three phases just distinguished above. In each successive phase, the previous "fourth vertices" do not successively disappear, but rather, what happens is that a former non-player achieves prominence and drives events. From 1993 to 1998, this was the United States; from 1999 to 2004, it was the EU or at least several of its member-states (and their "national champions" such as BP for the United Kingdom and Eni for Italy); and from 2005 to 2010, this has been China. With the addition of a "fourth vertex" in each phase, quadrilateral relations in fact become characteristic. However, the internal structure of the quadrilateral of each phase may be regarded as a composite of four triangles. Each of these four triangles in each phase would omit one of the phase's four vertices. The foundational Kazakhstan-Russia-Turkmenistan triangle is a constant throughout every chronological phase of the analysis.

During the first phase, then, in addition to the basic Kazakhstan-Russia-Turkmenistan triangle, the US was the fourth player. Its presence was most immediately in evidence over the question of an export pipeline for Tengiz crude: American offshore terminals in the Gulf of Mexico were the first intended targets of Kazakhstani oil shipments. Also during the first phase, the US embassy in (the then-capital) Almaty provided essential help to Russia and Kazakhstan for the restructuring of the Caspian Pipeline Consortium (CPC), enabling its pipeline to be subsequently built.

Western interest in Turkmenistan at this time was exclusively US interest, and it concentrated on ameliorating Ukraine's payments situation as an importer from Turkmenistan as well as on the incipient promotion of the first attempt to negotiate a Trans-Caspian Gas Pipeline (TCGP) between Turkmenistan and Azerbaijan. The US companies GE Capital, Bechtel and PSG were the driving forces behind the TCGP project in the 1990s. The US-Kazakhstan-Turkmenistan triangle remained undeveloped.

From 1999 to 2004, the EU became the driver, the "fourth vertex," of the fundamental Central Asian energy triangle. This evolution manifested, as before, in three new triangles. The Russia-Turkmenistan-EU triangle was animated by new EU interest in gas from Ashgabat in the first decade of the 21st century, after the American-sponsored TCGP project had failed. The current initiative for such a pipeline, led by the German company RWE, derives indirectly from this. Second was the EU-Russia-Kazakhstan triangle: it manifested itself in European and Russian interest to develop the Kashagan deposit and other northern Caspian Sea fields in Kazakhstan's offshore that came into prominence at that time. Finally, the EU-Turkmenistan-Kazakhstan triangle manifested also in the failed TCGP project as well as in other designs still on the drawing-board.

Finally in the third phase, from 2005 to 2010, China has come into a prominence that it did not earlier enjoy, as the fourth vertex of yet another quadrilateral, the newest one. The triangles into which it is decomposable manifest as follows. The China-Turkmenistan-Russia triangle is animated by rivalry between China and Russia over Turkmenistan's natural gas, as in the competition between Russia's unrealized project for a refurbished Caspian Coastal ("Prikaspiiskii") Pipeline on the one hand and, on the other hand, the now-operating Turkmenistan-China gas pipeline and other export vectors. The China-Kazakhstan-Russia triangle, also animated by the China-Russia contradiction, manifested in the China-Russia competition to buy out the Canadian firm Petrokazakhstan (previously Hurricane Hydrocarbons) and other similar industrial competition.

Petrokazakhstan happened to own a piece of the pipeline that China needed to put together its Tengiz-Xinjiang oil pipeline (itself a westward extension of the pipeline from eastern Kazakhstan to China, agreed in the late 1990s, which entered into service after long negotiations over implementation). Finally, the China-Kazakhstan-Turkmenistan triangle is manifest in the gas pipeline, negotiated on the basis of a bi-lateral China-Kazakhstan project, from Turkmenistan (through Uzbekistan then) through Kazakhstan to western China, where it will join up with the "West-East" Gas Pipeline in China (actually its second string) running to the coast, which Beijing constructed earlier this decade, for precisely this reason, at a financial loss.

*Greater Southwest Asia*

An analogous three-phase chronological evolution has occurred in Greater Southwest Asia over the same time frame, with the same phases but with different actors. The fundamental basis for the evolution of energy geo-economics in Greater Southwest Asia is, by contrast, the triangle Azerbaijan-Russia-Turkey. Other international actors have also added their presence to this triangle over time: these being the United States beginning in 1993, Georgia beginning in 1999 and the European Union beginning in 2005.

From 1993 to 1998, the US was the principal external player in Greater Southwest Asian energy geo-economics through its diplomatic promotion of what became the Baku-Tbilisi-Ceyhan oil pipeline (BTC) as well as the Baku-Tbilisi-Erzurum natural gas pipeline, also called the South Caucasus Pipeline (SCP), and also of the then-failed TCGP from Turkmenistan to Azerbaijan. From 1999 to 2004, Georgia became the additional vertex of that triangle (now quadrilateral with the US), as the construction of the BTC and then the SCP confirmed the country's crucial contribution to energy security in the region and beyond. Then from 2005 to 2010, the EU finally manifested its interest in the region with the more definite promotion of the Nabucco pipeline, the foundation of the European Energy Community with Georgia as an observer, and eventuating in the strategic Southern Corridor initiative that includes the White Stream pipeline along with Nabucco as integral elements.

The evolving response by Russia and Turkey to these developments has been to establish cooperation, followed by an entente (if not an alliance), in energy geo-economics (amongst other important economics sectors) – part of a broader diplomatic rapprochement between the two sides over a number of issues including South Caucasus geopolitics. Their agreement to build the Blue Stream natural gas pipeline in the late 1990s was intended to block the efforts of the TCGP negotiations then ongoing, and it succeeded in that goal.[4] Indeed, until recently, the Russo-Turkish project for the South

---

[4] For details, see "Turkey and the Geopolitics of Turkmenistan's Natural Gas," *Review of International Affairs*, vol. 1, no. 2 (Winter 2001): 20-33, available at <http://www.robertcutler.org/download/html/ar01ria.html>, accessed May 30, 2010.

Stream pipeline was widely and correctly viewed as a competitor to the Nabucco pipeline. The Blue Stream project appears as the origin of such an entente; but, only under the regimes of Russia's Prime Minister Vladimir Putin and Turkey's Prime Minister Recep Tayyip Erdogan, has it begun to acquire characteristics of institutionalization.

### 3. The Present: Azerbaijan in the South Caucasus Crucible

Contrary to expectations fifteen years ago, it is not Azerbaijani crude oil but rather its natural gas – and, primarily, the Shah Deniz deposit – that is at the center of international attention today.[5] The Shah Deniz deposit began production in 2005, and gas from its Phase One began flowing for international sale in 2007. Azerbaijan produces between 8 and 9 billion cubic metres per year (bcm/y) from this source, of which 6.6 bcm/y are sold to Turkey. Shah Deniz One has been scheduled to peak in 2011 at a production level of 8.6 bcm. It is Shah Deniz Two that will fill the Nabucco pipeline. It is projected to come on line in 2016, with a volume of between 10 and 15 bcm/y, ramping up later to 22 bcm/y.

The price agreed at the time of signature of the original contract between the two parties was USD 120 per thousand cubic metres (tcm). In the meantime, the world price reached well over double that figure. The contract between the two sides gave Azerbaijan the right to renegotiate the price but did not impose upon Turkey the obligation to renegotiate. After the original price agreement lapsed, Turkey still continued to receive gas, agreeing to pay for it retroactively after agreement on the price was later reached. Another, formally separate set of negotiations involved increased quantities of Azerbaijani gas putatively destined for Turkey, also from Shah Deniz but from its Phase Two development.

Turkey remained patient, expecting that Azerbaijan would be unable to find enough other customers to take the planned increased production from Shah Deniz. Ankara was confident that Baku would eventually recognize the need to come to terms, recognizing the Anatolian peninsula's key geo-

---

[5] For documentation of individual facts in the following narrative, please contact the author, who bases it upon contemporary press reports and other documents and his own consultations and interviews.

economic situation. Ankara even played a game trying to convince Baku that the Nabucco project might not even need Azerbaijan. Thus Turkey's energy minister Taner Yildiz was in Turkmenistan in January 2010 for the opening of the new short pipeline expanding the volumes of natural gas that Turkmenistan will sell to Iran. His government wanted Azerbaijan to think that a pipeline under the Caspian Sea was not the only route by which Turkmenistan's natural gas could reach Turkey for transhipment on to Europe.

In such tactics, Ankara appears to have been encouraged by Moscow at the highest levels of government. The Nabucco Intergovernmental Agreement gave Turkey the authority to define its own domestic legal regime for regulating transit revenues, even if this contravened the principle that all parties should pay the same fixed price for each mile of pipeline through which their gas flows. Nevertheless, after Erdogan had agreed with the EU in principle (Prague summit, early May 2009) on terms of pricing and legal regulation for the Nabucco pipeline and the gas it would carry, he reversed course just days later and re-raised the previously solved issues, following a summit meeting soon thereafter in Sochi with Putin. This was, to all appearances, a quid pro quo for Russia's agreement to sponsor construction of the Samsun-Ceyhan ("trans-Anatolian") oil pipeline and to consider two non-mutually exclusive variants for a "Blue Stream Two" gas pipeline extending the original Blue Stream to the west and/or south (called Med Stream in Turkish reference).

Azerbaijan diversified its customer base whilst awaiting a successful conclusion to the negotiations with Turkey. Russia had signalled in 2008 its readiness to purchase the entirety of Azerbaijan's natural gas production into the indefinite future: an offer that would have killed Nabucco. However, Baku declined this "commercial" (i.e. taking the world market as a basis for setting prices) offer explicitly for geopolitical reasons. The State Oil Company of the Azerbaijan Republic (SOCAR) nevertheless signed in March 2009 a Memorandum of Understanding (MoU) concerning the supply of gas to Russia at market prices. The timing reflected then-diminishing hopes for overcoming the Turkey-EU disagreements over Nabucco terms, in addition to awaiting agreement itself with Turkey over the price and conditions of sale of Shah Deniz Two gas destined for Nabucco.

The original agreement with Russia provided for the sale of 500 million cubic meters (mcm) of gas per year as of January 1, 2010, with the gas coming from Shah Deniz One. This was subsequently doubled to 1 bcm for 2010 and doubled again to 2 bcm for 2011. Azerbaijan also agreed, separately, to sell 500 mcm in 2010 to Iran, and perhaps more as the Baku-Astara pipeline is refurbished – but, this is unlikely ever to approach the figure of 5 bcm/y that the Iranian ambassador mentioned in 2009 in Baku.

Azerbaijan also has agreed to sell 1 bcm/y to Bulgaria. The gas would transit the Black Sea from Georgia using relatively new compressed natural gas (CNG) technology, which is, however, as yet untried over long maritime distances. The CNG option, discussed at the Batumi conference in January 2010, could easily be less expensive than liquefied natural gas (LNG), but CNG technology has not been used for such large-scale marine transportation before. Its tankers are more expensive than those for LNG, but CNG does not require expensive gasification and de-gasification infrastructure. The Batumi energy conference discussed specific projects for construction of CNG terminals, although not LNG. Industry analysts are currently at work calculating and verifying costs of transport that will likely govern which technology may be chosen in the long run. The bi-lateral MoU with Bulgaria sees the 1 bcm/y export level in 2011 rising eventually to 8 bcm/y.

Even if Azerbaijan is capable of supplying Nabucco and/or White Stream exclusively from its own offshore deposits, it is incumbent to address the position of Turkmenistan, which international energy companies and Western diplomatic players have long invoked as a source of gas for various trans-Caspian pipeline projects. Turkmenistan has recently set in motion a long-term tectonic shift in Caspian energy geo-economics by initiating the decisive strategic direction to diversify its gas exports not only beyond Russia but also beyond China.

At the end of May 2010, the Turkmenistan government announced that the state enterprise Turkmengaz will fund the renovation and reconstruction of the East-West Pipeline inside the country, using Turkmenistan's own human and physical resources. Coincidentally, the announcement also effectively kills the tri-lateral project including Kazakhstan to renovate and refurbish the segment of the Central Asia-Centre pipeline that the three countries had, at Russia's behest, designated the Caspian Coastal Pipeline, also called "Prikaspiiskii." Turkmenistan's internal East-West Pipeline will be designed for a capacity of 30 bcm/y. This is, coincidentally, the minimum volume necessary to justify economically a TCGP from Turkmenistan to Azerbaijan. The East-West Pipeline's design phase will start immediately, and it is anticipated that the construction will be finished in five years. The gas will come from the South Yolotan field, which the British firm Gaffney Cline estimates holds six trillion cubic meters (Tcm), within a possible range of four to 14 Tcm.

Also at the end of May, the first visit by Turkmenistan President Gurbanguly Berdimuhamedov to India included discussions of the Turkmenistan-Afghanistan-Pakistan-India (TAPI) pipeline project. While he agreed to promote a bi-lateral intergovernmental commission as a principal forum for economic cooperation with attention to energy questions, India declared its interest in the implementation without delay of the TAPI project. New Delhi, in particular, hopes that its experts in hydrocarbon exploration, development and production might participate in the project in Turkmenistan. The Indian government is also preparing to host a meeting of technical experts to discuss the project with the participation of the Asian Development Bank, which has declared support for it.

India has also brought up the possibility of gas swaps with Iran, specifically from the South Pars deposit that figured in the defunct Iran-Pakistan-India (IPI) project, in return for increased Turkmen exports to northeast Iran. However, Iran needs those imports for domestic consumption, and moreover suspended all oil swaps with foreign partners just two weeks ago. Therefore, it is unlikely that the swap scheme will be implemented, all the more so in view of the inability of Iran and India to agree on prices, quantities and quality of gas in the negotiations over the IPI project.

In addition, the United Arab Emirates (UAE) is also entering the field of competition for Turkmenistan's gas with a sovereign wealth fund reportedly exceeding $300 billion. Using the Dubai-based firm Dragon Oil as its vehicle, the UAE has been exploring for oil in Turkmenistan for a decade and now has an inside track to win exploration rights for offshore gas exploration blocks. Moreover, as a 20 percent shareholder in the Austrian firm OMV, which leads the Nabucco project, the UAE is well placed to find easy export routes for any offshore gas that it finds.

**4. Linking Central and Southwest Asia: The Trans-Caspian Gas Pipeline**

In May 2008, presidents Ilham Aliyev of Azerbaijan and Gurbanguly Berdimuhamedov of Turkmenistan held their countries' first bi-lateral summit in over a decade. Symbolically, the day the summit began, a ship from the Azerbaijani state oil company SOCAR delivered equipment to a Turkmen oil rig located in Turkmenistan's Caspian offshore. In a concluding joint press conference, the two presidents declared "all issues resolved" between their countries. Turkmenistan reopened its embassy in Baku, and Azerbaijan paid off its $45 million gas debt to Ashgabat. Moreover, at another energy summit just a few days later in Kyiv, Aliyev underlined Azerbaijan's role as both a producer and a transit country, leading many observers to believe that a bi-lateral Caspian delimitation agreement with Turkmenistan was in the works. Such an agreement would likely adopt the "modified median line" rule already in force under bi-lateral agreements between Azerbaijan and Russia, between Russia and Kazakhstan, and between Azerbaijan and Kazakhstan. Even if formalized only on an ad hoc basis in the beginning, such a procedure would allow Azerbaijan and Turkmenistan to settle their dispute over ownership of the Kyapaz/Serdar field in the Caspian Sea (probably providing for its development under a joint venture), not to mention resurrection of the TCGP project.

The TCGP project, which failed in the 1990s due to the insistence of Turkmenistan's then-president Saparmurad Niyazov on leading personally his country's negotiations (combined with his inability to grasp the technical details of project planning and financing), is now integrated as a principal variant of the Nabucco pipeline led by Austrian concerns. The route of the 2,100-mile Nabucco pipeline would run from Turkey's eastern border (with Georgia and/or Nakhchivan, in two non-mutually exclusive variants) through Ankara and Istanbul into eastern Greece, then northward through central Bulgaria and western Romania, finally snaking across Hungary from southeast to the northwest and terminating at Austria's Baumgarten gas hub.

How, then, is it that the MoU that Berdimuhamedov signed in Brussels in November 2007 refers to Europe importing gas from Turkmenistan as early as possible? There is only one answer: interconnecting the natural gas rigs from the Turkmen sector of the Caspian Sea to those in the Azerbaijani sector, which are already part of the international network of gas pipelines from the Caspian Sea basin to Europe. This arrangement would not require authoritative resolution of the issue of delimiting the Turkmen and Azerbaijani sectors of the Caspian Sea subsoil resources. Any working agreement could easily include the provision that such an arrangement creates no legal precedent for resolution of the matter, and the creation of facts on the ground would have enormous political significance and knock-on demonstration effects. It is perhaps no coincidence that Berdimuhamedov learned in November 2007, on his visit to EU headquarters in Brussels, that Belgian companies in particular specialize in such technology.

For Turkmenistan, this MoU has been an important bargaining chip as the country has proceeded with negotiations with other potential partners: another flag in the terrain of what we may call the ongoing War of the Memoranda. No MoU is legally binding; it only establishes some certainty in the business environment. The MoU with the EU is an agreement in principle, a declaration of intent and political support at the highest levels. It is up to companies and consortia to realize its intent on a market basis, knowing that favorable political will now exists.

An undersea ridge spanning the Caspian from Azerbaijan's Apsheron peninsula to Turkmenistan's port of Turkmenbashi, which divides the Caspian into deeper southern and shallower northern halves, is the best and most feasible route for a TCGP between the two countries. This was determined in the 1990s, when PSG, a joint venture between Bechtel and the GE Capital unit of General Electric (later joined by Royal Dutch Shell), first sketched out the project that would see gas ultimately reaching world markets via a Georgian-Turkish gas route. Now, as then, technical specifications can minimize the risk of ecological damage from pipeline construction and operation.

The only complicating factor is some minor seismic activity, and design features of the pipeline can easily take them into account. (The 1990s project foresaw the pipe diameter varying from 28 to 52 inches.) Such objections were raised by Brussels Eurocrats in the late 1990s, but the real origin of their opposition was a wish to exclude US influence from the region. Now that Russia – after the gas imbroglios with Ukraine – has turned out not to be the uncritical friend that the EU expected, the Europeans are hungry for Turkmen gas to feed the Nabucco pipeline that has been on the drawing board for some years.

No agreement will be possible, however, until Ashgabat and Baku resolve their disagreement over the oilfield that the former called Serdar and the latter calls Kyapaz. The Caspian Sea legal regime was regulated through 1991 by two Soviet-Iranian treaties signed in 1935 and 1940, and one Russian-Iranian treaty signed in 1921 by the Russian Soviet Federated Socialist Republic (before the USSR was created in 1922). Since the disintegration of the Soviet Union, the status of the sea under international law has been discussed at numerous ministerial and sub-ministerial meetings of the five countries, without resolution.

The two main agreements, those of 1921 and 1940, remain in force. Those agreements, however, neither established national sectors of the sea or seabed nor addressed energy development questions in any way, addressing only fishing and shipping issues, although there is an expert consensus that the 1940 treaty prohibits Iran from deploying naval vessels in the Sea. Agreements that have come into force since 1991 over other issues are not invalidated by the fact of pre-existing accords. Indeed, the Russian Federation has demarcated sub-sea sectors (with the right to exploit sub-sea resources) with Kazakhstan (in 1998) and with Azerbaijan (in 2001), following the established principle in international law of the "modified median line."

Also called the "equidistance method", the method of the modified median line involves drawing a line equidistant from the closest mainland points of each of two adjacent countries, and then adjusting ("modifying") the result so as either to take de facto boundaries into account or to avoid such problems as would result from dividing a single oil field between two states. The implementation of the agreement between Russia and Kazakhstan, for example, has been exemplary, and the two countries have even devised administrative methods for joint development of "shared" fields in the north Caspian. Kazakhstan and Azerbaijan have also agreed on the demarcation of their sub-sea sectors according to the modified median line principle.

Establishing a joint economic zone can resolve the problem. This is in fact a standard procedure for implementing the "modified median line" principle for demarcating maritime rights to subsoil resources; Kazakhstan and Russia have used it to common advantage in the north Caspian. However, such a joint economic zone can be implemented even without a bi-lateral agreement over subsoil rights. In other words, Azerbaijan and Turkmenistan do not have to agree on every detail of their Caspian offshore sectors if they wish just to declare Kyapaz/Serdar to be such a joint economic zone. Resolving the Kyapaz/Serdar issue is the necessary condition for international energy companies and consortia to begin to treat the TCGP as a project that has the true potential of springing from the drawing-board into reality. It could indeed clinch the deal.

In this connection, it is proper to note that Austrian Chancellor Werner Faymann was one of the few observers not to attribute, correctly, great significance to the July 2009 Turkmen declaration, that it would take its Caspian Sea demarcation dispute with Azerbaijan over the Kyapaz/Serdar field to "the International Court of Arbitration." In actuality, there is no "International Court of Arbitration." The two best-known juridical forums that could possibly be relevant here are the London Court of International Arbitration and the Stockholm International Arbitration Court, the latter of which specializes in energy issues. However, the competence of these courts is limited to questions of contract fulfilment, to which territoriality issues are foreign and extraneous.

The only international judicial forum competent to treat territorial disagreements, including jurisdictional issues over the continental shelf (which is what these matters are, given the present legal status of the Caspian Sea), is the International Court of Justice (ICJ, also World Court, not to be confused with the recently better-known International Criminal Court) in The Hague. For the ICJ in fact to have that authority, however, would require that both Azerbaijan and Turkmenistan accept its jurisdiction in the particular case at hand; and neither at present does. It is worth recalling that in 1999, during the last flare-up of disagreement between the two countries over sectoral demarcation in the Caspian Sea, Turkmenistan's then-president Saparmurad Niyazov declared that he would take the case to the ICJ, but no case was ever submitted, undoubtedly for the reasons just given if not additionally others.

The unresolved legal status of the Caspian Sea is a stumbling block insofar as Kazakhstan feels obliged to take Russia's interests into account in formulating its own energy export policy. Talks amongst the five Caspian littoral countries over the status of the Sea in international law have been dragging along for well over a decade, although a number of important bilateral agreements have been reached on different issues. The most notable of these concerns the allocation of national sectors of the seabed's subsoil resources. It is such an agreement between Moscow and Astana that permitted resource development to move ahead notably in the northern Caspian offshore between Kazakhstan and Russia.

Russia insists, as a way of blocking the TCGP, that the agreement of all five littoral states is necessary for any trans-Caspian pipeline to be built. But of course no development at all would have occurred over the past two decades, if unanimity were required before. One way to finesse this problem could be to offer to include in the pipeline gas from fields that were assigned to Russia (but now developed jointly with Kazakhstan) during the process of Russian-Kazakh Caspian border demarcation. However, that is unlikely to work insofar as it would require not just an economic but rather a political decision on Russia's part.

Consequently, the EU has also been looking at exploring other means for conducting Central Asian gas from the eastern to the western coast of the Caspian Sea. The three methods available are liquefaction, compression, and gas-to-liquids. They would all be more expensive than constructing the TCGP, and the break-even price of the gas to the end consumer would be higher than the TCGP in every case, complicating the prospects of each in a different way.

In the attempt to overcome this difference between Turkmenistan and Azerbaijan, one of the variants of the TCGP that has been recently mooted is the construction of a gas pipeline from Kazakhstan under the Caspian Sea to Azerbaijan from Karachaganak, Tengiz or the offshore Kashagan project, where a large amount of associated gas will need to be somehow captured as the underlying crude oil is developed. A pipeline from Turkmenistan could then join that Kazakhstan-Azerbaijan pipeline in the Kazakh offshore sector. This manner of proceeding would enable Turkmenistan's gas to enter Nabucco without the need for it to cross directly into the Azerbaijani sector.

The undersea portion of the TCGP from Kazakhstan would run from the country's Caspian Sea coast at Aqtau, whither gas from Tengiz would be brought overland, to Baku, connecting there to the South Caucasus Pipeline (Baku-Tbilisi-Erzurum) and eventually on to Europe. At the same time, a spur from this main line to the port at Turkmenbashi would connect Turkmenistan's gas fields to the TCGP. At present, the pipeline is projected to have an initial capacity of 20 bcm per year, possibly increasing to 30 bcm per year. Its total length would be almost 1,600 kilometers, of which only 300 would actually be underwater.

Due to delays with Kashagan, and with Karachaganak still dedicated to Orenburg for the foreseeable future, associated gas from the onshore Tengiz oil deposit is now the best candidate to supply Kazakh gas in a revamped TCGP project. Industry practice has been to flare Tengiz gas into the atmosphere, but now this must cease by 2011. The government in Astana considers the practice to be environmentally unsound (there is legislation against it) and, moreover, wishes to recover the gas for domestic use and revenue enhancement through export.

Kazakhstan has been working together with Azerbaijan and the EU to address concretely the realistic prospects for Kazakhstan's gas to reach Europe and the available techniques for this, ever since the agreement of the multi-lateral "Road Map" in Astana in November 2006 by the Second Energy Interministerial Conference of the Littoral States of the Black and Caspian Seas (a process set into motion under the EU-sponsored 2004 "Baku Initiative," but which acquired true momentum following the January 2006 suspension by Russia of natural gas exports to Ukraine).

## 5. The Near Future: Stakes Around the Black Sea

Azerbaijan has also investigated means for liquefying its gas production for export across the Black Sea into Europe. The energy conference held in early 2010 in Batumi set the framework for establishing the company Azerbaijan-Georgia-Romania Interconnector (AGRI) in Bucharest, charged with evaluating such a project's commercial, financial, legal and technological aspects, including a feasibility study. The project itself would involve construction of a liquefaction plant, probably at Kulevi on the Georgian Black Sea coast where the Azerbaijan state company SOCAR owns an oil export terminal, and a re-gasification plant at Constanta, Romania. AGRI's throughput estimate is set at 7 bcm/y, of which Romania would require only about 2 bcm/y. The remainder could go into pipelines and connectors for export to other EU countries. Connections through Romania to Hungary (such as the Arad-Szeged connector) and Central Europe are in particular being considered.

The LNG and CNG projects across the Black Sea are not trivial. Taking the LNG and CNG projects together (even though they need not be implemented together), a combined first phase would amount to 8 bcm/y, with a combined total up to 15-20 bcm/y when fully deployed. This is not enough to replace either White Stream or Nabucco individually. The demonstration of viability of CNG technology would factor into discussions concerning the development of Turkmenistan's natural gas deposits for export across the Caspian Sea and South Caucasus to European markets. The LNG and CNG trans-Black Sea projects are, however, no substitute for implementation of the EU's "Southern Corridor" strategy. They are properly understood as work-arounds in the short- to medium-term for diversification of Azerbaijan's gas export routes whilst awaiting the resolution and co-ordination of decisions on the other, more "strategic" projects.

Either project would likely be significantly more expensive than the White Stream undersea pipeline project for the truly large quantities that Europe would like to receive via Azerbaijan from Turkmenistan and, eventually, Kazakhstan. But a series of offshore discoveries in the Azerbaijani sector of the Caspian Sea over the last few years make it possible that even as much as 24-32 bcm/y (equivalent to the full first string projected for White

Stream, an undersea pipeline that would run from Supsa to Constanta) could eventually be sourced exclusively, or almost so, through Sangachal without requiring recourse to trans-Caspian deposits that could come on line later.

The ratification of the Nabucco Intergovernmental Agreement by Turkey's Grand National Assembly has catalyzed new developments in the maturation of Euro-Caspian pipeline network. One of the more interesting results is seen in the public comment by Eni's chief executive officer Paolo Scaroni, that it should be conceivable to merge the Nabucco and South Stream projects. Even more interesting is Gazprom's categorical public rejection of his proposal. For the two companies supposedly engaged in a strategic alliance over so potentially important a project as South Stream to find themselves in public opposition over so fundamental a question, inevitably raises doubts over the degree of the real seriousness of the project itself, which is slated to cost twice as much as Nabucco and the signature of which Erdogan unilaterally postponed until, ostensibly, later in 2010.

It should be recalled that Eni and Gazprom together built the Blue Stream pipeline under the Black Sea from Russia to Turkey in the late 1990s. Blue Stream was and remains uneconomical; it was a political enterprise from Russia's standpoint, intended, with success, to block the project at that time being negotiated for construction of a TCGP under the Caspian Sea from Turkmenistan to Azerbaijan (for subsequent transhipment to Europe).

To fill Nabucco, Azerbaijan has been ready to supply 8 bcm/y and recently declared its capacity to supply 15.5 bcm/y, half of design capacity. Iraq is contracted for 8 bcm/y, although disputes between the central government in Baghdad and the Kurdistan Regional Government (KRG) over the division of revenues may complicate implementation. That leaves 7.5 bcm/y out of Nabucco's 31 bcm/y volume to be accounted for, although the KRG has recently mentioned the possibility of a 15.5 bcm/y contribution. Together with Azerbaijan's 15.5 bcm/y commitment, that would totally fill Nabucco. But the first stage of Nabucco requires only 10-15 bcm/y.

As mentioned previously, Turkmenistan has an agreement to supply 10 bcm/y to Europe through interconnecting its own offshore Caspian rigs with offshore Azerbaijani rigs, which are in turn already connected up to networks capable of moving the gas to Europe. It remains to find practical means to put this last-mentioned agreement into effect, or to await strikes by companies now exploring Turkmenistan's offshore blocks.

Russia, besides implementing a "divide and conquer" strategy appealing to the national interests of selected EU members to the detriment of others, has countered Europe's emerging recognition of its situation by encouraging Turkey's relatively new ambitions to assert its status as a relatively autonomous regional Power. In particular, this countermove has eventuated most recently in a diplomatic waltz where various figures on both sides variously endorse the idea that the Nabucco and South Stream projects may co-exist and even prosper together. The subtext to this concerted initiative is to the detriment of White Stream and similar projects. It is a replay of the situation twelve years ago, when Russia induced Turkey to build the Blue Stream pipeline between the two countries under the Black Sea, in order to block at that time the project for the TCGP from Turkmenistan to Azerbaijan: a project that evolving political and economic conditions have, over the course of the last few years, made again feasible in principle, and which may also now be associated with White Stream.

The novelty of a Russo-Turkish entente, pointed out at the beginning of this article, may account for the failure of some major players in the European Union to seize more quickly the essence of the situation. Some of them, however, have been wilfully blind: indeed, those European countries historically most sympathetic to Great Power ententes have done the most, until recently, to restrain concerted EU energy diplomacy in the region; however, this has been changing. In particular, the EU officially endorsed in 2009 a so-called "Southern Corridor" strategy that includes not only the Nabucco project but also the White Stream pipeline project under the Black Sea from Georgia to Romania, the latter now an EU member.

Whereas ten years ago Turkey's energy minister could be forced from office and accused of corruption in the transactions surrounding the Blue Stream agreement, today the corresponding interests in each of the two countries are well established in their government responsibilities. With the institutionalization of a bi-lateral grand commission for economic co-operation, the Putin-Erdogan entente will not be confined to energy and other economic matters. It may evolve into a real Russo-Turkish geo-economic alliance as the two leaders continue to entrench themselves and their social circles in the offices of state responsibility, and so become still more able to defend the unofficial interests to which they are sociologically linked.

### 6. Conclusion: Azerbaijan and the Further Future of Central Eurasian Energy

The beginning of this article pointed out three phases (bubbling up, settling down and running deep) in the development of Caspian Sea basin energy geo-economics from 1993 through 2010. It is incumbent now to say what follows. These three phases together represent a "meta-phase" of bubbling up, to be followed by a meta-phase of settling down (which we are now entering), which will in turn subdivide into three phases. To recall the slightly more technical language of complex-systems theory from the beginning of the article, these phases and meta-phases are a progression of emergence, goal-oriented self-definition and self-organized coherence.

The phase we are now about to enter, in the structuration of energy geo-economics in the Caspian Sea basin, is the emergence of "settling down." If the past is any guide, this phase will also last for five years, from 2011 through 2016, followed by a phase of the self-defining of the orienting direction (of the settling down, from 2017-22) and then self-organized coherence (of the settling down, 2023-28). Then a meta-phase of "running deep," subdivided into three phases, should follow, from 2029 to 2046. Coincidentally, the years around 2040 are independently projected by international relations analysts to be the next period of global-systemic transformation, which will undoubtedly be felt also in the Caspian Sea basin, and also in the geo-economics of the region.[6]

If all this is so, then we are now at the start of a settling-down metaphase of the present international system, including international energy geo-economics. The settling-down metaphase that we are now entering also lasts more or less 16 years, then a third, running-deep metaphase will

---

[6] Robert A. Denemark, "World System History: From Traditional International Politics to the Study of Global Relations," *International Studies Review*, vol. 1, no. 2 (June 1999): 167-199.

succeed it, likewise running about 16 years, bringing us up to the aforementioned period of the early 2040s, when there will appear a period of transformational turmoil equivalent in quality and extent to the end of the Cold War, but which cannot yet be described, as its nature will depend upon the system's evolution, including energy geo-economics, in the interim.

This is the perspective in which the oncoming "settling-down metaphase" of Eurasian energy geo-economics must be seen. It is the perspective in which such issues as the Nabucco and South Stream gas pipelines, or White Stream, the broader significance of the "Trans-Anatolian" (Samsun-Ceyhan) oil pipeline, and other similar issues should be seen.

The central phase in this nested progression is clearly the middle phase of the middle meta-phase, i.e. 2017 through 2022. It follows that the projects today being planned for construction and entry into service during those years will be the defining axes of development for the entire energy production sector from Central Europe to Central Asia, for the whole half-century following the disintegration of the Soviet state.

In the longer perspective, it was pointed out that the current international situation in Greater Southwest Asia is, in light of the Russo-Turkish energy entente, unprecedented. Such a situation affects not only Azerbaijan but also Europe. The Southern Corridor strategy is Europe's only option if it wishes to avoid a dual chokehold by Russia and Turkey on its own natural gas supply. Of the various cross-Black Sea projects discussed above, White Stream is the only strategic one; yet for that reason there is greater difficulty in ensuring the tectonic shift in geo-economics that its realization would require. This shift may be finally under way with the most recent reorientation of Turkmenistan's export policy toward a diversification of customer base. This re-orientation only enhanced Azerbaijan's centrality, which makes it well placed not only to promote its own interests in such a context but also to participate in the shaping of the Euro-Caspian geo-economic space into the future.

Much of the present chapter has focussed on natural gas, but the Kazakhstan-Caspian Transportation System (KCTS) deserves mention in closing. The KCTS is designed to reduce Kazakhstan's dependence on the

Moscow-controlled CPC, which runs from the Tengiz to the Black Sea. The KCTS would include expanded and upgraded ports as well as construction of tanker fleets and, if necessary, additional pipelines within Kazakhstan itself. About 80 percent of Kazakhstan's oil has nowhere to go today, other than through Russia's pipeline system. Half the remainder is exported through the Georgian Black Sea port of Batumi, the seaside capital of the Georgian autonomous province of Ajaria; the rest goes to China.

Kazakhstan has now decided to construct a 590-mile pipeline, for Kashagan oil in particular, running from Eskene, where Kashagan's onshore processing facility will be located once full-field development gets under way, to the port of Kuryk, near Aqtau. Starting at 500,000 barrels per day (bpd), its volume would later be increased to 750,000 bpd; to this, another 400,000 bpd may be added by doubling the capacity of the Aqtau port itself. The oil it carries would enter the BTC pipeline, turning it into the Aqtau-Baku-Ceyhan (ABC) pipeline, terminating near the Turkish Mediterranean coast. This project would be a manifestation of the EU-Kazakhstan-Turkmenistan triangle mentioned near the beginning of the chapter, and it could be integrated with the Turkmenistan-Kazakhstan-Azerbaijan gas pipeline also just discussed. As such, it also requires deeper European involvement to be realized.

# NATURAL RESOURCES INVESTMENT RELATIONS AND REGIONAL ENERGY STRATEGIES

**Albert Bressand,**
Director,
Center for Energy, Marine Transportation and Public Policy,
Columbia University

Natural resources – particularly the oil and gas resources – will play an essential role in the development of the South Caucasus countries, namely Azerbaijan, and will influence the development and international relations of the region as a whole. In this respect, the fate of the region is closely intertwined with that of the broader Caspian region, which is in many ways the most relevant geographic context when considering the development of energy resources. Similarly, the development of Caspian oil and gas resources and the transit of energy resources through the South Caucasus will be significantly influenced by the strategies followed by one transit country – Turkey – and by three major oil and gas producers, most notably the Russian Federation but also Iran and, increasingly, Iraq. Overall, how Azerbaijani energy resources are developed and transported and how investment and transit relations evolve in the broader Caspian region will have repercussions well beyond the energy field.

Let us therefore review the general context for energy resources development in the Caspian region before focusing on the essential role of the export and transit of natural gas in this complex nexus of multi-lateral energy relations. We will then offer some views on possible developments to 2021 by looking at how tensions between the Russian, EU and Turkish jurisdictions may or may not be resolved – with the source of such tensions lying not only in geopolitical rivalry but also in conflicting views regarding how large-scale energy investments should be financed, as well as the lack of a genuine external policy perspective behind the EU policy of gas market liberalization. The chapter will conclude with a discussion of initiatives that South Caucasus countries could take to overcome such tensions and provide a lasting foundation for regional cooperation, as well as global investment and trade.

**Significant Energy Resources**

The history of the modern energy industry has involved the South Caucasus region since the beginning. Azerbaijan is indeed the world's oldest oil producer – an oil well was drilled in Bibi Heybat in 1847, twelve years before the first oil well in Titusville, Pennsylvania – and for a few years at the beginning of the twentieth century, Azerbaijan was the source of half of the world's oil production.

At a time when many other regions of the world have either reached a production plateau or have begun to experience a significant decrease in their production, the Caspian region has again become one of the most active parts of the new oil and gas frontier. While the region has not come to rival the Middle East and the Russian Federation in importance, off-shore fields like Kashagan in Kazakhstan and Shah Deniz in Azerbaijan are among the largest discovered, and have the potential to contribute significantly to global hydrocarbon supply at least until 2021. The region's proximity to the large European market as well as to the rapidly developing Chinese and Indian markets gives added importance to the Caspian's gas resources. Present and future investment levels are also among the most significant in the world. The 1994 "Contract of the Century," which led to the development of the Azeri-Chirag-Guneshli (ACG) fields and the construction of the Baku-Tblilsi-Ceyhan (BTC) export pipeline, represented a $20 billion investment and had profound implications on the Caspian region. The ACG project raised the profile of the Caspian basin as a new oil and gas frontier; the BTC pipeline created an opportunity to export Caspian oil through the Mediterranean port of Ceyhan; Azerbaijan started to generate significant revenues, with positive spillover effects on the Georgian economy as a result of transit fees and of investment by Azerbaijani companies. An estimated $22 billion will be invested in the second round of development of the Shah Deniz field in the Azerbaijani off-shore, which is expected to feed the Nabucco pipeline. Across the Caspian, the supergiant Kashagan field in Kazakhstan with a $130 billion price tag is probably the most fascinating and challenging oil and gas project on earth. Meanwhile, in spite of known reserves being developed at a controlled pace, the majority of Turkmen gas reserves remain largely unexplored and could be the source of renewed developments of great importance in reshaping trade and investment patterns in the region and beyond.

The landlocked geographic situation of key producer countries makes transit in the greater Caspian region more dependent on foreign policy considerations and on regional cooperation than would be the case for countries with open access to the sea. This is even more the case for the South Caucasus, situated as it is at the intersection of the Russian, Turkish, Iranian, European and potentially in the future Chinese and Indian spheres of influence, as well as being of great interest to the United States – a quite unique situation in today's world. Investment relations in the region are therefore multi-lateral in nature, calling for a different type of approach than in cases such as Algeria, Egypt, or many other producer countries for which the multi-lateral nature of commercial relations is absent or secondary.

**Golden Age for Natural Gas**

While the Azerbaijani oil resources are significant, the strategic importance of the region is even more noticeable regarding natural gas. Indeed, how natural gas is developed, transported, marketed and sold will be an essential consideration in shaping the region's economic and strategic future.

The wealth of natural gas resources in the region and in countries immediately adjacent to it (notably Russia, Turkmenistan, Iran and Iraq) is being developed on a large scale at a time when natural gas assumes a renewed importance in the global energy mix. In addition to being still relatively plentiful compared to oil, natural gas is also a more attractive energy source from a carbon emissions mitigation perspective: power plants of the combined cycle (CCGS) type achieve a much higher level of energy efficiency than power plants using other fuels; furthermore, natural gas emits only half the amount of greenhouse gases that coal emits per unit of energy produced. Even in America, a country with very large coal reserves and no cap-and-trade rules, no less than 206 of the 372 power plants that are expected to be built between 2010 and 2012 are designed to be gas-fired, while only 31 are to be coal-fired. The combination of carbon taxes and carbon emissions-rights markets that can be expected to develop on a global scale by 2021 will open important possibilities for continued fuel-switching toward natural gas. One way or another, the positive environmental externalities associated with natural gas will be internalized, at least in part, into the relative prices of the various energy sources. Financing gas projects in the region – in the distribution but also possibly in the upstream sector – is likely to be facilitated by the various carbon-related instruments that will develop as a result of international and regional climate negotiations, most prominently those currently under way in the United Nations Framework Convention on Climate Change (UNFCCC).

The global production of natural gas is expected to grow at a rate of 1.8 percent per year. The demand growth figure is much higher, particularly in China where demand growth is expected to proceed at 5.8 percent annually, in line with the objective of increasing the share of natural gas in Chinese primary energy consumption from 3.2 percent in 2008 to 12.5 percent by 2020. Even in Western Europe, where gas accounted for 24 percent of the EUs primary energy consumption in 2006, the one percent growth rate anticipated for the demand of gas over the 2006-2030 period compares more than favorably with the decreases of 0.4 percent per year and 0.5 percent per year in the demand for oil and coal over the same period.

Looking to 2021, an essential question is then whether investment and transit relations in oil and gas in the South Caucasus will still be as strongly informed by geopolitical considerations as is the case today. Natural gas became a key driver in the relations between the two halves of the European continent in spite of the geopolitical tension of the Cold War and Reagan periods. While the Chinese factor will loom increasingly large in the energy balance equation, for historic and geographic regions the development of the South Caucasus natural gas resources must largely be seen in the context of the broader architecture of investment and trade relations that will emerge within the Former Soviet Union (FSU) and in the multi-lateral relations between Russia, Central Asia and the European Union.

So far, efforts by South Caucasus countries to develop their resources – practically speaking, this includes Azerbaijan as well as Georgia as a transit country – have taken place in an international context that has tended to exacerbate the tension that exists between two visions of the legal and regulatory organization of the Euro-Asian space. These two visions reflect, respectively, the EU and the Russian market philosophies and geopolitical perspectives. They differ not just in the traditional sense of national interest, but also in a different philosophical understanding of what fair and balanced relations imply. Writing in the 2008 Centre for European Reform report, *Pipelines, politics and power: The Future of EU-Russian energy relations*, Christian Cleutinx and Jeffery Piper note:

> One often hears both in the EU and in Russia that more 'reciprocity' is required. Unfortunately, this term means different things to different people. In Russia, it means equality in end-results, that is to say, asset swaps of equivalent financial or commercial value; for the EU, it means commonly agreed principles and access to markets and investments – a level playing field, with the end result being left to free competition.

The EU approach is perceived by many Russian observers and policy-makers as strongly determined by a broader Euro-Atlantic perspective in which the American voice matters at least as much as the European one, and often differs from what would be the national perspective of key EU member countries. As observed by Alexander Rahr and Sebastian Rieder in their 2009 article for *Azerbaijan Focus*, "Moscow saw the construction of the BTC pipeline as a US project aimed at reducing Russian influence in the region and tried to impede it." Similarly, the first crisis between Ukraine and Russia over Ukraine's payment of Russian gas deliveries led to Western reactions that Russians interpreted in ways well-captured by Dmitri Trenin writing in *Pipelines, politics and power*: "Many Europeans and Americans subsequently accused Moscow of using energy as a weapon. Energy security became synonymous with security against Russia." Russians were also concerned to see that, in Trenin's words again, "Speaking on the eve of the NATO summit in Riga in November 2006, US Senator Richard Lugar proposed the creation of an 'energy NATO.'"

It remains to be seen whether the Russian and EU perspectives will continue to drift away from one another, as was the case in August 2009 when Russia made the decision not to ratify the Energy Charter Treaty. The Energy Charter intended to foster convergence and, at a minimum, to protect commercial relations from the political risk associated with these tensions between the EU and Russian market philosophies and geopolitical perspectives. Whether some alternative framework can be developed is an important question for all three South Caucasus countries.

Conflicts within the region itself further compound the situation. The recent war in Georgia raised significant concerns as to how quickly conflicts in the region can escalate, and what potential severe implications such conflicts could have on relations between Russia and NATO member states. The growing role of Russia in the Armenian economy, and particularly in the energy sector, significantly contrasts with Georgia's pro-Western orientations and with the efforts by Azerbaijan to preserve some balance in its foreign and energy relations. Such contrast, as well as the ongoing occupation of Azerbaijan's territories by Armenia serve as a stumbling block for the integration of the three South Caucasus economies.

This has resulted in Armenia basically being left out of major regional transit projects, and impedes Azerbajan's ambitions to play the role it aspires to in the region. To quote Alexander Rahr and Sebastian Rieder again, "as long as [the Nagorno Karabakh] conflict is not settled between Armenia and Azerbaijan, Azerbaijan will not be able to tap its potential as a bridge between cultures." The role of Turkey as the only transit country that could rival in importance with Russia in shaping the architecture of gas export routes generates an additional layer of opportunities as well as complexities for the South Caucasus region. By 2021, Turkey will either have been admitted into the EU, with the EU liberalized energy rules applying to Turkish territory, or will have given up on such hopes, which may encourage the development of a regulatory approach granting a much higher degree of control to the Turkish state. Consequences for the South Caucasus countries will be important, as the first scenario is more likely to foster the development of a Turkish gas hub while the second may add an element of unpredictability to the export of gas from the South Caucasus region. One should not forget also that Turkey is dependent on Russian gas for about two thirds of its needs, a high proportion that contrasts with the role that Turkey plays in the development of those alternative supply 'corridors' that the EU endeavors to develop in order to reduce its own dependence on Russian gas.

By 2021, the present 'spaghetti bowl' of pipelines will have further densified, and other physical hubs will likely have emerged. Turkmenistan in particular could be a more important nexus of five routes, namely toward China, the Russian Federation, the South Caucasus (via Trans-Caspian pipelines), Northern Iran and the Indian subcontinent through the Afghanistan route.

Seen in this context, how natural resources will influence the further development of the South Caucasus region to 2021 raises three major issues. The first issue is about the relative importance that South Caucasus oil and gas resources will assume by 2021 in the relevant markets – with these markets today being the global market for oil and the regional markets for natural gas in the EU, Russia, China and, to a lesser extent, Turkey and South Asia. Whether gas markets will remain as fragmented as they are today compared to oil markets is also a relevant question within the 2021 timeframe. A second major issue is geopolitical in nature, and regards the conditions under which Russia, the EU and Turkey could develop more harmonious relations over transit and trade in natural resources. A third issue, potentially of great significance, is the extent to which the South Caucasus countries themselves – or possibly countries like Turkey, Kazakhstan and particularly the US – could take initiatives that could contribute to a transformation in these relations.

### An investment Environment in Search of a Foundation

Commercial relations over natural resources in the South Caucasus region and in the adjacent countries cover a large spectrum, and so do the legal conditions under which international investors can develop upstream exploration and development activities. At one extreme lies Azerbaijan and its open investment regime, which includes stable conditions of access and pace-setting efforts to abide by international norms, such as the Extractive Industry Transparency Initiative (EITI). Closer to the other extreme of the spectrum lies Turkmenistan, where only a handful of international investors have been able to establish access and where economic opening is presently proceeding at a very controlled pace.

A large part of the resources of the region are located under the Caspian Sea bed, which further tightens the interdependence of the countries in the broader region, even if for the wrong reason. A number of off-shore fields are located in parts of the South Caspian for which delimitation is still hotly contested. The Islamic Republic of Iran is a significant source of legal complexities in this respect. One may still hear the extreme view that Iran and the USSR once were the only two countries to share the Caspian Sea, and that they de facto agreed to granting each other an equal share of the Caspian under an agreement that should still be enforceable vis a vis the successor states to the USSR. A milder and more seriously-conveyed version of this argument is that the Caspian Sea should be treated as a lake (a closed body of water) under the United Nations Convention on the Law of the Sea (UNCLOS). If such were indeed the legal situation, an equal sharing of the Caspian economic resources would be the norm. Iran therefore promotes a consortium approach to the development of the Caspian Sea bed, in the hope that this would open the door for an equal sharing – or at least some negotiated sharing – of revenues among the countries represented in the consortium. Iran, however, is not the only country to challenge mainstream views on how the UNCLOS rules should be applied to the Caspian. Turkmenistan also insists that the Absheron peninsula on which Baku is located should not be taken into account when drawing the border between the Exclusive Economic Zones (EEZ) of Azerbaijan and Turkmenistan. As a result, the development of projects and agreements that could give a further boost to Azerbaijan's production, such as the Alov and Sardar/Kapaz Production Sharing Agreements, will be strongly influenced by the extent to which the Caspian littoral states will be willing and able to achieve a consensus on the sea's legal status.

Nonetheless, given delayed Shah Deniz Stage Two development in addition to requiring the agreement of transit countries, the financing and construction of transport infrastructure may also depend on the participation of other gas producers that are able and willing to supply the quantities of oil and gas needed for such infrastructure to be economically viable. In this context, an importance of reaching an agreement between Turkmenistan and Azerbaijan is vital. Moreover, the Caspian legal issue, as such, adds to the complexity of development of South Caucasus energy corridor.

The proven reserves of the Caspian and neighboring countries, as indicated in the BP 2009 statistical review, are the following:

*Proven Caspian Region Oil and Gas Reserves*

|  | Oil (in bboe) | Gas (in tcm) |
|---|---|---|
| Caspian region Azerbaijan | 7.0 | 1.2 |
| Iran | 137.6 | 29.6 |
| Kazakhstan | 39.8 | 1.8 |
| Turkmenistan | 0.6 | 7.9 |
| Key Neighboring Countries (Iraq) | 115.0 | 3.2 |
| Russian Federation | 79.0 | 43.3 |
| Uzbekistan | 0.6 | 1.6 |

Source: BP Statistical Review of World Energy 2009

In designing the Nabucco project as a tool to reduce its dependency on Russian natural gas, the EU has set for itself the relatively modest objective of transporting 31 bcm/y of non-Russian gas in what it calls "the Southern Energy Corridor." This will come in addition to gas shipped through the Baku-Tbilisi-Erzurum pipeline. By comparison, before declining as a result of the global recession, imports of Russian gas by the EU reached more than 160 bcm/y, and the total Russian gas production is on the order of 600 bcm/y. Other Eurasian midstream projects under discussion are also significantly larger than is envisioned for Nabucco. The Nord Stream gas pipeline project, intended to link Russia and Germany while bypassing Ukraine, is being designed for a 55 bcm capacity, and the South Stream project has recently been expanded to a 64 bcm capacity.

While the South Caucasus and the Caspian region could be a middle-sized supplier to the EU, it has the potential to be among the largest suppliers of natural gas to the less-developed but rapidly growing market of China.

The Central Asia–China gas pipeline that that is being built now, carrying Turkmen and at later stages Kazakh gas, will have a capacity of 30 bcm. Obviously, in the timeframe addressed here, the amount of natural gas flowing through that West-East corridor can be greatly expanded, and it is not unthinkable that the Trans-Caspian pipeline could be working in reverse by 2021 – namely so that Azeri gas would join Turkmen and Kazakh gas and flow to China. At this stage, however, the Chinese market is not unified, although this will likely happen by 2021. Presently, South Caucasus and Caspian gas is not intended for the coastal Chinese market, where prices are now close to international prices. Rather, it is destined for the market of Western China. In light of the development needs of these poorer regions, Chinese authorities and companies tend to place a glass ceiling on acceptable import prices on the Western Chinese market. By 2021, such differences can be expected to have subsided, with China having become a more mature market. At that time, the present efforts by China to establish closer relations with Arab countries and with the broader Caspian region will have also borne fruit. China will therefore be involved in the multi-lateral set of interactions within and about the South Caucasus region far more than today.

A discussion of the relative importance of South Caucasus gas resources would not be complete if it did not include a dynamic element related not just to the rapid development of a particular market, but also to the sequencing of the development of natural gas resources in the broader Eurasian region, including Russia. From a pure market perspective, the lower-cost natural resources would be developed first, and the higher-cost resources later. Yet, from a national perspective, Russia may find an advantage in developing expensive resources it controls in the Yamal peninsula and in the Arctic Sea earlier than such an economic-optimum sequence would suggest. In addition, according to a World Bank study, 38 bcm of gas is annually being flared, mainly due to lack of access to the Gazprom-controlled network of gas pipelines. Another source of added gas supply for the Russian market stems from the significant energy efficiency gains that can be expected to take place in the Russian domestic market as Russian authorities continue to close the gap between Russian domestic prices and European prices. The substitution of coal for gas where economically feasible adds one more reason to look at Russian policies as being of critical importance in influencing the relative importance of South Caucasus and Caspian gas. Much will depend on Russia's capacity and willingness to develop greenfields such as Yamal, as it faces high decline rates in the regions that currently account for the largest share of its exports.

As a result, the economic value of South Caucasus gas will not be set simply between the exporting countries and their European and Chinese clients. It will also reflect strategies on the part of all countries involved, most notably Russia, a situation better understood in game theory terms than in simple supply and demand terms.

**South Caucasus and Future Foreign Relations**

In the previous section we have looked at how the investment relations in the South Caucasus and adjacent regions are influenced by a multi-lateral context rich in tensions and in still-to-be-adjudicated border disputes. We have also stressed how different approaches to fair and balanced relations in energy could create major misunderstandings and tensions between the key producer – Russia – and the key importing region – namely the EU. This partial review has already suggested that the economic development of the natural resources of the South Caucasus will be influenced by much more than the economists' favored reference to a global economic first best. A strategy game is underway that can point to contrasted scenarios for the state of the South Caucasus in 2021.

To develop such scenarios, however, one needs to consider another major source of departure from the economic first best, namely jurisdictional discontinuity – in other words, the economic impact on trade flows resulting from the fact that buyers and sellers are operating in different jurisdictions rather than within the same country or jurisdiction. Even in the case of an integrated economic region like North America, trade volumes between a US state and a Canadian province are significantly lower than they would be between two US states or between two Canadian provinces. Obviously, looking at Eurasia as a whole brings to light jurisdictional discontinuities that are orders of magnitude higher than this example. Whether the various jurisdictions converge in regulatory terms or continue to operate along very different rules will be one of the essential conditions affecting the development and exports of South Caucasus resources.

During the 1990s, such discontinuities were in the process of eroding as a result of the whole-hearted embrace of market principles within the FSU, and even of the regulatory convergence process fostered by the EU within and beyond its borders. Consisting of no less than 80,000 pages of regulation in more than 30 domains, the EU "acquis communautaire" has provided the legislative and legal equivalent of a bulldozer to reduce jurisdictional discontinuities. The "deeper integration" that follows from the implementation of the acquis brings down the transaction costs that such discontinuities generate. Countries like Turkey, which are not members of the EU, are pursuing policies of convergence to ease their way into the EU 'club.' After completing its enlargement to Central and Eastern Europe, the EU put in place a Neighborhood Policy that intends, inter alia, to promote convergence between the EU and a number of countries in the region in terms of standards and of some regulations. This policy is complemented with more targeted programs toward the Black Sea (of which Azerbaijan is considered a part), such as the Black Sea Synergy initiative.

The Baku Initiative of the INOGATE program also includes countries in the South Caucasus and its broader Caspian-Central Asian environs, including those involved in the new transit corridor promoted by the EU. By and large, however, these well-intended European policies have so far disappointed participating states, and have not amounted to a significant support for convergence and deeper integration. Part of the reason for this has been that these initiatives have been devoid of the necessary political clout to create a common vision for the region that supersedes regional political tensions while simultaneously fostering (as they do presently) integration on more technical grounds, such as harmonization of legal and market structures. A more ambitious Eastern Partnership (EaP), launched by the EU at the initiative of Poland and Sweden may, however, restore the integration momentum by infusing a higher-order political aspect to relations with its South Caucasus neighborhood.

Yet, a major turning point in these integration dynamics took place at the beginning of the second presidential mandate of Vladimir Putin in Russia. Some form of convergence between the Russian Federation and the European Union was encouraged in the Yeltsin years, and was still considered positively in the early years of the Putin presidency. By contrast, the present image of the EU in Russia has strongly deteriorated. In his report, "Toward a New Euro-Atlantic 'Hard' Security Agenda: Prospects for Trilateral US-EU-Russia Cooperation," Dmitri Trenin of the Carnegie Moscow Center makes the point that the EU legal and regulatory order – the EU acquis – is now seen in Russia as a form of "normative imperialism" that must be resisted. Not only is convergence with the EU jurisdiction considered against Russian interests, but it is also seen by conservative groups in Russia in the more dramatic light of an effort by foreigners to grab Russian natural resources under less than equal and fair terms. In the interview he gave to the Wall Street Journal on March 31, 2009, Russian Deputy Prime Minister Igor Sechin found it appropriate to remind his fellow countrymen and would-be international partners that "Russian resources are a God-given good that should be used effectively... somebody is always wanting to take them away."

Seen from the perspective of South Caucasus countries, the impact of jurisdictional discontinuities between the EU and Russia goes well beyond the increase in transaction costs lamented by economists. The exports of energy resources from Azerbaijan and neighboring Caspian countries in particular depends on a large-scale energy transportation system that has become a bone of contention between the EU and Russia. By 2021, this tension will have been resolved, one way or another – whether through some form of accommodation or though a redirection of Caucasus and Caspian exports toward East and South Asia or the Russian domestic market. Let us therefore reflect on the various manners in which these jurisdictional discontinuities may be handled, and in a manner that is not limited to the usual opposition between transit routes controlled by Russia or circumventing Russia. After all, pipelines are one form of network in today's global networked economy, and there is more to a network than its physical location.

Developing competitive advantages in a networked economy is dependent on a complex, multilayered, multi-lateral context that each player may be more or less able to influence. In a previous work, we defined a network as consisting of three components: a physical infrastructure, a set of rules and a set of mutual expectations and commitments to deal with issues beyond the existing rules. The Internet for instance depends, in a nutshell, on telecommunication links, on addressing rules such as the world wide web (www), and on a new culture of information-sharing and connectedness. Seen in this light, the pipeline network in Eurasia raises issues in all three dimensions: the EU and Russia presently disagree as to the physical infrastructure and its geographic location; they disagree over the rules that should apply to the use of these infrastructures, with the EU favoring third-party access and Russia favoring monopoly control; and they have also failed to develop the mutual expectations and commitments that would help manage conflicts and unresolved issues fostered by their energy interdependence. This last point was well illustrated by the abrupt manner in which Prime Minister Putin announced on July 30, 2009 that Russia would not become a signatory and, therefore, would terminate the provisional application of the Energy Charter Treaty.

Much of the public discussion of countries' efforts to gain the upper hand in this networked economic context has centered on the first dimension: namely, the routes along which pipelines should be laid. In reality, the second dimension is probably more critical as third party access would make the geographic location irrelevant, at least beyond straightforward issues of construction and transit costs. The Energy Charter Treaty (ECT), adopted in 1994 but not ratified and now denounced by Russia, would have been an important step in addressing these issues and in laying the ground work for a common culture based on arbitrage and due process; yet, the hopes generated by the ECT have been largely met with disappointment. The EU and Russia are now separated by different visions of interdependence which feed themselves different views of which rules are most appropriate for the networks that would connect to them.

While the EU and Russia are both penalized by this growing rift and this inability to articulate a common vision of their interdependence, and while this situation certainly benefits third-parties like China, the impact on the South Caucasus is more complex. On the one hand, jurisdictional discontinuities, as well as outright conflicts, are delaying the development of significant resources in the region, as could be seen with the continuous postponement of the commercial exploitation of the Shah Deniz Two field. On the other hand, Russia – and to some extent the EU – has been ready to pay a security premium when acquiring Caspian resources. The term security premium refers to the "energy security" concerns of both parties, meaning, on one hand, security of supply for the EU, and on the other hand, the implications for Caspian producers of what Russia defines as its security of demand. The latter covers not only outlets for Russian supply – which would not affect third-party producers – but also reflects Russian concerns about Russia's market share in the European market. Part of the attractiveness of the direct route to European markets for Central Asian countries lies in the access it can give these countries to the higher prices for gas paid in the European market. Russia, however, has increased the price at which it is ready to purchase Central Asian gas to the equivalent of the European market price, net of transportation costs. Russia has also learned from its successful Wingas venture with Wintershall/BASF that it could ostensibly see the price of its gas diminish as competition develops between different resellers of Russian gas (in this case Wingas and Ruhrgas, which had previously enjoyed a monopoly over sales of Russian gas in Germany). Russia therefore seems to go out of its way – including by offering higher prices than it could – to avoid recreating situations in which Russian, or even FSU gas, competes with itself or other FSU exporters.

As our three-dimensional analysis of networks would suggest, the fundamental insecurity at play in these relations is not so much about interdependence as it is the rules that should govern it. Looking at energy security as a symptom of a deeper interdependence insecurity sheds a different light on the relationship between the EU's energy market legalization drive and the EU external energy relations policy. It also suggests some directions in which to reflect on the possible initiatives that South Caucasus countries could take to foster the win-win developments in energy relations that have not materialized so far.

**The EU's Internal Energy Market Liberalization: Implications for Russia**

In an economist's idealized world, politics should be about the facilitation of economic transactions with a view to reaching the economic optimum. Such a view comes even more natural to the EU, where the political legitimacy of the Commission and of EU supra-national arrangements is grounded most clearly in the promotion of free-trade and of "the four freedoms" of movements of people, goods, information and money. In designing its internal rules for the EU energy market, the EU assumed that its liberalization drive would be supported by a broader trend toward market-based relations with its major energy suppliers. In the words of Jacques de Jong and Coby van der Linde in their Swedish Institute for European Policy Studies report, "EU Energy Policy in a Supply-Constrained World," the EU was of the view that:

...international markets would become the dominant and efficient way to connect demand and supply in the world. With that expectation came the underlying assumption that private companies would be the main players in the international energy arena. This idea was mainly based on the expectation that the resources of the FSU would become available for foreign direct investments of private international oil companies and they would thus be able to create a counterweight to the impending market power of the NOCs of the OPEC and some other countries, where IOCs could not access new reserves.

As the world did not conform to this implicit assumption by the EU Commission – in practice, the EU Directorates-General for Competition (DSG Comp) – the EU began to adapt and modify its approach in 'band-aid' mode. The band-aid was the now famous 'Gazprom clause' that makes some of the benefits of EU market liberalization – in this case the possibility to acquire transmission assets previously owned by vertically integrated monopolies – conditional to the adoption of a similarly liberalized framework in the acquirer's home country. While this sounds natural to EU minds, surprised as they were that Russia had not followed the EU on the liberalization road, this was bound to be more difficult to understand and accept for Russians who had never shared this feeling about the superior value of an unbundled industry structure. Hence Sergey Yastrzhembsky's predictable reaction in *Pipelines, politics and power: The future of EU-Russia energy relations*:

> While the EU is seeking full access to Russian resources and pipelines, the European Parliament is unwilling to let Russian investors buy into the EU energy sector. Would the EU be happy if the Russian parliament adopted a similar approach?

The EU DG COMP would have done Europe a service by not rushing to implement a not-fully tested doctrine in the absence of some deeper analysis of its internal implications. Integrating the external policy and internal market perspective is better done ex ante rather than on the band-aid mode.

From the South Caucasus countries' perspective, an important question will be whether the EU, hopefully strengthened by the adoption of the Lisbon Treaty, will be able to open its eyes to the geopolitical and economic complexity of the Caspian region. The challenge for the EU is to overcome what Pawel Swieboda, writing in *Pipelines, politics and power: The future of EU-Russia energy relations*, cleverly labeled the Frank Sinatra strategy: "The Sinatra strategy of 'do it my way' has been at the core of today's inability to build a strong and coherent European energy policy."

### Initiatives That South Caucasus States Could Take

The multi-lateral nature of the energy relations in which they are engaged provides high-powered starting points for initiatives on the part of South Caucasus states. As observed by Elmar Mammadyarov, the Foreign Minister of Azerbaijan, the construction of the present energy infrastructure "generates additional incentives for regional cooperation." For obvious reasons, this cooperation has been limited to Georgia and Turkey, and will remain fragile as long as the Nagorno Karabakh issue has not found a mutually satisfactory solution. Making progress on the "infostructure" dimension of the Eurasian energy network is a field in which South Caucasus countries could take more of a leadership role. Obviously, Russia will take some time to adjust to what has been a relatively emotional attitude concerning the ECT, a treaty that includes little of the more-demanding European and North American approach to pipeline regulation, and which may in fact lock the EU into a second-best world. Precisely because they have some freedom to move their natural resources through different routes, the South Caucasus countries could play a role in a gradual return to business-like discussions among Eurasian parties.

The way in which natural gas is sold will certainly evolve significantly between now and the year 2021. Presently, the global market for gas is still fragmented, with the North American market being the only one in which prices are set through 'gas to gas' competition. In Eurasia and in the Pacific basin, prices are set in the framework of long-term contracts that embody a reference to substitute fuels like diesel and heating oil. In practice, Eurasian gas prices are therefore indexed on a basket heavily influenced by oil prices, with a time lag of as long as nine months. An important question for South Caucasus and Caspian producers is whether these circumstances will persist or whether Eurasia will witness the emergence of a more liquid market in which natural gas can be traded as it is in the US, and in which gas prices are therefore far more autonomous from oil prices. The move to a US-style market would require the development of "gas hubs" such as the Henry Hub in the US, with important geopolitical, strategic, and economic implications for producer countries.

Turkey has often described its role in Eurasia as that of becoming not simply a major transit country but also a full-fledged energy hub. At this stage, however, this terminology does not reflect the actual role of Turkey in the energy value chain. An energy hub is not defined simply by the interconnection of important pipelines and terminals; it also requires that buyers and sellers can enter into a whole set of different contracts, including short-term ones. They also need to have access to the array of sophisticated services – from gas storage to financial futures contracts – needed in support of what is in fact a marketplace for natural gas. It is possible to imagine that Turkey and the Caucasus region develop such a function by 2021. This would require that various streams of natural gas be traded far more flexibly than is possible today in the region. If Caspian gas, Iraqi gas, Egyptian gas and Iranian gas (including in the form of swaps with Iranian gas delivered in the Gulf) could be traded in the region – as well as possibly off-shore gas from Turkey itself, if exploration of the Turkish off-shore domain is successful – the South Caucasus would truly become an energy hub for Eurasia. Needless to say, such a scenario assumes a full normalization of political and economic relations between all countries in the broader region, including even Syria and Iran. Countries like Azerbaijan, which already enjoy a diversified set of relations with gas producers and importers in the region, could certainly play a role in accelerating the type of economic integration that would be required in this 'energy hub' scenario.

The European Union's integration model is certainly one from which the region could seek incentives, with proper adaptation, in this respect. After all, Europe did not begin with the Schengen Treaty, which establishes free movement for people, or with the common currency. It began with a pooling of resources in the coal and steel industry that, at the time, were industries of strategic importance to Europe. Natural gas is, in many ways, a similarly strategic resource for the region as well as one over which tensions, not to mention conflicts, have tended to intensify in the recent past. The term 'energy weapon' is even used, although often in a fairly loose manner, which suggests an analogy with what was said of steel in Europe after the Second World War. Promoting cooperation over gas could therefore be a major avenue for the region to take its future in its own hands and also contribute to a pacified architecture for Eurasia as a whole. As was done in Europe, such a strategy needs to begin not with the most controversial and conflict-prone aspects on the agenda, but with a number of more technical issues on which agreement can be more easily fostered. The development of common approaches on contracts and on the various aspects of an 'energy hub' could provide such a technical platform for a more ambitious strategy. In this sense, natural resources would contribute to the well-being of the South Caucasus countries in 2021, not just in terms of export revenues, but also in terms of a qualitative change in their role in the international division of labor and the political structure of Eurasia as a whole.

# Part Three:

# External Influences and Foreign Policy Strategies

# TURKEY'S POLICIES IN ITS HISTORICAL HINTERLAND

Udo Steinbach,
Professor of International Politics,
University of Hamburg

Turkey shares numerous historical, cultural, religious and linguistic commonalities with the political map that emerged in the southern Caucasus after the collapse of the Soviet Union. According to Ismail Cem, Turkey's foreign minister from 1997 to 2002, it provides Turkey with a new international environment of historical and cultural dimensions. For centuries, the Ottoman Empire exerted its influence over the Caucasus; some of the peoples – among them the Azerbaijanis – were Turkish speaking, and Islam was one of the most widely distributed religions. All of these facts – beyond current political and economic interests – made Turkey into one of the main shapers of the political landscape in the Caucasus.

A look at the history books shows us that after the Sunni Ottoman Empire and the newly emerging Shia Safavid Empire of Persia established their long-term borders in the aftermath of the Battle of Chaldiran (1514), the Caucasus remained a region dominated by the rival influences of the Ottomans and the Persians until the end of the Safavid Dynasty (1736). When Ivan IV ("The Terrible," 1547-1584) conquered the Khanates of Kazan (1552) and Astrakhan (1556), the Russians also made their presence felt, especially in the North Caucasus. For Constantinople (Istanbul) the Caucasus was a strategically important region for curbing Iranian expansion. As part of the Peace of Constantinople Agreement (1700), the Ottomans and the Russians divided up those areas of the Caucasus that had until then belonged to Persia. Even if the Peace of Constantinople was advantageous to the Ottomans, it legitimated the Russian presence in the Caucasian territories. In the 1740s, Nadir Shah (1736-1747) succeeded in wrenching the Azerbaijani territories away from the Ottomans. After his death, however, the Khanate in Azerbaijan returned to the Ottomans. The loss of the Crimea to Russia in 1774 began the extensive Russian annexation of North and South Caucasus, a process completed in the mid-19$^{th}$ century.

Russian power in the Caucasus was strengthened still further by the Peace of Turkmenchai (1828), agreed in the wake of the Second Russian-Iranian War. Iran had to cede North Azerbaijan, including Karabakh and Nakhchivan, to the Russians. Besides, Yerevan Khanate and the center of Armenian Church Ejmiatsin, which are located in today's Armenian territory, were also ceded to the Russians. A year later, the Ottomans were forced by the Peace of Adrianopel to cede further territories in the Caucasus to the Russians. Following the Russian-Turkish War of 1877–1878, Russia was awarded Turkish provinces of Kars, Batumi and Ardahan at the Conference of San Stefano. Kars and Ardahan returned to the Turks as a result of the Peace Agreement of Brest-Litovsk on March 3, 1918 and were occupied by the Turks on April 25, 1918.

As early as the mid-19$^{th}$ century, the increasingly tight grip exerted by Russia over the North Caucasus had led to the migration of large groups of Turkic and/or Islamic populations of the Caucasus into the Ottoman Empire; among them, the Cherkess formed the largest group.

With the incorporation of the short-lived South Caucasian states, which had declared independence after the Bolshevik October Revolution, into the Russian Socialist Federation of Soviet Republics (known from 1923 as the USSR), the Turkish Republic, founded in 1923, was hermetically sealed off from the Caucasian territories. In 1945 the Caucasian question seemed to have returned to the political agenda as Stalin demanded that the "Armenian" territories of Kars and Ardahan, which had been hotly disputed since the 19$^{th}$ century, be returned to the Soviet Union. Given the Soviet pressure, Turkey began to make approaches to the US and the Western military alliance; in 1952 it joined NATO.

### Turkey: A Regional Power with a Caucasian Aura

Immediately after the Soviet Union broke up, Ankara turned its attention to the newly independent states of the Caucasus. When Turkey recognized Azerbaijan's independence on December 9, 1991 – one week before recognizing the other Islamic states situated on former Soviet Union territory – it became the first country to pay its respects to the new republics' independence. Diplomatic ties were established soon after – except with Armenia. Moreover, the creation of the Agency for Turkish Cooperation and Development (Türk İşbirliği ve Kalkınma Ajansı, TIKA) in January 1992 provided Ankara with an instrument for economic and developmental cooperation with the new states in the Caucasus.

The end of the Soviet Union and the newly found independence of the South Caucasus states, however, did not only open up a hinterland to Turkey in which the Ottoman Empire had exerted influence for centuries. By joining the alliance against Iraqi dictator, Saddam Hussein, to free Kuwait in the autumn of 1990, Turkey began to take on the role of a regional power whose political influence radiates through the Near and Middle East, into central Asia and the Balkans. Thus, from that time on, Ankara's invigorating policies in the Caucasus had to be seen within a wider context that was defined, in particular, by Russia's presence in the Caucasus and the (energy) interests of the US and the European Union.

Among the most important external powers in the Caucasus, rivalries broke out once again. Ankara was afraid that Tehran might be tempted to exploit a politicized Islam to exert influence over Muslims in the Caucasus (Azerbaijan, like Iran, has a Shia majority), a fear that was shared by Moscow. Iran for its part was concerned that Turkey's active role in the region might lead to the hegemony of Pan-Turkism on Iran's borders. Moscow also feared that the advance of Turkish influence, perhaps in coordination with American interests, might come at the expense of conventional Russian influences in the region. Moscow countered by exploiting the imminent conflicts in the South Caucasus to gain influence.

### Strategic Partnership with Azerbaijan

At first, Turkey's Caucasus policies concentrated on Azerbaijan. By becoming Shiite after the Safavids had come to power in 1501, it is true, a wedge had been driven between Azerbaijan and the Ottoman Empire, the leading Sunni power of the time. On the other hand, of the Turkic languages, the Turkish spoken in Azerbaijan is the most similar to that spoken in Turkey. Pan-Turkish ideas in the 19$^{th}$ and 20$^{th}$ centuries also encouraged Azerbaijani Turks to dream of a greater Turkey – Turks had assisted Azerbaijani nationalists in their struggle against Bolshevik forces in Baku, while at the same time hundreds of thousands of Azerbaijanis fled from the Soviets onto Turkish territory, where there is still a largely integrated and discreet community (and political lobby). Finally, since 1991, Pan-Turkish aspirations to set up a union of Turkish states from the "Tyrrhenian Sea to the Chinese Wall" have been evident on both sides.

It was not only for historical, linguistic and cultural reasons, but also because of common political, economic and strategic interests that Azerbaijan was the main item on Ankara's Caucasus agenda. Turkey was the only country to support Azerbaijan in its struggle for Nagorno Karabakh, and in doing so, it was willing to accept a strain in its relations with Russia. This development reached its zenith during Azeri President Abulfaz Elchibey's time in office (1992-93). Despite repeated efforts, however, he was not able to persuade Turkey to provide military assistance in the conflict with Armenia.

After Elchibey was overthrown in a coup in which Russia quite evidently had its hand, bi-lateral relations became more pragmatic. In the area of cultural policies, Ankara created or strengthened organizations whose task it was to keep relations with the Turkish speaking peoples of Central Asia alive. These included the Joint Administration of Turkic Arts and Culture, which was set up to strengthen cultural relations between the Turkish-speaking countries and societies and to carry out research into "shared Turkish culture." Fresh impetus was given to the Institute for Research on the Turkic World, which distinguished itself by publishing the *Handbook of the Turkic World*. Furthermore, Azerbaijan and Turkey began to concentrate on developing their economic and energy cooperation. Besides the Baku-Tbilisi-Ceyhan (BTC) Pipeline, the rail link currently being built between Baku in Azerbaijan to Turkish Kars via Akhalkalaki in Georgia will reinforce long-lasting ties between the two countries.

### Armenia – Ghosts of the Past

From the very start, relations between Turkey and Armenia have been burdened by both the Nagorno Karabakh conflict and the events of 1915. It is true that on December 16, 1991 Ankara recognized Armenia's independence. Their rapprochement for a time even led to the preparation of a Turkish-Armenian treaty of friendship. The escalation of the Karabakh conflict and Turkey's close ties with Azerbaijan, however, encouraged Ankara to distance itself from Yerevan. Relations were decisively strained when the Armenian parliament contested the border between the two countries, which had been set down in the Treaty of Kars in October 1921, and which is still internationally recognized today. As a consequence, the borders between Turkey and Armenia were closed in 1993. The atmosphere worsened in the wake of Yerevan's efforts to persuade the international community to recognize the events of 1915-16 as genocide and to condemn Turkey's refusal to do so. Yerevan was successful; in 2006, the French parliament passed a law making it a punishable offence to deny that genocide had been perpetrated on the Armenians.

When the Party for Justice and Development (AKP) came to power in autumn 2002, relations between Turkey and Armenia, however, did become more practical; Armenia declared that the current border was "a political reality," and offered Ankara unlimited and unconditional diplomatic ties. As a result, room could be created for initiatives aimed at easing tensions. Indeed the existing constellation no longer matches the interests of either Turkey or Armenia. From Turkey's point of view, the continuing conflict in the South Caucasus is obstructing a strengthening of its political and economic role in that region. From Armenia's perspective, the border blockade is putting a strain on its economy as it is making imports more expensive and making closer economic ties between Armenia and its neighbors more difficult.

As is quite often the case in Turkish politics, the initial signals suggesting a possible change of direction came from the Turkish commercial sector. Quite a long time ago the Turkish-Armenian Business Council had begun to take small steps to improve business relations with Armenia. Armenia would be the natural transit country connecting Turkey to Azerbaijan, Russia and Central Asia. Trade between Turkey and Armenia is done unofficially via Iran and Georgia. In keeping with plans made by the Turkish Industrialists' and Businessmen's Association (TUSIAD) and the Armenian Union of Manufacturers and Businessmen of Armenia, the Turkish economy would like to invest in the textile, energy and telecommunication sectors.

Other developments that indicate future improvements in the Turkish-Armenian relationship were of a social and cultural nature. Thus, high level representatives of the Turkish government and society took part in the festivities to celebrate the reopening of the completely renovated Armenian Church on the Island of Akdamar in the East Anatolian Lake Van in March 2007; but, government and religious leaders from Armenia were also invited. They did not accept their invitations, however. The event was to be a sign that relations were to be revived.

Even in the "Armenian Question" progress is noticeable. Prime Minister Erdogan proposed setting up a joint commission to clarify the Armenian Question scientifically. This proposal is in one of the two protocols that were signed by the foreign ministers of both countries in Zurich on October 10, 2009 (see below). Turkish academics and journalists – also of Armenian descent – are dealing with the issue free from taboos. The murder of Hrant Dink, the publisher of the Armenian language newspaper *Agos*, on January 9, 2007 by a young Turkish nationalist fanatic led to an unprecedented outpouring of solidarity with the Armenian minority by a section of the Turkish public.

Despite these signs of improvement in Turkish-Armenian relations, the visit by President Abdullah Gul to Yerevan on September 6, 2008 came as a surprise. It was the very first visit by a Turkish state president to Armenia. Even if the occasion, a qualification game between the two countries' national football teams for the World Championship, was a sporting one, it prompted a process of political negotiation concerning opening borders between the two countries as a first step toward normalizing bi-lateral relations.

On October 10, 2009, two protocols were signed by Turkey's and Armenia's foreign ministers in Zurich in which both parties agreed to a process leading to normalization of relations. The key issues were: the opening of the borders, which had been closed since 1993; the establishment of diplomatic relations; and the development of political, economic, scientific and cultural relations between the two countries. The agreements are to come into effect once they are ratified by the parliaments in Ankara and Yerevan. Owing to nationalist resistance on both sides, considerable difficulties are to be expected in implementing the agreements upon completion of the treaties.

Relations between Ankara and Baku have not gone unaffected by this development: in Azerbaijan it is feared that in the wake of Turkish-Armenian rapprochement, the pressure on Yerevan to find a mainly political solution to the Nagorno Karabakh conflict might be removed.

### Georgia's Growing Importance

After the end of the Soviet Union, Georgia swiftly became a close foreign partner to Turkey in its immediate geopolitical environment. Georgia sought political support from Turkey to counter the pressure being put on it by Russia; the Georgian government assisted in completing the Baku-Tbilisi-Ceyhan Pipeline Project and showed interest in working together with Turkey in a multiplicity of areas from tourism to national security. Turkey saw political, economic and military support for Georgia as a way of spreading Ankara's influence to the South Caucasus and of opening the gateway to Central Asia.

The Turkish government recognized Georgia's independence in November 1991; diplomatic relations followed in May 1992 after Eduard Shevardnadze's return to Georgia. In 1992, the two countries signed a Treaty of Friendship and Cooperation. The civil war in Georgia and the enormous pressure exerted on that country by Russia, which insisted on maintaining military bases in Georgia for the following 25 years, encouraged Ankara and Tbilisi to draw even closer together. In January 1994, Shevardnadze visited Ankara; a joint communiqué was signed in which the two parties pledged to promote independence, peace, stability, democracy and to develop closer economic ties.

Over the years, Turkey became Georgia's most important economic partner. In May 2007, Georgian President Mikheil Saakashvili and Turkey's Foreign Minister Abdullah Gul opened Batumi Airport, which was built by a Turkish consortium and which serves direct flights to Istanbul among others. Shortly before that, the Turkish TAV Airport Holding had completed the construction of Tbilisi's international airport.

The two countries are also working together on military matters. Within the Partnership for Peace programs, Ankara is advising and assisting Georgia in its efforts to build up its army. These programs include military training, and the modernizing of military airports and the equipping of military bases. In addition, Turkey is backing Georgia's efforts to become a member of NATO.

In the last few years, Turkey's bi-lateral relations with Azerbaijan and Georgia have begun to acquire a tri-lateral dimension. On February 7, 2007, the presidents of Azerbaijan and Georgia and the Prime Minister of Turkey signed the "Tbilisi Declaration," setting out their joint vision for regional cooperation. The main focus is on: the oil and gas sectors, the power grid, free movement of people and goods and, in particular, the railway project mentioned above. Especially the latter is being accorded ever more significance. The financing of the railway – in contrast to the BTC – is a joint regional project, which therefore probably involves a military component; in the case of renewed military conflict in Nagorno Karabakh, Azerbaijani troops could be supplied via the railway from Turkey and Georgia. Furthermore, after Russia's embargo threatened Georgia's gas supply, Turkey and Azerbaijan pledged to supply Georgia with natural gas if need be.

**European and American Interests**

The development of bi-lateral relations into an Ankara-Baku-Tbilisi axis has been advanced in part by a series of pipeline projects. The plan to build an oil pipeline from Baku to the Turkish terminal in Ceyhan was launched in the mid-1990s by Washington, whose aim it was to maintain access to the Central Asian oil and gas reserves and at the same time to keep the transport routes out of Russian and Iranian control.

Only after numerous political and economic doubts (concerning the length of the pipeline, the land to be crossed, the high costs and the relatively high price for the oil in comparison to oil from the Gulf) were overcome, could the construction be approved at the OECD Summit meeting in Istanbul in November 1999. Due to the exclusion of Russia and Iran, plus Armenia (through which in fact the shortest route between Baku and Ceyhan could have been built), the project took on considerable political significance. In autumn 2005, the BTC pipeline was opened. The oil pipeline project was enhanced by the building of a gas pipeline parallel to the BTC from Baku via Tbilisi to Erzurum, where this pipeline joined another pipeline coming from Iran.

The idea of Turkey as a "bridge" for Caspian oil and gas has also spurred on the imagination of European energy planners since the end of the 1990s, and they have begun to take considerable interest in raw materials from the Caspian area. The Caucasus and Central Asian regions are to be linked more closely to Europe by two transport corridors. While the TRACECA is to be a transport corridor for goods and people between China's western border and Bulgaria, the Nabucco Pipeline should transport Caspian gas to Europe. Devised in 2002 as the first project of a joint European energy policy, the 3,300-km pipeline is to start at the Turkish border to Iran and Georgia and end in Austria.

**The Russian Factor**

If nothing else, these above-mentioned pipeline projects draw attention to Russia since they so obviously, deliberately and completely circumvent Russian territory. Nevertheless, Russia is still a part of the South Caucasus's constellation of powers since Russia's decisions also affect Turkey's Caucasus policies. When the Soviet Union came to an end and the hermetically sealed-off Caucasus borders were opened, Moscow and Ankara competed for influence in the new South Caucasus states. With respect to the Turkic peoples of the Caucasus and Central Asia, Russia feared Turkey would increasingly exert ideologically- (Pan-Turkish) underpinned influence.

Simultaneously, Turkey was Washington's closest ally in the region. Along the Black Sea, it seemed intermittently that a maritime arms race was beginning. While Moscow was openly and militarily supporting the Abkhazian and the South Ossetian separatists in Georgia, Ankara and Tbilisi, as already described, were rapidly developing closer relations. Ankara's backing for Baku in the struggle for Nagorno Karabakh stood counter to Moscow's support for Yerevan. With regard to the conflicts in the North Caucasus, especially in Chechnya, Russia feared, in particular, that the lobby formed by the Caucasian peoples, which had fled Russian annexation in the 19th century and settled in the Ottoman Empire, would attempt to move the Turkish government to influence events. Most certainly, one of Ankara's key principles must have been to ensure that Russia's influence in the Caucasus was kept to a minimum in order to keep the gateway to Central Asia as wide open as possible.

Continuous rivalry resulting from divergent political interests and the simultaneous development of bi-lateral relations is the formula that could be used to describe Turkish-Russian relations during the Putin era. The backbone of the relationship is made up of trade and cooperation in the energy sector. The Blue Stream Pipeline running under the Black Sea from the Russian Black Sea coast to the Turkish harbor town of Samsun (with an extension to Ankara) is the cornerstone of their energy partnership. At the same time, Ankara has made it clear that Turkey will work together with Russia to build the so-called South Stream pipeline that should transport Russian oil to southern Europe through the Black Sea. This willingness is all the more significant since the pipeline is indisputably a rival Russian project to the Nabucco Pipeline in which Turkey plays a pre-eminent role. It is also significant that after the estrangement of Turkey and the USA in the wake of the Iraq War, Washington is no longer primarily relying on military cooperation with Turkey but is building up its own military presence in the Caucasus.

Both militarily and politically, Ankara has completely refrained from getting involved in the conflicts in the North Caucasus, despite occasional pressure exerted by lobbies in Turkey, especially by those of Chechen origin. Nevertheless, divergences in Turkish and Russian interests, especially with regards to energy, are becoming apparent. The BTC pipeline was built and commissioned to create an energy corridor that did not touch Russian territory. Thus, the short war between Russia and Georgia that began on August 8, 2008 when Georgia attacked South Ossetia fed the assumption that Russia's military operations might be targeted at gaining control of the BTC pipeline. Even if this assumption has not been confirmed, Moscow, not least by giving recognition to the secessionist provinces of Abkhazia and South Ossetia, has been able to consolidate its influence in the South Caucasus. Ankara responded to the war by proposing the creation of a Caucasus Stability and Cooperation Platform on which Turkey, Russia and the three Caucasus states would cooperate.

This initiative would have been a suitable way of providing the Black Sea Economic Cooperation (BSEC) with greater importance. It was set up in 1992, primarily as the result of Turkey's initiative. For a long time the BSCE, which currently has 12 members and 13 observers, languished in the shadow cast by economic and political rivalries. In the last few years, the organization, whose aim is to strengthen economic cooperation, gained in importance. It was one of the few forums on which Armenians and Azerbaijanis could meet. It was also given fresh impetus by the fact the region became an intersection for energy interests.

## The New Parameters of Turkish Politics

The signing of the two protocols on whose foundations relations between Turkey and Armenia were to be built in October 2009 illustrated Ankara's determination to redefine Turkey's place in the whole region. At the same time, this step is a result of far-reaching changes in Turkey's domestic politics and society since the Party for Justice and Development came to power at the end of 2002. In particular, the legal, social, cultural and religious reforms initiated between 2003 and 2005 have changed the face of the country in a way that is indeed comparable to the Kemalist reforms of the 1920s. The breadth and depth of the changes should be attributed to two issues: the "Kurdish Issue" and the position occupied by Islamic religion in politics and society. Unlike the Kemalist tabooing of the subject, today there is public admission that there is a Kurdish problem; it is felt that to solve the problem it will not be enough to combat terror waged by the Kurdish Workers' Party (KWP), but rather it will primarily require that democratic structures be strengthened. At the same time, Islam, after being filtered out of public view for decades, has clearly begun to determine individual and societal behavior and the sense of identity of many citizens in Turkey. The state has diminished as a source of behavioral norms and self-image; this has freed space within which society can re-determine and redefine itself. The gradual withdrawal of the military as the refuge of a state-centered definition of the citizen based on nationalism and rigorous Laicism is one symptom of that.

One facet of this complex re-organization of the state and society is a new way of dealing with the events of 1915. Until very recently the idea that serious crimes had been committed in the course of the "resettlements" was still being disputed. In particular, any state involvement was always denied. For a number of years now, especially among academics and liberal publishers, discussions have revolved around seeing the "events" differently and investigating the involvement of the state bodies in the planning and carrying out of the massacre. After the murder of the Turkish-Armenian journalist, Hrant Dink, by a nationalist fanatic, tens of thousands took to the streets and chanted: "We are Hrant Dink." They were expressing their mutual solidarity against state forces, which are still determined to make a taboo of socially sensitive issues even if they have to resort to physical repression. Turkish President Abdullah Gul took into account this altered and, in some respects, more relaxed perception of the "Armenian Issue" when he accepted an invitation to attend the football game between Turkey and Armenia in Yerevan in September 2008. Since a psychological taboo developed holes as a result, it was only a matter of time until the hermetically sealed physical border between the two countries became porous.

The developments in Turkish-Armenian relations are exemplary of the connection between the changes within Turkey itself and those in its whole regional environment. While observers in the 1990s were able to describe the geopolitical environment around Turkey as a "360-degree nightmare," the prospects are different today. Relations with its Arab neighbors (including the Palestinians) and Israel are marked by dynamic interaction. This is not only true of economic relations. In Ankara, there is much more talk of a strategic quality that not only contains political elements but even military ones. For decades, Ankara's foreign policy was almost exclusively directed toward NATO and the European Union. That only began to change in the early 1990s. After 2002, the new political powers completely altered their perceptions of the immediate area. The Kemalist powers had relocated Turkey in the West. Just as they had separated themselves from the Ottoman Empire's past, they had kept their distance from those neighbors with whom they associated wars and conflicts, some of them lasting centuries.

In contrast to that view, the new elite sees in this past a chance in a profoundly changing world to reposition Turkey. This does not mean a break with the coordinates of the last few decades. However, the parameters of Turkey's foreign policy are to be expanded to include that region with which the Turks within the Ottoman Empire shared a common history over centuries. From a perception of instability and threat, Turkey is being challenged to help stabilize its neighboring area. That this involves giving significance to comprehensive economic cooperation is the pragmatic aspect of this vision. This combination of vision and pragmatism also includes Iran. Closer political and economic ties to this – historically so alien – state are perceived as being the better strategy with which to work to counter the threat posed by Iran's atomic program. This political re-orientation is based on a new understanding of history, culture and religion. It results in new – also emotional – solidarities. That this may cause friction and differences with existing partners lies in the nature of the matter. One symptom of that is the cooling of Turkey's relations with Israel as a result of Israel's policies with respect to the Palestinians, and its excessive military force used during the 2008 Gaza War.

The intense dynamic in Ankara's foreign policy toward its neighboring countries shows why the Turkish government has continued to cooperate and ease tensions with Armenia despite Azerbaijan's disquiet and uncertainties about what will happen to the further process of ratification of the Zurich Protocol in Ankara and Yerevan. The normalization of relations with Armenia has come at a time (autumn 2009) when the government is starting a campaign to intensify democracy in Turkey. With these steps toward normalization of relations with Armenia, the AKP government is trying to regulate a situation that has been restricting the scope of its policies in the Caucasus since the early 1990s and which has continuously taxed Turkey's relations with the US and the EU. In domestic politics, the unresolved Armenian Question is inhibiting the development of a liberal and open society in which pluralism and protection of minorities are not habitually seen as a threat to national unity and the state's existence.

Since autumn 2008, there have been talks between Ankara and Yerevan concerning the normalization of relations. These consultations seemed for a time to have hit a dead end in both countries in spring of 2009 since national resistance reared its head and, moreover, Turkey had to consider Azerbaijan, which was seen as a "brother state" and which finds itself in a "frozen conflict" with Armenia over the Azerbaijani territory of Nagorno Karabakh. It was all the more surprising when Turkey, Armenia and Switzerland jointly declared on August 31, 2009 that Turkey and Armenia had agreed to two protocols. The first foresees the opening of the borders and the establishment of diplomatic ties. Both sides also recognized their mutual borders. As a result, Turkey's often repeated reservations that Armenia, at least implicitly, was laying claim to territories in eastern Turkey that had been assigned to the new Turkish Republic after the First World War, were rendered groundless.

The second protocol contains details on how the political, economic, scientific and cultural relations are to be developed. To this end, a bi-lateral governmental commission (with various sub-committees) is to be set up, which, three months after the protocol takes effect, should begin to devise the content of the different areas of bi-lateral relations. At the end of the process, the protocols are to be ratified by both parliaments.

The public's attention will probably also focus on an agreement that the commission should discuss the "historical dimension" with a view to "restoring mutual trust between the two nations." This choice of words addresses the hotly disputed question of whether and how one can come to an agreement on how to judge the massacre of Armenian citizens in the Ottoman Empire in 1915 – as a deliberate act of genocide by the empire's leaders of that time, as claimed by the Armenians and a large section of the international public, or as a regrettable side-effect of the warlike conflicts of that time, as is the official Turkish interpretation.

Most past efforts to attain a settlement in this matter, in which the international Diaspora has played an important part, were doomed to failure from the very beginning. The two sides in this matter remained rigidly opposed to one another. The Armenian Diaspora, which is extremely important for Armenian politics, draws its identity from the genocide. On the other side, the categorical denial of the genocide is seen by many Turks as an integral part of the Turkish Republic's national identity. This is hardly surprising since numerous leaders of the "first generation" of the Kemalist state were more or less involved in the massacre of the Armenians.

As a result, this historical issue is of immense political and existential importance for both sides. Should the process, which is still in its early stages, produce a Turkish-Armenian agreement, it would not only provide bi-lateral relations with a new foundation; in Turkey a further cornerstone would be removed from the nationalist Turkish political and intellectual edifice, which had been hugely obstructive for the development of a democratic order that includes broad social acceptance of free opinion. That is why nationalist groups will mobilize considerable resistance against the signing and subsequent ratification of the two protocols by the Turkish National Assembly. Nationalist Armenian opposition in Yerevan with similar aims will almost certainly play into their hands.

If the protocols were to be successfully ratified and implemented in both countries, however, that would not only set the course in domestic politics but might also have significant implications for the politics of the region.

Initially the AKP's policy of normalizing political relations with Turkey's neighbors seemed to have been successful once more. Furthermore, repercussions for the Nagorno Karabakh conflict are inevitable. By signing the protocols, Turkey would find itself in a situation in which it would more or less be obliged to mediate between Armenia and Azerbaijan. If the latently violent tensions between its Caucasian neighbors continue, however, these could threaten ratification by the Turkish parliament.

Moreover, Ankara would hardly be able to maintain problem-free bi-lateral relations with both countries at the same time. Either the consolidation of the policy of settlement with Yerevan would constantly be in peril or Turkey's regional energy policies, which are closely tied to its relations with Azerbaijan, would be latently threatened. The worst-case scenario would see both happening simultaneously.

For Baku and Yerevan, Russia is the only possible alternative to good relations with Turkey and the "opening to the West" associated with them (if one regards the theoretically possible build-up and expansion of special relations with Iran as unlikely). Yet, neither South Caucasian state shows any increased interest in sacrificing itself to Russia's political influence in the long-term.

Therein lies the chance for Turkey, backed by the EU and the US, to intensify its politics of mediation. If the Nagorno Karabakh Conflict were to enjoy long-lasting calm, this would alter the power structure in the South Caucasus in favor of a more autonomous regional development in which Turkey could play an important role. In that case, the geo-strategic situation of the Caspian energy producing states would also be transformed: the transport of energy through the South Caucasus would be easier. However, such a development would be at the expense of Russian influence in the region. The unanswered question therefore is how Moscow would react to tendencies of that kind. The outcome of the Georgia War in August 2008 helped to significantly reinforce its position in the South Caucasus. The Turkish plan for a Stability and Cooperation Platform for the Caucasus would confirm and define Russia's role in the region. However, Russia in return would have to recognize Turkey's political ambitions in the South Caucasus. The image that appears behind that of a Russian-Turkish "condominium" in the region not only stirs up considerable resistance in the states of South Caucasus: It would also be an expression of Turkey's over-estimation of itself. Reconciliation between Turkey and Armenia opens up the prospect of comprehensive regional stabilization and the development of a new political order. Nevertheless, it is only the first step of a longer, extremely uncertain journey. Turkey alone cannot produce a new long-lasting regional order, let alone guarantee one. Nevertheless, Ankara and Yerevan have been able to make an important start.

That is why the latest developments in relations between Russia and Turkey can also be seen as a preventative act of reassurance by Ankara. In August 2009, Prime Minister Putin visited Turkey. In the course of the visit, a range of agreements in the energy sector were made. Thus, Erdogan's government gave Russia, or more precisely Gazprom, the right to use Turkey's exclusive business zone to lay the planned South Stream east-west pipeline through the Black Sea. The development of the South Stream project has thus been freed of any potential obstacles. In addition, the Turkish government stressed it would award a Russian-Turkish consortium with the construction of the first Turkish atomic power station. In return, Putin approved Russian participation in a planned Trans-Anatolian Oil Pipeline with which a consortium consisting of the Italian energy giant ENI and the Turkish firm Calik wants to connect the Turkish Black Sea harbor Samsun with the Ceyhan oil terminal on the Mediterranean. Russia now wants to guarantee this pipeline's previously uncertain oil supply.

The agreements made during Putin's visit, will reinforce existing Turkish-Russian-Italian energy cooperation and, in doing so, also the political and economic interdependence of Russia and Turkey. Given the geopolitical importance of energy issues, this would also help to underpin Turkey's regional policies in the South Caucasus in the long term. The EU-planned Nabucco gas pipeline, an alternative to South Stream, has contributed to this process by making significant progress: on July 13, 2009 the representatives of six participating states signed the necessary treaties.

Ankara is keeping several options open in the energy question. Their realization would not remain completely unaffected by reconciliation between Turkey and Armenia and the shift in the regional order associated with it. Turkey has been able to use its room for maneuver to influence development in the region unhindered.

**Conclusion**

It is obvious that Turkey is in the middle of a dynamic transitional phase, both in its domestic and foreign relations. In domestic politics, this means the consolidation of democracy and the continued reinforcement of stability. In its foreign policies targeted at its neighbors, extensive interdependence with all those involved strengthens the country's security. This in turn has repercussions for the expansion of economic ties and the geopolitical location of Turkey. The Kemalist principle "Peace at home, peace in the world" has received an added dimension. Old patterns of perception of friends and foes that rested on ethnic or ideological foundations are currently shifting. They are making way for a pragmatically guided shaping of relations.

This provides new prospects for relations between Turkey and the EU. Turkey is contributing to the stability of a region that is important for the political and economic foreign relations of the EU. It is impossible to overlook the fact that Ankara has become more confident in its dealings with Brussels in these matters. Membership in the EU is still the number one item on Ankara's foreign policy agenda. This will remain true, however, only so long as Brussels is willing to give recognition and backing to Turkey's new role. How relations are shaped in the future will depend on how attractive the EU becomes or remains as a multi-lateral actor. In the long-term, it is possible that Ankara will reassess its relations with the EU. Turkey may decide to give preference to seeking a secure place within its geopolitical environment than to striving for membership in the EU, which obviously still has problems with accepting Turkey as a possible member.

# GEOPOLITICAL DYNAMICS OF THE CAUCASUS-CASPIAN BASIN AND THE TURKISH FOREIGN AND SECURITY POLICIES

**Mustafa Aydin,**
Rector,
Kadir Has University, Turkey

A new geopolitical region has emerged at the heart of Eurasia since the collapse of the Soviet Empire. Variously labeled as the Caspian Basin Region, Trans-Caspian, Central Eurasia or simply Central Asia and the Caucasus, it stretches from the Black Sea into Western China and Mongolia. The states within the region are experiencing similar economic, political and social changes and difficulties. Their situation is further exacerbated by the rivalry among a number of countries that aim to fill the power vacuum, which emerged in the wake of Soviet collapse. Many have labeled the struggle to define this region's future as the new "Great Game."

Situated at the western side of this area, the South Caucasus, hosting three independent countries since 1991, have witnessed all the particulars of "great gaming," including rivalry of external powers over energy resources and influence in the region, competition of multinational companies, contested borders and identities, territorial claims, active and cold wars, economically motivated out-migration, refugee movements, rise of transnational crime networks, infusion of outside investment and consequent rise of wealth, and bad economic and political governance. Taking into consideration that all these are happening at the same time in a very small part of the world with a total population of approximately 15 million people, it has not been surprising to see various conflicts emerge in the region.

The Caucasus Region, encompassing the North and South Caucasus as well as the Caspian Basin, is one of the most coveted pieces of territory in the world, thanks to its geo-strategic significance between Central Asia and Europe and, more importantly, on the historic invasion routes of Russia. The land corridor of the Trans-Caucasus fosters contact or confrontation between Russia in the north and Turkey and Iran in the south. On this same axis, various forms of Christianity face Sunni and Shia branches of Islam. Furthermore, the fact that the area possesses large oil and gas deposits can be reason for further cooperation or competition and conflict between regional powers and their external allies. These conditions make the area a unified strategic and security complex as well as a site of conflict.

Even a rudimentary study of Caucasian history reveals a region that has been full of complexities and diversity. And to an extent, the region is still suffering from the after-effects of Tsarist conquest and colonial rule. Social fabric of the region was distorted earlier on by the mass deportation of people toward the end of World War II. It remains a region where the implication of sudden independence and realization of ethnic identities by titular nationalities ensured the onset of ethnic strife, forced population movements and economic hardships.

In addition to the general potential for conflict in the Caucasus, new strains have emerged due to conflicting interests of a number of regional and extra-regional powers since the exploration of the Caspian Basin has revealed significant deposits of oil and gas. The possibility of transferring large-scale oil and gas deposits mainly to Europe raised hopes for regional economic development and prosperity. At the same time, however, "the belief that whoever secures the major share of oil pipeline transit will gain enhanced influence not only throughout the Caucasus and Central Asia but also on a global political scale," highlighted the concerns about the future stability of the region. In terms of geopolitics, control of the region represents a prize of considerable value. Thus the competition for influence among regional states, with its ideological, religious and political dimensions, made possible armed conflicts more likely.

The independence of the Caucasian states after the collapse of the Soviet system has changed the geopolitics of the region immensely. When the Soviet Union collapsed, newly independent Caucasian countries started to define their geopolitical orientation. There was no doubt that the outcome would fundamentally alter political and military equations throughout

Eurasia. Earlier geopolitical domino theories for the region suggested various scenarios of explosive instability. Given the unstable nature of the region in general, the prospects for widespread destabilization have been real indeed. The consequences of such an event would be felt throughout Eurasia and would inevitably have a significant impact even on the remote powers of the North Atlantic. Moreover, the West, especially the US, has important economic and commercial interests connected with the exploitation of hydrocarbon deposits in the Caspian Basin.

The developments in the region since the September 11, 2001 terrorist attacks and the August 2008 conflict between Russian and Georgia demonstrated once again that the geopolitical realignment has not yet ended and the rivalry of the outsiders over the region's future still continues. Among the regional stakeholders for stability, Turkey and its policies have drawn a lot of attention. Yet, there remains a certain amount of ambiguity and suspicion toward Turkish policies in the region; thus a reassessment of Turkish foreign and security policy toward the Caucasus and the Caspian Basin is in order, taking into account especially recent activity and various initiatives of the current Turkish government.

### Turkey's Approach to the Caucasus-Caspian Region

Since the late 1980s, Turkey, once an outpost of the West against the Soviet Bloc, found itself at the epicenter of rapidly changing Eurasian geopolitics. It has been cited as an important actor because of its strong historical, cultural, ethnic and linguistic bonds with the newly independent states of Eurasia. Its positive role was discussed not only within Turkey but also in the West, which feared that radical Islam, instigated and/or supported by Iran, might fill the power vacuum left behind by the collapsing Soviet Union. This led the West to encourage the newly independent states to adopt a "Turkish model" of secular democracy and liberal economy.

On the other hand, while the emergence of liberal democracies in Eastern Europe created a buffer zone between Western Europe and Russia, Turkey still felt threatened by the lingering uncertainties in its neighborhood, especially in the Caucasus. Thus Turkey felt the urgency to create new openings in its foreign and security policies based on advantages of its geo-strategic location bordering the region.

After almost two decades of practice, the main lines of Turkish policy that emerged in the first half of the 1990s have started to evolve based on a more complex understanding of regional dynamics. Nevertheless, to understand basic contours of the current Turkish policies toward the region, the analysis should start from the basic parameters developed earlier.

First of all, from the beginning Turkey strongly endorsed the sovereignty and independence of all three Caucasian countries. This included calls for reinforcing their political institutions and building up their economic welfare, outside autonomy and internal social accord. Rather than being a simple rhetoric, this was seen as a strategic priority for Turkey's Caucasian policy. Turkish decision-makers assumed that if these countries could be empowered enough to resist outside pressure and interventions, then Turkey's historical, political, economic and strategic regional pull would gently push them toward Ankara's orbit.

Secondly, strengthening national unity and territorial integrity of the three South Caucasian countries were emphasized. Conceiving of itself as a status quo power, Turkey approached any change in its surrounding regions as an undesirable challenge. As a country that emphasizes unitary state formation internally, Turkey is keen to see surrounding countries behave in a similar fashion. Thus, even peaceful evolutions toward federative structures in its neighborhood are watched apprehensively. Moreover, Turkey is very sensitive to attempts to challenge the long-established balances around its borders, particularly through force. As most of these balances are based on international agreements or treaties signed in the early 1920s, frictions can emerge between Turkey and its neighboring countries that wish to contest the continued validity of these agreements.

As independent countries, Azerbaijan, Armenia and Georgia create a buffer zone between Turkey and its historic rival in the Caucasus: Russia. It was Tsarist Russia and the Soviet Union that threatened the Ottoman Empire and Turkey for centuries. At the end of the Cold War, however, for the first time in history, Turkey found itself not sharing a land border with its big neighbor in the north and believed that the best way to reinforce this position was to support the independence, stability and territorial integrity of the newly independent Caucasian states. For similar reasons, Turkey opposed moves from the Russian Federation to stage a political comeback in the region, either through socio-economic inroads it had been able to develop or in the form of Russian soldiers on Turkish borders. It was also understood that as long these states maintain their independence and political stability, it would be difficult for the Russian Federation to have a domineering influence over them near the Turkish border. As a result, when the Caucasian countries declared their independence from the Soviet Union, Turkey extended its recognition immediately.

There has also been an understanding in Turkey that stability in the countries bordering Turkey would affect Turkey's own security and stability. If any of the Caucasian countries succumb to instability, that could, if not spill over into Turkey, at least easily affect trade and transport relations with a number of countries in the east. It became clear during the early 1990s that, even if Turkey did not wish to be involved in regional conflicts, it was almost impossible for Ankara to be completely aloof from the developments. Many Turkish citizens, in fact, had Caucasian ancestry and thus remained interested in the region. Moreover, the Turkish public had developed a sense of close kinship especially with Azerbaijan.

Another priority for Turkey has been to turn itself into an energy and transport hub, facilitating transfer of Caspian oil and gas to Europe through shipments from the Ceyhan port and via pipelines, as well as air passengers through Istanbul airport. Turkish Airlines was the first international company to fly regular direct flights to regional capitals, and is still the most-used company for air passengers traveling west. Another important move was the renovation and opening of Georgia's Batumi Airport, operated by a Turkish company. Turkish Airlines allows Turkish passengers to fly to and from Batumi without passports on their way to nearby Turkish towns, a novel approach for cooperation in the region.

The Baku-Tbilisi-Ceyhan (BTC) oil and the Baku-Tbilisi-Erzurum (BTE) gas pipelines, as well as the Blue Stream natural gas pipeline from Russia and all the other planned connections (Kazakh oil to BTC, Turkmen, Iranian and Iraqi gas, further Russian gas through Blue Stream II, and connecting all this to Europe through Nabucco) are aimed at making Turkey a regional energy player. However, Turkey has not been without competition. It is not only the oil and gas transit revenues that heighten countries' interest to have pipeline routes pass through their territories. They have been seen by many players as one of the key factors in securing and maintaining influence throughout the region. American determination to undermine Russian influence was a clear strategic goal during the BTC negotiations. Moreover, though the shortest pipeline route from Azerbaijan to the Mediterranean is through Armenia, the unresolved Nagorno Karabakh conflict made this route unrealizable. Coupled with US opposition to passing the pipeline through Iran, this left Georgia as the only possible route for the westward pipeline. Turkey, Azerbaijan and Georgia have become strategic partners due to pipeline politics.

Beyond deriving economic benefits from hosting outlets for the region's hydrocarbon resources, Turkey hoped that such connections would create interdependences in the region that could strengthen Turkey's standing in this troubled neighborhood. Moreover, the Caucasus was also considered an important gateway of Turkey to the Central Asian Turkic world and beyond. Thus the Caucasian region needed to be secure and stable.

Another aim has been to encourage the economic, political, social and security sector transformation of the Caucasian countries and their integration into the wider European structures. It was thought that this would create inroads for Turkey to become a more influential regional player. In fact, with the support of its strong construction companies busy building roads, airports and other infrastructure, as well as trading and operating companies, Turkey has already become the biggest trade partner of both Georgia and Azerbaijan. It has also become the second biggest investor in Georgia, having built road networks and a couple of airport terminals, as well as having invested in a glass factory, cell phone and airport operation businesses, and numerous small and medium-scale companies. Although the land border with Armenia is currently closed to traffic, trade is booming between the two countries, mainly through Georgia. According to reports in the Turkish press and by Armenian sources, approximately 400 trucks per month passing through Georgia are actually destined to Armenia, and there are about 10,000 Armenians engaged in so-called "luggage trade" with Turkey, as well about 40,000 Armenians working in Turkey, mostly illegally, and sending back remittances.

In its policy toward the region, another important element for Turkey to take into consideration has been the position and policies of the Russian Federation (RF). Russia's 'near abroad' policy, announced at the end of 1993, clearly indicated its continued interest in the former-Soviet states of Central Asia and the Caucasus. Subsequent economic and political recovery brought Russia back onto the scene. Though Turkey had the support of the West, especially of the US, it did not possess adequate economic resources and political power to compete against Russia. As a result, since 1994, Turkey has become more conscious of the dangers of confrontation with the RF and adopted a policy stressing the benefits of cooperation and co-existence with Russia, increasing trade and political connections.

### AKP Government and Turkey's Relationship with the Caucasus

In the general elections of November 3, 2002, the Justice and Development Party (AKP) won 34.28 percent of the general vote and 363 out of 550 seats in the parliament. Even though the general lines of Turkish policy toward the Caucasian states stayed unchanged, domestic and global developments affected the priorities of the AKP. When it came to power, questions were raised about Turkey's commitments to the region. There were speculations that the AKP would not be as strongly predisposed to closer relations with the Caucasian and Central Asian republics as the party's predecessors had been because of its holistic Islamic rhetoric.

Indeed, instead of highlighting the historical and cultural ties with the region, the AKP government preferred to focus on the development of economic relations especially on pipeline projects. However, it has become clear that the apparent non-interest of the AKP government toward the region was a result of other priorities like the American intervention in Iraq, ups and downs in Turkish-EU relations, Cyprus-related domestic discussions, PKK terror, the Kurdish issue and lastly the possibility of closure of the AKP.

The only area of interest to the AKP government was the issue of energy. The AKP pursued an active policy of bringing alternative resources to Turkey for both Turkish consumption and transit to Europe through Turkey. The idea of Turkey becoming a "regional energy hub" was given much support and Turkey undertook policies designed to strengthen its connections to Caspian resources through Georgia and Azerbaijan.

Another idea that affected the AKP's Caucasian policy has been Turkey's "neighborhood policy," which emphasizes zero-problems with neighbors and region-based foreign policy. These were formulated toward the middle of the first AKP government and came to signify its foreign policy understanding. Accordingly, Turkey's foreign policy under AKP refocused on regional matters from 2006 onwards. In this, Turkey's inability to make substantial progress in its negotiations with the EU, American operation in Iraq and its repercussions, as well as the AKP's own general preferences have played a role. In the end, Turkey was actively involved in the Middle East in general, but less active in other regions, including the Caucasus, until after the July 2007 general elections.

With this background, 2007 was an interesting and difficult year for the Turkish politics in terms of both domestic and international developments. In addition to general and presidential elections, EU relations and developments in Cyprus and the Middle East continued to occupy the political agenda for Turkish policy-makers.

Presidential elections and the related political and constitutional crisis kept Turkey busy for most of 2007. A severe political crisis started in the Parliament in April 2007, when Abdullah Gul, then the foreign minister, decided to run for president. This led to the general elections of July 22 and ended with the victory of the AKP, which obtained 46.7 percent of the vote. After the elections, multiple political crises continued to rock the country one after the other, culminating in a Constitutional Court closure case against the AKP, which took another eight months to resolve. As a result of these multiple domestic political crises, the government grew hesitant to take prominent steps in foreign policy, including toward the Caucasus, throughout 2007.

However, once these multiple crises were somewhat contained – and especially after the August 2008 crisis between Georgia and Russia, which showed once again the very volatile nature of the region – Turkey started to pay more attention to regional developments and to work out its own initiative regarding the future of the Caucasus. Its Caucasus Stability and

Economic Cooperation Platform brought together Turkey and Russia with the three Caucasian states. Although it was not an altogether new idea, the Platform initiative took a long-term view and a region-wide approach. Almost impossible to realize in the short term due to hot scars in the region, it provided the necessary background for Turkey's opening toward Armenia in 2009.

There was one important initiative that took place in 2007, despite the AKP government's general inactivity in the Caucasus. The lack of political relations between Turkey and Armenia and the closed situation of the Turkish-Armenian border since 1993 created problems for Turkey's relations with the Caucasus and its link with Central Asian countries. However, it has also forced Turkey to search for alternative ways to develop ties with the rest of the Caucasian and Central Asian countries. The routes of the BTE natural gas and BTC oil pipelines were chosen as a result of this search and appeared as successful projects. Obviously, the realization of these projects had effects on regional development and security going far beyond the energy sector. In the same vien, another project had been developed and an agreement was signed between Turkey, Georgia and Azerbaijan to construct an international railroad, bypassing Armenia and linking Turkey with these countries as well as Central Asia.

In fact, a railroad corridor linking Europe to Asia already existed, passing through Turkey and Armenia then branching out to three different lines. However, use of this railroad link was discontinued as a result of border closure, and thus the railroad connection between Turkey and Asia was routed through Iran, which created many logistical problems as well as political complications. The establishment of a rail connection between Kars and Tbilisi was proposed as an alternative first in July 1993 during a Turkish-Georgian Transportation Commission meeting. Azerbaijan joined in the meetings of the Commission in 2004, leading to the expansion of the project.

The project aimed to create direct railroad transportation between Turkey, Georgia and Azerbaijan in order to facilitate and increase the overland transportation between Turkey and the Caucasus and between Europe and Asia. The strongest opposition to the project understandably came from Armenia and the Armenian Diaspora around the world since the project would have further isolated Armenia in the region both strategically and economically. The Russian Federation was also not in favor of the project since it would have increased Turkey's influence in the regional politics. Nevertheless, the tri-lateral declaration of intention to build the Kars-Tbilisi-Baku Railroad Connection was signed in Baku on May 25, 2005 by the heads of state of Azerbaijan, Georgia and Turkey. Although the implementation of the project was somewhat slowed as a result of financial and political obstacles, the framework agreement was finally signed in February 2007 by Turkish Prime Minister Erdogan and the heads of state of Azerbaijan and Georgia, aiming to conclude the project by 2010.

In the meantime, the BTE gas pipeline became operational in March 2007 with the delivery of gas from Shah Deniz of Azerbaijan, effectively ending Georgia's gas dependency on Russia and providing an alternative source to Turkey. In fact, natural gas that was destined for Turkey was initially diverted to Georgia, in agreement with Turkey, when Georgia was experiencing gas shortages due to its heightened tension with Russia in the winter of 2007.

In addition to advantages the project brought to the relations of the three countries and their strategic importance to each other, it also showed an important alternative route for gas transportation to Europe and enabled Turkey to start dreaming about becoming an energy corridor. In this, Turkey was also emboldened by the construction and operation of the BTC oil pipeline, which had became operational in 2006, even before the BTE. Another pipeline project that captured the attention of the world at large has been the Nabucco project linking natural gas resources of Azerbaijan and possibly Iran, Iraq and Turkmenistan to Europe. After many delays, an intergovernmental agreement and a joint declaration was signed between Turkey, Austria, Bulgaria and Hungary, and witnessed by the representatives of other countries on July 13, 2009, providing a legal framework and highlighting the intention of these countries to build the pipeline. The planned 4,042-km pipeline, expected to cost some 7.9 billion euros and to carry 31 billion cubic meters of gas annually by the end of the decade, is planned to come online in 2014.

Although the Nabucco agreement was hailed as an alternative gas route bypassing Russia in the wider energy game, the picture was complicated again when Turkey signed several agreements with the visiting Russian premier Vladimir Putin on August 7, 2009. With these agreements, Turkey allowed Russia to begin studying the feasibility of a Turkish economic zone in the Black Sea regarding the South Stream gas pipeline project, which many consider as a direct competitor to the proposed Nabucco line. There was also an agreement to build a new oil pipeline between the Black and Mediterranean Sea coasts of Turkey to transport Russian oil to the Mediterranean on to Israel, the Red Sea and eventually to carry it to India.

Although the picture regarding energy deals signed by Turkey or proposed pipelines going through or around Turkey looks rather confusing, Turkey has leveraged these deals to successfully position itself as the link between the energy-producing countries of the East and the energy-hungry countries of the West. The political implications of these projects and their effects on Caucasian politics will no doubt be felt in the coming years.

### Recent Developments and Repositioning Turkish Policies

The August 2008 war between Georgia and Russia has affected Turkish politics toward the Caucasus in multiple ways. The conflict showed clearly that the "frozen" conflicts of the Caucasus were not so frozen and could ignite at any moment. Thus, given the heavy military procurements of involved parties, simply waiting for the problems to solve themselves was not an option. Moreover, Russia gave a clear indication of its intentions regarding regional hotspots. Finally, Turkey realized that unless it became active and somehow pacified the region, the Caucasus could easily succumb to instability and oblivion, a situation that does not serve Turkish interests politically, economically or security-wise.

Although Turkey's bi-lateral economic and political relations with Azerbaijan and Georgia continue to improve, its overall Caucasian policies seem to be convoluted by developments beyond Turkey's control.

Turkey and Georgia have formed strong political and economic bonds in recent years, mostly due to the new oil pipelines. Because these routes provide more secure energy for Europe and the US, they have been supported by the West. Besides their political relations, economic relations between Turkey and Georgia have improved rapidly, with Turkey becoming both the biggest trade partner and the second largest investor in Georgia, leading to a Free Trade Agreement between the two countries in 2007. Moreover, Turkish companies took an important role in developing Georgian infrastructure, forming 23 percent of the total foreign investment in that country. The movement of people between the two countries was enhanced by lifting visa requirement for 90-day stays in 2007 and the opening of the Batumi airport, which was built and operated by a Turkish company as a domestic destination for Turkish citizens.

While economic and political relations between Turkey and Georgia continued to improve, the uneasy situation in Georgia caused by the Abkhazia dispute stayed unsolved and somewhat colored its relations with Turkey. Even though Turkey continued to support the territorial integrity of Georgia, it also pushed for a peaceful resolution of the dispute. Turkey attempted to bring to sides together and offered alternative openings. However, the existence of Turkish citizens of both Georgian and North Caucasian origin complicated Turkey's stance, creating suspicions on both sides, thus preventing repeated Turkish attempts to create a platform for peaceful resolution to bear fruit. What is more, Turkey faced an increasingly volatile domestic situation as both Georgian and North Caucasian Diasporas became more vocal in recent years in their demands for action. This forced Turkey to be even more cautious in its dealings with Georgia.

The August 2008 crisis showed Turkey's weaknesses and limitations. When Georgia and Russia started exchanging fire, Turkey found its policy options limited on three grounds. First of all, the Turkish government was lobbied by Turkish citizens of Georgian and North Caucasian origin, both sides wishing to stir Turkey toward their supported causes. Though Turkey had little direct power, proponents of both sides took to Turkey's streets in protest. Secondly, Turkey was pressed between its strategically important partner Georgia and economically and politically important neighbor Russia. Territorial integrity of Georgia was important to Turkey for various political, strategic, psychological and historic reasons. But Russia has become an important trade and political partner to Turkey in recent years. Thirdly, Turkey was squeezed between the demands of its newly-emerging partner, the Russian Federation, and long-term allies, the US and NATO countries. Faced with all these pressures, Turkey's initial reaction to the crisis was quite mute, though it became rather active later on when Prime

Minister Erdogan got directly involved with his Platform idea. Though the idea did not make much headway, it prepared the ground for Turkish-Armenian reconnection.

Armenia has been the only Caucasian country with which Turkey's bilateral relations did not show serious improvement until recently. While both sides were keen on developing relations in the early 1990s, suspicion and distrust began to grow in the mid-1990s because of regional and domestic developments and historical baggage. As a result, the land border between the countries remains closed and diplomatic relations have not yet been established, although air connections expanded significantly in recent years and dialogue on the civil society level has lately started to develop.

The already complex nature of the relations is further complicated by the fact that third parties have a stake in the continuation of stalemate. On the one hand, the Armenian Diaspora continues to try to isolate Turkey internationally because of the events of 1915. On the other hand, Azerbaijan resents any move on the Turkish side to improve its relations with Armenia so long as the Nagorno Karabakh conflict remains unsolved.

However, after the assassination of Hrant Dink, a prominent and outspoken Turkish citizen of Armenian origin, on January 19 2007, an interesting thawing process began. Even though a successful solution to the disagreements between the two states has not yet come out of this thaw, important human-to-human connections and dialogue between the Turkish and Armenian civil societies appeared.

Armenia's problematic relations with Turkey and Azerbaijan, as well as its isolation from enhanced cooperation in the region, have negatively affected the economic recovery of Armenia. Worsening conditions have sent many Armenians to seek employment in neighboring countries. As a result, even though the land border still remained closed, some forty thousands Armenians came to Turkey by the end of 2006 looking for work. By the end of 2007, Turkish officials were regularly reporting that 70,000 Armenian citizens were working illegally in Turkey. Besides providing jobs and livelihood for the families of these workers, this illegal but "condoned" immigration has further created opportunities of contact between ordinary Armenians and Turks.

Under these circumstances, political relations took an interesting turn when newly-elected Armenian President Serzh Sarkisyan invited President Abdullah Gul to watch the football game between Turkish and Armenian nationals team in Yerevan on September 6, 2008. President Gul's acceptance of the invitation and his visit to Yerevan marked an interesting watershed in Turkish-Armenian relations and raised hopes for reconciliation.

The initiative seemed to pave the way for a Turkish-Armenian framework agreement toward reconciliation on April 22, 2009. The brief statement, posted on the web sites of both Turkish and Armenian foreign ministries, said that "the two parties have achieved tangible progress and ... have agreed on a comprehensive framework for the normalization of their bilateral relations." However, Azerbaijani reaction to opening the Turkish-Armenian border without improvement on Karabakh created a strong backlash in Turkey, forcing Prime Minister Erdogan to halt developments when he visited Baku on May 13, 2009, and announce that Turkey will not proceed with the opening of its land border with Armenia unless the latter ends the occupation of Azerbaijani territory. By the time Turkey and Armenia were ready to announce on August 31st that they agreed on two protocols and would sign them in due time, it seems that Turkey was better able to explain its position to Azerbaijan. As a result, the Azerbaijani reactions were more muted this time around and Turkey signed the protocols on October 11, 2009. Nonetheless, it was made clear inside the country that the government would not try to force the ratification of the protocols by the Turkish Parliament, where a majority still opposes such a move unless positive developments are seen toward the solution of the Nagorno Karabakh dispute.

Although relations with Azerbaijan seemed to sour recently over Turkish moves towards Armenia, the overall relationship could still be classified as a strategic partnership. With cultural, linguistic and historical affinities as important driving forces, Turkish-Azeri relations have easily developed not only in terms of strategic, economic and military relations deriving from national interests but also in terms of cultural and social relations of the two societies.

The BTC and BTE pipelines and impending Kars-Tbilisi-Baku railroad connection link the two countries to each other. Economic relations have also been booming, with the trade volume recording an average yearly increase of 40 percent since 2003, and reaching over $1.2 billion in 2007. This makes Turkey Azerbaijan's biggest trading partner. Moreover, Turkey has become the biggest investor in Azerbaijan in non-energy fields, investing $2.5 billion in 2007. Investments in the energy sector are also around this number, which brings total Turkish financing in Azerbaijan close to $5 billion. However, as indicated above, the relationship has increasingly come under stress from Turkey's opening toward Armenia. This shows once again that Turkey's policy options in the Caucasus are rather limited and its different aspects are usually interrelated, limiting maneuverability.

**Conclusion**

The collapse of the USSR has been a mixed blessing for Turkey. While the century-old Soviet threat to Turkey's security has disappeared, the vacuum created by this departure has turned Eurasia into a breeding ground for potential border risks and threats to regional security.

It is clear that Turkey has undergone a dramatic shift away from its traditional policy of isolationism since the end of the Cold War, and that Turkish foreign policy is increasingly focusing on the Caucasus, alongside other surrounding regions. Even if Turkey's initial vision toward the wider Eurasia proved somewhat unrealistic, the effects it generated set the tone for Turkish policy for the rest of the 1990s and early 2000s. While Turkey has not necessarily become a model to which the new states of Eurasia aspire, its thriving private sector, secular approach to religion and its functioning democracy continue to have their appeal in the region.

The emergence of independent republics in the Caucasus represented a turning point in Turkey's regional role and policies. Turkey has become one of the important players in a region where it previously had only a marginal influence and no active involvement. Although economic and political conditions in the region are unlikely to stabilize for some years, Turkish policymakers will continue with their efforts to create new networks of interdependency between Ankara and the regional capitals. It is also clear that the tensions in the region will continue to be contributing factors for Turkish security planning.

There are a number of challenges that need to be tackled before any country, including Turkey, is able to operate fruitfully in the region. In view of the continued potential for conflicts and overarching difficulties, Turkey tries to follow a multi-layered and multi-dimensional policy in the region in order to realize its stated goals. Whether Turkey will be successful in its new opening is still an open question and will depend on various regional and international developments, sometimes beyond the control of Turkey or the regional countries. In this limited opportunity environment, Turkey, by creating innovative solutions to regional problems and by putting the region into a wider context, can contribute to the creation of a larger geography where stable countries cooperate with each other in multi-lateral conventions as well as in their bi-lateral relationships. Various Turkish initiatives in and around the Black Sea and the Caucasus promises to do so. Their positive results will have a multiplying impact all around, just as negative results will have repercussions in a much wider area.

# SECURITY ISSUES AND US INTERESTS IN THE SOUTH CAUCASUS

**Dr. Ariel Cohen,**
Senior Research Fellow,
The Heritage Foundation

**Kevin DeCorla-Souza,**
Senior Associate,
IFC International

Since the fall of the Soviet Union, the United States has had significant strategic, economic and energy interests in the South Caucasus. In 1992, within months of the Soviet Union's collapse, the first Bush administration opened embassies in all 11 non-Russian Newly Independent States (NIS), including the three countries of the South Caucasus – Armenia, Azerbaijan and Georgia. The first Bush administration clearly saw the energy wealth of the Caspian Sea and the geopolitical importance of the Caucasian land bridge between the Middle East, Turkey and Russia, which also connected Europe with Central Asia along the ancient Silk Road. The historic aspirations and presence of the German and the British Empires in the Caucasus a century ago may have been on the minds of strategic planners in Washington in the early 1990s. Since then, US engagement in the region has intensified under the Clinton and second Bush administrations through military cooperation and the development of energy infrastructure.

US interests in the South Caucasus are a function of the region's strategic location at the crossroads of Europe, Russia, the Middle East and Central Asia (see *Figure 1*). Strong, independent, pro-Western states in the South Caucasus serve to contain expansionary anti-American regimes in Russia and Iran; allow the secure transit of energy resources from the Caspian to the Black Sea and the Mediterranean via Turkey; and encourage the expansion of democratic and free-market principles and institutions in Eurasia.

*Figure 1: The South Caucasus and its Neighbors*

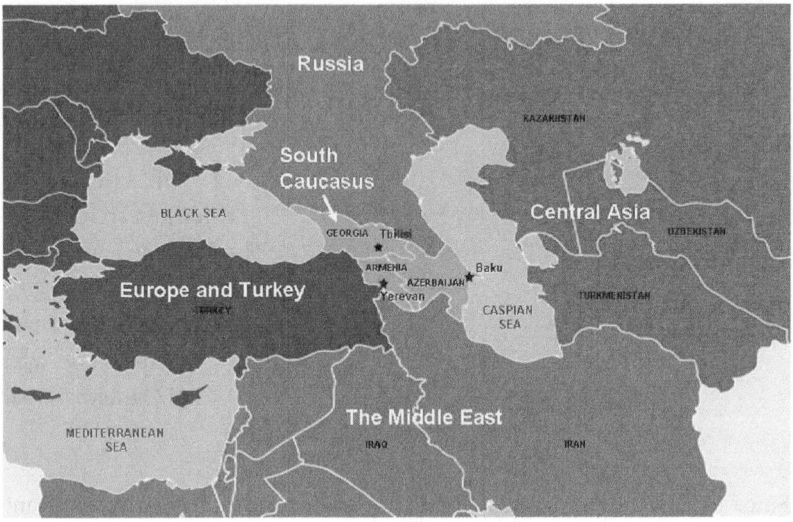

Source: DeCorla-Souza, 2009

Despite abundant strategic concerns, the South Caucasus are generally viewed as a secondary consideration to US interests vis-à-vis the region's larger, more important neighbors such as Russia, Turkey and Iran. As a result, policy toward the South Caucasus risks taking a backseat to other US priorities. For example, critics blamed the Clinton administration, especially during its first term, for prioritizing a "Russia first" policy, allegedly pursued under Strobe Talbott, special advisor to the Secretary of State on the former Soviet states and later Deputy Secretary of State, rather than engaging interests in the South Caucasus.[1] Greater emphasis on the region, particularly the promotion of a strategic East-West energy corridor, began during Clinton's second term and intensified under George W. Bush's administration, which developed close relations with all South Caucasus countries, and particularly with Georgia. However, policy toward the South Caucasus again appears to be shifting under the Obama administration, which has prioritized "resetting" frayed relations with Russia in order to win its help on such issues as Afghanistan, Iran and arms

---

[1] Hill, Fiona, "A Not-So-Grand Strategy: US Policy in the Caucasus and Central Asia Since 1991," *Foreign Policy, Asia,* February 2001, <http://www.brookings.edu/articles/2001/02foreignpolicy_hill.aspx> (October 27, 2009).

control. This policy has a led to fears that the Obama administration may be weakening US ties with allies in the South Caucasus in favor of strengthening relations with Moscow.

A July 2009 trip by Vice President Joe Biden to war-ravaged Georgia did little to reassure the region of America's support. Although Biden correctly rejected Moscow's claims to what Russian President Dmitry Medvedev has called an "exclusive sphere of interests,"[2] he fell short of offering the nation an American "physical security guarantee," nor did he offer any concrete road map to restore Georgia's sovereignty over Abkhazia and South Ossetia. Biden also presented no plan for holding Moscow to its commitments in the Medvedev-Sarkozy peace accord of August 2008, which requires Russia to pull back to its pre-war positions.[3]

The absence of an elaborate and engaged US foreign policy in the South Caucasus puts US security and commercial interests, and the sovereignty and independence of US allies in the region at risk. Weakened ties between the South Caucasus and the US, NATO, EU and other principal trans-Atlantic institutions emboldens Russia and Iran to extend their influence, puts the reliability of energy flows and new pipeline projects at risk, and threatens the development of democratic and free market institutions. The Turkish-Armenian rapprochement, which is occurring against the background of increasing Turkish-Russian security and energy cooperation, and simmering security conflicts in the South Caucasus, such as the status of breakaway Georgian provinces of Abkhazia and South Ossetia and the dispute over Nagorno Karabakh, make strong US engagement in the region essential. The Obama administration needs to understand the strategic importance of the South Caucasus and give US friends there the same firm support that its predecessors did.

---

[2] "Interview given by Dmitry Medvedev to Television Channel One, Rossia, NTV," Sochi, August 31, 2008, at
<http://www.un.int/russia/new/MainRoot/docs/warfare/statement310808en.htm> (October 27, 2009).
[3] "Biden pledges support for Georgia," BBC News, July 22, 2009,
<http://news.bbc.co.uk/2/hi/8163876.stm> (October 27, 2009).

**US Interests in the South Caucasus**

US interests in the South Caucasus can be divided into three broad and interrelated categories: security, energy and democracy. These strategic interests shape US foreign policy toward the region. Coordination and integration of these priorities, which occasionally clash, are the main challenges facing US policy in the region.

*Security*

Security in the South Caucasus is of great importance to the United States in that it affects the balance of power in Eurasia and the Middle East. Central to this concern is the goal of checking the power of increasingly anti-American regimes in Russia and Iran. Strong, independent states in the South Caucasus serve to keep Moscow and Tehran from running roughshod over the region, provide access to the Caspian and Central Asian energy resources, and allow presence for electronic and other intelligence gathering capabilities.

The South Caucasus remained a priority for Moscow even after the collapse of the Soviet Union disabled or weakened Russian influence elsewhere along the Russian periphery. Political leadership, senior experts and military brass laid down plans to reintegrate parts of the former USSR as early as 1993, when Moscow supported Abkhaz separatists, and even allowed independence-minded Chechens to fight on the side of Sukhumi against Georgia.

The expansion of Russian power and influence in the South Caucasus is a major security concern of the US Since the mid-1990s, Russia has endorsed a "multi-polar" world view, as articulated by the then-Foreign Minister and Prime Minister Yevgeny Primakov, and launched a thinly veiled attempt to dilute American influence in world affairs after the Iraq war. Under the banner of multi-polarity, Moscow seeks to give legitimacy to its efforts to restore a "privileged sphere of influence" in the post-Soviet space; and to this end, a resurgent Russia is actively seeking to reverse the Westward shift of its former satellite states by influencing their domestic political processes and threatening their security and territorial integrity. These actions run directly counter to US policy interests, which seek independent and sovereign countries along Russia's borders, combining Western orientation with good relations with Moscow, if possible. This conflict between US and Russian interests was brought to the forefront of international relations during the August 2008 war when Russia effectively annexed Georgia's breakaway provinces of South Ossetia and Abkhazia.

Despite the Obama administration's attempt to "reset" frayed US-Russian relations, the security interests of the two powers are likely to continue to clash in the South Caucasus. Russia, observing the lack of a forceful US response in the wake of the Georgia conflict, will be emboldened to again exercise its muscle in a part of the world that it considers its backyard. Future US-Russian flashpoints in the South Caucasus may include a repeat performance over Georgia's breakaway republics and the independent status of Nagorno Karabakh, which is officially part of Azerbaijan but under de facto occupation of Armenia. The US, preoccupied with Afghanistan, Pakistan, Iran and Iraq, as well as the global war on terrorism, has neither the attention span nor resources to deploy sufficient diplomatic power and foreign assistance to counter aggressive moves by Moscow in the South Caucasus or to avert proxy conflicts. Instead, the Obama administration will employ diplomacy and seek help from European allies and Turkey to resolve future conflicts. Strategists in the Kremlin, who view geopolitics as a zero-sum game, will perceive a tepid US response to Russian encroachment and aggression as a sign of weakness and will push harder to expand Moscow's power in the post-Soviet space.

A second security concern of the United States in the South Caucasus involves Iran. For decades, Iran vied for power in the Middle East against Saddam Hussein's tyrannical regime in Iraq. In the 1980s, Tehran sought Moscow's support against US-allied Iraq, while in the 1990s, Iran's priority in dealing with Russia was technical assistance for its missile and nuclear sectors, as well as arms deals, which involved modern fighter aircraft and anti-aircraft missile systems. It was not interested in upsetting the apple cart and meddling in either Central Asia or the Caucasus against Russian interests – even when Muslim Chechens were slaughtered in the hundreds of thousands.

This balance was upset by the US-led Operation Iraqi Freedom in 2003, which plunged Iran's once formidable adversary further into chaos and removed Saddam from power. The eventual withdrawal of US troops from Iraq and the rather fragile Iraqi government that remains in place, as well as the strength of the Shia in Iraq, with their traditional ties to Iran, will give Iran a strategic opening to gain greater power in the Middle East. Iran already has a considerable military advantage over its neighbors in the Gulf and its intelligence services have an active presence in Shia areas of Lebanon, Saudi Arabia's Eastern Province, in Iraq and Azerbaijan. If Iran manages to successfully develop nuclear weapons, it could emerge as a regional hegemon in the Middle East with the ability to threaten US allies as far away as Israel, Egypt, and southern Europe. Iran already has the ability to threaten the world economy by shutting off oil tanker traffic in the Strait of Hormuz. Were the US to pursue or even threaten a military option against Iran, the countries of the South Caucasus, particularly Azerbaijan, would be needed as a staging ground for US intelligence collection, military pressure, or contingencies to contain Iran or disarm it of its nuclear weapons program.

The US can help contain Iran by promoting peace in the disputed territory of Nagorno Karabakh. Officially, Iran holds a neutral position on the Nagorno Karabakh conflict that divides Armenia and Azerbaijan, its two Caucasian neighbors to the north. Unofficially, however, Iran desires that Azerbaijan remain embroiled in the dispute, thus making the nation less attractive to Iran's Azerbaijani minority and diverting resources from a campaign for South Azerbaijan's autonomy or even independence, which could cause the Azeri-populated territory in northwest Iran to demand independence.[4] By helping Azerbaijan and Armenia obtain peace in Nagorno Karabakh, the US could help both Baku and Yerevan, and weaken the anti-American regime in Tehran.

A final security consideration for the United States in the South Caucasus is the threat of Islamist terrorism. Since the attacks of September 11, 2001, the US has prioritized disrupting the activities of terrorist groups that could

---

[4] Schaffer, Brenda, "Iran's Role in the South Caucasus and Caspian Region: Diverging Views of the US and Europe," *Iran and Its Neighbors: Diverging Views on a Strategic Region*, Eugene Whitlock (Ed.), Stiftung Wissenschaft und Politik/German Institute for International and Security Affairs, Berlin, July 2003, p. 19, <http://belfercenter.ksg.harvard.edu/files/tfpd_divergingviews_whitlock.pdf> (October 1, 2009).

endanger the United States and its allies. The threat of Islamic radicals gaining a foothold in the South Caucasus is less acute than in the North Caucasus, where *jamaats* are active throughout the region, especially in Dagestan and Ingushetia, or in Central Asia. The only predominantly Muslim nation among the South Caucasus is Azerbaijan, and the country's traditionally tolerant population for now makes it an unlikely breeding ground for Islamic radicalism. Nonetheless, some Muslim activists in the Sunni north of Azerbaijan belong to the Salafi (also known as Wahhabi) sect of Islam, one of the strictest forms of the faith, whose adherents include Osama bin Laden and the 9/11 attackers. Iranian-controlled Shia groups in southern Azerbaijan are also a growing concern. Russia shares the terrorist concern with the United States, and the Global War on Terror (or "Overseas Contingency Operations" as the Obama administration has renamed it) can provide a platform through which US and Russian interests coincide and where cooperation between the two powers in the South Caucasus is possible.

*Energy*

Energy is a critical US interest in the South Caucasus because of the region's role as a strategic transit corridor that can bring energy from Azerbaijan and Central Asia (Kazakhstan and Turkmenistan in particular) to Western markets. Non-OPEC oil supply has been flat in recent years and many, including Fatih Birol, the chief economist at the International Energy Agency, believe that conventional non-OPEC oil production will peak in the next few years if it has not already.[5] As a result, world oil markets are expected to grow increasingly dependent on the OPEC oil supply (found primarily in the Middle East) to meet growing demand. Greater dependence on OPEC is a danger for the US and its allies because OPEC has used its oil exports as a weapon in the past and because OPEC is a cartel that sets production quotas in order to maintain high prices, thus harming Western consumers. The non-Russian, non-Iranian Caspian region, which includes Azerbaijan and the Central Asian nations of Kazakhstan and Turkmenistan, has moderate proven oil reserves of about 38 billion barrels. However, estimates of this region's possible reserves – a less precise

---

[5] "IEA Warns Non-OPEC Oil Could Peak in Two Years," *The Times*, July 21, 2008, <http://business.timesonline.co.uk/tol/business/industry_sectors/natural_resources/article436 8523.ece#> (October 1, 2009).

measure of in-ground resources that includes reserves found through extensions, divisions and new discoveries – indicate that the Caspian could hold as much as 162 billion barrels of crude oil, making it a potential energy superpower (see *Table 1*).

*Table 1: Proven and Possible Crude Oil Reserves (billion barrels)*[6]

|  | Proven Reserves | Possible Reserves |
|---|---|---|
| Azerbaijan | 7.00 | 32.00 |
| Kazakhstan | 30.00 | 92.00 |
| Turkmenistan | 0.60 | 38.00 |
| Caspian 3 | 37.60 | 162.00 |
| Russia | 60.00 | |

Source: US EIA

In addition to oil, the Caspian region also holds significant proven and possible natural gas reserves, which can be tapped to diversify Europe's natural gas supplies (see *Table 2*). Dependence on Russian natural gas is a key energy security concern for US allies in Europe. Russia is Europe's single largest source of natural gas, supplying more than 40 percent of total EU natural gas imports in 2006, or about 25 percent of total EU gas consumption.[7] Russia's state-controlled Gazprom is the monopoly supplier to many Eastern, Central, and Southern European countries, and many Western European countries rely on Russia for substantial portions of their total natural gas needs; and their dependence is growing.

---

[6] Proven Reserves as of 2009 from "International Energy Statistics," US Energy Information Administration,"
<http://tonto.eia.doe.gov/cfapps/ipdbproject/IEDIndex3.cfm?tid=5&pid=57&aid=6>
(November 3, 2009). Possible Reserves as of 2005 from "Caspian Sea Region: Survey of Key Oil and Gas Statistics and Forecasts," US Energy Information Administration, July 2005,
http://www.eia.doe.gov/emeu/cabs/caspian_balances.htm (November 3, 2009).
[7] "EU Energy in Figures 2009," Directorate-General for Energy and Transport, European Commission,
<http://ec.europa.eu/energy/publications/doc/statistics/part_2_energy_pocket_book_2009.pdf> (October 27, 2009).

*Table 2: Proved Natural Gas Reserves (billion cubic meters)*

|  | Gas Reserves |
|---|---|
| Azerbaijan | 850 |
| Kazakhstan | 2,408 |
| Turkmenistan | 2,663 |
| Caspian 3 | 5,921 |

Source: US EIA

Russian gas pipelines already reach deep into Europe from the north and the south and with additional large pipeline projects – such as the North Stream and South Stream pipelines – underway, Russia hopes to further consolidate its grip on the European natural gas market. This dependence on Russian natural gas is worrisome, not only because of its magnitude but also because of Moscow's history of using energy exports as a tool of its foreign policy. New natural gas exports from the Caspian region have the potential to diversify Europe's natural gas supply away from Russia and enhance the continent's energy security.

The US has a strategic interest in developing the Caspian region's oil and gas resources and bringing those resources to Western markets without traversing Russian or Iranian territory. The key export route for these resources is a path of friendly countries – Azerbaijan, Georgia and Turkey – that can connect the Caspian region's gas supply to Europe and the Mediterranean Sea. This path, known as the "Southern Corridor," already has two key pipeline systems: the Baku-Tbilisi-Ceyhan (BTC) pipeline, which can carry up to 1 million barrels per day of oil to the Turkish port of Ceyhan on the Mediterranean Sea, and the South Caucasus Pipeline, which can deliver up to 8.8 billion cubic meters of natural gas per year to the Turkish pipeline system at Erzurum.[8] Begun in November 2007, an extension of the South Caucasus Pipeline now transports natural gas from Turkey to Greece.[9] The US and its European allies hope to expand exports

---

[8] "Azerbaijan Country Analysis Brief," US Energy Information Administration, <http://www.eia.doe.gov/emeu/cabs/Azerbaijan/Background.html> (October 1, 2009).

[9] "Turkey-Greece Pipeline Delivering Azerbaijani Gas to Europe Inaugurated," *APA News Agency*, UNDP Azerbaijan Development Bulletin, November 19, 2007, <http://www.un-az.org/undp/bulnews54/rg1.php> (October 1, 2009).

along the Southern Corridor to bring more Caspian energy to Western markets. Integral to this goal is the 7.9-billion-Euro (US $11.5 billion) proposed Nabucco gas pipeline that would expand and extend the South Caucasus Pipeline to bring up to 31 billion cubic meters of natural gas from the Caspian to Europe.[10] Other important projects include proposed Trans-Caspian oil and gas pipelines that would bring energy resources from Turkmenistan and Kazakhstan to the BTC and Nabucco through pipelines beneath the Caspian Sea.

Russia allowed the BTC pipeline to break its monopoly on Caspian oil resources and does not want to see Nabucco do the same for natural gas despite the statements of Russia's captains of gas industry to the contrary. Russia is aggressively contracting Caspian gas volumes, including recent agreements to export Azerbaijani gas along Russian pipeline systems in order to starve the Nabucco project of needed volumes.[11] Turkey's demands for higher transit tariffs and lower gas sale prices force Azerbaijan to look for alternative routes.

Moscow has also proposed a competing project – the South Stream pipeline – that would supply gas to Europe from essentially the same sources (plus Russian gas) and along the same route as Nabucco. US and EU energy security interests will continue to clash with Russia's desire to control energy flows in Eurasia. The energy "chess game" that has played out between Russia and the West will continue to intensify.

*Democracy*

The promotion of democracy and market principles in the South Caucasus is an important component of US policy in the South Caucasus. There was a long-standing belief in US foreign policy circles during the Clinton and George W. Bush administrations that democracy and free trade bring stability and economic growth. There is less commitment to democracy

---

[10] "Project Description / Pipeline Route," Nabucco Gas Pipeline Project, Nabucco Gas Pipeline International GmbH, <http://www.nabucco-pipeline.com/project/project-description-pipeline-route/project-description.html> (October 1, 2009).

[11] Erkan Oz, "Azerbaijan Looks For Gas Routes To Europe Bypassing Turkey", *The Wall Street Journal,* October 17, 2009, <http://online.wsj.com/article/BT-CO-20091017-701339.html>.

promotion under the prevailing "neo-realism" of the Obama administration.

Empirical evidence shows that democracies go to war with each other considerably less often and are internally more stable than brittle autocratic regimes.[12] Liberal theory also predicts that trade creates common interests for countries, thus raising the costs of going to war and reducing its occurrence.[13] Furthermore, strong, independent democracies in the South Caucasus would help to ward off external attempts to influence and control relatively new and weak states. Strong democracies in the South Caucasus would also bolster America's broader strategy to bring peace and stability to the turbulent Greater Middle East. The US strongly supported the 2003 "Rose Revolution" that replaced Georgian President Eduard Shevardnadze with a government led by President Mikheil Saakashvili. During the 2008 Georgia War, Russia sought not only to create conditions for Abkhaz and South Ossetian independence, which is likely to lead to *Anschluss* by Russia in the future, but also to undermine the Rose Revolution by forcing out President Saakashvili. This conflict over democracy (and independence) in the South Caucasus will continue to be a source of tension between the US and Russia.

**Security Concerns in the South Caucasus**

US interests in the South Caucasus are threatened by the region's simmering insecurity, including the conflict between Russia and Georgia over the latter's breakaway provinces, the ongoing dispute between Armenia and Azerbaijan over Nagorno-Karabakh and the occupation of Azeri territories, and the worrisome emergence of Islamic fundamentalism in Azerbaijan.

*The August War*

Who started the war between Russia and Georgia in August 2008 is subject to debate between the warring parties and experts around the globe. Clearly,

---

[12] Rummel, R. J., "Democracies Don't Fight Democracies," Peace Magazine, May-June 1999, <http://archive.peacemagazine.org/v15n3p10.htm> (October 27, 2009).

[13] Friedman, Thomas L., "The Lexus and the Olive Tree," Farrar, Straus and Giroux, 1999, p. 240.

Russia prepared for this war for years and provoked Georgia to escalate in response to the ongoing shooting and shelling of Georgian-controlled villages in South Ossetia. However, there is no question that the brief but intense events that unfolded in the summer of 2008 damaged US interests regarding security, energy and democracy in the South Caucasus. Although the conflict was formally ended by the peace plan brokered by French President Nicolas Sarkozy, Russia did not implement many fundamental components of the plan, and the debate over the self-proclaimed "independence" of the Georgian provinces of South Ossetia and Abkhazia has not yet been resolved. At the time of the writing, only Russia recognized the secessionist territories, while Nicaragua and Venezuela promised to follow suit. The simmering conflict is liable to flare up again, and there is a high probability that the issue will further impact US interests in the region.

During the August War, Moscow's response went beyond fighting in South Ossetia when Russian forces destroyed key military and civilian infrastructure in Georgia, and caused thousands of causalities. Russia's systematic attack on Georgia's military bases and capabilities clearly weakened the country's ability to defend itself in future conflict. More importantly, the obliteration of Georgia's nascent military power and the heightened insecurity of its borders have made some NATO member countries – particularly those in Western Europe – less willing to extend a Membership Action Plan (MAP) to Georgia and have raised questions about NATO membership for Ukraine.[14] MAP is the last formal step on the way to possible future membership in NATO. By keeping NATO out of the South Caucasus, Russia reserves the right to intervene militarily in the region without the fear of a treaty-obligated allied response under Article 5 of the NATO Charter. In a recapitulation of the principle of collective defense, NATO announced that Article 5 is at the basis of a fundamental principle of the North Atlantic Treaty Organization. It provides that if a NATO Ally is the victim of an armed attack, each and every other member of the Alliance will consider this act of violence as an armed attack against

---

[14] Kucera, Joshua. "Georgia: No Discussion of MAP for Tbilisi During NATO Meeting," *Eurasia Insight*, December 4, 2008, <http://www.eurasianet.org/departments/insightb/articles/eav120408c.shtml> (October 1, 2009).

all members and will take the actions it deems necessary to assist the Ally attacked.[15]

For now, this principle will not apply to Georgia. As Vice President Joe Biden stated during his visit there in July 2009, the US will not provide a "physical security guarantee" to Tbilisi.[16] Future instability in Georgia's breakaway provinces or another war could further strengthen Russia's hand in the region at the direct expense of Georgia's sovereignty and the interests of the US and its Western allies.

Security and energy in the Caucasus are inexorably linked. The August War between Russia and Georgia was ostensibly fought over the breakaway province of South Ossetia. However, many speculate that Russia's disproportionate use of force in Georgia was designed to cast doubt on the security of the strategic pipeline corridor linking the energy resources of the Caspian with Western markets. The BTC oil pipeline, which runs from Azerbaijan through Georgia to Ceyhan, a Turkish port on the Mediterranean Sea, was shut prior to the start of the August War due to an explosion at a pump station in eastern Turkey. However, this did not stop Russian forces from targeting the pipeline. Media sources reported that Russian jets dropped more than 50 bombs in the vicinity of the BTC pipeline south of Baku but failed to damage the buried line.[17]

Overall, the BTC shutdown had a minimal effect on world oil markets. Despite the restriction of oil flows from Azerbaijan during the August War, oil prices continued to fall due to the bursting of the financial bubble, including energy prices and a steadily worsening global economic outlook. The real long-term effect of the August War has been to cast doubt on the security of future energy projects in the South Caucasus, particularly the proposed Nabucco gas pipeline, which the US and EU see as a necessity to meet Europe's growing demand for natural gas and to diversify the supply

[15] "What is Article 5?" NATO website, http://www.nato.int/terrorism/five.htm (October 27, 2009)

[16] Cohen, Ariel, "Biden Should Treat Poland with Respect," *The Foundry*, The Heritage Foundation, October 21, 2009, <http://blog.heritage.org/2009/10/21/biden-should-treat-poland-with-respect/> (October 27, 2009)

[17] "Georgia: Russia Targets Key Oil Pipeline With Over 50 Missiles," *U.K. Telegraph*, August 10, 2008, <http://www.telegraph.co.uk/news/worldnews/europe/georgia/2534767/Georgia-Russia-targets-key-oil-pipeline-with-over-50-missiles.html> (October 1, 2009).

of gas away from Russia. By causing instability in the South Caucasus, Russia has effectively increased Nabucco's security risk, making the project less palatable to investors and giving an advantage to Gazprom's competing South Stream pipeline.

The August War also threatened democracy in the South Caucasus. Russia's leadership disdains pro-Western Georgian President Mikhail Saakashvili, who came to power during the "Rose Revolution" of 2003. Russia's heavy-handed response to the relatively low-level dispute between Georgia and South Ossetia was partly designed to embarrass Saakashvili and force a change in the country's leadership. Toward the end of the August War, Russia's UN ambassador reportedly told then US Secretary of State Condoleezza Rice that Saakashvili "must go."[18] Russia would like nothing more than to replace Saakashvili's pro-Western government with a leadership that tilts toward Moscow.

In January 2009, the outgoing Bush administration showed strong support for Georgia by signing the "US-Georgia Charter on Strategic Partnership," which states that "our two countries share a vital interest in a strong, independent, sovereign, unified, and democratic Georgia."[19] The charter, among other things, emphasized cooperation on defense and security matters to defeat threats and to "promote peace and stability" in the South Caucasus and to increase "the physical security of energy transit through Georgia to European markets." The Obama administration's support for Georgia has been more muted and Obama's push to "reset" relations with Moscow has raised fears in some quarters that the US is abandoning its Georgian ally.[20]

---

[18] "US: Russia Trying to Topple Georgian Government," CNN.com, August 11, 2008, <http://www.cnn.com/2008/WORLD/europe/08/10/un.georgia/> (October 1, 2009).

[19] "United States-Georgia Charter on Strategic Partnership," US State Department, America.gov, January 9, 2009, <http://www.america.gov/st/texttrans-english/2009/January/20090109145313eaifas0.2139093.html> (October 1, 2009).

[20] "Diplomacy 'reset' worries some US allies," Wall Street Journal, March 9, 2009, <http://online.wsj.com/article/SB123655154931965237.html> (October 27, 2009).

*Nagorno-Karabakh*

The Armenian-occupied and disputed territory of Nagorno Karabakh is another potential flashpoint in the South Caucasus that could threaten US interests. Azerbaijan and Armenia are still technically at war over Nagorno Karabakh, but a ceasefire has kept the region under de facto Armenian control since 1994. In the short-term, the threat of the conflict resuming is low. Armenia, which has been heavily armed with the help of Russia, still has a significant military advantage over Azerbaijan despite Baku's large increases in military expenditures, which have been fueled by surging oil and gas earnings over past several years (see *Table 3*).[21]

*Table 3: Military Expenditures by Country, 2000-2008*[22]
*(Constant 2005 US$, in millions)*

|      | Armenia | Azerbaijan | Georgia |
|------|---------|------------|---------|
| 2000 | 94.3    | [141]      | [27.2]  |
| 2001 | 91.5    | [160]      | [34.5]  |
| 2002 | 90.5    | [172]      | 49.3    |
| 2003 | 104     | [215]      | 57.7    |
| 2004 | 115     | [260]      | 80.6    |
| 2005 | 141     | 305        | 214     |
| 2006 | 166     | 625        | 363     |
| 2007 | 195     | 680        | 720     |
| 2008 | [217]   | 697        | 651     |

[] = uncertain number

Source: SIPRI

---

[21] Daly, John C. K., "Growing Azeri Defense Budget Buildup—In Earnest or for Show?" *Eurasia Daily Monitor*, Vol. 5, Issue 209, October 31, 2008, <http://www.jamestown.org/single/?no_cache=1&tx_ttnews%5Btt_news%5D=34069> (October 1, 2009) and Giragosian R., "The Military Balance of Power in the South Caucasus," ACNIS Policy Brief Number Two, April 2009, <http://www.acnis.am/publications/2009/THE%20MILITARY%20BALANCE%20OF%20PO WER%20IN%20THE%20SOUTH%20CAUCASUS.pdf> (October 30, 2009).
[22] Information from the Stockholm International Peace Research Institute (SIPRI), <http://www.sipri.org/databases/milex> (November 3, 2009).

Nevertheless, violations of the 1994 ceasefire have increased in 2008-2009, and the departure of the US and Russian envoys to the Minsk Group – the Organization for Security and Cooperation in Europe (OSCE) body responsible for Nagorno Karabakh negotiations in 2009 – has made the prospect for peace increasingly unclear.[23] A resumed conflict between Azerbaijan and Armenia would directly impact US strategic interests in the South Caucasus.

In the meantime, both the Turkish-Armenian and Azeri-Russian rapprochement open new vistas for the Karabakh settlement. In October 2009, Turkey and Armenia signed accords to establish diplomatic relations, reopen their shared border, which has been shut since the Armenian occupation of Nagorno Karabakh in 1994, and establish a joint historical commission to investigate the massacre of Armenians by Ottoman Turks during the First World War. The protocol received support from both Washington and Moscow but, as of this writing, awaits parliamentary approval in both Armenia and Turkey. It is unclear whether the agreement has enough support on both sides to succeed. In Armenia, the rapprochement faces vehement opposition from nationalists at home and from the Armenian Diaspora abroad, while Turkey is facing pressure from Azerbaijan to condition the deal on the withdrawal of Armenian troops and the restoration of displaced Azerbaijanis in Nagorno Karabakh.[24] Though some in Baku felt betrayed by Ankara, many international analysts see the Turkish-Armenian rapprochement as a positive factor that may finally lead to a breakthrough in the Nagorno Karabakh dispute.[25]

---

[23] Abbasov, Shahin, "Azerbaijan: With Departure of Two Karabakh Mediators, Future of Talks Unclear", Eurasianet.org *Eurasia Insight*, August 6, 2009, <http://www.eurasianet.org/departments/insightb/articles/eav080609a.shtml> (October 1, 2009).

[24] "Statement of the Ministry of Foreign Affairs of the Republic of Azerbaijan," Republic of Azerbaijan, Ministry of Foreign Affairs, October 10, 2009, <http://mfa.gov.az/eng/index.php?option=com_content&task=view&id=580&Itemid=1> (October 29, 2009) and "Turkey-Armenia rapprochement far from guaranteed," Reuters, October 12, 2009, <http://www.reuters.com/article/vcCandidateFeed1/idUSTRE59B3GY20091012> (October 29, 2009).

[25] "Turkish-Armenian rapprochement might cause breakthrough in Nagorno-Karabakh," *Sunday's Zaman*, October 29, 2009, <http://www.sundayszaman.com/sunday/detaylar.do?load=detay&link=182043> (October 29, 2009).

Moscow's support of the Turkish-Armenian agreement is curious, and there is doubt as to how strongly Moscow actually supports the rapprochement. A resumed conflict between Azerbaijan and Armenia would benefit both Russia and Iran at the expense of the US. Russia would benefit if Russian "peacekeepers" are called in to mediate a ceasefire between Baku and Yerevan and an increased Russian military presence would further increase Moscow's leverage and influence in the region.[26] Moscow already enjoys strong influence in Armenia due to the latter's political and economic isolation from its neighbors. Meanwhile, Iran stands to gain if Azerbaijan remains preoccupied with the conflict over Nagorno Karabakh rather than turning its attention to interacting with Iran's Azerbaijani minority, which reportedly numbers 25 million and has complained of rights abuses.[27] The US would rather see Armenia and Azerbaijan reach a peaceful compromise over Nagorno Karabakh, thus limiting Moscow and Tehran's leverage in the region and allowing the countries of the South Caucasus to integrate economically with the West.

Much like a second Georgian war, a resumed conflict between Azerbaijan and Armenia would cast doubt on the ability of the US to protect its friends and on the security of US and EU-backed energy projects in the South Caucasus. Should the Nagorno Karabakh conflict erupt into all-out war between Azerbaijan and Armenia, Azerbaijan's energy exports (its source of hard cash reserves) would become a strategic target for Armenia.[28] Under such a scenario, Armenia would likely target the BTC pipeline or Azerbaijan's Sangachal Terminal – where oil and gas from Azerbaijan's offshore fields are stored and processed before export.[29] A successful attack on the processing plants at Sangachal would shut Azeri exports for a much

---

[26] "Russia Steps Up Efforts on Nagorno-Karabakh," Radio Free Europe Radio Liberty, October 29, 2008,
<http://www.rferl.org/content/Russia_Steps_Up_Efforts_On_NagornoKarabakh/1336149.htm l> (October 1, 2009).
[27] Vatanka, Alex, "Azerbaijan-Iran Tensions Create Obstacle to Caspian Resolution", Eurasianet.org Eurasia Insight, January 29, 2003,
<http://www.eurasianet.org/departments/business/articles/eav012903.shtml> (October 1, 2009).
[28] Karagiannis, Emmanuel, Energy and Security in the Caucasus, (New York: RoutledgeCurzon, 2002), p. 45.
[29] "BP Caspian - Sangachal Terminal," BP website,
<http://www.bp.com/sectiongenericarticle.do?categoryId=9006674&contentId=7015100> (October 1, 2009).

longer time than a direct attack on the pipeline, putting billions of dollars of Western investments at risk. An attack on the BTC or Sangachal would also increase the political risk on the proposed Nabucco gas pipeline and other future energy projects in the region.

*Terrorism*

Controlling the spread of Islamic terrorism in the South Caucasus is another important foreign policy concern of the US. To date, there has been limited evidence of international terrorist groups operating in the South Caucasus. Azerbaijan is the only country in the region with a majority Islamic population, but its traditionally secular government and elites make it less prone to radicalism. Nevertheless, Islamist ideology has gained ground in recent years due to internal factors, such as disillusionment with the current government and increased levels of poverty despite booming oil and gas revenues, as well as external factors, such as the penetration of Hezbollah and sponsorship of Islamic schools from Middle East donors and foundations connected with radical Sunni circles, which also support al-Qaeda and other terrorist organizations.

The rise of Salafi Islam among the country's Sunnis is a worrying phenomenon. Of particular concern is a radical Wahhabi movement that has taken hold among the ethnic Lezgin minority in northern Azerbaijan, which has been sponsored by wealthy Saudis, Kuwaitis and natives of other Gulf States.[30] The Wahhabi movement has been active in the North Caucasus – Chechnya and Dagestan – for over a decade and has grown in Azerbaijan alongside Lezgin nationalist sentiments.[31] In 2007, Azeri security forces detained a group of Wahabbi militants armed with grenade launchers and automatic weapons that was planning to launch an attack on US and British embassies in Baku, as well as the Baku offices of several

---

[30] Geybullayeva, Arzu, "Is Azerbaijan Becoming a Hub of Radical Islam?", *Turkish Policy Quarterly,* Spring 2007, p. 109, <http://www.turkishpolicy.com/images/stories/2007-03-caucasus/TPQ2007-3-geybullayeva.pdf> (October 1, 2009).

[31] Kotchikian, Asbed, "Secular Nationalism Versus Political Islam in Azerbaijan," Jamestown Foundation *Terrorism Monitor,* Vol. 3, Issue 3, February 9, 2005. <http://www.jamestown.org/single/?no_cache=1&tx_ttnews%5Btt_news%5D=27525> (October 1, 2009).

major oil companies.[32] Authorities have also detained several dozen suspected militants accused of attending militant camps outside of the country.

The rise of Wahhabi radicalism in Azerbaijan could endanger energy infrastructure in the region. Energy assets have become a popular target for Islamic terrorists in the Middle East because they are high-value Western investments, which, if successfully attacked, could impact economies around the world. In February 2006, Saudi forces foiled an al-Qaeda attack on the Abqaiq oil gathering and processing facility through which flows two-thirds of the country's oil output.[33] More recently, in July 2009, Egyptian authorities arrested 26 al-Qaeda-linked men suspected of planning to attack oil pipelines and tankers transiting the Suez Canal with remote-controlled detonators and explosives.[34] If al-Qaeda gains a foothold in Azerbaijan, oil and gas assets, such as the BTC pipeline and the Sangachal oil and gas terminal, could become potential targets.

Radical Shia groups sponsored by Iran and Hezbollah are another potential concern in Azerbaijan, particularly in southern Azerbaijan along the border with Iran. Baku has repeatedly accused Teheran of interfering in its internal affairs. In 2002, Azeri authorities shut down many extremist Shia madrasas (religious schools) sponsored by Iran, which glorify the theocratic regime in Tehran, but a large number of schools reportedly remain in operation.[35] In 2006, 15 Azeris, who received training from Iranian security forces, were charged with plotting violence against Israelis and Westerners. In 2008, surveillance, which was instituted as a result of that case, uncovered links between local militants and Hezbollah operatives and helped Azeri security forces foil a plot to blow up the Israeli Embassy in Azerbaijan. The foiled plot was reportedly mobilized by Hezbollah and Iranian intelligence as

---

[32] Yevgrashina, Lada, "Analysis: Azerbaijan Plot Shows Radicals' Threat Has Teeth," Reuters, November 8, 2007, <http://www.reuters.com/article/latestCrisis/idUSL08191665> (October 1, 2009) and Cohen, A. and Kushnir, K., "Azerbaijan," World Almanac of Islamism (2010, forthcoming).

[33] "Saudi Arabia: Explosion Near Oil Refinery," Stratfor, February 24, 2006, <http://www.stratfor.com/saudi_arabia_explosion_near_oil_refinery> (October 1, 2009).

[34] "Egypt Arrests 26 Over Suspected Suez Canal Plot," Al Arabiya, July 9, 2009, <http://www.alarabiya.net/articles/2009/07/09/78285.html#> (October 1, 2009).

[35] Geybullayeva, p. 114.

revenge for the alleged Israeli assassination of Imad Mughniyeh, chief operations officer of Hezbollah, who died from a car bomb in Damascus.[36]

## The Caspian Energy Game

The South Caucasus region is of high importance to the US and its Western allies because it provides a corridor free of hostile influence for oil and gas exports from the Caspian Basin – a region that includes Azerbaijan, Kazakhstan and Turkmenistan. Historically, all energy exports from this landlocked region have flowed through the Russian Empire to end markets in Europe or, after the 1917 Bolshevik Revolution, into the Soviet Union. This arrangement has benefited Russia in two ways. First, as the sole export route for Caspian energy until the mid-2000s, Russia has wielded significant economic and political leverage over the Caspian Basin countries. Secondly, Russia has been able to increase the total volume of energy resources under its control, allowing it to secure monopoly power over gas supply and political leverage in Eastern and Southeastern Europe and expand its market share and political clout in Western Europe.

Russia's control of Caspian energy began to crack with the opening of the Southern Corridor's BTC oil pipeline in 2005 and the South Caucasus Pipeline (SCP) gas line in 2006. The BTC pipeline, in particular, was heavily supported by the Clinton and Bush administrations (1993-2008) (see *Figure 2*). These projects allowed Azeri oil and gas exports to bypass Russia on the way to consuming markets in the West. Other Caspian producers remain dependent on Russian oil and gas export routes, although this dynamic may be altered by proposed Trans-Caspian oil and gas pipelines, which would run beneath the Caspian Sea, linking up with the BTC oil pipeline and the South Caucasus/Nabucco gas pipeline in Azerbaijan. Kazakhstan, the Caspian region's largest oil exporter and reserve holder, currently relies on Russian pipeline routes for the majority of its crude exports, including the Russian pipeline network operated by the state-owned Transneft and the Caspian Pipeline Consortium (CPC) Project, a pipeline developed by Russian and Kazakh governments and a consortium of national and

---

[36] "Azerbaijan Seen as a New Front in Mideast Conflict," *Los Angeles Times*. May 30, 2009, <http://articles.latimes.com/2009/may/30/world/fg-shadow30> (October 29, 2009).

international oil companies, which carries oil from western Kazakhstan to Russia's Black Sea port of Novorossiysk.[37]

*Figure 2: Map of Oil Pipelines in the South Caucasus*[38]

Source: Energy Information Administration

Russia has aggressively worked to prevent a proposed Trans-Caspian oil pipeline, which would transport 150,000 to 400,000 barrels per day from Kazakhstan's massive Kashagan oil field beneath the Caspian Sea to the BTC pipeline in Azerbaijan, allowing Kazakhstan to reduce its dependence on Russian export routes.[39] Some Kazakh oil – roughly 100,000 barrels per day – is already shipped to the BTC pipeline via tanker across the Caspian,

---

[37] "Kazakhstan Country Analysis Brief," US Energy Information Administration, <http://www.eia.doe.gov/emeu/cabs/Kazakhstan/Oil.html> (October 1, 2009).

[38] The Baku-Tbilisi-Ceyhan pipeline was completed in 2005 and is not "planned" as indicated in the map

[39] "Kashagan Partners Eye US$4-bil. Trans-Caspian Oil Transport System to Connect to BTC Pipeline," IHS Global Insight, <http://www.ihsglobalinsight.com/SDA/SDADetail6096.htm> (October 1, 2009).

and plans are underway to expand these shipments.[40] Russia and Iran – another suitor of Kazakh oil – both oppose a Trans-Caspian oil pipeline and have thrown a roadblock at the project by challenging the legal status of the Caspian Sea.[41] Furthermore, Moscow is also working to ensure that Kazakh production is exported via Russian-controlled pipelines. Following the leadership of Russia's pipeline monopoly Transneft, after excruciating negotiations, CPC pipeline shareholders agreed in December 2008 to double the capacity of the pipeline from 700,000 barrels per day (b/d) to 1.4 million b/d by 2013 to accommodate rising oil output from Kazakhstan.[42] Increased capacity on Russian-controlled routes makes the Trans-Caspian oil pipeline increasingly unlikely.

Kazakh oil exports east to China are another concern. A 613-mile pipeline exported about 85,000 b/d of oil to China in 2007 and plans are underway to double the nameplate capacity on the line from 200,000 b/d to 400,000 b/d by filling the line with crude from the Kashagan field.[43] Exports along this route are effectively locked up by internal Chinese markets, making less oil available for Western-oriented export routes.

Russia's opposition to the US and EU-backed Nabucco gas pipeline has been even more forceful. In recent years, Russia has offered to buy natural gas from Caspian producers, especially the key supplier Turkmenistan, at prices that are near the average prices paid by European Union customers to Gazprom (less transit fees) and has proposed a competing project – the South Stream pipeline – designed to obviate the need for Nabucco (see *Figure 3*).[44] Given the limited number of potential suppliers in the Caspian region, it is unlikely that there is enough gas to supply Nabucco and

[40] "Kazakhstan Country Analysis Brief," US Energy Information Administration, <http://www.eia.doe.gov/emeu/cabs/Kazakhstan/Oil.html>.

[41] "Kashagan Partners Eye US$4-bil. Trans-Caspian Oil Transport System to Connect to BTC Pipeline," IHS Global Insight, <http://www.ihsglobalinsight.com/SDA/SDADetail6096.htm>.

[42] "CPC agrees on pipeline expansion, BP exit terms," Reuters, December 17, 2008. <http://uk.biz.yahoo.com/17122008/323/update-1-cpc-agrees-pipeline-expansion-bp-exit-terms.html> (October 1, 2009).

[43] "Kazakhstan Country Analysis Brief," US Energy Information Administration, <http://www.eia.doe.gov/emeu/cabs/Kazakhstan/Oil.html>.

[44] Socor, Vladimir, "Russia to Increase Purchase Prices for Central Asian Gas: Outlook and Implications," *Eurasia Daily Monitor*, Volume 5, Issue 50, March 16, 2008, <http://www.jamestown.org/single/?no_cache=1&tx_ttnews[tt_news]=33464> (October 27, 2009).

Russian pipelines. Azerbaijan and Turkmenistan are the primary potential suppliers for the Nabucco project, and although supplies from Iraq and Iran could conceivably contribute to the pipeline, political and security concerns make their participation highly speculative. Specifically, Iran is under US sanctions, which severely limit foreign investment into the Islamic Republic of Iran's energy industry, while the security situation in Iraq, including the relations between the Kurdistan Regional Government and the central government in Baghdad, are far from stable. In the long term, the likelihood of Iraqi gas being exported via Nabucco is higher than the Iranian product.

*Figure 3: Proposed Nabucco and South Stream Pipeline Routes*

Source: BBC News

Russia has acted assertively to ensure that its South Stream project, which would flow from Russia across the length of the Black Sea to Bulgaria and further to Serbia, Hungary and Austria, has the upper hand over Nabucco. In 2007, Gazprom agreed to buy up new supplies of Kazakh and Turkmen gas at near European prices beginning in 2009 – a move that effectively doubled the price that Gazprom paid in 2008. [45] Russia, Turkmenistan and Kazakhstan also agreed to expand the existing northbound Caspian coastal

---

[45] Socor, "Russia to Increase Purchase Prices for Central Asian Gas: Outlook and Implications," *Eurasia Daily Monitor*,
<http://www.jamestown.org/single/?no_cache=1&tx_ttnews[tt_news]=33464>.

gas pipeline, the Prikaspiisky pipeline, which will increase capacity to accommodate 10 billion cubic meters (bcm) per year of Turkmen gas and equivalent quantities of Kazakh gas by 2010. This move will leave less Central Asian production available for the Western-backed Trans-Caspian gas pipeline that is necessary to fill Nabucco and will set the framework for greater cooperation between Russia and Caspian producers to fulfill the South Stream project.[46] Gazprom's willingness to pay higher prices for Central Asian gas despite the resulting reduction in its profit margins on re-exports to Europe highlights the company's willingness to sacrifice short-term profits for long-term control of the Central Asian gas supply and its European market share.

Despite the financial crisis and the crash in energy prices, Gazprom in May 2009 announced with project partner Eni SPA of Italy that it planned to double the capacity of the South Stream pipeline to 63 bcm per year, up from the original capacity of 31 bcm per year.[47] Shortly before the plans were announced, Russian Energy Minister Sergei Shmatko told reporters that he thought that the South Stream project, currently slated to launch in 2015, would be realized before the 31 bcm per year Nabucco project, which has an in-service date of 2014.[48] The South Stream project scored a major victory in October 2009 when Russia announced that Turkey had granted all of the permits necessary for Gazprom to construct South Stream along the Turkish-controlled seabed beneath the Black Sea.[49] The agreement, which allows Gazprom to redirect the South Stream through Turkish rather than Ukrainian waters (at higher cost), follows recent deals signed with Italy, Bulgaria, Greece, Serbia and Slovenia to start building the onshore European segments of the pipeline and gives the project a clear leg up over the Nabucco project. The agreement also caused speculation, fueled largely by Russian media outlets, that Moscow was planning to bypass Bulgaria and

---

[46] "Turkmenistan to Launch Russia Gas Pipeline in 2010," Reuters, July 15, 2008. <http://uk.reuters.com/article/oilRpt/idUKL1563346520080715> (October 1, 2009).
[47] "South Stream Pipeline Capacity to be Doubled," *Oil & Gas Journal*, May 21, 2009.
[48] Ibid.
[49] "Russian Pipelines Win Key Approvals," *Wall Street Journal*, October 21, 2009, <http://online.wsj.com/article/SB125605250259596613.html> (November 3, 2009).

run the pipeline ashore in Turkey. The rumors may have been designed to put pressure on Bulgaria.[50]

Russia is also seeking to poach potential Nabucco supply from Azerbaijan. In June 2009, Gazprom signed an agreement to import 500 million cubic meters per year of natural gas from Azerbaijan and ship it by pipeline to Europe beginning in 2010.[51] Although the contracted amount is relatively small, Alexei Miller, Gazprom's CEO, said that Azerbaijan had also promised the company priority in buying gas from the second phase of Azerbaijan's Shah Deniz gas field – the main source of supply that the EU hopes will fill the Nabucco pipeline.[52] Setting the framework for future Russian purchases from Shah Deniz Two, the sale and purchase agreement for the Azeri gas deal, signed in October 2009, indicated that initial purchase volumes would increase subsequent to increases in Azerbaijan's export potential.[53]

The US and EU have thus far not responded to Russia's assertive actions in the Caspian, although both have continued to give strong support to the Nabucco project, which has struggled to move forward amid numerous challenges. There are a large number of actors that need to be brought fully onboard for Nabucco to succeed, including multiple suppliers, transit nations, and customers across several regions, including Central Asia, the South Caucasus and Europe. In September 2009, Joschka Fischer, a political communication adviser to Nabucco and a former German vice chancellor and foreign minister, said the project had not yet received the necessary political backing to move forward.[54] While the EU as a whole supports Nabucco, some European countries and companies have acted

---

[50] "Ivan Kostov: The publications in Russian media about South Stream is a tactic to put pressure on Bulgaria," Focus Information Agency, October 21, 2009, <http://www.focus-fen.net/index.php?id=n197893> (November 3, 2009).

[51] "Gazprom Seeks to Rattle EU with Azerbaijan Gas Agreement," *Oil & Gas Journal*, June 30, 2009.

[52] Ibid.

[53] "Gazprom and SOCAR sign purchase and sale contract for Azerbaijani gas," Gazprom Press Release, October 14, 2009,
<http://www.gazprom.com/press/news/2009/october/article69312/> (October 27, 2009).

[54] "Nabucco Needs More Support, Fischer Says," *Hurriet Daily News*, September 8, 2009,
<http://www.hurriyetdailynews.com/n.php?n=nabucco-needs-more-support-fischer-says-2009-09-08#> (October 1, 2009).

opportunistically, choosing to support both Nabucco and Gazprom's South Stream project. Suppliers from the Caspian and Middle East have not yet signed supply agreements with Nabucco, while Russia has inked several important gas deals with Caspian producers over the last few years that are likely to limit supply available for Nabucco. In particular, the recent gas deal between Gazprom and the State Oil Company of Azerbaijan (SOCAR) has raised questions about Azerbaijan's commitment to supply the initial 8 bcm to the Nabucco project from Shah Deniz Two.

European concerns were partially eased in July 2009, when Azerbaijan, along with Turkmenistan, affirmed that they had enough supplies available to fill Nabucco, although neither has signed a supply agreement with the project.[55] A few days later, the governments of participating EU countries signed an intergovernmental agreement with Turkey authorizing the Nabucco project. Following the agreement, Russian state television echoed earlier statements from Prime Minister Vladimir Putin that questioned the feasibility of the project. In May 2009, Putin derided Nabucco saying: "Before putting millions of dollars into a pipeline and burying it in the ground, you have to know where the gas for this pipeline is going to come from."[56] Gazprom's head Alexei Miller voiced a similar sentiment at the meeting with the members of the Valday Club in September 2009.[57]

Russia's moves in the Caspian energy game are a direct challenge to US energy interests in the South Caucasus. If Gazprom's South Stream project succeeds at the expense of Nabucco, Russia could consolidate its grasp on Caspian gas for decades to come and provide Moscow with enhanced energy clout and bargaining power vis-à-vis European capitals and Brussels. Given the strategic economic and political benefits at stake, Russia will continue to push South Stream regardless of the cost, which many experts expect to be at least double that of Nabucco. Russia will also continue to offer potential Nabucco suppliers, transit countries and customers better conditions than the non-Russian route alternative provides. The US and the EU are likely to stand in firm support of Nabucco but will have difficulty managing the myriad diplomatic and financial prerequisites necessary for

---

[55] "Caspian Gas Producers Affirm Supplies for Nabucco," *Oil & Gas Journal*, July 10, 2009.

[56] "EU Nations, Turkey Sign Nabucco Gas Line Treaty," *Oil & Gas Journal*, July 14, 2009.

[57] Ariel Cohen's personal notes, meeting with Alexei Miller, September 2009, Moscow.

launching Nabucco, particularly in the face of determined Russian attempts to kill the project.

If Russia is unable to derail the Nabucco and Trans-Caspian pipelines economically and politically, it may resort to violence – by stirring up the simmering territorial conflicts in Georgia, Nagorno Karabakh, or even the Caspian Sea – in order to increase the security risk in the Southern Corridor. Iran, another Caspian littoral state, is Moscow's ally in this regard. In July 2009, Russia and Iran held a joint military exercise in the Caspian Sea involving some 30 vessels, a signal that the two nations' Caspian interests are beginning to align. Iran wants a greater stake in the Caspian's energy riches – up to 20 percent if the Caspian Sea is legally classified as a lake – while Russia would like to block the Trans-Caspian pipelines designed to bypass Russian territory.[58]

## Conclusion

Since the fall of the Soviet Union, the US has had significant strategic and economic interests in the South Caucasus, including containing revisionist anti-American regimes in Russia and Iran, securing the transit of oil and gas exports from the Caspian, and promoting democratic principles, transparency, good governance and markets based on property rights and the rule of law in Eurasia. These interests are threatened by region-wide security concerns, including Russia's push against the states perceived to be US-friendly, such as Georgia and Azerbaijan. The August 2008 conflict between Russia and Georgia over Georgia's breakaway provinces and the conflict between Armenia and Azerbaijan over Nagorno Karabakh should be viewed on their merits, as well as through the prism of the Russian-American competition in the region. US energy interests are threatened by Moscow's determination to monopolize the Caspian's oil and gas resources and control key energy routes to Europe. A careful approach is required for examining the roles of Iran and Turkey in the region, especially as Turkish society, government and policy assume a more pronounced Islamic character and the country distances itself from the US

---

[58] Afrasiabi, Kaveh L., "Russia and Iran Join Hands," Asia Times Online, July 30, 2009, <http://www.atimes.com/atimes/Middle_East/KG30Ak01.html> (October 1, 2009).

The rise of Islamic fundamentalism in Azerbaijan should be seen through the prism of the global rise of radicalism and the Sunni-Shia confrontation. In the foreseeable future, Iranian and Sunni interests will clash in the Greater Middle East and around the world, and Azerbaijan, the South Caucasus and the Russian North Caucasus are no exceptions.

Despite these strategic concerns, the Obama administration has reduced US support for allies in the South Caucasus, seeking instead to prioritize relations with Russia. This is the "neo-realism" of the Obama administration, and it may take a while until the White House recognizes that the policy does not bear desired fruit – or, on the contrary, is a success. Nevertheless, this divergence from the foreign policies of previous administrations is putting significant US interests at risk. In order to defend US interests regarding security, energy and democracy in the South Caucasus, the Obama administration should:

- **Re-think the "Reset" Policy.** The Obama administration should reassess its policy of "resetting" relations with Russia. Maintaining a working relationship with a country that still has enough nuclear weapons to destroy the world several times over should continue to be an important goal of the US. However, this goal should not come at the expense of US allies in the South Caucasus or elsewhere in the former Soviet Union. Although the Cold War has long been concluded, strategists in the Kremlin still view the "near abroad" as Russia's "zone of privileged interests" and international politics as a zero-sum game. The Putin-Medvedev "tandemocracy" as well as post-Soviet elites who direct Russia's foreign policy will undoubtedly see friendly overtures and unilateral concessions by the US – such as the cancellation of the missile defense program in Eastern Europe – as a sign of weakness, if not naïveté, and a signal that the US may not seek to contain a resurgent Russia in the post-Soviet space. The losers in this equation are the countries that belong in what Moscow considers its "sphere of interests," including those in the Southern Caucasus. Georgia and, to a lesser degree, Ukraine have already felt the heavy hand of Moscow. The Obama administration should show firm support for the nations of the South Caucasus, including boosting political-military relations, and send a clear signal to Moscow that attacks on the integrity and independence of friendly nations will come at a price.

- **Offer a NATO Membership Action Plan to Georgia.** NATO's failure to offer Georgia a MAP – a prelude to NATO membership – at its April 2008 summit in Bucharest may have emboldened Russia to act aggressively towards Georgia in August of that year. The Obama administration should coordinate policy to immediately extend a MAP to Georgia and should continue to offer bi-lateral military train-and-equip programs and economic support to the country. Bringing Georgia into the NATO alliance would be a clear signal to Moscow that the West is not willing to recognize a "sphere of privileged influence" in the South Caucasus. The Obama administration should also work on expanding Armenia's and Azerbaijan's ties to NATO, conditioned on the peaceful settlement of the Nagorno Karabakh issue, moves to improve democratic governance in both countries and efforts to reform their militaries.

- **Negotiate a Nagorno Karabakh Peace Settlement.** Settlement of the dispute over Nagorno-Karabakh would help bring stability to the South Caucasus, diffuse the "frozen conflict" between Armenia and Azerbaijan, and reduce political risk in the strategic Southern Corridor. Provided Azerbaijani sovereignty over occupied lands is restored, Armenia and Azerbaijan would be able to forge closer relations with the West and eventually join NATO and/or the EU. The Obama administration should work inside and outside of the OSCE's Minsk Group to negotiate a peace settlement between Baku and Yerevan. The Turkish-Armenian rapprochement and the September 2009 appointment of Robert Bradtke as envoy to the Minsk Group are a good start.[59]

- **Cooperate on Anti-Terror Measures with Azerbaijan.** The Obama administration should continue to support bi-lateral and multi-lateral cooperation with Azerbaijan to combat the rise of

---

[59] "Armenia and Azerbaijan: Appointment of US OSCE Minsk Group Co-Chair," US Department of State, September 7, 2009, <http://www.state.gov/r/pa/prs/ps/2009/sept/128680.htm> (October 1, 2009).

Islamic fundamentalism and terrorism. Intelligence sharing between US and Azerbaijan should be expanded, while Azerbaijan should further undertake financial measures to uncover and intercept terrorist financing. Although Azerbaijan is making progress in this realm, the Council of Europe, through its Committee of Experts on the Evaluation of Anti-Money Laundering Measures and the Financing of Terrorism mechanism, issued a negative assessment of Azerbaijan's anti-money laundering reform effort in January 2009.[60] In view of the Turkish-Armenian rapprochement and in order to continue anti-terror support that began under the Bush administration, the Obama administration must permanently waive sanctions – the so-called "Section 907 of the Freedom Support Act of 1992" – that the US levied against Azerbaijan in response to its blockade of Armenia. Section 907 bans any kind of direct US aid to the Azerbaijani government. In October 2001, the Senate gave the president the ability to waive Section 907, and President Bush used this authority to provide counterterrorism support to Azerbaijan.

- **Help Europe to Take a Leadership Role on Nabucco.** The US should help Europe push forward the Nabucco pipeline project that will diversify Europe's natural gas supplies away from Russia. The US, perhaps more than the EU, has a unified and coherent policy toward Nabucco, as well as the political leverage to bring all the necessary actors together. Yet, it is a European project and should be run by and for European companies, consumers and governments. Without sidetracking European actors, the Obama administration should boost US involvement in Nabucco, encouraging all actors to cooperate in getting the project from the negotiation room to the field.

The South Caucasus will remain a crucial geopolitical area, in which East-West and North-South interests intersect. The US today is involved in Iraq, Afghanistan, Pakistan and the global war on terrorism. Washington is trying, with great care, to push the "reset button" in its relations with

---

[60] "MONEYVAL publishes its second report on Azerbaijan," Council of Europe, <http://www.coe.az/Latest-News/123.html> (November 2, 2009).

Moscow and has a confrontational and highly problematic relationship with the Islamic Republic of Iran. The South Caucasus will continue to play sensitive and important roles in all these arenas. In management of US interests in the region, diplomatic, defense, energy and intelligence establishments will play an important role. As Russia, Iran, and Turkey increase their involvement in the South Caucasus, US policy toward the region will also require adequate resource allocation and ample executive time, understanding, compassion and toughness at the highest level.

# THE MIDDLE EAST AND AZERBAIJAN: THE IMPACT OF REGIONAL EVENTS

**Barry Rubin,**
Director,
Global Research in International Affairs (GLORIA) Interdisciplinary Center

To what extent will the strategic interests and situation of Azerbaijan depend on developments in the Middle East? There are important developments in the region that will affect Azerbaijan in international terms and others that may also have internal consequences.

The most important issue in the region today is the war between nationalism and Islamism. Islamists have become the main opposition movement and are challenging the dominant nationalist governments in every Arab country. Islamists are reacting both to the failures of the existing regimes and to their own revolutionary ambitions. Nationalist forces also cast the struggle in sectarian terms, identifying their radical Islamist opponents with the Shia branch of Islam.

Islamism also opposes Jewish nationalism in Israel (Zionism), Turkish nationalism (Kemalism) and Azeri nationalism. It seeks to replace them with Islamist-ruled states. Thus, while Islamism seeks to rule individual states, its overall goal is an Islamist-ruled region. Islamist groups help each other across national lines and some Islamist movements – the Muslim Brotherhood, al-Qaeda, Iranian-backed groups – are transnational.

The main, but not the sole, radical Islamist factor is an alliance led by Iran that includes Syria, Hamas, Hezbollah, Iraqi insurgents and other elements is seeking regional hegemony. Other Islamists, however, such as the Muslim Brotherhoods and al-Qaeda, oppose the Iranian-led bloc and are trying to stage their own revolutionary takeovers. In Turkey, an elected government is bent on transforming the society in an Islamist direction. In Lebanon, the political battle is being fought among a range of political forces that include an alignment of Shia Muslims, Hezbollah, Amal, traditional pro-Syrian politicians and even a Christian faction led by Michel Aoun.

While there is an ideological Islamist aspect to the conflict, there is also a more opportunist conflict of those competing to take power in their own country. Another dimension is that of a Shia versus Sunni conflict. Yet, as noted, the Iranian-led bloc includes Alawites (the Syrian regime), Sunni Muslims (notably Hamas) and even Christians (Aoun's forces in Lebanon).

This great battle is the central feature of contemporary regional politics. The situation can be compared to the Communist factor in the previous century. But the Islamist movement has several advantages over Communism. It is far less complex for the masses to grasp, coincides with traditional and religious attitudes, and includes a wide variety of streams that adjust to the conditions in specific countries or among different sects (that is, Sunni and Shia Muslims).

The victory of Islamism in any country tips the balance further in the direction of Islamist forces and thus endangers the security and stability of Azerbaijan. It weakens Western influence, encourages many individuals (including within Azerbaijan itself) to join radical Islamist groups, makes Islamist states stronger and more aggressive, and inspires more support to subversive revolutionary movements elsewhere.

In this regard, there are two countries that are particularly important for Azerbaijan, both in their own right and relating to the role of Islamism in governing them: Iran and Turkey.

**Iran**

As Azerbaijan's neighbor whose citizens include a large portion of ethnic Azeris, Iran's fate and policies are of tremendous importance. They will be shaped by a number of issues, which should be considered separately: Iran's ambitions, possession and usage of nuclear weapons, domestic political stability, and relations with Western and Arabic-speaking powers, as well as bi-lateral relations with Azerbaijan itself.

*Iranian Nuclear Weapons*

Iran's drive for nuclear weapons and missiles capable of delivering them poses possibly the single greatest challenge to US policy today. Additionally, this is an issue of pressing importance, because Iran may acquire the ability to use such weapons within three years.

The problems this poses for US policy involves much more than just the possibility that Iran might use such weapons against Israel or that Israel might launch a preemptive attack. Having such weapons will greatly increase Tehran's leverage in the Middle East because it will be able to intimidate Arab and Western states into acquiescing to its demands. Equally worrisome, this breakthrough would be seen by radical Islamist forces and the general Muslim publics as a great victory. Groups would become more aggressive, their memberships and bases of support would increase sharply as millions of people concluded that Islamism was the wave of the future and – in many though not all cases – that Iran was its leader.

The result would be a rise in the level of violence and instability throughout the region and even expanding terrorism in Europe. Another potential outcome could be the the the fall of one or more Arab states to an Islamist revolution, either completely independent-minded or as part of Iran's bloc. Oil prices would rise due both to the perception of dangerous crises and enhanced Iranian influence on pushing prices upward to increase its own revenue.

It is easy to say, as the Obama administration does, that it will try to talk Iran out of its nuclear weapons program. Still, no matter how friendly the United States is, no matter how much it offers or apologizes, there will be no serious likelihood that Iran will stop. Then what should the United States and Europe do? With a military response probably ruled out by Washington, the United States is most likely to accede to a fait accompli and accept Tehran as a nuclear power with devastating consequences and horrifying longer-range ones.

In short, Iran having a nuclear arsenal would be a disaster for Azerbaijani as well as Western interests because it would transform the regional situation in a number of ways:

1. A nuclear Iran will make it impossible for the West to protect its interests in the Middle East. All Western countries would be too intimidated to act in any way contrary to Iran's desires out of concern that Iran would use nuclear weapons against them, their troops or others.

2. A nuclear Iran would intimidate all Arab regimes to appease Iran including, for example, rejecting Western basing rights or alliances. They might well believe that the United States is unlikely to go to nuclear war for them and instead strive to get the best surrender terms from Tehran. This would prohibit any Arab-Israeli peace. Arab cooperation with the West would plummet. Arab states would be afraid to cooperate with the United States in resisting the expansion of the Iran-Syria bloc and would be far more likely to join it. Islamist regimes would be more likely to take over in many countries.

3. A nuclear Iran would lead to a huge upsurge in radical Islamist movements and their recruiting. With hundreds of thousands of Muslims joining such groups, the existence of every Arab regime would be jeopardized; terrorism and regional instability would rise.

4. Large numbers of Muslims living in the West would also join radical Islamist groups, believing the day of victory was at hand and that Iran had shown the way. Terrorism would rise throughout the West.

5. A nuclear Iran, or an Iran on the verge of obtaining nuclear weapons, might attack Israel either directly or by giving weapons to terrorist groups. This could set off an incredibly bloody and destabilizing war. Alternatively, Israel might wage a preemptive attack on Iran, which also would have some effect on instability and a war of some sort between them.

6. The price of oil, given understandable belief by consumers that the region will be more unstable, could climb even higher than it is now. In addition, the tremendous power that Iran – a price hawk – would have ensures that it would push up the price and the Saudis

would be too intimidated to try to push it down. This would benefit Azerbaijan financially, though not enough to overcome the other negatives. The resulting unstable situation might well threaten Azerbaijan's ability to export and transport oil products.

7. A nuclear arms race would be triggered in the region, greatly increasing the likelihood of a nuclear war between two or more Middle Eastern countries and the potential that such weapons might get into the hands of terrorists.

*Iranian Ambitions*

The threat posed by Iranian nuclear weapons is only part of a larger picture; nuclear arms are being sought as an additional means to further existing Iranian goals. Tehran, because of its Islamist ideology, nationalist sentiments, and the regime's definition of its own interests, seeks to expand its influence throughout the region. In this context, it has created an alliance including Syria, Hamas, Hezbollah and important forces in Iraq as well. This bloc opposes US and Western interests, seeks to destroy Israel and is trying to gain primary influence over Iraq, Lebanon and the Palestinians.

Iran and its allies use subversion, sponsorship of opposition and revolutionary groups, bribery, terrorism, assassination of opposing leaders, and an ideologically consistent propaganda campaign against neighbors. As Tehran's sense of success increases and as its regime needs more foreign policy triumphs or distractions to ensure domestic support, neighbors could be increasingly jeopardized.

*The Internal Situation*

Iran's regime underwent a major transition in 2009 to become far more extreme. Elements in this situation include:

1. The stealing of the election by the regime in a particularly bold way.

2. The repression of large, peaceful demonstrations protesting the balloting.

3. Putting on trial large numbers of dissidents and even establishment figures with heavy sentences against them.

4. Purging or pushing out less extreme members of the ruling group.

5. The appointment of a man wanted by Interpol for terrorism as defense minister.

6. Increasing consolidating of power for President Mahmoud Ahmadinejad and his supporters, the most radical grouping in the government.

7. Growing numbers of appointments for Islamic Revolutionary Guard Corps' officers to the extent that many Iranians speak of a silent coup.

This has resulted in a much more radical government willing to undertake bold actions abroad and determined to complete Iran's nuclear weapons' program. By the same token, the Iranian leadership is far less likely to make compromises with the West over the nuclear program or other issues.

The continuation of a radical regime will sooner or later become a menace to Azerbaijan either directly or, more likely, indirectly. If the hard-line regime continues in power, it will try to spread both Iranian hegemony and radical Islamist revolution – which are not contradictory – to other states, including Azerbaijan.

Indirectly, if Iran's overall regional power increases and that of the United States declines, Azerbaijan will be simultaneously exposed to a more dangerous environment and can expect less protection from Tehran's ambitions. The choice becomes one of resistance, with the possibility of increased subversion or direct threats, or appeasement, either of which is unpalatable.

**Turkey**

Turkey is very important for Azerbaijan as neighbor and role model. That country's success in developing as a secular, democratic and rapidly developing society has inspired Azerbaijan's own efforts. But now that Turkey itself had a de facto Islamist government, it threatens to turn from a benefit and helpf for Azerbaijan into a problem.

True, Turkey's ruling party has, up until now, denied that it is Islamist and calls itself a center-right good government party. Behind the scenes, however, it has been transforming key institutions such as government departments, courts and media. Increasingly it has become more open about its intention of transforming Turkey from a secular republic to an Islamic-oriented or even Islamist state.

This strategy has included mobilizing intense hostility toward Israel, growing anti-Americanism, intimidation of the media, infiltration of the army along with trials of officers for alleged coup plans, and other steps to consolidate its authority, perhaps irreversibly. Iranian, Sudanese and Hamas leaders have been warmly received in Teheran. Faced with a choice between attending the moderate Arabs' Kuwait summit or the radicals' Qatar meeting, Ankara chose the latter.

Since Turkey has so long been secular in politics and moderate in Islam, a NATO member and a candidate for the European Union, the shift is especially shocking. One indication of how much things have changed is that the current Turkish government feels more comfortable with Iran than the United States. It has been substituting links with Israel to a cozy relationship with Syria. If Turkey is increasingly aligned with the radical forces, it would tilt the power balance in the region toward the Islamist forces in general and the Iran-led bloc in particular.

On top of this, the Turkish-Armenia rapprochement also poses problems for Azerbaijan.

A number of other countries are also at this crossroad. Will countries like Afghanistan, Lebanon and Egypt be taken over by radical Islamist regimes – whether or not aligned with Iran – and to what degree will they achieve stability?

## Afghanistan

Western troops are in Afghanistan to ensure the survival of the existing moderate regime, to ensure that the Taliban does not return to power and, most ambitiously, to try to help Afghanistan become a stable and developing country.

There are two key decisions regarding Afghanistan. First, will the United States and its European allies maintain their major military role in that country to keep the Taliban at bay? Second, will this effort suffice? If the West continues its role in Afghanistan, and perhaps even if it doesn't, the regime will probably survive. Yet actual victory there is impossible. The fighting will not go away and the emergence of a stable regime – especially if Western forces are withdrawn – is unlikely. There is a real danger of the radical Taliban reappearing, even accompanied by a reemergence of its al-Qaeda allies who hit the United States on September 11, 2001. There is no good solution to Afghanistan. Foreign troops will either stay or be withdrawn. Either way, the result will be at best a long-term holding action, at worst a major defeat.

## Egypt

While more distant from Azerbaijan, Egypt's position as the most important country in the Arabic-speaking world means Cairo's leaders are important to Azerbaijan, even if only indirectly. President Hosni Mubarak is likely to leave the scene in the next few years. He has not yet made clear his choice of successor, though his son is one possibility. Egypt is in no danger of a radical Islamist takeover in the near to medium future, but could be headed down that road. In the hands of the current regime, Egypt provides at least some counterforce to Islamist and Iranian ambitions.

## Iraq

The future of Iraq is also important for Azerbaijan, not just as a battleground between extremist Islamist Sunni forces and the ruling Shia-Kurdish coalition, but also as a test case for Iran's expanding influence.

In contrast with Afghanistan, a US and Western troop presence is less necessary at this point and a stable moderate regime is more likely to succeed. Iraq's government has had more than four years to consolidate power and to defend itself, though bloody violence will continue.

But what if things do go wrong? It is difficult to formulate a response even under the best of circumstances. How would the United States and the West respond if Iran and Syria, as the sponsors or allies of large forces in Iraq on both the Shia and Sunni sides, raised the level of violence? How would the West respond to ethnic massacres or a destabilized regime?

Moreover, would Iran be able to fill the vacuum with its own influence on a Shia-led government? There are no easy answers, but the situation looks positive right now.

### Lebanon

The battle between Islamists and secularists in Lebanon is also relevant to Baku. The power of the moderate March 14 coalition government steadily eroded, in large part because it lacked real Western support. In contrast, its adversaries enjoyed full backing from Tehran and Damascus, including weapons and support for terrorist activities.

In the 2009 elections, Hezbollah and its allies did not win but gained enough votes to bargain for a coalition in which it had one-third of the power plus a veto on major policies. In the future, a combination of Hezbollah, Amal, Michel Aoun's Christian forces, pro-Syrian Sunni politicians and others could take over Lebanon, pushing the country into the Iran-Syria bloc and strengthening radical forces in the region. Some are willing to use a combination of force, bribery, and elections to make sure this happens. Another war resulting from Hezbollah's attacks on Israel would also destabilize the region.

### Pakistan

This issue also poses a paradox. On one hand, Pakistan is considered a friendly country for the West and especially the United States as well as an important ally in fighting al-Qaeda and the Taliban in neighboring

Afghanistan. Indeed, the United States depends on Pakistan to control the border and prevent terrorists like Osama bin Laden from finding safe haven among Pakistan's tribes. Consequently, it provides Pakistan with billions of dollars in aid and wants to ensure the current government's survival even when it is less than helpful on critical matters.

However, the Pakistani government has not been very cooperative. There is evidence that it has been less than energetic in trying to help find Afghanistani terrorists. Pakistan even released another top-priority enemy of regional stability and friend of radical Islamist forces, the rogue nuclear scientist Abdul Qadir Khan, from house arrest in February 2009, and then cut a deal to allow the Taliban to control the Swat Valley, near its own capital city.

Descent into anarchy or radical Islamism by Pakistan, especially given its possession of nuclear weapons, would be dangerous for Azerbaijan because it would give the Islamist side more assets and expand its power and influence.

**Other Factors**

In addition to the Islamist threats in specific countries, several regional issues also play a role. These include:

*The Israeli-Palestinian Conflict*

Though this conflict is of little direct importance to Azerbaijan, it is worth examining because it receives so much attention. It is beset by two myths. First, it seems that many people overestimate of the importance of the question, treating it as if it were the main problem of the region or at least the key to resolving all others. Actually, while regimes find the issue useful for proving their nationalist credentials and mobilizing mass support, Arab governments have little direct involvement in the conflict.

In the Middle East, all the usual principles of politics have not been suspended. Revolutionary movements, factions, and individuals seek power; different ideologies compete; countries strive for influence, hegemony, or survival. The Arab-Israeli conflict does not trump all these factors. Indeed,

Egypt and Jordan have opted out through peace treaties with Israel. These and other states have more pressing concerns. Even inasmuch as they would like to see the issue resolved, they do little to help but merely insist the West fix the problem for them. Indeed, the Arab states have not been very helpful in pursuing a resolution, as seen so visibly during the 1990s peace process. One reason is that they do not feel that ending the conflict – especially if that would cost them anything – is in fact such a high priority.

The second myth is that the issue can be quickly and easily settled. In fact, as the events of the 1993-2000 peace process showed, achieving any real progress is quite difficult. Today, there are many barriers, particularly from the Palestinian side. These include the continuing radicalism in Fatah; the overwhelming dominance of hardline views in educational, media and religious institutions; the weakness of the Palestinian Authority leadership; the lack of any real debate on Palestinian options; and a dozen other points. Most obvious of all is Hamas' control of one of the two sections of Palestinian-ruled territory, its rejection of all prior agreements, and its insistence on Israel's destruction and replacement by an Islamist Palestine.

It is clear that there is no quick fix for this dispute, and solving it is no panacea for the long list of other regional problems. Having said this, whether the Palestinian leadership is seized by Islamist Hamas is another important element figuring into the overall regional equation of the Islamist versus nationalist conflict. While a broader Arab-Israeli war is possible, it is very unlikely.

*Oil and Natural Gas*

The consistent availability of petroleum and natural gas at affordable prices is a major strategic and economic need for the industrialized world. This does not, of course, require the West to have direct control over these resources. Rather, what is important is constant access.

As such, it is preferable that control of oil resources does not fall to revolutionary Islamist. Most important is that no single country – notably Iran – be able to "turn off the tap" by controlling production levels or blocking transit routes. Both the 1991 and 2003 wars in Iraq were motivated in part by the need to prevent a radical regime from taking control over Gulf oil.

Here, Azerbaijan plays an important rule and, in contrast to other issues, a level of tension and instability in the Middle East makes Azerbaijan all the more central in providing alternative sources of supply.

With an at least temporary decline in prices from recently high levels, the problems of energy supply have become less urgent for the United States. Still, there is no major campaign to achieve energy independence or to develop alternative fuels, which means that the West will continue to rely on the Middle East for much of its energy. Consequently, oil will remain a central issue for Western involvements in the Middle East.

In addition to the effect of instability and conflict on petroleum and natural gas supplies, more radical regimes tend to be price hawks, while more moderate ones are more likely to invest in the West, engage in mutually profitable trade, and prefer lower prices because they take a longer-term perspective.

*The Growing Role of Russia*

Russia's reemergence on the Middle Eastern scene is, of course less alarming than its powerful role during the Soviet and Cold War days. Still, Moscow seems to put a priority on complicating US efforts by, for example, paying the Kyrgyzstan government to push America out of the Manas airbase so critical for supplying its forces in Afghanistan. Russia has also watered down UN sanctions on Iran and continued to supply that country with nuclear technology while becoming a major arms supplier for Syria.

Russian Middle East policy and involvement is of great importance to Azerbaijan. If Russia increasingly becomes aligned with Iran and Syria, as well as Armenia, this poses an increased threat to Azerbaijan. This is true not only because of the strengthening of radical forces and higher prospects for regional instability but also due to possible coordination of anti-Azerbaijan factors.

*Terrorism*

Of course, terrorism is not an ideology or a strategy in itself, but a means of waging war, building a mass of popular support, and intimidating real or potential opponents. At a minimum, the war against terrorism was a campaign to destroy al-Qaeda and overthrow the Taliban in Afghanistan. The Iraq invasion, although it overthrew a government that was a sponsor of terrorism, was in part related to Persian Gulf security. Yet extending the war on terrorism has often been essentially a distraction from the key issue: the battle against the radical Islamist forces that threaten to overthrow all regimes in the Middle East.

For Azerbaijan, as a relatively secular and Western-oriented state, the strengthening of terrorist groups and the legitimization of such methods in the Middle East, poses a threat. It is equally important that Western states take a strong stand against terrorist ideology and groups since Azerbaijan needs this support against subversive attacks, whether internal or cross-border.

## Solutions

The Islamist tidal wave is being ridden by Iran, Syria, Hamas and Hezbollah. It blocks a solution to the Arab-Israeli conflict, promotes terrorism, takes advantage of the weaknesses of the region's ruling dictatorships, and causes increases in the prices of oil and natural gas while threatening the supply. If Russia aligns with the radical Islamist bloc, the danger will increase further.

A key question will be what counter-forces emerge. The United States could, with European cooperation, unite all those who oppose radical Islamism and regional instability. A broad coalition must be assembled, consisting of European allies, Arab regimes, Israel and all the moderate forces that can be mustered within each country – including those who oppose the Iranian regime at home.

The optimum policy could be to make moderate regimes feel secure that America would support them, in order to toughen their resolve in the face of an enemy that threatens their very lives.

Unfortunately, the Obama administration's policy is the precise and exact opposite of what is needed. Instead of emphasizing the need to combat the radicals and reinforce the moderates, it focuses on conciliating the radicals, which undermines the moderates.

This basic strategy includes the following elements, though these may only ultimately characterize the administration's first year or two:

1.  Emphasizing engagement with radical forces, notably Iran and Syria. If the United States' sanctions fail to deter Iran from obtaining nuclear weapons, they will convince many regional states that Washington is not a reliable or effective ally, and that they must appease – or at least not displease – Iran.

2.  The effort to avoid friction with Russia even at the cost of unilateral concessions, albeit in the hope that they will be reciprocated in future.

3.  A declared ending of the "War on Terrorism" against all groups except al-Qaeda. It is not clear whether the United States would then view revolutionary groups seeking to subvert or overthrow the Azerbaijani government as enemies against whom it would take action.

4.  An emphasis on enhancing Obama's popularity with Muslims which – whatever its intentions – might play into the hands of Islamists.

5.  The effort to reach a quick resolution of the Arab-Israeli and Israeli-Palestinian conflict has already visibly failed.

Underlying this basic approach is a failure to create and lead a broad coalition of countries who oppose extremism and revolution. Instead, the emphasis is placed on engaging radicals, which will be viewed locally as strengthening these forces and undermining moderates. At least, radicals will use the time bought by American conciliation attempts to try to obtain nuclear weapons, gain control over Lebanon and Iraq, consolidate their leverage among the Palestinians, and bring Turkey into cooperation with them.

Here is the central point and problem for the United States: its interests and allies are increasingly menaced by a growing threat, whose existence, meaning and scope, current US policy does not even recognize yet, much less counter effectively.

# PART FOUR:

## CONFLICT RESOLUTION PROSPECTS AND NEW REGIONAL SECURITY ARCHITECTURE

# OPPORTUNITIES GAINED AND LOST: SOUTH CAUCASUS SECURITY SINCE INDEPENDENCE

Gerard Libaridian,
Professor of History,
University of Michigan

The South Caucasus along with the Baltic states, came into prominence worldwide at about the same time as the unification of Germany and the dissolution of the Warsaw Pact were progressing. To be sure, the Caucasus was not as significant then for the remainder of the international community as Central and Eastern Europe were; nonetheless the rise of popular movements in the Caucasus indicated that the USSR might have been weaker and more vulnerable than unrest on the Western front indicated.

For the international community, in this case meaning the Western world, the South Caucasus acquired a strategic significance as a region somewhat late. Cornered between Russia, Turkey and Iran and cut off for decades from its Near Eastern geography, the emerging republics of Armenia, Azerbaijan and Georgia initially presented a collective challenge. They were not viewed as individual states moved by their own dynamics or by an inter-state dynamics that encouraged collective policies or paths of evolution. That is, the region was a region despite what the inhabitants and masters of the region thought and did. Even for Turkey and Iran, immediate neighbors of the region and historically connected to it in various ways, the Soviet period was one when the Caucasus could be forgotten; all was determined in Moscow. To be fair, Washington remembered the Soviet republics of Armenia, Azerbaijan and Georgia briefly in 1979, during the presidency of Jimmy Carter; during that year his National Security Advisor, Zbigniew Brzezinski, and his deputy, Paul Henze, organized a one day conference in Washington, DC on the region. It was an intelligent though mild attempt to bring that region to the attention of policy makers in the US capital.

Almost two decades of development of and experimentation with foreign and security policies by Armenia, Azerbaijan and Georgia should indicate that ultimately their security will depend on their ability to resolve the problems between themselves and with their immediate neighbors. The initial impulse and lingering tendency to rely on outside forces did not stop a war involving Armenia and Azerbaijan, militarized conflicts in Abkhazia and South Ossetia at the start of this period, and a war between Georgia and Russia more recently. The first three episodes were directly related to local conflicts, while the last was occasioned by them.

In attempting to understand this region and project its future, we often focus on the fault lines, which that area represents on the larger map of history: a region that separates Europe from Asia; a sharp point of contact between Islam and Christianity; a region at the crossroads of East and West, North and South, whatever these terms may mean in any given context. The history of relations between the three major ethnic groups – Armenians, Azerbaijanis and Georgians – as indeed between major and small groups has been troublesome. Differences of language and religion and strong senses of nationalism have often been pointed out as sources of conflict and antagonism that are insurmountable.

However, one has to be careful not to view these factors as fatal and irreparable fault lines. It is not pre-determined that differences in language and religion will produce irreconcilable differences, or antagonisms and nationalist ideologies that are mutually exclusive and lead to war.

For those who took charge of these republics between 1988 and 1991, there was no escaping the geopolitical considerations, the implications of Caspian hydro-carbon resources, and expectations of grand futures, thought to be independent and prosperous. Yet, in addition to independence and freedom, the dynamics of history included secessionist movements, economic collapse and massive social and political transformations.

The period immediately following independence was not conducive to thinking about regional concerns and long-term security interests. In

Georgia, Zviad Gamsakhurdia – the country's first democratically-elected President – developed rhetoric and policies that alienated significant non-Georgian groups in the country, including Abkhazians, South Ossetians, Armenians and Azeris; his approach to state and nation building ensured that Russia and others would regard Georgia as a hostile future neighbor. In Azerbaijan Abulfaz Elchibey – the first post-Soviet Azeri President – antagonized Russia and Iran, manifestly considering Azerbaijan a mere extension of Turkey, while attempting to drive Armenians of Nagorno Karabakh out of their homes for their expressed desire to be part of Armenia. Armenia's first post-Communist leader, Levon Ter-Petrossian, adjusted the country's policies regarding Nagorno Karabakh – moving from a demand for unification to the more flexible principle of support for the security of Armenians there and their right to self-determination. Moreover, while seeking to normalize relations with Turkey, he also insisted on maintaining the security umbrella of Russia, considering the relations with Ankara to be uncertain.

With all its problems and faults, the Soviet system constituted a security system for all concerned in the region, a system that came to an end with the fragmentation and fracturing of the USSR. Whether we consider it imposed or otherwise, the Soviet Union kept peace in the region until its last couple of years, when it started falling apart from within. Governing constituent republics of the Soviet federation, the leaders of Armenia, Azerbaijan and Georgia thought it was their mandate to maintain the status quo, i.e., "brotherly" relations with their neighbors – particular local inequities were deemed insignificant compared with the larger picture of peace, stability and development that the system provided through the Communist Party of which they were part. Autonomous republics and regions within constituent republics by and large had acquiesced to the Soviet arrangement as it provided for an authority above the republican center: the Abkhaz and South Ossetians could always appeal to Moscow above and beyond Tbilisi, just as Armenians in Karabakh could appeal to the Soviet capital, above and beyond Baku.

The increasing demands for a larger share of power by the constituent republics entailed a similar move by the autonomous republics and regions, a process that contributed to the weakening of the center and, consequently, to the sense of insecurity. The weakening and then the demise of Moscow as the ultimate authority created a vacuum, which each unit tried to fill in its own way, though the larger tendency was gravitating toward centers outside the region – Moscow, Ankara, and beyond to Brussels and Washington.

## Popular Movements Challenge the Soviet System

Though to different degrees and by differing formulas of mixture, in all three republics the popular movements were sustained by anti-imperialism, anti-Russianism, and anti-Communism. As a result, in all three republics, independence, national regeneration, democracy and even the free market system were the answers to the future.

The oppositional movement in Armenia, first manifest in an environmental demonstration at the end of 1987, returned with a force in 1988 in support of the demand by Nagorno Karabakh Armenians to have their autonomous region attached to Armenia. Within a few months the "Karabakh Movement" had been transformed into a force for democratic, economic and social renewal and, eventually, independence.

In Georgia, the Round Table-Free Georgia reformist coalition came into prominence and led Zviad Gamsakhurdia into the presidency. By 1992, the nationalist leader, elected overwhelmingly, was hounded out of office after showing serious signs of movement toward dictatorial rule and having contributed, at least in part, to the rise of the secessionist movements in Abkhazia and South Ossetia.

In Azerbaijan the Azerbaijani Popular Front and reborn Musavat Party claimed the street and eventually placed Abulfaz Elchibey in the presidency. Similar to his counterpart in Georgia, Elchibey's nationalist ideology drove the Karabakh conflict toward full militarization, declared Russia and Iran mortal enemies and Turkey the eternal friend. Elchibey was driven out of office in 1993.

In Azerbaijan and Georgia, the leaderships were replaced by the former communist bosses of these republics, Heydar Aliyev and Eduard Shevardnadze, respectively. Both leaders brought some kind of a balance to their foreign and domestic policies and instituted a degree of pragmatism.

It was only in Armenia that the initial leaders of the popular democratic movement remained in power. Their anti-imperial instincts were tempered by Armenia's security needs regarding Turkey. With regard to the Karabakh problem, the government of Levon Ter-Petrossian moved toward arguing not for annexation but for negotiations with Azerbaijan based on the need to reconcile the two principles of territorial integrity and the right of peoples to self-determination. The Ter-Petrossian administration had also declared its policy of seeking the normalization of relations with Turkey without pre-conditions.

Thus it took a number of domestic crises, conflicts and wars for the promises of the independence and renewal movements to be crystallized. This brings the narrative to the year when the opportunities for regional cooperation were at their highest and were, by and large, lost – 1995.

**Opportunities following the cease-fires**

The cease-fire agreements reached in 1994, addressing the three militarized conflicts in the region – Abkhazia, South Ossetia and Nagorno Karabakh – proved durable. President Heydar Aliyev was able to stabilize the internal situation in Azerbaijan, having neutralized a restless military commander and taken charge of the state apparatus; Aliyev was working hard on the development of the country's hydrocarbon resources and their transport to international markets. President Eduard Shevardnadze was close to stabilizing Georgia, having eliminated para-military elements and warlords who had brought him to power. Levon Ter-Petrossian, in Armenia, had eliminated any threat of para-military activity in 1990 and headed a stable country that tolerated an active opposition.

Furthermore, all three presidents could claim a comfortable degree of legitimacy. Despite the extra-legal means by which Aliyev and Shevardnadze had achieved power, both had been welcome by their peoples and elected comfortably in 1993 and 1995, respectively, as presidents with enough authority to secure an atmosphere within which it was possible to look at the future. Ter-Petrossian had been elected in 1991 with an overwhelming majority; although he had lost some support mainly due to economic hardships and the effect of the Karabakh war, he felt confident enough to reverse the economic collapse, deepen the systemic economic reforms initiated earlier, and focus on the resolution of the Nagorno Karabakh problem.

The focus on the conflicts in the region and failure to resolve them has obscured two important dimensions. Firstly, the three presidents shared a moderation with regard to the problems they were facing and a revulsion of extreme nationalism. In fact, they shared the ability to make good judgments and to be circumspect. Both characteristics were vital due to the fragility of their young states, the fragility of the peace processes and the vulnerability of the region to external stimuli. Though they were successful politicians, the three presidents emerged also as statesmen with a deep sense of their regional identity and interests.

**A Wide Spectrum of Agreement**

The second dimension, which is a result of the first and validates that assessment, was their agreement on a wide spectrum of issues, especially regarding foreign and security policies. In this sense, 1995 was a good year for the region because the respite from instability and wars provided an opportunity for the three leaders to think of the future of their countries, the relevance of the region to them, and the larger problems that would define the perimeters of their security, stability and long-term development.

If we consider 1995 as the first year of stability in the region, this is what we find:

All three presidents were committed to state building rather than nationalist ideology as the ultimate goal, and they had determined that the conflicts needed to be resolved; by and large they had ruled out the use of force to do so. Shevardnadze relied on diplomacy and negotiations to achieve reunification; Aliyev added diplomatic and economic pressure to find a solution. All three realized that important concessions had to be made for solutions to be found and did not rule out interim or temporary solutions.

While aware of mutual differences and historical antagonisms, all three presidents could see the significance of geography and that they were condemned to live together; they could not imagine a future without some form of close cooperation, or possibly even political and economic association. Azerbaijan was ready to see its oil pipeline go to Turkey through Armenia and, in fact, may have preferred that route, should the Karabakh issue be resolved. Such a possibility was formulated by Azerbaijan and the United States as a quid pro quo: Armenia would agree to concessions on the Karabakh issue in return for the pipeline. This formulation made the offer appear as a bribe for concessions, which the Armenian side may or may not have been ready to make; it made the offer politically unpalatable. The Armenian side insisted on negotiating the terms of a solution to the conflict on its merits and leaving aside extraneous issues, as interested as Armenia was in becoming the transit country for Azerbaijan's oil exports. Nonetheless Aliyev's vision for the future did not preclude such close association with Armenia in an area as critical as its oil exports.

All three presidents regarded integration in European structures as the ideal future – a European type of society constituting their vision of the state. The paths chosen to achieve that goal differed as did the level and depth of the commitment of each to democratic principles. At the least, all three accepted being judged by European standards.

All three wished to maintain good relations with Russia, concerns regarding Russian goals notwithstanding, especially in Georgia and Azerbaijan. Shevardnadze and Aliyev set aside the virulent anti-Russian rhetoric of their predecessors, Zviad Gamsakhurdia and Abulfaz Elchibey, respectively, and adopted a more realistic attitude based not only on power relations but also on an appreciation of Russia's legitimate concerns. Armenia had always maintained close relations with Russia; their divorce had been a friendly one. All three were members of the Commonwealth of Independent States and, until 1999, signatories to the Collective Security Treaty led by Russia, although Azerbaijan and Georgia had become part of that treaty somewhat under duress in 1993.

All three maintained normal relations with the Islamic Republic of Iran, though Azerbaijan was dissatisfied by Iran's role in the conflict over the Karabakh issue. Nonetheless Aliyev discarded his predecessor's anti-Iranian and irredentist policies of wishing to annex northern Iran. Unlike his predecessor Elchibey, Aliyev did not see Turkish ethnicity as the determining factor of the identity of his people; he emphasized, rather, an Azerbaijani identity.

All three maintained or wished to establish normal relations with Turkey. Turkey had recognized the independence of all three republics and established diplomatic relations with Azerbaijan and Georgia. Armenia and Turkey initiated negotiations for the normalization of relations between them in the summer of 1992; despite serious historical and political antagonisms, Ter-Petrossian had adopted a policy of normalizing relations with Turkey without preconditions, inviting much criticism from some Armenian quarters but also overcoming probably the thorniest impediment to the relations of the three republics with their immediate neighbors. In April 1993, following the extension of Armenian military control over Azerbaijan's Kelbajar district, Turkey linked normalization of relations with Armenia to a solution or, at the least, serious steps toward a resolution of the Karabakh conflict, in support of Azerbaijan.

All three developed relations with NATO, first through the North Atlantic Cooperation Council, and later the Partnership for Peace (PfP) program. The menu of joint activities with NATO that each republic adopted might have been longer for Georgia and shorter for Armenia. Yet even Armenia made clear that it did not view its membership in the Russian-led Collective Security treaty as a limiting factor to Yerevan's general concept of national security, nor did it view NATO as an antagonistic structure. Armenia may have needed strategic relations with Russia, but did not feel that such relations limited its option of developing relations with the West or all of its neighbors.

All three were weary of the Kurdish issue, which was critical for Turkey, Iran and the wider Near East. Armenian sympathies for the fate of Kurds and full recognition of its Kurdish minority did not translate into a policy of support for the PKK in Turkey, however.

Both Armenia and Azerbaijan were careful not to encourage the secessionist tendencies of their respective Armenian and Azeri minorities in Georgia, thus leaving the Karabakh problem the only conflict between any of two of the three republics, an anomaly rather than the rule.

By and large both Armenia and Azerbaijan labored hard to make sure the Nagorno Karabakh conflict was not perceived as a religious conflict; in this effort, they had a partner in Iran, whose neutrality, however much resented by Azerbaijan, contributed to keeping religion out of the definition of the conflict.

Although speaking altogether unrelated languages, the Presidents and the elites in the three republics used Russian as a lingua franca in their discussions and communications. This was a fact that stressed their common history of the last two centuries, the promotion of national histories in each republic notwithstanding.

All three republics were careful not to engage deeply in the Israeli-Palestinian conflict. Georgia and Azerbaijan may have developed closer relations with Israel than Armenia did, while Armenia had better relations with the Arab countries and Iran. But that conflict was not internalized and did not become a determining factor in the security concept of the three republics.

All three projected a security system that was based, ultimately, on the resolution of conflicts and close cooperation between them.

Thus, if for a moment we leave aside the Karabakh conflict, we see a remarkable spectrum of agreement between the three republics on major issues relevant to them and to the wider Near East, of which they are part. Differences were limited to degree and emphasis; none would have prevented them from pursuing a common foreign policy.

This wide spectrum of agreement evolved despite the differences in ethnicity, language and religion, despite the long history of antagonisms, and despite the renationalization of cultures. The areas of agreement also evolved without collective work or extensive consultation between them; it was the result of the maturity and circumspection of the three leaders and the considerable forces behind them in their respective countries.

There was even a degree of agreement on the difficult problem of Karabakh. Although, on occasion, Heydar Aliyev did evoke his country's ultimate right to resort to the use of force should negotiations fail, he believed that the problem should and could be resolved through diplomacy; in direct negotiations with the Armenian side in July and August of 1994, he had agreed that the cease-fire agreement brokered by Russia and signed earlier in May that same year was a permanent cease-fire, one that would be effective until the signing of a larger political agreement. The Armenian side had no reason to resort to a military solution, since it had the advantage on the ground. The more important point here is that the concessions Ter-Petrossian was ready to make, if Azerbaijan had reached a similar point in its evolving position, would have been sufficient to solve that problem too.

**Personalities Matter**

Both capable Communist party leaders, Aliyev and Shevardnadze had matured as politicians and master bureaucrats in their own republics, and had gone on to achieve USSR-level positions. Aliyev was removed by Gorbachev as KGB chief and Politburo member; Shevardnadze was elevated to a federal position by Gorbachev and would eventually resign that position in protest against the hardening of the Soviet leader's domestic policies. Aliyev and Shevardnadze returned from obscurity to take charge of the republics they had left behind for Moscow. The devoted Communists from the despised Caucasus region returned as saviors of their republics, moving then on the nationalist track for collisions with the others' nationalisms.

Aliyev and Shevardnadze returned to their republics – the first for being too conservative and the second for being too liberal – and ended up with the same synthesis: there was something valuable in the overrated internationalism of the Soviet era. Yet, something in the nationalism of their countrymen, beyond the desire for independence, had mired them in conflicts that could have been avoided or dealt with differently. Both ended up with the concept of state building – the very old and very new nation-state and, in their case, the state-nation.

Aliyev and Shevardnadze charted a middle ground between whatever they could rescue from the obtuse and discredited internationalism of the Soviet absurd and the nationalism that replaced it in their republics.

The youngest of the three presidents, Ter-Petrossian of Armenia, had not held any political office and was not even a member of the Communist Party when he became one of the leaders of the national movement in Armenia in 1988, led the country to independence and became its first president. Ter-Petrossian and his colleagues had reached the same conclusion as to the primacy of statehood and state-building from a completely different perspective than his colleagues in Georgia and Azerbaijan: a radical re-reading of Armenian history and the security challenges the Armenian people had faced in its long history. Ter-Petrossian and his colleagues had debunked the myth of Armenian security being based on the "eternal friendship" with Russia and its threat coming from the "eternal enemy," Turkey. This was a revolution in Armenian political thinking that brought Armenia's position close to that of its two neighbors and would make "regional thinking" possible.

Anyone who observed the interaction between the three presidents when they met at regional or international gatherings, beyond joint official statements or the lack thereof, could sense or should have sensed the significance of special historical moments – three kindred minds, though not kindred personalities.

There were, then, also no personality clashes between these three leaders. All three were endowed with large but secure egos; they were aware of the place history would assign them in the building of their countries; and, in their case, that awareness acted as a brake on any temptation to adopt extremism or brinkmanship.

It was possible to imagine that the combination of the wide spectrum of agreement on foreign policy issues and the personalities of these three presidents could have produced joint statements on a common foreign policy more often than even members of the European Union could.

### 1995 Was a Good Year

That would have been the only way to counteract the sense the three presidents and others had that, while the larger Cold War had ended, a mini cold war continued, as applied to the South Caucasus region where both Russia and the United States acted as the Great Powers did in the 19th century. It is also true that, each in his own way, the three presidents tried to maximize their benefits from the big players. Clearly, Washington and Brussels had replaced Moscow as the center that must be engaged, at least as far as Azerbaijan and Georgia were concerned. These centers of power would provide technology and capital needed for the exploitation and transportation of hydrocarbon resources as well as forces to balance the Russian advantage in the region. Even Armenia's quest for normalization of relations with Turkey was based on a dual consideration: not only to diminish any threat Turkey might represent by normalizing relations, but also, by doing so, diminish the degree of dependence on Russia for its security.

1995 was a good year for the South Caucasus because of the opportunities it presented for the development of a sense of regional identity. And the development of a regional identity was critical for the welfare of the three republics and the peoples in the region, particularly for the ability to help shape their own destinies. Their destiny would no longer have to be shaped, for the most part, by larger regional and international forces that had already designated the region as an arena for competition and rivalry.

**Obstacles and Loss of Opportunities**

We can now ask the question: why was this rare opportunity offered in 1995 not realized?

Clearly, it was difficult for many of the players in the new great game to see the opportunity the coincident concurrency of these three presidencies provided. Even Germany, which tried hard to shape a European policy that would compel the three countries to act jointly when dealing with Europe, was not conscious of the underlying strength of such a policy; Germany perceived regional cooperation as a policy that needed be imposed from above for practical reasons rather than for a policy that had indigenous foundations and needed to be nurtured.

One can also argue that even the three presidents themselves were not fully conscious to what extent they agreed on so many issues; when localized, their thinking was focused on the conflicts; when looking at the international arena, their concern was how to make their country relevant to the big players, and how to prevent becoming fully dependent on one state; after all, that was the meaning of independence. The localized and international thinking met on two levels: how to connect to the international community to assure maximal support for their efforts to reset their shattered economies; and how to use the international community in support of their solution to the conflicts.

These points of junction lead us to the policies of the regional and international players themselves toward the South Caucasus.

My first argument was already introduced above: neighboring and geographically more distant powers by and large viewed the region as an arena where their interests collided with those of others, where increased influence of one power meant the decrease of the power of another or others. Even the most disinterested of the powers – the EU, which preached the religion of regionalism – was still made up of members who tried to exploit the benefits of their influence on one or the other country. Most external powers continued to look at the region in terms of how it could contribute to their national interest. The "it" here could be the whole region or one single country; if the interest was in the Caspian hydro carbon resources, Azerbaijan was important. If the interest consisted in the transport of Caspian oil to the West, bypassing Russia and Iran, then the interest consisted in engaging either Armenian or Georgia. Either one would do. If the transit country could not be Armenia, Georgia would do and Armenia could become, for all practical purposes, irrelevant, except to make sure it does not destabilize the region. Regardless, that value was centered in the perception of each capital of the value of the South Caucasus. By definition, therefore, the region itself and how its leaders might imagine their future was relevant to the external forces only to the extent that such visions might run counter to the strategic functions and roles assigned to these republics by the strategic thinking of the external powers.

For the regional and more distant powers, the Nagorno Karabakh conflict was not just another obstacle to more propitious developments in the region; it was not just another independent variable that was difficult to manage because of the hard-line positions of the parties to the conflict; the resolution of the conflict was made more difficult because of the use of the conflict by external powers for pursuing their own interests through their involvement in the conflict resolution process. The question on the missed opportunity of 1995 is reduced then to a question on why was it not possible to resolve the Karabakh problem or, at the least, make serious progress beyond the maintenance of the cease-fire. At the least, outside powers looked upon the conflict from the perspective of their larger interests; whether a solution was desired or not depended on that perspective. More commonly, the character and content of proposed solutions were measured by the degree to which their interests would be promoted or harmed.

Specifically, while all concerned professed their goal of achieving peace in the region, major players were reluctant to support any solution to the Karabakh conflict that might have reduced their influence or increased the influence of the "other." This was true of the US as well as of Russia, of Turkey as well as of Iran. When in a weaker position in the international arena, Russia was reluctant to use its influence to solve the problem since, under the circumstances, a solution might lead to the loss of its influence in the region. More often than not, analysts have thought Russia was weak in general, since it was weak relative to the US and the West in general. For this mistaken and ill-fated notion, the Caucasus countries and peoples as well as the West have paid very dearly: from Chechnya in the 1990s, to Georgia in the summer of 2008.

Of the major players in the region, Russia is the best positioned to compel the Armenian side to make concessions. And, in the medium-term and long-term, peace, as opposed to the existing cease-fire, depends on concessions on the ground by the Armenian side.

An ascendant US during the 1990s decided to become a major player in the region, and the role of a mediator in the Karabakh conflict (membership in the OSCE Minsk Group) provided that initial opportunity. From that point on, statements to the contrary notwithstanding, the US viewed the great game at least in this region as a zero sum game: for the US to gain, Russia had to lose. In addition to a schizophrenic policy toward Russia, the US had plans for Caspian Sea hydrocarbon resources and NATO expansion, and a sanctions policy toward Iran.

Turkey subjected its South Caucasus policy to identity politics. Instead of rising to the occasion and recognizing Armenia's readiness to establish diplomatic relations without preconditions, Turkey decided to link the process to the settlement of the Karabakh problem, thus making Turkish policy hostage to Azerbaijani intransigence and, in fact, inviting such intransigence. That linkage, while giving successive Turkish governments short-term political security, diminished Turkey's ability to be a full strength regional player and certainly made it impossible for that country to become a major intermediary in the conflict. It is difficult to determine whether this policy was due to the weak coalition governments that succeeded each other or to an exaggerated sense of what that policy of continuing closed borders with Armenia could accomplish. The fact remains that such a policy did not contribute to the resolution of the conflict; compared to Russia and Iran, Turkey looked very much like a party to the conflict.

That issue continues to create problems even after Armenia and Turkey signed two protocols in October 2009 for the establishment and development of normal relations and opening of the border, protocols that do not directly refer to the conflict.

Despite its religious affinities with the majority of the population in Azerbaijan, Iran was able to transcend identity politics and pursue a neutral policy in the region; at one point in 1992, it emerged as the mediator in the conflict. That effort was torpedoed by Russia, the US and Turkey – separately, but equally forcefully. Increasingly Iran viewed Azerbaijan as a rival oil and gas exporter with competing claims on some offshore fields in the Caspian. Subsequently, Iran looked upon the status quo as the best solution, lest a solution increase US and/or Turkish influence or even bring NATO into the region. An Azerbaijan freed of its Karabakh wound may be ready for NATO; and Armenia would have less need for Iran.

The regional powers and the US did not disabuse the governments of the region from their notion that they each could translate their leaning toward one or the other outside powers into diplomatic or military advantages in their conflicts with secessionist regions.

Within a short few years, there were significant changes also within the region as two of the three republics witnessed regime changes that also produced important policy changes.

Armenia's Ter-Petrossian was compelled to submit his resignation in early 1998 under pressure from power ministries led by Prime Minister Robert Kocharian; Ter-Petrossian had accepted a Minsk Group proposal for the resolution of the Nagorno Karabakh conflict as a basis for negotiations, a proposal that involved significant compromises but ensured the security of Karabakh and its people. Kocharian, former leader of Karabakh, became president of Armenia. In a formal way he continued Armenia's foreign policy in all matters except for an uncompromising line on Karabakh and raising the issue of Genocide recognition by Turkey to the level of state policy. But these two items were sufficient to sabotage the rest of his policies, at the least making them less credible and certainly less practicable or meaningful. At the end, the Kocharian policies made Armenia far more dependent on Russia and kept Armenia out of regional and international development projects.

Kocharian would replace Ter-Petrossian as president and rule for a decade without a realistic strategy for the resolution of the Karabakh conflict while complicating discussions with Turkey by catering to a particular form diasporan mentality.

In Georgia, Shevardnadze was removed by a group of young leaders he had brought to power, supported by street demonstrators, in 2003. The reasons given in this case of rebellion were authoritarianism, corruption, and lack of national will and leadership. The new president, Mikheil Saakashvili, while formally maintaining the outline of his predecessor's foreign policy, introduced two changes: integration of the secessionist states by any means; and, making Georgia's membership in NATO the linchpin of his strategy and Georgia's security. But, as in the case of Armenia, these two changes made all other dimensions of his foreign policy quite irrelevant, statements to the contrary notwithstanding.

Shevardnadze was replaced by Mikheil Saakashvili, whose harsh anti-Russian rhetoric, ideologized NATO aspirations and brinkmanship with use of army power would provide Russia with the excuse to humiliate Georgia in 2008.

The problem with the changes in Armenia and Georgia was quite clear, though possibly not clearly seen: Armenia insisted on its independence and an independent policy vis-à-vis Europe and the US while pursuing a policy that made it more and more dependent on Russia in more and more areas; and Georgia insisted on independence from Russia and did so by offering to be completely dependent on the US and NATO.

### Regional Cooperation: A Victim of Circumstance?

For all practical purposes, the possibility of a regional cooperative effort based on a common perception of foreign policy issues became impossible. That impossibility was secured by recklessness in Armenia and Georgia. In Armenia, recklessness consisted of the belief that no change was the best policy; in Georgia, it consisted of the belief that change at any cost and at any price was the best policy.

In both cases there was a connection between the changes introduced. Offering oneself to the US and NATO was supposed to provide security and support in brinkmanship: Georgia "belongs" to NATO and the US and, therefore, if for any reason, including those related to its secessionist states, its sovereignty is violated by Russia, NATO and the US will come to its assistance. In Armenia, the hope for support was not for any action it might take regarding the resolution of the Karabakh problem, but its inaction. That is, should there be pressure to compel Armenia to accept a resolution of the Karabakh problem that required any changes on the ground, Russia would secure Armenia's back.

Both Armenia and Georgia were mistaken, of course. When the Georgian strategy was tested in the short war of the summer of 2008, the US failed to provide military assistance. And Russia, feeling more secure and aggressive, has been able to compel Armenia to accept concessions that it would not have otherwise accepted in the case of the Karabakh conflict, for the right price, which at the present appears to be eventual Russian control of the strategic Lachin corridor.

After the decade of a de facto policy of preserving the status quo followed by his predecessor Robert Kocharian, Armenia's new president, Serzh Sargsyan, has in a very awkward manner, and at least on paper, returned to active diplomacy. This year, Sargsyan's foreign minister signed the two protocols that provide the framework for the establishment and development of diplomatic relations with Turkey, 20 years after the foundation was laid for a pragmatic regional policy in Armenia. The question is whether attempting to normalize relations with Turkey before serious progress is made in the resolution of the Karabakh conflict was a practical one. Events proved otherwise, and neither problem has been resolved, as of this writing.

Interestingly, Azerbaijan is the one country that has shown continuity of policies in general, even when with Heydar Aliyev's death, his son Ilham Aliyev succeeded him. Though largely inexperienced and less authoritative than his father, Ilham Aliyev has proven to be an adept pragmatic politician and diplomat.

There have been a number of opportunities for the settlement of a given conflict in the history of post-Soviet Caucasus that can be considered lost. The resolution of the regional conflicts could also have provided an impetus to the processes of democratization: the imbalance in state budgets favoring defense expenditures, the increasing significance of the military establishment, the incendiary politics of conflict resolution requiring undemocratic methods of control would eventually decrease and the initial vision may be restored gradually.

This article tries to indicate that there are also larger moments, moments that may go unnoticed and unmarked by major events, bounded by the better know dates. With some imagination and political will, much more than a single conflict could have been resolved; 1995 and possibly a year or two following it constituted such a "moment" when the larger congruencies could have driven the actors to resolve the specific conflicts because the list of benefits ready to be harvested was far longer.

This does not mean that diplomatic activities diminished following that moment – 1995-1997. Indeed, one can see more activities and ideas generated toward the end of the decade. Initiatives by Russia, Georgia, the

European Union and the US abounded, each engendering conferences and meetings, declarations of principles and expressions of good will. But these were well-intentioned schemes that failed to provide for the resolution of the Karabakh conflict; the visions and benefits of peaceful coexistence were not sufficient – and, could not have been, on their own, sufficient – to transcend the real problems that remained to be resolved.

Since that unmarked year of 1995, we have also witnessed the recognition of Kosovo as an independent state by most of the West, which at least contributed to Russia's recognition of the independence of Abkhazia and South Ossetia. One cannot say with certainty that such recognition marks the solution of these two conflicts. It is clear, though, that these two conflicts do not involve Armenia and Azerbaijan, neither of which followed Russia in its policy regarding these regions. It is clear, however, that these partial recognitions of secessionist states have made the solution to the others much more difficult.

The Nagorno Karabakh issue clearly remains the main obstacle to the development of regional cooperation and consolidation. Negotiations since the assumption of power in Armenia by Serzh Sargsyan seem to be more serious than any during the last decade. The main obstacle there seems to be the inclusion of some wording that would refer to the methodology of determining the status of the territory in the future – a compromise between the "step-by-step" and "package deal" approaches. It is easy to imagine that the parties cannot find a common language when they are trying to pre-determine the outcome of any "referendum" or "expression of the will of the people," even while pretending not to do so. Once parties recognize that acceptable wording to both sides must indicate an uncertain future status for the territory – the core problem – solutions to the conflict become possible. Such an understanding is necessary, though not sufficient, for peace to break out and for regional cooperation to be possible.

The resolution of the Karabakh problem will be necessary for the development of a real security policy that, as indicated earlier, cannot be just a regional policy. It is necessary to recognize opportunities when they arise and manifest political will as well as wisdom. Regional or international actors can contribute to the security of these republics or to a system developed by them; they cannot, in the long run, constitute the basis of such a security system.

# A LANDSCAPE AFTER THE BATTLE: THE VARIABLE GEOPOLITICS OF THE SOUTH CAUCASUS

**Dmitri Trenin,**
Director,
Carnegie Moscow Center

This chapter will assess the changes in the geopolitical landscape of the South Caucasus following the Russo-Georgian war over South Ossetia; analyze the prospects for further evolution of relations among the local, regional and global actors in the Caucasus area; and conclude, somewhat arrogantly, perhaps, with a set of ideas, or "recommendations" to policy-makers in the relevant countries.

## Situation Assessment

The Russo-Georgian war of August 2008 was brief. It did not change the world, as some feared, but it has ushered in a new phase in the post-imperial – i.e. post-Soviet – evolution of the Caucasus. The principal features of this phase include: a palpable decrease in Washington's interest in the South Caucasus; an even more marked rise in Turkey's regional activism, exemplified by Ankara's contacts with Armenia; the European Union's growing institutional proximity to the countries in its eastern neighborhood, moderated, however, by the EU's uncertainty as to what its role ought actually to be; Russia's somewhat disjointed approach to the South Caucasus, against the background of growing instability in its own North Caucasus borderlands; Abkhazia's subtly modified independence agenda – now, increasingly, vis-à-vis Russia; South Ossetia's utter failure at nation-building; Georgia's growing frustration, both domestic and international; and a fresh attempt by outsiders at promoting a provisional settlement for Nagorno-Karabakh, which so far has left the parties to the conflict confused.

The Obama administration has reset the entire foreign policy agenda of the George W. Bush era. US diplomacy has been refocused toward core American national interests and the US's global and regional priorities that derive from them. The strange situation in which Washington's support for Georgia's Rose Revolution came to mean essentially a compensation for the collapse of the Republican administration's democracy promotion agenda in the Greater Middle East is no more. President Obama and the Democrats, of course, stand by Georgia's territorial integrity and continue to support Tbilisi, including in the military sphere, but they refuse to see the Saakashvili government as a beacon of democracy in that part of the world. While Vice President Joe Biden traveled to Tbilisi in 2009 as part of a region-wide tour, Barack Obama has been holding Mikheil Saakashvili at an arm's length. In the context of an improved US-Russian relationship, differences between Washington and Moscow over Georgia have been bracketed, and the US side has gone out of its way to reassure the Russians that the US-Georgian collaboration poses no danger to Russia. Most importantly, while the promise of NATO membership given to Georgia and Ukraine at the 2008 NATO Summit in Bucharest has not been withdrawn, it is widely understood that there will be no movement toward that goal in the foreseeable future – which may well mean within the lifetime of the Obama administration.

For some time now, Turkey has been on the rise as a regional power. Frustrated by the European Union's continued unwillingness to embrace its country as a member, the Turkish leadership has decided to demonstrate Ankara's geopolitical prowess and economic clout and thus confound the European naysayers. This may not necessarily be the best accession strategy on behalf of Turkey, but – quite apart from the EU issue – Turkey has emerged as a major actor at the juncture of Europe and the Middle East. Within its expanded geopolitical horizons, Ankara sees the South Caucasus as a region where it should naturally play an enhanced, more pro-active role. Even as hostilities were still raging between Russia and Georgia, President Gul traveled to Moscow to present his stability plan for the South Caucasus. In the following year, a series of bi-lateral summits led to a breakthrough in Turkish-Armenian relations. The process has paused just short of a full normalization of the historically afflicted relations and the lifting of the economic blockade imposed on Armenia by Turkey at the height of the Karabakh war in 1993. Characteristically of this bolder approach, Turkey even shrugged off Azerbaijan's concerns over its rapprochement with Armenia: Ankara no longer wants to be boxed in a certain corner or pinned down to a certain position in a region so close and so important to itself. What it wants now is access to all, freedom of maneuver and regional leadership. In its dealings with Russia and Iran in particular, Turkey has also demonstrated its ambition to become an economic powerhouse and an energy hub at the crossroads of Europe and the Greater Middle East.

The European Union, during – or rather due to - its French Presidency in the second half of 2008, became directly involved in negotiating an end to hostilities in the Russo-Georgian crisis over South Ossetia. With the departure in 2008 of both the UN and the OSCE missions from the zones of conflict in Akhazia and South Ossetia, EU monitors, now de facto dispatched only to Georgia proper, became the only third-party observers in the area. However, the EU's structural deficiencies prevented the Union from playing a more serious, and sustained part in the regional developments. While President Nicolas Sarkozy of France mediated between Moscow and Tbilisi, several Central and Eastern European leaders paraded their solidarity with Georgia. When France was succeeded by the Czech Republic at the helm of the EU, Europe's role diminished considerably. Part of the time it was presiding over the Union, Prague did not even have a government.

It is also true, however, that the Czech Presidency was marked by the launch in May 2009 of the EU's Eastern Partnership (EaP) with six ex-Soviet countries, three of them in the South Caucasus. The fate of the project however will depend on whether it will be seen – above all by the EU itself – as an early bid for integrating those countries with Europe, or a means of keeping them at a safe distance from the already widely expanded Union. The ratification of the Lisbon Treaty by the end of 2009 and the uninspiring choices for the EU President and its Foreign Minister have suggested that the Union still prefers to be less than the sum of its member states. This may be the only way a consensus could be reached within the EU, but the result was certainly not lost on Europe's partners.

It appeared in the aftermath of the Georgia war that Russia had greatly strengthened its position in the region through a swift, decisive and relatively bloodless victory in its neighborhood, but that at the same time Russia had sustained irreparable damage to its relations with the West, particularly the United States. By the early 2010, the situation looks exactly the opposite. Relations with the US have been famously "reset," with both the US President and the NATO Secretary General traveling to Moscow in the second half of 2009. By contrast, the situation in the Caucasus is now less comfortable for Moscow than in 2008. Above all, the Russian leadership has been troubled by the worsening instability in the North Caucasus. The Russian republics of Ingushetia and Dagestan have become scenes of virtually daily bombings, assassination attempts and unrest. Ruled by its iron-fisted strongman, Chechnya has also experienced a spate of terrorist activity. Other republics have not become safe havens either. The Kremlin has been able to modify the law "On Defense" to ease the President's decisions to send forces abroad, but Moscow's successes on the diplomatic front have been few.

By promising loans, Moscow was able to sway Nicaragua and Venezuela to recognize Abkhazia and South Ossetia as independent states. However, it stumbled to procure Ecuador's support, and did not hear from Bolivia, the fourth member of the Latin American left-wing bloc, ALBA. Cuba, too, has stayed away. Tiny Nauru in the Pacific has extended recognition in exchange for Russian aid, but all the countries of the CIS have balked. Their message to Moscow could not have been clearer: not a single Russian ally/partner wants to be seen sitting in Moscow's pouch. Defiant Russia, of course, vows never to withdraw its recognition, which is fully consistent with its image as a great power, but it recognizes the difficulties of the two enclaves' new status, including for itself. South Ossetia is obviously not sustainable as a state. By contrast, Abkhazia both can and wants to be independent, and eventually will seek to rebalance its relations with Russia. So far, Moscow has allowed Sukhumi to carry out reasonably free and fair presidential elections in December 2009, thus learning from Russia's own mistakes of five years previously. Moscow initially backed a candidate who failed to win, and had to then acquiesce to the Abkhazians' choice.

In another attempt to learn from recent history, Moscow has increased its efforts toward conflict settlement in Transnistria and Nagorno Karabakh. Abkhazia and South Ossetia were declared "special cases," rather than representing a change in Russia's basic approach to separatism. To underline that point, President Medvedev in 2008-09 organized several Armenian-Azeri summits. Yet, Russia does not attempt to pose as a peacemaker-in-chief there and is content to be a team player within the Minsk group. At the same time, predictably, Russia's own participation in the Geneva talks on Georgia, Abkhazia and South Ossetia has not yielded any breakthrough. Moscow refuses to deal with Mikheil Saakashvili or his cabinet which they see as the Georgian President's mere extension. Even as informal "congresses of Georgian people" are organized by ethnic Georgian businessmen close to the Kremlin, the Russians have to admit, reluctantly, that Saakashvili is in control of the country and is unlikely to be unseated by the fractious and ineffective domestic opposition before his second presidential mandate runs out in 2014. Yet, in a bitter irony, Saakashvili's staying power may be a blessing in disguise for the Russians. As long as he remains in office, he will be tainted in the eyes of many in the West as the one who fired the first shot in the war over Ossetia. It would follow that, as mentioned above, NATO membership or even a Membership Action Plan will be out of reach for Georgia, and Abkhazia's and South Ossetia's break from Georgia will grow permanent. In 2008, the Kremlin wanted Saakashvili in the dock. In 2009, it discovered the man was more useful in the presidential palace in Tbilisi.

If it is really dawning on the Georgians that Abkhazia and South Ossetia are definitely lost, the process of this realization is extremely slow. Very few Georgians dare to accept today's reality as finality. All Georgia is deeply frustrated with the military defeat; President Saakashvili, once a darling of the Western media, experienced a certain fall from grace: not only are there fewer red carpets for him abroad, but even his phone calls sometimes go unanswered; the Georgian opposition feels impotent vis-à-vis the President; and both the president and the opposition fear, irrationally, a US-Russian collusion at the expense of Georgia. Furthermore, the new activism of Turkey and its rapprochement with Armenia undermine Georgia's once privileged position as the vital connecting link between the Caspian basin and the European energy market. Tbilisi looks confused, unsure of what to do on any of these fronts.

Azerbaijan and Armenia, of course, stayed out of the Russo-Georgian conflict. Yet, the break in relations between Moscow and Tbilisi resulted in a substantial deterioration in Armenia's geopolitical situation. Against this background, Turkey's willingness to normalize relations with Armenia and to lift the blockade is salvation for Yerevan. The signing of the protocol on establishing diplomatic relations met with approval in the major capitals, including Washington, Moscow and Brussels. This salvation, however, comes with a price. Any movement on the Nagorno Karabakh conflict settlement will require Armenian material concessions, such as troop withdrawals. Yerevan and Stepanakert, however, are afraid that an Armenian withdrawal from the regions around Karabakh will make their overall military and political bargaining position weaker in the interim, while guaranteeing them nothing in terms of the final solution.

What is not good enough for Armenia is not good enough for Azerbaijan, either. Baku felt upstaged by Ankara's activism, and also by the Turkish ambition to become the energy hub of the region. It realized that Turkey will follow its national interest, and could no longer be relied upon to automatically protect Azerbaijan's in all cases. With regard to the international efforts toward an interim solution to the Karabakh conflict, the Azeris' concern is that such a settlement would defuse the issue, deprioritize it in the eyes of the international community and threaten to turn the interim state into a permanent one, thus depriving Azerbaijan of Karabakh forever.

Though essentially unrecognized, except by Russia, Abkhazia has made important steps toward consolidating its statehood. In December 2009, as already noted, it held a free and fair election. It is a pluralist polity with a strong sense of national (ethnic) identity, with largely free media and a vibrant civil society – ironically, so much more so than its protector's. Even while it remains de facto a Russian protectorate, Abkhazia is careful about ceding too much property rights to the Russians. By contrast, South Ossetia remains a sorry story. In terms of domestic politics, it is a de facto one-man show, with opposition decimated and exiled. The 2009 South Ossetian elections – in contrast to Abkhazia's – were anything but free and fair. Economically, South Ossetia is a mess, with the reconstruction effort stalled and corruption stifling. Residents continue to leave the area for North Ossetia and other parts of Russia. Nevertheless, Abkhazia and South Ossetia are the only part of the former Soviet Union, which could be called Russia's zone of influence.

## Future Prospects

What lies ahead for the South Caucasus? With so many conflicts unresolved, wars are still possible among several players there, but they are unlikely, for the time being. The war scare in August 2009 was more of a psychological phenomenon than anything else. The Russo-Georgian conflict may certainly erupt again, arising from renewed hostilities on the frozen and now unusually quiet frontlines of Abkhazia and South Ossetia patrolled by Russian border guards. However, Tbilisi is in a far worse position, domestically and internationally, to initiate military action than it was in 2008. By contrast, Russia, even more so than in 2008, has basically what it wants, and has no reason to attack. Also, the present US administration is much more competent in Georgian affairs than its dysfunctional predecessor. Even if there were an armed incident somewhere, or a "provocation" due to the activity of some rogue elements, no major attack is likely. There have also been dire warnings with respect to the eventuality of resumed hostilities over Karabakh, in the absence of a final settlement there. Yet, despite the obvious nervousness in Baku and Yerevan, both parties know full well that they would lose massively if the 15-year truce collapsed.

Unfortunately, stable peace is even less likely to "break out" in the region. Russo-Georgian relations are in tatters, and will probably take a long time to recover. Even as Moscow continues to treat Georgia, not just Saakashvili, with contempt, it has been reluctant to reach out to the ordinary Georgian people. The present chill is likely to survive the change of leadership in Georgia, when it is finally due. A conversation may be resumed, but Tbilisi's geopolitical orientation toward the West will probably continue. Abkhazia and South Ossetia will be permanent factors in Russo-Georgian relations, and while Moscow, if it feels the need, can push its protectorates to make steps to meet Tbilisi, it will not surrender Abkhazia and South Ossetia to Saakashvili's successors. For now and the near future, the prospects for a settlement on Nagorno Karabakh are not particularly bright, all the mediation/facilitation activities of the third parties notwithstanding. Security cooperation in the region will be patchy and constrained.

In terms of geo-economics, the South Caucasus could maintain and even expand its role as a conduit of Caspian energy exports to Europe, via

Turkey. The competition between the EU-favored Nabucco gas project and the Gazprom-promoted South Stream will continue, but neither of the two extreme options: a Russian domination of the EU's gas supply chain or Russia being cut out of the South European gas market by the more successful Nabucco – seems likely. A more complex picture will probably emerge, with multiple suppliers and multiple routes. At some point, gas pipeline politics may help resolve old conflicts, such as the one over Nagorno Karabakh. Armenia's inclusion into the energy transit system, of course, can only happen as part of a general package agreement. Another economic project with wide-ranging geopolitical implications would be to reopen the North-South overland transit corridor, linking Russia – via Georgia, Abkhazia and South Ossetia – to Armenia, and extending it to eastern Turkey, Syria and Israel in the west, and Iran, Iraq and the Gulf in the east. Having invested heavily in Armenia, Russia has not only provided it with a relief loan during the economic crisis in 2009, but has a clear interest in lifting the isolation of its client.

Developments on the immediate periphery of the South Caucasus can impact heavily on the situation in the region. To the south, the big unknown is the evolution of Iran and of its relations with the outside world. However the Iranian nuclear issue is resolved, Iran is likely to continue to rise as a regional power, with more influence along its perimeter, including the South Caucasus and the Caspian. In the future, Iran, alongside Turkey, will play an increasingly active role in the Caucasus. Russia, for its part, will not disappear or fully retrench from the South Caucasus, but its ability to exercise influence there will depend on how successful Russian policies will be in the North Caucasus.

### Policy Recommendations

Under the leadership of Barack Obama, the United States has embarked on a pragmatic course toward the countries of the South Caucasus that serves larger US interests. It stands by Georgia and its territorial unity, but subtly distances itself from President Saakashvili. It supports the efforts of the Minsk Group on Nagorno Karabakh. It welcomes the expansion of Armenia's token participation in the US-led coalition in Afghanistan. It makes its moves in the region more transparent to Moscow.

However, Washington is not the only relevant player, and it has to watch all others closely. Certainly, it will need to pay attention to its friends and partners in the region and the wider Black Sea neighborhood, particularly Ukraine. A Ukraine that is pursuing a confrontational course vis-à-vis Russia would be a problem for the United States. It will be more difficult, but even more crucial to manage US relations with Russia in the region so sensitive to Moscow. No geopolitical "bargains" or "swaps" are advisable, and they will not stick anyway, but developing an understanding for the various countries' interests and perceptions is indispensable.

The United States would also do well to coordinate with its principal regional allies, notably Turkey, whose role is becoming more important than it has ever been since the end of World War I; reassure its friends in the South Caucasus, such as Georgia, and help them, including in structuring more stable polities; and establish a better mutual understanding with Russia. Without prejudice to its legal position, the United States would need to maintain working-level contacts with the Abkhaz, who are evolving into a nation.

The European Union, now endowed with a President of the European Council and an EU foreign minister, also needs to develop a geopolitical vision for the future. The Eastern Partnership is a step in the right direction, but it needs to be enhanced, and the participants' prospects for eventual EU membership need to be clarified. The crucial geopolitical issue for the EU is, of course, Turkey's membership. It is there that United Europe's geopolitical acumen is being tested. As to now, the EU appears more likely to fail that test than to pass it. Yet, the EU will only be what its members want it to be. There will be fundamental obstacles to the Union playing a strategic role even on its own periphery, but the EU preserves an enormous capacity for soft power projection, especially in its neighborhood. Association agreements with all South Caucasus countries would be a new step forward. For many countries there, the EU will remain the only game in town, even if their own membership in the Union will appear extremely distant and uncertain.

Turkey has managed to emerge as a regional power. It will seek to maintain its de facto (if not unproblematic) alliance with Azerbaijan; develop solid relations with Georgia; exploit the breakthrough in relations with Armenia;

and relate to Iran and Russia as its equals in the region. A key NATO ally, a regional economic powerhouse and an energy hub, Turkey needs to define its new role in terms other than a supplicant at the EU's doorstep. The Turkey of the 21$^{st}$ century is neither a new Ottoman empire nor a Byzantium redux, but it will inherit some elements of both, and will demand a great power worldview.

While asserting its influence, Turkey has to be careful in order not to overreach itself politically: attempting to resolve the Caucasus conflicts single-handedly would be a waste of time, and court a diplomatic failure. Turkey has an excellent opportunity to further increase its economic attractiveness in all countries in the South Caucasus. It can become a vital partner to Russia and Iran. By providing an obvious alternative to Russia in Abkhazia, Turkey can decisively contribute to Abkhazia's gradual consolidation – and in the very distant future, to its reconciliation with Georgia.

Russia's most pressing business is north of the Main Caucasus Ridge. The main challenge is improving governance. Russia needs: more development aid reaching the population instead of being stolen by the officials, either in Moscow or in the region; more job-creation projects to absorb the bulging youth population; more accountability on behalf of the authorities; more expert managing of clan and ethnic relationships instead of money-based favoritism; more openness in discussing the issues instead of formal shows of 99 percent support for the Kremlin policies; better intelligence and more sophistication in addressing radicalism; more professionalism in the police force and among the security organs and the military; more coordination within the federal government; etc., etc. All of this is fairly obvious, but extremely hard to implement due to the constraints of the established system of control and the power-money nexus.

South of the border, Russia could gain more by being nice, for a change, than by trying to look tough and arrogant. One clear set of opportunities is expanding human contacts with Georgia. It makes all the sense in the world to drop the politically-motivated sanctions against Georgian wines, and mineral water. Another winning step would be abolishing or drastically easing the visa regime for Georgian citizens. Direct air travel and postal connections need to be resumed. These measures would help engage

Georgian elites in a conversation with their Russian counterparts about the future of Russo-Georgian relations and the future of the region as a whole. Russia would win a lot from promoting cultural, sports and other human contacts with the Georgians. That would help restore Moscow and St. Petersburg as traditional cultural magnets for the Georgian artists and intellectuals. Better relations with Georgia are necessary for Russia with respect to its WTO bid, which one day will become topical again; and in the context of the dialogue on European security that has started as a result of President Medvedev's initiative, enhanced by the Georgia war.

A new departure in Russia's relations with Georgia should not come at the expense of Abkhazia's statehood. Moscow needs to develop a respectful relationship with Sukhumi, and treat Abkhazia as an emerging sovereign nation state. Clearly, Russia ought to respect its own recognition of Abkhazia's independence. Even though the current situation of quasi-unilateral recognition of Abkhazian sovereignty by Moscow gives Russia a certain advantage, it is not in the Russian long-term interest to block Abkhazia's relations with third parties, which would eventually dilute the exclusivity of Abkhaz-Russian ties. In a distant future, Russia would benefit from facilitating, maybe in a tandem with Turkey, Georgian-Abkhaz reconciliation. That reconciliation might require another border change, in which the Georgian-populated district of Gali, now under Abkhaz control, could revert to Georgia, as part of the normalization/recognition process.

South Ossetia, the casus belli in August 2009, is a much more difficult case. South Ossetia is not viable as a sovereign nation. Its only reason to exist is to make it off limits to a hostile regime in Tbilisi, but this is not enough for nation-building. The logical solution – merging South Ossetia with its bigger sister republic in the Russian North Caucasus – would have disastrous consequences. Russia would have to absorb a piece of territory it liberated from Georgian control: an annexation totally unnecessary and utterly disastrous. Russia's borders will be moving outward again: beware, Ukrainians, Kazakhs, Estonians, Azeris and others! A different context for a merger, in which North Ossetia would secede from the Russian Federation first, before absorbing its southern neighbor, would be equally disastrous for Russia, although for different reasons. Moscow would be dismantling its position in the North Caucasus with its own hands: unthinkable!

The taboo on border changes was broken as a result of the 2008 war, and regional geopolitics has become more fluid. Ideally, a solution of the Ossetian issue could be found along the lines of an "Andorra model," under which a nominally independent South Ossetian statelet would form a condominium jointly managed by Russia and Georgia. If it could also be turned into a ski resort and a duty-free paradise, the analogy would be even closer. Alas, for the time being there is no prospect of this idea even being discussed, given the current state of relations between Moscow and Tbilisi.

So far, Russia has been generally a team player on the Karabakh issue, occasionally coming up with initiatives of its own to facilitate top-level contacts between the parties to the conflict. This role is in accordance with both Russia's interests and its available resources. It should be continued. Even though Armenia is a formal ally of the Russian Federation, with Russian forces stationed there, and Azerbaijan is not, with Russian forces withdrawn from it in 1993, Moscow needs to treat both countries above all as neighbors with long-standing links with Russia. Imposing a solution on the Azeris and the Armenians is out of the question, of course, but helping them with a solution that both sides would be able to live with is in the Russian interest.

In general, however, Russia needs to engage in more serious thinking about the region. Its policies would benefit from closer monitoring of the developments there and deeper research into their roots and causes. Russian diplomats would need to study the local languages, and not rely on the local people's knowledge of Russian or the Russians' use of people with the local background. Places like Rostov (for the North Caucasus and Black Sea region), Krasnodar (for economic relations), Astrakhan (for the Caspian region), and Sochi (for high-level diplomatic contacts) could become regional expertise/contact centers, functioning as channels for multilevel intercourse between the Russian Federation and the countries of the South Caucasus.

The town of Sochi was chosen as the venue of the 2014 Winter Olympics. This is a serious challenge to the Russian authorities and developers. But it should also be a challenge to Russian policy-makers. Making sure that Russia is able not only to defeat and deter, but also to attract its neighbors would be a major contribution to a rehabilitation of the region, which has suffered most in the turbulence that followed the collapse of the Soviet Union two decades ago.

# TOWARD A NEW STRATEGY FOR ADDRESSING REGIONAL CONFLICTS IN THE SOUTH CAUCASUS

**Oksana Antonenko**,
Senior Research Fellow, Program Director,
International Institute for Strategic Studies (UK)

The South Caucasus region comprising, Georgia, Armenia and Azerbaijan, represents the most problematic sub-region within the post-Soviet area in terms of regional security concerns. This fact has been highlighted in August last year during the five-day Russia-Georgia war, which broke out after Georgia used military force in an attempt to bring its break-away republic of South Ossetia under Tbilisi's control. Russia's recognition of Abkhazia and South Ossetia as independent states – while the rest of the international community with the exception of Nicaragua continue to recognize them as part of Georgia – only entrenched the unresolved status of the Georgian-South Ossetia and Georgian-Abkhaz conflicts, adding a layer of the Georgian-Russian conflict on top of them. Moreover, the South Caucasus region also features the only unresolved inter-state conflict in post-Soviet Eurasia – the conflict between Armenia and Azerbaijan over the status of Nagorno Karabakh.

The presence of protracted inter-ethnic and territorial conflicts, which have a long history and flared up again after the end of the Soviet Union, has prevented the South Caucasus region from developing any meaningful regional cooperation. However the regional states have developed extensive ties with regional (Organization for Security and Cooperation in Europe – OSCE, Commonwealth of Independent States – CIS, Collective Security Treaty Organization – CSTO, Black Sea Economic Cooperation – BSEC), extra-regional (European Union – EU, North Atlantic Treaty Organization – NATO) and global (United Nations – UN) institutions, which have been involved in different capacities in promoting conflict resolution agenda in the South Caucasus, but so far with no real success.

This section examines the legacy of engagement by different institutions, the current security challenges faced by the region, and the outlook on future policy options for different regional and international actors engaged in the South Caucasus.

## Failures of Conflict Resolution

The outbreaks of conflicts in Abkhazia, South Ossetia and Nagorno Karabakh in the first years after the dissolution of the Soviet Union, have taken the international community by surprise. For many decades during the Cold War period, the South Caucasus region – known at that time by its Russian name the Transcaucasus – was closed to any international actors including the UN and the Charter for Security and Cooperation in Europe (CSCE), to which the Soviet Union belonged.

Russia, which has emerged as a successor state to the Soviet Union, had assumed the key role in managing and ending the violent conflicts being fought on its borders. Many experts and residents of states where the conflicts took place believe that Russian security forces have also played a role in provoking these conflicts and in assuring the victory of 'separatist' forces – as a tool to retain its influence in the 'near abroad.' This view, as well as the ability of the Russian state (or the Soviet Union in its last years) to control all of its agencies, particularly those in the security sector, and to implement such a policy remains a matter of dispute. What, however, is not disputed is that the dissolution of the Soviet Union has provoked a wave of nationalist revivals in which both larger nations – like Georgians – and smaller ones – like South Ossetians and Abkhaz – have been empowered to fight by all means to implement their national projects. The conflicts were also fueled by the fact that post-Soviet borders in the Caucasus have not been properly legalized in the chaos that followed the Soviet collapse, and the rights of ethnic minorities in South Caucasus states have become subservient to the larger nationalist agendas of titular nations in Georgia, Azerbaijan and Armenia.

In the absence of political will on the part of other international actors to intervene decisively to end the conflicts, Russia used its own diplomacy and military power as well as the political framework offered by the newly established Commonwealth of Independent States to negotiate the ceasefires and to establish post-conflict peace-keeping mechanisms. These conserved the conflicts – leaving them in a state of no peace and no war for over a decade until the August 2008 war changed the status quo by Russia's recognition of Abkhazia and South Ossetia – to a, yet again, unilaterally imposed outcome.

Given that Russia was seen by some regional states as a party to their conflicts – particularly Georgia and Azerbaijan, which have lost de facto control over parts of their territory as a result of these conflicts – Russia's engagement in the role of peace-maker had to be complemented by other institutions such as the OSCE and the UN. Both organizations have had only a marginal role in shaping developments on the ground in the midst of the most violent phases of the conflicts in Nagorno Karabakh, Abkhazia and South Ossetia. However, the OSCE and the UN have played an important role in developing multi-lateral negotiating mechanisms and deploying observer missions, which accompanied Russian-brokered ceasefire regimes and subsequent conflict resolution processes.

Today, over 15 years since all three ceasefire agreements were signed and one year after the new war broke out between Georgia and Russia, the role of the UN and the OSCE in the conflict resolution process has significantly diminished. Russia's veto blocked the extension of UN and OSCE missions in Abkhazia and South Ossetia in 2008, and the OSCE Minsk Group has failed to produce any tangible progress in over 10 years of its activities on the resolution of Nagorno Karabakh, despite being perhaps the most politically prominent group than in any other conflict around the world in terms of its composition – including Russia, the US and France as co-chairs. Moreover, the long-standing engagement of many international players and institutions did not contribute in any meaningful way to effective prevention or even containment of the new outbreak of conflict in South Ossetia and consequent full scale war between Russia and Georgia in August 2008. Nor had the UN engagement in Abkhazia prevented Russia, a member of the UN Security Council, from unilateral recognition of

Abkhazia and South Ossetia as independent states in violation of key principles of international law, which the UN is tasked to promote.

This rather negative result of a long-standing institutional engagement is not, however, the failure of the institutions themselves. Both UN and OSCE missions, deployed respectively in Abkhazia and South Ossetia, as well as a small team of OSCE observers acting in Nagorno Karabakh have done a very good job promoting confidence-building and helping to prevent new conflict escalation within rather limited means that they had at their disposal. Russian peace-keeping forces deployed in Abkhazia and South Ossetia have, too, contributed positively to stabilizing the situation on the ground for over a decade that the conflicts remained unresolved. The lack of progress in conflict settlement is not a function of institutional failure, but of the way individual member states of these multi-lateral institutions demonstrated unwillingness and inability to find new creative ways for bringing about sustainable peace and security to the region.

The effectiveness of the UN and the OSCE has been hampered by fundamentally different perception of threats and interests on the part of their key members including Russia, the US and the EU states. The CIS has been used as a fig leaf to cover what were essentially Russian policy objectives in relation to conflict in Abkhazia and made the organization hostage to Russia' role as a party to this conflict. Other regional institutions like GUAM aspired to promote conflict resolution, but lacked capacity and never followed their political statements with practical responses necessary to affect the situation on the ground. Finally, the EU, as a new player, has been slow in building consensus within the organization on the need to commit more resources to stabilizing the situation in the South Caucasus. The deployment of the EU Monitoring Mission in Georgia in the aftermath of the August war could mark the beginning of a more active EU engagement. However, the EU's leverage is limited by the fact that it is in no position to offer a clear membership perspective to any of the South Caucasus states.

Another problem for the credibility of international institutions is the selectivity in which the international law principles have been applied by different actors. The push for a unilateral recognition of Kosovo, although legally speaking not constituting a precedent for the South Caucasus, has had a major impact on the dynamic of regional conflicts. On one hand, it has made unrecognized states like Abkhazia and South Ossetia more intransigent in rejecting any consideration of Georgia's sovereignty over them. If was difficult to explain to the people living in these region, who endured bloody conflicts with Georgia and over a decade of existence in isolation as de facto states, that Kosovo has a better case for independence than they do. On the other hand, the Kosovo decision has made both Georgia and Azerbaijan nervous and more open to considering a military solution to their internal conflict, fearing that international support for their territorial integrity could be a matter of political decision or a potential trade off with Russia over a deal on Kosovo. Moreover, the Russian President has explicitly warned on numerous occasions that Russia sees a link between Kosovo and Abkhazia and South Ossetia. Western decision to ignore Russian opposition on Kosovo pushed Moscow toward asserting its own unilateral solutions for conflicts it considers vital to its security interests, just as the US and the EU consider Kosovo. Finally, the Bush administration's decision to use force in Iraq without an explicit authorization by a UN Security Council resolution has emboldened Russia to do the same when Georgia used force against its citizens and its peace-keepers in South Ossetia. Even if most experts believe that Georgia was provoked into using force by separatist forces and their Russian backers, Russia's initial response to Georgia's attack had a veil of legitimacy, if one applies the logic of unilateral interpretation of threat versus a multi-lateral sanction on the use of force.[1]

The August war and its aftermath have changed the entire institutional picture in the South Caucasus, particularly in Georgia. On June 30, the lack of consensus between Russia and other members of the OSCE, particularly the US and EU states, on the mechanics of the extension of the OSCE's mandate after Russia's recognition of South Ossetia, forced the mission to close down. The OSCE mission in Georgia played a key role in supporting efforts to promote conflict resolution in South Ossetia, it had offices in Tbilisi and Tskhinvali, deployed eight unarmed observers into the conflict zone defined by the Sochi agreement, produced regular reports for the OSCE in Vienna on the security situation on the ground, liased with the tri-

---

[1] For analysis of Russia's legal arguments for its use of force in Georgia see Nikolai Petro "The legal Case for Russian Intervention in Georgia," *Fordham International Law Journal*, vol. 32, Issue 5 (May 2009), pp. 1524-1549.

lateral peace-keeping force (JPKF) deployed in the zone of conflict (consisting of Russian, North Ossetian and Georgia units each up to 500-man strong), and participated in the workings of the Joint Control Commission (JCC) which, until 2008, was the main mechanism for negotiating the political settlement to the conflict (it included representatives of Georgia, de facto South Ossetian authorities, Russia, North Ossetia and the OSCE; EU representative attended as observers and, in some cases, UN agencies like UNHCR were also invited to attend). The OSCE has been often blamed for failing to prevent the conflict escalation in August, and South Ossetians and Russians accused its observers of biased reporting. On occasion, Georgians, who sought to undermine both the JCC and JPKKF mechanisms and to replace them with others where Russia is no longer a dominant player, also criticized the OSCE for its limited mandate, which did not cover the entire territory of South Ossetia (or Tskhinvali region, as Georgians referred to it). However, limited numbers of observers and their limited mandate issued by the OSCE has been the reason why the mission's role was so restricted. Although its observers had been reporting on the escalation of violence leading to the August 2008 war, the lack of political consensus among members in Vienna prevented the OSCE from intervening early and decisively to prevent the large-scale violence. There is no doubt that even with a limited and far from perfect mission mandate, the OSCE played an important role in helping to investigate and thus prevent violent incidents, and to promote dialogue across the conflict divide. The closure of the mission was motivated by Moscow's insistence that the OSCE open two totally separate missions to South Ossetia and to Georgia – a possibility, which was not acceptable to Georgia and those states within the OSCE that support Georgia's territorial integrity and consider South Ossetia part of Georgia. Active mediation by the Greek OSCE chairmanship, which made a number of proposals for a status neutral arrangement, has been rejected. The closure of the OSCE mission will leave a major gap in post-conflict international stabilization efforts in and around South Ossetia. The OSCE mission and its military observers have been denied access to South Ossetia immediately after the end of the August war; the absence of the OSCE means that no independent international organization will be able to observe the activities of Russian and South Ossetian forces operating inside the administrative border line (or behind the official border, as Russia considers it) between South Ossetia and

Georgia. This could make it more likely that violent incidents continue to take place and undermine stability.

The closure of the UN Mission in Georgia (UNOMIG), which was deployed on both sides of Georgian-Abkhazian administrative border for 16 years, was even more unexpected than the closure of OSCE mission. On June 15, the UN Security Council failed to reach a consensus on the new mandate for UNOMIG after Russia vetoed the resolution submitted by the US, UK and France. As a result, UNOMIG is now in the process of winding down its operations and is expected to close completely by the end of August 2009. UNOMIG had over 90 observers deployed in Gali (Georgian populated region in Abkhazia) and in Zugdidi (Georgian region bordering Abkhazia).[2] In addition to conducting regular patrolling in areas where violence has taken place in the past, UNOMIG also participated in political dialogue between the two sides of conflict, particularly after the formal Geneva process was interrupted following a Georgian operation in Kodori in 2006. The UN Secretary General's Special Representative has been compiling regular reports to the UN Security Council on developments in the Georgian-Abkhazian conflict. These reports were important for keeping the conflict on the international agenda and for presenting an objective analysis, which was available for both parties to the conflict and which helped to dispel one-sided and often inaccurate reporting. The closure of UNOMIG was again linked to the contradiction regarding the current status of Abkahzia. Russia demanded that following its recognition a special separate mission should be established in Abkhazia with no reference to Georgia, while the US and European states supported Georgia's position that no compromise should be made that in any way could be considered as undermining the principle of Georgia's territorial integrity with Abkhazia as its integral part. These political disagreements have made it impossible to find a consensus on the term of a new mandate for the UN mission. After the closure of UNOMIG, no international organization will be present inside Abkhazia and no objective analysis will be available on developments there, making it more isolated and subject of Georgia's often less than accurate reporting on developments there, addressed both to the Georgians and to the international community.

---

[2] 56 observers were deployed in Gali and 35 in Zugdidi. Source: <http://www.unomig.org/operations/>.

The closure of the OSCE mission and UNOMIG was accompanied by the change in the status of Russian forces in Abkhazia and South Ossetia. While in the past they were present there in a limited capacity – up to 3,000 in Abkhazia under the CIS mandate and 500 (or 1,000 if one counts the North Ossetian part of the JPKF) under the1992 Sochi agreements[3] – now they will be stationed there on official Russian military bases under 'inter-state' agreements reached with Abkhazian and South Ossetian governments. The original plans announced by Russia include 3,700 troops in each territory, representing a major increase in numbers from the time of peace-keeping forces, but later there were reports that the overall numbers will be reduced.[4] These agreements are not recognized as legitimate by the rest of the international community (except for Nicaragua), and the US and the EU continue to insist that Russia withdraw all its forces from Georgia (including Abkhazia and South Ossetia) as agreed in the August 12 Medvedev-Sarkozy memorandum. Russia claims that it has implemented all its commitments under the Medvedev-Sarkozy agreement on October 10 when it pulled its troops out of Georgia-proper. These disagreements are likely to persist with no prospect for finding a formula for a commonly agreed security regime inside Abkhazia and South Ossetia.

Following the Sarkozy-mediated ceasefire agreement in August 2008, the EU has deployed a 246-strong police force to Georgia (which has no access to either Abkhazia or South Ossetia). The EU role is important given the closure of the UN and OSCE missions, but it cannot be fully effective as a security-enhancing and confidence-building tool as long as it has access only to one side of the conflict divide. Given the EU's unequivocal recognition of Abkhazia and South Ossetia as part of Georgia, it is unlikely that its monitors will receive access to these territories. The EU is also trying to establish a new status-neutral negotiating mechanism – known as the Geneva discussions – in which all key parties participate. Formally the EU Special Representative together with SRs of the UN and the OSCE co-chair these discussions in which Georgia, Abkahzia, South Ossetia, Russia and the US participate. However, the progress has been slow and incident prevention mechanisms agreed in Geneva – not as a legally binding document – have been sluggish to start functioning. Its capacity to address

---

[3] "Соглашение о принципах урегулирования грузинско-осетинского конфликта." Text available at: <http://www.peacekeeper.ru/index.php?id=84>.
[4] <http://en.rian.ru/world/20090617/155274434.html>.

crises will continue to be hampered by disagreements on status as well as by the voluntary nature of the commitment to it by key parties in the Geneva dialogue.

With the current role of all institutions diminished, new forms of confidence-building and conflict-management should be developed, which are able to address current and future threats to regional security.

**Unresolved Conflict as the Key Threat to Security in the Region**

Security threats in the South Caucasus will remain serious, complex and urgent. At the center of these concerns are three protracted unresolved conflicts in Abkhazia, South Ossetia and Nagorno Karabakh. These conflicts pose major risk to regional states, populations and regional security as a whole. In my judgment, which is shared by many experts working on these conflict for many years, there are few hopes that these conflicts will be resolved through a mutually agreed settlement in the foreseeable future – the only possible exception is the Nagorno Karabakh conflict, but even there the positions of Armenia and Azerbaijan remain irreconcilable on a number of important issues concerning even the Basic Principles of the Conflict resolution. Therefore, the key task for regional actors, as well as for international ones, is to find effective mechanisms to manage inherent instability rooted in the unresolved nature of these conflicts, while creating conditions in which it will be possible to reach and implement a comprehensive settlement agreement and move toward a sustainable peace.

*Abkhazia*

Russia's recognition of Abkhazia and deployment of Russian troops there have removed the immediate threat of large-scale conflict escalation. Abkhaz authorities have welcomed Russia's new role as explicit security guarantor against any new Georgian attack. For many people who currently reside in Abkhazia, Russia's military presence means that for the first time in over 15 years they feel secure and no longer fear for their lives and those of their families. However, Russia's new military bases do not provide the Russian forces with a formal responsibility for promoting stability and preventing violence within Abkhazia. This is particularly important given that thousands of ethnic Georgians still live in the break-away territory (the exact number of those who returned to Gali has not been confirmed but their numbers are estimated to be up to 45,000).[5] The Georgian authorities, who have adopted the law on occupied territories and consider Russian forces to be an occupying force, on the contrary, now hold Russian forces responsible for any violence that might be perpetrated toward the Georgian population in Gali and on both sides of the Georgian-Abkhazian (administrative) border. With the withdrawal of UNOMIG monitors from Gali and the deployment of Abkhazian forces there, the likelihood of such violence both in Gali and Kodori (a region in Abkhazia, which before August was controlled by Georgian authorities) remains high. Moreover, no unbiased reporting on the situation there will be available following the withdrawal of UNOMIG, thus limiting the possibilities for violence prevention and effective containment. The closure of border crossing points on the (administrative) border will make it harder for members of the Gali population to visit their families or receive medical treatment in Georgia. Finally, Abkhazian authorities continue to accuse Georgian security forces of attempting to foment violence in Gali and Kodori.[6] In the past, Georgian paramilitary groups regularly crossed the border along the Inguri River and targeted some Georgians who cooperated with Abkhazian authorities and whom they considered 'traitors.'

In addition to potential violence in Gali, there are growing concerns in Abkhazia about the political implications of its new de facto status as a Russian protectorate. Abkhazians were concerned about the closure of the UN mission, which left them isolated and open to de facto absorption by Russia. Russia has claimed control over Abkhazian railways and its airport, and wants Abkhazia to lift limitation for Russian citizens to own land and property in Abkhazia. Moreover, Russia's economic expansion in Abkhazia

---

[5] The ICG Report states 40,000, source:
<http://www.crisisgroup.org/library/documents/europe/caucasus/b53_georgia_russia___still_i nsecure_and_dangerous.pdf>, p.5; the IDMC gives 45,000: <http://www.internal-displacement.org/idmc/website/countries.nsf/(httpEnvelopes)/E8EEFB4402BF144DC12575EC 00366C07?OpenDocument>; UNHCR also gives the latest figures at 45,000 in 2008: <http://www.unhcr.org/48ff51084.html>.
[6] "ПРИОРИТЕТЫ РАЗВИТИЯ," VPK N29, available at:
<http://www.vpk-news.ru/index.php?option=com_content&task=view&id=619&Itemid=7>.

is likely to increase further in the context of its preparation for the 2014 Olympic Games in Sochi, located just few kilometers from Abkhazia. The Abkhazian opposition has already critised the Abkhaz government for ceding too much control to Russia and thus undermining the chances for achieving true independence for Abkhazia.

To counterbalance Russia's growing influence, Abkhazia is encouraging its large diaspora, which consists of the descendants of the Abkhazians who fled Russian imperial occupation in 19ᵗʰ century and currently reside in Turkey and Middle East, to return to Abkhazia. If such a return begins in earnest, new conflicts might emerge due to the distinct culture and religion of these people, who speak no Russian and are predominantly Muslim. However, in the foreseeable future no such massive return is predicted as long as Abkhazia remains isolated.

The challenge for the international community is how to engage with Abkhazia in a status neutral way and thus seek to influence both its internal security situation and its attitudes to continuing seeking an agreed settlement with Georgia. If no such engagement takes place, it is likely that in the next decade Abkhazia will be irreversibly separated from Georgia and de facto absorbed into Russian economic, political and military spheres. In these circumstances it might be a matter of time before a new violent conflict might occur – be it as a result of a decision by a future Georgian leadership, which is unlikely to voluntarily accept the partition of its territory, or by internal conflict within Abkhazia, which could be used by Georgia and Russia.

*South Ossetia*

The situation in South Ossetia is even more complicated than in Abkhazia, with fewer chances of meaningful progress toward an agreed conflict settlement between Tbilisi and Tskhinvali. Unlike Abkhazians, the majority of the South Ossetian population, which after the August war now consists predominantly of ethnic Ossetians (with many ethnic Georgians expelled and their villages burned down), does not seek to establish an independent statehood but rather to become part of Russia by unifying with the Republic of North Ossetia, where the majority of Ossetians currently reside. Unlike Abkhazia which seeks to assert its independence and develop ties with the outside world to guarantee it, South Ossetia's relations with the international community have never been particularly important for its authorities, who are happy for their break-away territory to become a de facto part of Russia.

Secondly, the fact that the August war took place primarily on the territory of South Ossetia (with only small operations conducted in Abkhazia) makes it harder to contemplate any quick reconciliation between Ossetians and Georgians. Ossetians, who three times in the past 18 years were subjected to Georgian military attacks, have no desire to seek any relations with the Georgian state. Hostility toward Georgians, which was widespread even before the August war, has increased further after the recent devastation of their territory and large civilian casualties. Therefore Georgian-South Ossetian reconciliation is likely to be a long-term project for future generations. With a new border being erected between South Ossetia and the neighboring Gori region of Georgia, the former will be fully dependent on Russia for its existence – not only for security guarantees but also for economic development as its role as a transit region alongside the strategic highway connecting the South and the North Caucasus will be undermined by the new border.

Finally, Russia's military deployments in South Ossetia will continue to challenge Georgia's own sense of security given South Ossetia's location just over 100 kilometers form Georgia's capital Tbilisi. The new wave of IDPs from South Ossetia will continue to create political pressure on the Georgian government, while their return is unlikely to be accepted by the South Ossetians even in the medium- to long-term perspective. Moreover, the dispute over the status of the Akhalgori (Ossetian name Leningori) region remains a source of tensions and possibly even violence.

The options for developing an effective security management mechanism, or a viable political dialogue between Tbilisi and Tskhinvali are very limited and should be considered as a long-term objective. The access to South Ossetia by any international organizations will be similarly difficult in the foreseeable future. In the short term, it is important to develop effective and regular low-level contacts between all parties operating on both sides of the (administrative) border – including Georgian, South Ossetians, Russians and the EU bodies – and to maintain a dialogue on IDP return. It is unlikely that the EU or other international actors will be able to implement their economic programs in South Ossetia or to gain easy access to the region. Therefore a continuation of the Geneva discussions remains critical for keeping even a nominal line of communication in place. Developing contacts between the EU Monitoring mission and Russian forces (including border guards) are important as a tool for addressing potential violent incidents.

In the long run, new frameworks should be developed to stimulate people-to-people contacts between Ossetians and Georgian. This can be best achieved through informal multi-lateral mechanisms or NGO-led track two initiatives.

*Georgian-Russian Relations*

The August war has effectively transformed the Georgian-Abkhazian and Georgian-South Ossetian conflicts into one Russian-Georgian conflict. This new inter-state character of the conflict – combined with the unresolved inter-ethnic dimension of the two historic conflicts – makes the conflict resolution process more complicated and less likely to produce any progress in the short- to medium-term.

The August war has become the final chapter of the long developing 'cold war' between Russia and Georgia. The Georgian government has accused Moscow of interference in its internal affairs and support for separatism in Georgia. Russia accused Tbilisi of conducting anti-Russian policies and planning to use force against its citizens in Abkhazia and South Ossetia. Russia also resented the Georgian government for seeking to join NATO and backing so-called 'color' revolutions in post-Soviet Eurasia. Russia has long imposed an economic blockade on Georgia, closed down its border with Georgia and severed their direct transport links. Tbilisi has expelled several Russian diplomats on spy charges, blocked Russia's membership in the WTO and, in the past, supported Chechens who sought independence from Moscow.

The August war saw Georgian forces deliberately targeting and killing Russian peace-keepers in South Ossetia and Russian armed forces deploying in large numbers into South Ossetia and Abkhazia as well as to parts of Georgia proper. The Russian side bombed Georgian military facilities and some residential townships. Finally, after the end of armed hostilities, Russia recognized the independence of Abkhazia and South Ossetia.

Georgia accused Russia of occupation, cancelled its membership in the CIS and all ceasefire agreements of the 1990s, and finally broke-off all diplomatic relations with Moscow. Russian leaders announced that they would not have any relations with the Georgian government under President Saakashvili's leadership, calling him 'a political corpse.'

The break-down of Georgian-Russian relations represents a major challenge for implementing effective conflict management strategies in Abkhazia and South Ossetia. Moreover, the projection of the Georgian-Russian conflict into a diplomatic stand-off between the US and EU – which support Georgian territorial integrity – and Russia – which supports the independence of Abkhazia and South Ossetia – has already claimed OSCE and UNOMIG mandate as casualties. It is important to find ways for overcoming the currently entrenched zero-sum approach to any political decisions regarding conflicts – in which political definitions and titles (like the name of the OSCE and UN missions) become key obstacles for addressing real and urgent security challenges. One option could be to develop a clear policy on what "engagement without recognition" represents in practice. Georgia's law on occupied territories placed an unreasonable number of limitations for international actors, which are at odds with other cases of unrecognized entities, be it Taiwan or Kosovo or even Northern Cyprus.

Russia, too, is being unreasonable by limiting its contacts with Georgia. It is in the interests of Russia and its partners such as Armenia to see the Georgian-Russian border open and air links reestablished. Moreover, Russia should show more support for the Geneva discussions – currently the only platform for Georgian-Russian conflict dialogue – and help to transform them into into a long-term process for tackling practical issues related to security and IDPs.

Continuing speculations about a new conflict between Russia and Georgia are used by both sides to justify their uncompromising positions and to sustain their political conflict as well as manage their domestic political problems. Such speculations were particularly wide-spread in June-July 2009, when several Russian commentators accused the Russian government of preparing a new attack on Georgia.[7] Similarly, Russian officials and commentators accuse Georgia of building up forces near the borders of South Ossetia and rearming to prepare for a military revanche. These speculations can be stopped if the international community brokers a new "non-use-of-force agreement" between all parties to the conflict and develops regular consultations under the OSCE framework to address any concerns about new threats of attack on both sides.

*Nagorno Karabakh*

Unlike conflicts in Abkhazia and South Ossetia, which have entered a new status quo making new large scale escalation less likely, the Armenian-Azerbaijani conflict over Nagorno Karabakh territory remains vulnerable to escalation. Moreover change to the current status quo through an OSCE Minsk Group-mediated political agreement is also fraught with potential risks to stability and security in the region.

The Nagorno Karabakh conflict, which broke out in January 1992 and lasted for 2.5 years, was the bloodiest of post-Soviet conflicts, claiming an estimated 35,000 lives and over 1 million refugees and IDPs.[8] The conflict was fought between Armenia and Azerbaijan over the sovereignty of the Nagorno Karabakh region, which was populated predominantly by ethnic Armenians and was part of the Azerbaijan Soviet Socialist Republic in USSR. When the Soviet Union collapsed, Armenians fought to separate from Azerbaijan. Since the ceasefire was agreed in 1994, it has been controlled by Armenian forces, which also established control over seven other regions of the former AzSSR including the Lachin corridor

---

[7] See, for example, Pavel Felgenhauer:
<http://www.jamestown.org/single/?no_cache=1&tx_ttnews%5Btt_news%5D=35140>; Yulia Latynina: <http://www.ej.ru/?a=note&id=9213>; Andrei Illarionov (original):
<http://www.echo.msk.ru/programs/figure/600923-echo/>.

[8] There is no exact IDP number. Crisis Group (2005) puts the number at 413,000 Armenians and 724,000 Azerbaijanis (1,137,000 total) as a result of own research; same text refrerences UNHCR 2003 data with a total of 1,198,137:
<http://www.crisisgroup.org/library/documents/europe/caucasus/166_nagorno_karabakh_vie wing_the_conflict_from_the_ground.pdf>.

connecting Nagorno Karabakh with Armenia. As a result of the post-conflict status quo, the Azerbaijani region of Nakhichevan was separated from Azerbaijan, all Azeris were forced to leave Nagorno Karabakh and the occupied territories, and thousands of ethnic Armenians were expelled from Azerbaijan. A de facto state – the Republic of Nagorno Karabakh – was established, which exists due to economic and military assistance from Armenia, including its large diaspora in different parts of the world. Turkey supported Azerbaijan due to its ethnic links, and imposed a blockade on Armenia. Russia, in turn, has formal collective security guarantees with Armenia, which is a member of the CIS Collective Security Treaty Organisation.

Many years of negotiations brokered by the OSCE Minsk Group – consisting of co-chairs from Russia, US and France – have so far produced no political agreement. Several attempts to achieve a breakthrough, including the 2001 Key West summit hosted by the US administration and the 2006 Rambouillet talks, produced no results. In the past several years, negotiations have been focused around so-called Madrid Principles agreed on during the November 2007 annual OSCE foreign ministers meeting.[9] The core of these principles, which remain formally secret, includes the peace plan built around a two-stage process. The first stage stipulates Armenia's return of occupied territories outside Nagorno Karabakh and the allowed return of IDPs there and to Nagorno Karabakh (guaranteed by the deployment of an international stabilization force). In return, Azerbaijan and Turkey would lift the blockade on Armenia. In the second stage, the status of Nagorno Karabakh is addressed through a plebiscite with the involvement of residents of the contested area, including Azeri IDPs. The timing of the second stage and the modalities of the return of occupied territories – particularly Lachin and Kelbajar – represent the key sticking points, which have not been agreed by the parties.

Unlike conflicts in Abkhazia and South Ossetia, the Nagorno Karabakh conflict resolution process has witnessed pragmatic cooperation between all three co-chairs of the Minsk Group. However, no progress in securing the agreement has been achieved. As the negotiations continue to drag on –

---

[9] <http://www.rferl.org/content/Azerbaijan_Floats_Principles_For_Karabakh_Peace_Settlement_/1357686.html>.

with many experts believing that the parties only simulate the peace process and have no intention to actually make the concessions required to advance it – there are growing signs that other options are being considered by hardliners on both sides. In Azerbaijan, the President and other officials have repeatedly threatened to use force if negotiations fail to produce a peaceful agreement reaffirming its territorial integrity and reversing Armenia's occupation. In Armenia, political leaders are under intense pressure not to make any compromises; the country has a history of violence against supporters of a peace process. Armenia and Azerbaijan are locked in an arms race, which is threatening regional stability. The Azerbaijani defense budget grew at the fastest rate in the world in recent years as the country begins to receive large revenues from oil and gas exports. In Armenia, the diaspora is funding resettlement programs to occupied territories making it harder for Armenia's leaders to offer a compromise, which would require dismantling some of these settlements.

The August war has provided a reality check for proponents of a military solution. However, the normalization of Russian-Azerbaijani relations in 2008-2009 is being interpreted by some experts as an end to the guarantee of Russia's support for Armenia in the case of an Azeri military assault on Karabakh. This raises prospects for another prolonged and bloody conflict in this strategically important region. At present, there are no peace keeping forces deployed on the line of contact separating Armenian (NK army) and Azerbaijani forces. A five-man strong OSCE observer mission, which monitors the ceasefire, does not represent any significant deterrent for conflict escalation. At the same time the number of incidents of ceasefire violations continues to increase.[10] In these circumstances, new conflict escalation could take place quickly and with no early warning, making an effective international response problematic.

At the same time, the nature of governments in Armenia and Azerbaijan, which have not established their democratic credibility, makes it harder for them to agree to a compromise settlement. The secretive nature of negotiations only fuel resentment among populations, which have been, so far, excluded from any meaningful confidence-building or reconciliation

---

[10] Tom de Waal, "The Karabakh trap," p. 5, available at: <http://www.c-r.org/our-work/caucasus/documents/Karabakh_Trap_FINAL.pdf>.

process and subject to constant propaganda campaigns sustaining the enemy image on the other side of the conflict's divide. Authorities, who use the conflict in order to boost their power and legitimacy, are reluctant to delegate the role of peace-maker to their societies and therefore oppose any people-to-people contacts. Moreover, unlike Abkhazia and South Ossetia, where prior to the August war many international organizations had access and implemented some programs, Nagorno Karabakh remains isolated due to Azerbaijan's decision to block any engagement with it until there has been some progress on the return of the Armenian-occupied territories. In these circumstances Nagorno Karabakh residents and authorities, who are excluded from the official conflict resolution process, have developed much more uncompromising attitudes than those in Armenia-proper and are strongly critical of the Madrid principles and any concessions on their basis. The Karabakh position, in turn, has a strong influence on the Armenian public, which views it as a key nationalist project.

Following the August war and the election of President Barack Obama in the US, some promising signs have appeared, which could affect the dynamic of the Karabakh peace process. The main such development was the Armenian-Turkish rapprochement that started after the visit of Turkish President Abdulla Gul to Yerevan to attend a football match. Turkey and Armenia have themselves been locked in a political conflict over the legacy of the 1915-1917 massacre of Armenians, which the latter seeks to be recognized as genocide. Turkey opposes such a definition and criticizes Armenia for what it sees as its territorial claims on the eastern regions of Turkey where Armenians used to reside before the massacre. Following Gul's visit, a package of measures to normalize bi-lateral relations has been negotiated between the two sides, including the opening of the border and a normalization of diplomatic relations. Although offering much hope for transforming the atmosphere in which the Nagorno Karabakh resolution process has existed for over 15 years, many obstacles lie ahead. Azerbaijan has strongly criticized these steps as unilateral concessions to Armenia that has so far offered no real concession of its own on Nagorno Karabakh. Without any reciprocal progress, Ankara's parliament is unlikely to ratify the normalization of relations with Yerevan. In Armenia, many are also critical, including the country's powerful diaspora, and accuse Turkey of opportunistic moves set to derail US recognition of genocide, which was pledged by the Obama administration during his election campaign and supported by some powerful members of Congress.

The Nagorno Karabakh conflict represents an interesting case of, on the one hand, offering the most promise for some progress on a political settlement, compared with the new status quo that has crystallized in Abkhazia and South Ossetia. At the same time, it is also a conflict, which has the most potential to erupt once again into a full scale, inter-state war. The international community and key international organizations have high stakes in which way the conflict evolves in the coming years.

### Policies

In devising future policies to address regional conflicts, a number of key challenges need to be addressed:

1. **Territorial integrity vs. negotiated settlement.** For years, support for Georgia's and Azerbaijan's territorial integrity has been detrimental to any meaningful conflict resolution process as Abkhazia, South Ossetia and, to a lesser degree, Nagorno Karabakh (since it was excluded from the peace process altogether) saw no reason to engage in a process with a determined outcome and an outcome, which contradicted their interests and security concerns. Following the August war, the support of a settlement on the basis of Georgia's territorial integrity is even more at variance with reality (no experts and officials see it as a likely outcome in the any foreseeable future). Therefore this support contributes only to freezing the conflict and excluding any chances for involvement of consensus-based international organizations (as we have witnessed in the case of OSCE and UOMIG regional mission closures). It is important that while no recognition of Abkhazia and South Ossetia is made by the absolute majority of UN member states, there is also a meaningful support for finding a lasting and mutually agreed settlement of conflicts. This settlement should include many options starting from Georgian sovereignty, to more flexible models of a common state or a confederation and ending with a possibility of independent statehood, but only if recognized by Georgia. Such shift from insistence on a particular

outcome should be accompanied by clear stipulations of principles that would bar reaching any of these settlement alternatives – including foreign occupation (or presence of foreign troops), lack of progress on refugee/IDP return, and lack of a process for developing a civil society or access to independent sources of information. Other criteria could be considered, which could create incentives for restarting the peace process on a more sustainable and realistic footing.

2. **Dealing with de facto states – principle of engagement without recognition.** This paper argues that it is important to find ways to engage with de facto entities in order to affect their attitudes toward peaceful conflict resolution and generate progress toward reconciliation with their adversaries. Isolation only breeds extreme uncompromising attitudes. It is therefore important that international actors find ways to develop a common policy – or a norm – for engagement with Abkhazia, South Ossetia and Nagorno Karabakh, which would not constitute political recognition. There are a number of other cases to draw on, such as Taiwan, which is one of the largest EU trade partners. It is also important to give representatives of these entities a chance to have a dialogue with international organsiations such as the UN, OSCE and the EU (as do North Cyprus or Kosovo).

3. **Strengthening governments' capacities to reach a sustainable compromise.** This paper argues that existing governments that have not established their democratic credibility represent the major obstacle for a sustainable conflict resolution process. Moreover, the lack of engagement from the public and civil society makes it more likely that whatever compromise is agreed by governments will not be supported or implemented by their people. The international community should support democratic processes in Georgia, Azerbaijan and Armenia and encourage their leaders to support people-to-people contacts with representatives from conflict regions.

4. **Developing incentives for conflict settlement.** The lack of big strategic incentives constitutes a major problem for peace

processes in the South Caucasus. In the Balkans, the peace process and the implementation of peace agreements has been enhanced by the prospect for EU membership. It is important to develop a similar strategic vision for the South Caucasus, which would make it easier for the regional countries' leaders to persuade their societies on the need for compromise. Before the August 2008 war, the only thing that young Georgians and young Abkhazians agreed on is on a common desire to be part of Europe. Europeanization should still be considered a long-term realistic goal if a peace settlement is achieved.

5. **Addressing humanitarian problems – depoliticizing the refuge/IDP issue.** Given that a comprehensive settlement is unlikely to be achieved in the foreseeable future, it is important to develop a better strategy for addressing the humanitarian dimension of these conflicts. Hundreds of thousands of IDPs in Georgia and Azerbaijan are still living in temporary accommodations 15 years after the end of conflict. These people should not be kept as hostages to create pressure on the international community to press for settlement. They, together with new IDPs from the August conflict, should be offered options for integration while their undisputed right to return to their previous homes should also be guaranteed.

6. **Preventing conflict escalation/violence.** The lack of comprehensive security regimes in all three conflicts in the South Caucasus threatens to result in new violence and escalation. More efforts should be made to monitor the ceasefire regimes and to develop early warning systems for each of the conflicts. Both formal international organizations and NGOs can play a role in shaping new security regimes. Moreover, more efforts should be made to encourage all parties to the conflicts to sign no-use-of-force agreements and resolve on ways to monitor their implementation. Measures should be developed to stop the current arms race in the South Caucasus and make regional military expenditures open to international scrutiny, including by donors who provide these countries with credits and grants.

7. **Preventing conflicts in other regions.** While the old conflicts occupy the minds of policy-makers in South Caucasus and in international organizations, more effort should be exerted to prevent new potential inter-ethnic conflict from erupting. In particular, the situation of other ethnic minorities – Armenians in Javakheti (Georgia) and Azerbaijanis in Marneuli (Georgia) – should be monitored and improved by international organizations such as the office of the OSCE High Commissioner for National Minorities and the EU.

8. **Development of detailed plans for a post-settlement period.** In order for international organizations and states to appear credible in their efforts to push for a conflict settlement, it is important to draw up specific plans for post-conflict settlement, including economic incentives and peace-keeping forces. The current global financial crisis offers major challenges in his regard. Should Armenia and Azerbaijan agree on the terms of settlement tomorrow there is no gurantee that the international community would be able to find funds and forces required to aid with its implementation.

9. **Normalizing inter-state relations.** The South Caucasus is unique in the number of break-downs in inter-state relations, which exist in this small region. At present, the following states have no diplomatic relations with each other: Russia and Georgia, Armenia and Azerbaijan, and Armenia and Turkey. This lack of relations complicates the conflict resolution process. The tentative improvement of Turkish-Armenian relations offers a promise of change, and this process should be strongly supported by the US, the EU and Russia.

10. **Promoting regional cooperation – the Turkish initiative.** The lack of normal inter-state relations complicates the process of regional cooperation, which is necessary to support a regional security agenda as well as trade, energy and law enforcement cooperation. In the long-run, the development of regional cooperation initiatives between all regional states – along the lines of the Turkish initiative for a Regional Stability and Cooperation

Platform that includes the three South Caucasus states plus Russia and Turkey – should be encouraged. In the short-term, it is important to support the integration of regional states in wider initiatives and organizations such as the Organization for Black Sea Economic Cooperation (BSEC) and the OSCE. In some cases, status-neutral multi-lateral platforms could be open for representatives from Abkhazia, South Ossetia and Nagorno Karabakh to help promote mutual understanding and cooperation.

11. **Addressing wider regional challenges.** The region also faces potential threats of a spillover of insecurity from neighboring regions, particularly the Russian North Caucasus where the level of violence has been increasing in recent months. The prospect of a future conflict in Iran over its nuclear program would have a detrimental affect on the South Caucasus region and could trigger conflict escalation in places like Karabakh. This should be taken into account if any military action is considered in the future.

12. **Developing cooperation between external powers.** One of the major challenges for promoting a conflict resolution agenda in the South Caucasus was the lack of cooperation and, in some cases, open rivalry and zero sum thinking on the part of international actors engaged in the region. This was particularly strongly demonstrated in the dynamic of a proxy conflict between Russia and the US (under the Bush administration) over Georgia's Rose Revolution and its NATO membership prospects. It is important in the future to develop better cooperation among Russia, the US and the EU on issues related to regional conflict. Such cooperation is particularly promising in the case of Nagorno Karabakh since, following the August war, cooperation between Minsk Group co-chairs has improved. It is also important to find a modus vivendi between major external players on Abkhazia and South Ossetia, although it will be harder to achieve given that Russia has become a party to these conflicts.

# THE SOUTHERN CAUCASUS' INTEGRATION WITH NATO AND THE EU: CURRENT DEVELOPMENTS AND FUTURE PERSPECTIVES

**Uwe Halbach,**
Senior Research Fellow,
German Institute for Security and International Affairs

As a part of the Caspian as well as of the Black Sea region, the Southern Caucasus has become a target of increased attention by Euro-Atlantic institutions with regard to security policy, energy policy, intra- and inter-regional cooperation, and conflict resolution. The United States declared the region its "zone of strategic interest" already in 1997. NATO's engagement there was growing with security interests in the Black Sea and the Caspian Region, Central Asia and the Wider Middle East, since 2001, especially with those related to the war on terrorism.[1] The European Union was slower and more restrained in showing its colors there. It was not until 2003 that its Caucasus policy developed a broader tool box for getting more influence in this region. Armenia, Azerbaijan and Georgia differently positioned themselves between Russia and their Western partners, and between Eurasian and Euro-Atlantic vectors of their foreign and security policies. Notwithstanding these differences, all three countries developed cooperation with NATO and the European Union and demonstrated commitment to their integration with the Euro-Atlantic world.

## NATO and Security Cooperation with the Southern Caucasus

All three countries of the Southern Caucasus have been developing engagement with NATO – though on different levels of commitment.

---

[1] Svante Cornell: "NATO's Role in South Caucasus Regional Security,"
<http://www.silkroadstudies.org/docs/publications/2004/TPQ.pdf>.

Whereas after the "Rose Revolution," Georgia has been eager to become a full member of NATO as soon as possible, Armenia is interested in maintaining cooperation with the Alliance rather than in membership. Azerbaijan's security cooperation with external partners is more balanced than that of Georgia – with its one-sided Euro-Atlantic orientation – or Armenia's – with its strong leaning on Russia and its membership in the CSTO. Azerbaijan does not seek immediate NATO membership, but its relations with Western security partners are stronger than those of Armenia.[2]

In Georgia more than anywhere else in the post-Soviet area, NATO membership became a national project and an outstanding foreign policy and security topic. Orientation toward NATO was not only elite-driven. Before the war with Russia in August 2008, there was an overwhelming popular vote of more than 70 percent for NATO membership. It was higher than among actual applicant countries during the past decades (Estonia – 69 percent, Slovenia – 66 percent, Latvia – 60 percent, Lithuania – 46 percent). Before the war, the Georgian government has repeatedly fixed upcoming dates for access. President Mikheil Saakashvili tried to push Georgia into NATO on the same schedule as Romania and Bulgaria. Within NATO itself, this haste partly met with support, partly with scepticism. A nucleus of eight countries has developed within NATO and the European Union, which supports an active policy by both organisations toward Europe's East, generally, and toward Georgia, in particular. Initiated in 2005 in Tbilisi by the three Baltic states, Poland, Ukraine, Romania and Bulgaria and then joined by Sweden and the Czech Republic, this "New Friends of Georgia group" supported Georgia's goal to advance to a Membership Action Plan at NATO's summit in Bucharest in the spring of 2008.[3]

Some high NATO-representatives had a more cautious approach toward an early membership perspective for Georgia.[4] The political crisis in Georgia

---

[2] Alberto Priego: "NATO cooperation towards South Caucasus," in: *Caucasian Review of Internation Affairs*, Baku, 1/2008.

[3] Vladimir Socor, "Friends of Georgia Hold Strategy Session in Lithuania," *Eurasia Daily Monitor*, Jamestown Foundation, September 17, 2007, Vol. 4, Issue 171.

[4] In March 2006, Deputy General Secretary Jean Fournet stated that the access of Georgia and the Ukraine to NATO depends on overwhelming internal crises and conflicts within these

since autumn 2007 with the confrontation between the government and a growing opposition and the November 7th attacks of the riot police on demonstrators increased this scepticism. But nevertheless, Tbilisi worked very hard in its path to NATO, carrying out an ambitious Individual Partnership Action Plan (IPAP), being part of an Intensified Dialogue and working on the approval of its Membership Action Plan. With a contingent of 2000 troops, Georgia became the biggest provider for troops to Iraq if counted in per-capita terms of the providing country. It began perceiving itself as being in transition from a security-consumer to an international security-provider. But with its unresolved internal conflicts with Abkhazia and South Ossetia and a growing confrontation with Russia, it was far away from internal and external security.

The NATO Bucharest summit of April 2008, with Washington supporting a Membership Action Plan for Georgia (and Ukraine) and Moscow opposing it, raised tensions in the environment of Georgia's unresolved conflicts with Abkhazia and South Ossetia. At the end of the summit, when Georgia was promised that it would eventually become a member of the alliance but not given a firm pledge on MAP, Russian president Vladimir Putin made a blunt warning, saying: "The presence of a powerful military bloc on our borders...will be seen as direct threat to our national security."[5] The "Five Day War" between Russia and Georgia over South Ossetia did not dramatically change the conditions of Georgia's relationship with NATO.[6] But, after a short period of serious criticism toward Russia's military response to a Georgian offensive against Tskhinvali, the Alliance sought to normalize relations with Russia and to come back to "business as usual" with Moscow. Consequently, prospects for Georgian membership moved into an uncertain future. Moreover, after the war, the popular commitment to NATO membership in Georgia decreased somewhat.[7]

---

states and that this will take years. See Gulbaat Rzchiladse, "Russland und Georgien," in: *Osteuropa* 7/2007, 71-80, 75.

[5] Quoted by Thomas de Waal, "Abkhazia and South Ossetia," in: Adam Hug (Ed.), *Spotlight on Georgia*, Foreign Policy Center, London 2009, p. 111-121, quotation p. 115.

[6] Archil Gegeshidze, Post-War Georgia: Resetting Euro-Atlantic Aspirations? Caucasus Analytical Digest, Nko. 4, 16 April 2009, pp. 5-9.

[7] The vote for "full support" for NATO membership fell from 70 percent to 49 percent in February 2009; the vote for "strong opposition" increased from 4 percent to 10 percent. Georgian National Survey February 21-March 3, 2009: "Georgian Popular Opinion on NATO Membership and the Relationship with the West," Caucasus Analytical Digest 05/09, p.11.

Azerbaijan is more cautious in its public comments on NATO membership, emphasizing that the process of reaching Alliance-level standards is the main goal. Unlike Georgia, it tries to balance the Western vector in its foreign and security policy with a conflict-avoidance-policy toward Russia and Iran, two neighbors with an outspoken dislike for NATO-enlargement into the region. NATO and the US have been engaged in Azerbaijan's energy policy, supporting the construction and the security of the BTC oil pipeline, which opened up an "energy honeymoon" in Azerbaijan. Like Georgia, it is pressing ahead with plans to overhaul its armed forces in order to bring them up to Western standards. And like Georgia, Azerbaijan is aware that unresolved regional conflicts are the main hindrance for the entrance of South Caucasian states into Euro-Atlantic structures. In this case, it is the Nagorno Karabakh conflict and Azerbaijan's aggressive relationship with Armenia. Just like Tbilisi, Baku has multiplied its military budget within the last five years. Same as Gerogia, Azerbaijan has framed this military build-up as necessary to modernize its army and adapt it to Western military standards. However, Azerbaijan's higher defense spending also signalled a message of increased military capacity to its adversaries in the conflict on Nagorno Karabakh.

Noting that Azerbaijan's armed forces are the strongest in the region, the defense ministry in Baku in September 2009 stressed the intensity of cooperation with NATO, and the diversification of foreign defense assistance: allegedly the country has defense relations with 52 states and military agreements were signed with 26 countries.[8] Azerbaijan has steadily enhanced its level of cooperation with NATO through its membership in the Partnership for Peace (PfP) program and at a bi-lateral level with Alliance members. NATO would like to see a more concerted effort by Baku to strengthen civil control over the armed forces and make the security structures more accountable to parliament.[9]

In Armenia, integration with NATO is a tricky question. The country holds the closest security partnership with Russia in the region. It is party to the Collective Security Treaty Organization (CSTO). These ties impose certain

---

[8] Ayna, September 5 2009; quoted by Roger McDermott, "Azerbaijan Deepens Military Cooperation with US and NATO," *Eurasia Daily Monitor*, Jamestown Foudnation, Vol. 5, Issue 173, 22 Sep 2009.
[9] Roger Mc Dermott, ibid.

limitations on Armenia's integration with NATO.[10] While Georgia perceives Russia as a threatening power, Armenia regards it as a protector. Traditionally, Armenia had perceived NATO as an organization that strengthened its external enemy, Turkey. But it has since softened this historical aversion and demonstrated interest in security cooperation with the Alliance. It has changed its foreign policy from an exclusive orientation toward Russia to a policy of complementarism with different vectors to ensure its national interests. One of these vectors is the Atlantic one. According to a public survey from 2005 among 1,500 citizens from Yerevan and all Armenia, nearly 35 percent of the respondents affirmed that their country should become a member of NATO; 34 percent said "no." The results of an Expert Survey are even more outspoken for NATO-membership: 52.5 percent of the Armenian experts supported this perspective.[11] Though remaining an active member of the Russian-led CSTO, Armenia has enhanced its relations with NATO. It became involved in the PfP-program and started to participate in sessions of the NATO Parliamentary Assembly. Contacts between Armenian officials and NATO bodies became more active at all levels from 2005. Armenia obtained a NATO Individual Partnership Action Plan (IPAP) and intensified its cooperation with the Alliance in a number of areas. In 2008, soldiers from NATO-member states participated in a joint military exercise on Armenian territory. The August 2008 military conflict between Russia and Georgia put Armenia's policy of complementarism to a severe test. Like other of Russia's "allies" in the CSTO, Armenian officials were far away from any affirmative statement on Russia's military action in Georgia and from following its diplomatic step of recognizing Abkhazia and South Ossetia as "independent states."

All three states developed individualized relationships with NATO within the framework of Individual Partnership Agreements focusing on military reform, establishment of effective state institutions and certain democratization goals. There are diverging approaches to the linkage between NATO integration and conflict resolution. According to a poll in February 2007 in Georgia, the respondents gave the following answers to

---

[10] Alexander Iskandaryan, "NATO and Armenia: A Long Game of Complementarism," Caucasus Analytical Digest, no. 4, 16 April 2009, pp. 17-18.
[11] Armenian Center for National and International Studies: "Armenia's Place and Role in the Region." Presentation of Expert and Public Poll Results, July 2005, p. 647.

the question: What do you expect from NATO membership? (up to 3 answers): security guarantees – 57 percent; restoration of territorial integrity – 42 percent; social welfare – 22 percent; strengthening democracy – 16 percent.[12] NATO did not directly intervene in the unresolved regional conflicts and has no official plan to do so. Georgia's ambition for quick membership via a Membership Action Plan had, however, an impact on the relations among the conflicting parties. It increased the perception of a military threat for the breakaway entities, and Russia massively supported this perception. Unlike Georgia, Armenia and Azerbaijan did not expect an active role for NATO in the mediation and resolution of their conflict on Nagorno Karabakh.

### Dimensions of Insecurity in the Region

At the beginning of the post-Soviet period, the Western perception of regional security in the Caucasus was occupied by enormous difficulties in the process of state and nation building, secessionist wars, privatisation of violence, and the emergence of warlords on different conflict sides. With the cease fire agreements on South Ossetia (1992), Abkhazia and Nagorno Karabakh (1994), and the beginning of a process of political stabilization under new-old leaders like Eduard Shevardnadze and Haidar Aliyev, the focus shifted to the geo-economic and geo-strategic importance of the Caucasus. But instability remained with a profound lack of security in the region. Georgia and Russia became increasingly engaged in confrontation. The "frozen conflicts" were still far away from a political solution. More than one million people out of a population of 16 million in the South Caucasus remained displaced.

Insecurity in the Caucasus had two fundamental dimensions: ethno-territorial fragmentation and the "weak state" syndrome. The first dimension, with its focus on ethnicity and territory, recalled the simplistic Soviet concept of ethnic homelands, the matryoshka-like configuration of national autonomies as a substitute for political sovereignty. Conflict potential in this region appeared to be depicted on the map of its administrative entities as inherited from Soviet times. But it was too

---

[12] IRI (International Republic Institute), USAID etc.: Georgian National Voter Study. February 2007.

simplistic to reduce the analysis of regional instability to this dimension. Another dimension came into play: the syndrome of weak states with low legitimacy of political institutions, endemic corruption, political cultures dominated by personalities, and informal networks over institutions and policies. In a country like Georgia, these problems manifested themselves in the internal and external security structures. At the end of the Shevardnadze-era, actors and agencies officially responsible for "law and order" and for security were at the very center of the population's frustration. People felt that they were not living in a proper state.

In the first dimension, the unresolved conflicts in Abkhazia, South Ossetia and Nagorno Karabakh remain the most outstanding factor in the security analysis of the region. The problem with the established notion of the "frozen conflict" is that these conflicts were not reliably frozen but open to a risky "unfreezing." The scenario of falling back into open hostilities and war happened in the smallest of all conflict zones, in South Ossetia, which had been identified until 2004 as the regional conflict with the highest potential for confidence building between the conflicting sides. However, hostilities there resumed in summer 2004, and the security situation since then has become extremely volatile. The main suggestion of the adjective "frozen" conveys the notion that developments at a certain moment, with the ceasefire-agreements some 15 years ago, were stopped and put on ice. Nothing is more misleading than that notion. There have been manifold developments in the sovereign states as well as in the secessionist entities, which make the situation different from that at the time of ceasefire. Concerning the latter, the separation from the former de-jure state has been historicized: a new generation has grown up without any link to the former metropolitan state. To bring them back into a construction under the roof of one state would be extremely difficult. Another fundamental development was a growing "militariziation" of the South Caucasus on all conflict sides. The level of armament became fundamentally different from that in the period of secessionist wars at the beginning of the 1990s.

What about the second dimension – that of the "weak state?" In Georgia after the "Rose Revolution," the structures of internal and external security have been overhauled like no other sector of the state. Compared to the ancien regime, the condition of the police and the army changed remarkably. On the one hand, this could be seen as a positive aspect of a "stronger state" and "better governance." On the other hand, it was a manifestation of the already mentioned militarization of the region within the risky context of unresolved conflicts. For NATO, it was an ambigious challenge. Georgia, indeed, largely adapted its military structures to NATO standards, which was affirmed by NATO-monitoring missions in the region. As a consequence, Tbilisi – with strong support from Washington – demanded early accession to the Alliance. Yet at the same time, this process did not diminish the conflict potential in the region but aggravated tensions between Georgia and the breakaway entities of Abkhazia and South Ossetia, as well as between Georgia and Russia.

Growing militarization also applies to Azerbaijan, which now has by far the biggest military budget in the region.[13] But the unresolved conflict with Armenia on Nagorno Karabakh and Azerbaijan`s political culture sets certain limits to the transformation of security structures according to Western standards. NATO policies of democratization of the armed forces aim at putting the army under parliamentary control. Though the government allegedly worked on plans to promote civilian leadership of the defense ministry according to NATO standards, a speaker of the Defense and Security Committee attached the following reservation: "We did not undertake a commitment on this because the war between Armenia and Azerbaijan has not ended yet."[14]

One can hardly assess regional security in the Southern Caucasus without taking into consideration the developments in the Northern Caucasus. Though both halves of the region are separated by physically clear-cut borders running along a high mountain range, South and North Caucasian conflict dynamics are linked. That brings Russia into play, which holds in the Caucasus a position different from that in Central Asia or other parts of the post-Soviet space: Russia is part of this region. It has in the North Caucasus its own "internal abroad" with highly unstable entities like Dagestan, Chechnya, Ingushetia or Kabardino-Balkaria, and in the South Caucasus the most tense relationship in its "near abroad," that is with Georgia. And it feels itself geopolitically challenged in this region by a "far

---

[13] Jasur Mamedov: "Azerbaijan Flexes Military Muscles," in: *Caucasus Reporting Series*, No. 402, 19 Jul 2007.

[14] Quotation in: "Khazri Bakinsky, Mina Muradova: Azerbaijan Pursues NATO Integration," in: *Eurasia Insight*, 16 Mar 2007.

abroad," the United States. Before the 2008 "August War," some Russian Caucasus analysts believed that Russia was "trapped" by its own strategy concerning the conflicts with Abkhazia and South Ossetia. These analysts noted that while Moscow has been supporting the separatist governments for over a decade, any move to formally recognize the territories as well as any move to abandon the support to them would have far reaching implications for Russia's southern periphery in the North Caucasus.[15] After the war, Russia moved to formally recognize Abkhazia and South Ossetia. Moscow went from using the unresolved conflicts as its strongest leverage over Tbilisi by openly supporting the separatist parties to the conflict to changing the two contested territories into its military protectorates in the Southern Caucasus. Russia now presents itself as the guarantor of independence and security for these entities without being able to guarantee even a minimum level of stability to its own Federation citizens living in the Northern Caucasus.

Thus in the Caucasian region, NATO is approaching an area of antagonistic regional and international dynamics. Besides the regional antagonisms deriving from unresolved conflicts and the fundamentally poisoned relationship between Georgia and Russia, there are international antagonisms like that between the US and Iran, which is of growing concern for this region. There is a consensus even between Armenian and Azeri security experts, that a military escalation around Iran would be desastrous for their countries. Within this context, NATO-engagement in the Caucasus raises, above all, the question: how can it avoid becoming another antagonizing element of regional and international relations in this region.

### Integration with the European Union

The Southern Caucasus is located at intersecting zones of EU-regional projects and iniatives like the European Neighborhood Policy (ENP), the Black Sea Synergy initiative, and the most recent initiative of the Eastern Partnership (EaP) – encompassing Belarus, Ukraine, Moldova, and the three South Caucasus countries. A European Security Strategy adopted in

---

[15] Sergei Markedonov: "The Paradoxes of Russia's Georgia Policy," in: *Russia in Global Affairs*, vol. 5, no. 2, April-June 2007, 173-186.

December 2003 called on the EU to "take a stronger and more active interest in the problems in the Southern Caucasus."[16] The peaceful transfer of power in Georgia, with the new governing elite's strong commitment toward reform, good governance and a strengthening of statehood, was a stimulus for the EU to integrate the Southern Caucasus into its Neighborhood Policy in 2004. Since 2003, new tools and institutions for an EU policy toward this region emerged, including the EUSR (EU Special Representative) or the ENP-Action Plans. From the beginning of this process it became clear that an increased EU policy in this region would trigger a rivalry between the EU and Russia in their common neighborhood.[17]

All three countries commit to be part of Europe.[18] Their commitment to integration with Europe is accompanied by a low knowledge of European institutions and structures in the broader public. "It is not rare for an average person to confuse the EU with the Council of Europe, or the latter with the European Council. But this ignorance also represents an untapped opportunity for the EU. Unlike Russia and the United States, which are largely perceived in more controversial terms as being expansionist powers seeking to dominate others, the EU is perceived as a soft power that seeks to advance its interests by incentives rather than by pressure."[19]

In Armenia, the commitment to a European orientation has to be balanced with a special security policy relationship with Russia, the country's membership within Eurasian formats of security and economic cooperation centered on Moscow. Russia accounts for the lion's share of investment in Armenia. The telecommunications sector, the banking system, energy supply, the metal industry and the railway system are largely under Russian control. The country's budget and economy are highly dependent on

---

[16] "A Secure Europe in a Better World." European Security Strategy, European Council, Brussels, December 12, 2003, p. 8.

[17] Uwe Halbach: "Der Kaukasus in neuem Licht. Die EU und Rußland in ihrer schwierigsten Nachbarschaftsregion," SWP-Studie S 35, Berlin November 2005.

[18] Tigran Mkrtchyan, Tabib Huseynov, Kakha Gogolashvili: "The European Union and the South Caucasus. Three Perspectives on the Future of the European Project from the Caucasus." *Europe in Dialogue* 2009/ 01, Bertelsmann Stifung, Gütersloh 2009.

[19] Tabib Huseynov: "The EU and Azerbaijan. Destination Unclear," in: *Europe in Dialogue* 2009/01, pp. 49-89, quotation p. 63-64.

remittances from abroad. Though the Armenian diaspora is widespread and global, the lion's share of remittances to Armenia comes from Russia.[20]

Like both of its neighbors in the region, since its independence in 1991, Armenia got involved in bi-lateral and multi-lateral projects with the EU through the TACIS National Program, EU support for its institutional and administrative reforms, a food security program, regional infrastructure programs like TRACECA and INOGATE, a Partnership and Cooperation Agreement (PCA, signed 1996, in force since 1999), and recently the integration into the ENP via an action plan with eight high-priority areas for cooperation. The ENP Action Plan with Armenia focuses on 1) democratic structures, rule of law, judicial reforms and combating corruption, 2) respect for human rights and fundamental freedoms, 3) economic development and poverty reduction, environmental protection, improvement of investment climate, 5) the convergence of economic legislation and administrative practices, and 6) the development of an energy strategy. Only the last two priorities concern intra-regional relations and conflict resolution, topics which are more weighted in the Action Plans with Georgia and Azerbaijan.

Every year, Armenia's Foreign Minister states in his annual January briefings that a European orientation represents a top priority for the country. According to his ministry, the ENP is seen as a "useful anchor for reforms." Notwithstanding Armenia's economic dependence on Russia, the EU as a whole accounted for a 54.4 percent share of its exports, while 34.6 percent of its imports originated in EU member states.[21] The majority of parties in Armenia's last parliamentary elections in May 2007 said they see no alternative to European integration. But in Armenian society, the perception of this Western integration contains not only expectations, but also scepticism. Integration into European culture is seen as a certain threat to national identity of the most ethnically homogenous society in the post-Soviet space. Some Armenian intellectuals underline the spiritual "decadence" of Europe and present it as a challenge to Armenians' devotion

---

[20] Tigran Mkrtchyan: "Armenia's European Future," in: *Europe in Dialogue* 2009/01, pp. 14-48, on the economic dependence on Russia see p. 39.

[21] Statistical Yearbook of Armenia 2007; quoted by Tigran Mkrtchyan, op. cit., p.17.

to their families, church and community.[22] Nevertheless, a positive feeling toward the European Union prevails. The EU emerged from recent surveys among Armenian respondents as the most trusted external institution. Up to 38 percent of respondents replied that Armenia should definitely join it, while 51 percent voted for Armenia's possible access to the EU in the future.[23]

In Azerbaijan, the question "Are we Europeans?" is discussed by the political and academic elite. Different answers are given to this question: that the question mark does not exist at all and the discussion on the country's European identity has long been decided for Azerbaijani society; that Azerbaijan's regional identity is determied by its location between the East and Europe and that the factors affecting this identity are multifarious; that Azerbaijan is using the European experience for its strategy of modernism; that its Islamic tradition does not at all prevent Azerbaijan from moving towards integration with Europe as the issue of maintaining national traditions is generally accepted in the EU.[24] According to recent sociological surveys, the broader population supports integration into European structures. Among different offers for the direction of Azerbaijan's integration – CIS, EU, Organization of the Islamic Conference (OIC) – the largest share of respondents voted for the orientation toward the EU (38 percent, CIS – 13 percent, OIC – 7.2 percent, neutrality – 37 percent).[25] Among the respondents of a poll published in February 2008, only 6.9 percent opted for integration with NATO.[26]

In Azerbaijan, it is of interest whether the EU will be seeking a more active role in the resolution of regional conflicts, as can bee seen from its decision to send a mission to Georgia (EUMM) under the auspices of the European Security and Defense Policy (ESDP). In contrast to its greater involvement in the unresolved conflicts in Georgia, the EU's participation in the

---

[22] Tigran Matosyan: "Europe: A Model of Replication or a Threat to Identity? The Case of Armenia," in: Elena Marushiakova (ed.): *Dynamics of National Identity and Transnational Identities in the Process of European Integration*, Cambridge Scholars Publishing Newcastle 2008.

[23] Mkrtchyan, in: *Europe in Dialogue* 2009/01, pp. 22, 23.

[24] "Are We Europeans? National Discussions Spring Debates," "Iräli" Public Union Baku 2009.

[25] Ibid, p. 14.

[26] Tabib Huseynov: The EU and Azerbaijan. Destination Unclear, in: Europe in Dialogue 2009/01, p.63.

resolution of the Nagorno Karabakh conflict until now was minimal or non-existent. In Azerbaijan's perception on what are the main interests of EU in the region, the issue of energy supply diversification is of crucial importance. This issue pushed recent EU initiatives like the Black Sea Synergy of 2007 and the Eastern Partnership of 2009, and it is focusing on Azerbaijan as the only producer and a main transit country for Caspian oil and gas in the region. European markets represent the most profitable option for the export of Azerbaijani oil and gas. The EU-Azerbaijan energy memorandum of 2006 declared the country to be a "strategic partner" for the EU in the field of energy cooperation. The Azerbaijani elites view already existing pipelines like the Baku-Tbilisi-Ceyhan oil connection and future projects like the Nabucco-gas connection as "means for firmly attaching Azerbaijan to the political and economic map of Europe."[27]

However, the strongest commitment to Europe comes from Georgia and is closely and fatefully coupled with this country's emphasis on "fleeing the Russian empire." A majority of Georgians believe that the country has a "future in Europe." The Georgian historical narrative presents the country as a core of European civilization. "Europe started here," says a new map of Georgia for Western tourists. Public opinion polls carried out since the mid-1990s have shown high public trust accorded to European institutions, though a lack of the EU's visibility in the region and especially in the field of conflict resolution elicited complaints from Georgia's political community. With regard to security policy, the US and NATO were seen as closer Westerm partners. After the 2008 August war between Georgia and Russia, the EU's profile in the region has strengthened. The war showed political elites in Georgia that the country's security cannot only revolve around the US and a hypothetical accession to NATO. A scenario of "more EU, less NATO" evolved.[28]

The three South Caucasus countries differ widely in their reaction to a recent EU regional initative: the Black Sea Synergy (BSS) project, launched in April 2007. With Bulgaria's and Romania's accession, the EU turned from an outside player into a regional power in the Wider Black Sea Area, which not only encloses littoral states. Especially the issue of energy supply

---

[27] Ibid. p. 65.
[28] Oscar Pardo Sierra, "A point of no return? Georgia and the EU one year after the August War," Central Asia-Caucasus Institute Analyst 19 Aug 2009.

introduced a Black Sea dimension into the discourse on European integration and affected regional identities in the Southern Caucasus. It had the potential "to deconstruct the South Caucasus as a dominant geographical and mental concept for referring to the region."[29] For Georgia, "Black Sea," as a regional denominator, became more attractive than "Caucasian." The country has increasingly positioned itself as a Black Sea actor. Georgia is actively involved in cooperation efforts around the Black Sea in the areas of infrastructure developments (pipelines), security and stability (border protection, anti-terrorism, military, legal and conflict resolution issues), and scientific and environmental projects.[30] Its 2006 ENP Action Plan lays stress on this regional cooperation perspective.

Azerbaijan, on the other hand, has little sense of belonging to the Black Sea region; it portrays itself as a Caspian actor. And in Armenia there are practically no discussions on the BSS initiative. In nearly all critical areas of Black Sea cooperation (energy, transport, maritime security, environment, fisheries) Armenia has no participation at all.

**Future Perspectives**

With regard to democratization, regional cooperation, and peaceful resolution of perpetrated conflicts, the main European options for development in the Southern Caucasus are still far from implementation. With regard to democratization, the assessment of the domestic political developments even deteriorated recently. In the whole of the post-Soviet space, nearly every country saw its rankings drop in Freedom House's "Nations in Transit" 2009 report. According to numerical measurements that the organization developed to try to quantify democratization in several crucial areas, including civil society development, independent media, elections and corruption, Azerbaijan saw its aggregate score drop from 6.00 to 6.25 – the largest decline in recent years.[31] Georgia's front-runner image for democratization, which it had won with the "Rose

---

[29] Tabib Huseynov: "The EU and Azerbaijan. Destination Unclear," in: Europe in Dialogue 2009/01., p. 55.
[30] Kakha Gogolashvili: "The EU and Georgia. The Choice is in the Context," in: *Europe in Dialogue* 2009/01, pp. 101, 106-110.
[31] Joshua Kucera: "Central Asia and Caucasus: Dark Days for Democratization," Report, Eurasia Insight, 7 Jan 2009.

Revolution," was damaged by violent confrontations between the government and a growing opposition against authoritarian trends within the power elite around Mikheil Saakashvili. The same happened in Armenia with an even more violent confrontation between the government and the opposition in March 2008 and during contested presidential elections.

The trajectory of Georgian politics after the "Rose Revolution" demonstrated the tension between the principles of democratization/liberalisation and stabilization/state-building. The new Georgian government began consolidating executive authority by enlarging presidential power over the parliament and judiciary, centralized its influence over its Autonomous Republic of Ajara and restructered the system of local governance by centralizing political power in the provinces. Georgian civil society groups, once protagonists of the "Rose Revolution," now protest human rights violations by the power elite. They contested the balloting of the 2008 presidential and parliamentary contests. Nevertheless, over 70 percent of Georgians affirm that democratic institutions are the most appropriate mechanisms for governance. The mass level political culture is becoming more, not less, democratically oriented.[32] However, Georgia, just like other post-Soviet states, was struggling with the legacy of Soviet political culture and low-scale economic and social devolopment. It was thus unlikely to expect a rapid transformation.[33]

In this context, one may recall a prognosis, which a former standard-bearer of "democratization" in Central Asia made ten years ago. Askar Akaev, then president of Kyrgyzstan, said in an interview in 1999:

> Among the lessons of the transformation is what I call the collapse of illusions. The essence of this lesson is that both the West and the post-Communist nations naïvely expected too much in too short a time. The ruling elites in post-Communist nations obviously had an exaggerated and simplistic idea about the kind of support they

---

[32] Julie A. George: "One Year Later. Georgian Political Reform and the West after the War," CACI-Analyst, 14 Oct 2009; Hans Gutbrod, Koba Turmanidze: "'Is Georgia a Democracy Now?' Views of the Georgian Electorate," in: Adam Hug (ed.): *Spotlight on Georgia*, London 2009, pp. 20-33, <http://fpc.org.uk/fsblob/1079.pdf>.
[33] Kakha Gogolashvili: "The EU and Georgia. The Choice is in the Context," *Europe in Dialogue* 2009/01, p. 90.

could receive from the West... And the West underestimated the systemic complexity of change and the degree of resistance from old and still powerfull quarters. American aid programs first assumed that this transition period would last five years. Today Zbigniew Brzezinski writes about ten years of transition. In fact longer periods may be required.[34]

Ten years later Kyrgyzstan as well as other post-Soviet states is still far away from real and sustainable democratic institution building. In the already mentioned 2009 "Nations in Transit" report it, for the first time, left the category of "partly free" and joined the ranks of the "consolidated authoritarian regimes." With regard to this disillusionment on "rapid transformation," it is hard to dare a prognosis on the EU-membership perspective for Georgia, Armenia and Azerbaijan for the next ten years. Additionally, there are currently signs of a deep enlargement fatigue within the European Union.

In the Southern Caucasus, perspectives for democratization and good governance, as well as for good neighborly inter-state relations, are fatefully coupled with the situation around unresolved regional conflicts. After the August 2008 "Five Day War" in South Ossetia between Russian and Georgian troops, it has to be clear that no one should rely anymore on the "frozeness" of such conflicts. With regard to the South Caucasus regional conflicts, the EU as well as NATO were not, or were only indirectly, involved in conflict resolution and peacekeeping. The EU's role in this field of action was described by the International Crisis Group in 2006 as working around conflict, not working on conflict.[35] The EU spent over EUR 30 million before 2008 on reconstruction around conflict zones like South Ossetia in the hope of promoting reconciliation between the parties to the conflicts, but failed to develop a political and security strategy toward the South Caucasus as a region of unresolved conflicts. Some EU states feared that a greater EU role in this highly sensitive field of action – especially with regard to Georgia's separatist conflicts, where Russia was deeply involved – would complicate EU-Russia relations. Russia clearly opposed a greater EU role in conflict resolution and was eager to eliminate international presence

---

[34] <http://www.kyrgyzstan.org/public/01.html 28.6.1999>.
[35] Conflict Resolution in the South Caucasus: The EU's Role, ICG Europe Report No.173, 20 March 2006.

in the border regions between North and South Caucasus like an OSCE mission along the Georgian border with Chechnya, Ingushetia and Dagestan.[36] With its monitoring mission in Georgia (EUMM) since October 2008, the EU got more involved in the field of peacekeeping, which it cautiously abstained from before. With the 2008 August war, the EU had to learn that in a conflict-stricken region like the Southern Caucasus any external actor is eventually caught up by challenges of conflict management. This is true even if the external actor sets other regional priorities like good governance, rule of law, economic reform, support for intra-regional integration or energy cooperation. All of these issues from good governance to intra-regional cooperation are too much connected with, and hampered by, the implications of unresolved regional conflicts.

The EU's new approach to its Caucasian neighborhood is its first conflict-related Monitoring Mission in the framework of European Security and Defense Policy – the EUMM in Georgia with a staff of about 320 persons from nearly all EU-member states. The core task of this civilian, non-armed mission is monitoring, analyzing and reporting on the process of stabilization after the war, the reconstruction of infrastructure, the return of refugees as well as security and order throughout Georgia. But regarding the phrase "throughout Georgia," interpretations diverge, whith Russia and the Russian protected governments in Abkhazia and South Ossetia on one side, and the EU, Georgia and the rest of the international community on the other. The central point of reference for the mandate of this mission is the ceasefire agreement made by presidents Sarkozy and Medvedev in August and September 2008. But on central items of these agreements like the withdrawal of Russian troops to the status quo antebellum there are divergent interpretations. Instead of a withdrawal, there was an extension of Russian military forces in Abkhazia and South Ossetia. Instead of a European Monitoring Mission "throughout Georgia" there is no free access to the conflict zones. If the area of action of the EUMM remains limited to regions adjacent to Abkhazia and South Ossetia without unlimited access to both territories, the European Union is in a delicate position of contributing to the stability of borders that it itself does not recognize as state borders. And, without unlimited access to a still destabilized region

---

[36] Nicu Popescu: "The EU's Conflict Prevention Failure in Georgia," Central Asia-Caucasus Institute Analyst, 14 Oct 2009.

like South Ossetia, it can hardly fulfill its core function of monitoring, analyzing and reporting incidents. Thus, with regard to regional conflicts in their post-Soviet neighborhood, European actors remain confronted with one fundamental dilemma: nothing in this field goes without Russia, nothing in confrontation with Russia, but until now also practically nothing in cooperation with Russia.

If there are new dynamics of conflict transformation in the Southern Caucasus and the wider Black Sea Region, they concern Turkish-Armenian diplomatic approaches leading to the opening of the countries' mutual border. This approach, which began already before the 2008 August war, got an additional impulse by the "Georgian crisis." For Armenia, for instance, the war was a lesson on its transit dependence on Georgian territory and pushed the demand for the opening of closed borders. In Turkey, the war pushed ambitions for peace building activities in the Caucasus. In Azerbaijan, it toned down military rhetoric on resolving the problem of large parts of its territory beeing occupied by Armenian troops. In the Karabakh conflict itself, it opened a window of opportunity. There followed a year of vigorous shuttle diplomacy and an unprecedented frequency of summits between the presidents of Azerbaijan and Armenia.[37] Optimists see a breakthrough in the oldest regional conflict in the Southern Caucasus emerging. Pessimists see the connection between the unresolved conflict and the opening of the Turkish-Armenian border limiting the chances for rapid advances in Turkish-Armenian bi-lateral relations. Whenever there are new approaches they are quickly caught up by disillusioning realities deriving from unresolved conflicts.

In conclusion, the unresolved regional conflicts and their braking impact on the democratization of states in the Southern Caucasus make the short-term perspective for membership in NATO and the EU improbable. However, they also make "benign neglect" impossible. The conflicts challenge Armenia, Azerbaijan and Georgia to cooperate more closely with their Euro-Atlantic partners; EU and NATO members, meanwhile, realize the importance of their engagement for peace and development in the Caucasus.

---

[37] "Nagorno-Karabakh: Getting to a Breakthroug," ICG Policy Briefing, Europe Briefing No.55, 7 October 2009.

# BIBLIOGRAPHY

Acharya, Amitav. "Regionalism and Regional Security in the Third World: Comparing the Origins of the ASEAN and the GCC," in *The Insecurity Dilemma: National Security of Third World States*, ed. Brian Job. Boulder, CO: Lynne Rienner Publishers, 1992.

Acharya, Amitav. 1992. "Regionalism and Regional Security in the Third World: Comparing the Origins of the ASEAN and the GCC." in *The Insecurity Dilemma: National Security of Third World States*, ed. B. Job. Boulder, CO: Lynne Rienner.

Acharya, Amitav. *US Military Strategy in the Gulf* (London: Routledge, 1989).

Adamescu, A. A., and E. D. Silaev, eds. "Zakavkazskiy ekonomicheskiy raion. Ekonomiko-geograficheskiy ocherk" ("The Transcaucasian Economic Region. Economic and Geographical Essay"). Moscow.

Ansari, Ali M. 2006.*Confronting Iran: The Failure of American Foreign Policy and the Next Great Crisis in the Middle East*. New York: Basic Books.

Ansari, Ali M. *Confronting Iran: The Failure of American Foreign Policy and the Next Great Crisis in the Middle East*. New York: Basic Books, 2006.

Åslund, A. *How Capitalism was Built: The Transformation of Central and Eastern Europe, Russia, and Central Asia*. New York: Cambridge University Press, 2007.

Aydin M. (ed.). *KüreselPolitika'da Orta Asya* [*Central Asia in Global Politics*]. Ankara: Siyasal, 2004.

Aydin, M. "1990–2001 Kafkasya ve Orta Asya'yla Iliskiler," ["Relations with Central Asia and the Caucasus, 1990–2001"].

Aydin, M. "Foucault's Pendulum: Turkey in Central Asia and the Caucasus." *Turkish Studies*, Vol. 5, No. 2, summer 2004.

Aydın, M.: "Between Euphoria and Realpolitik. Turkish Policy toward Central Asia and the Caucasus." In: Ismael, T.Y./Aydın, M. (Hg.): *Turkey's Foreign Policy in the 21st Century*.

Ayoob, Mohammed. "Squaring the Circle: Collective Security in a System of States." *Collective Security in a Changing World*, ed. Thomas G. Weiss. Boulder, CO: Lynne Rienner, 1993.

Ayoob, Mohammed. "Squaring the Circle: Collective Security in a System of States." In *Collective Security in a Changing World*, ed. T. G. Weiss. Boulder, CO: Lynne Rienner, 1993.

B./Kirişci, K. (Hg.): *Turkey in World Politics. An Emerging Multiregional Power*. London/Boulder 2001.

Bahgat, Gawdat. 2008. "Security in the Persian Gulf: Two Conflicting Models." *Defense and Security Analysis* 24 (3).

Balcerowicz, L. *Socialism, Capitalism, Transformation*. Budapest: CEU, 1995.

Bartsch, G.K. et al. (Hg.), "Turkish Strategic Interests in the Transcaucasus."

Barysch, Katinka (ed.). *Pipelines, Politics and Power- The future of EU-Russia energy relations*. Centre for European Reform. London 2008.

Blandy, C. W. "The Caucasus Region and Caspian Basin: Change, Complication and Challenge," CSRC Report S36. Surrey: RMA Sandhurst, 1988.

Blix, Hans. 2004. *Disarming Iraq*. New York: Pantheon Books.

Bolukbasi, "The Caucasus within a Historical-Strategic Matrix. Russia, Iran and Turkey." *Foreign Policy* (Ankara) Vol. XVIII, 1994.

Borovalı, *A Changing Role in World Politics*. Burlington, 2003.

Bressand, Albert and Catherine Distler, *La Planete Relationnelle*, Le Seuil, 1995.

Brunner, Blake. "Russia And Turkey: Relations between equals?" *An Analytical Review*, Volume XV, Number 9, 5 Mar 2009.

Buszynski, Leszek. "Russia and the Commonwealth of Independent States in 2002: Going Separate Ways." *Asian Survey*, Vol. 43, No. 1, Jan.-Feb., 2003.

Caballero, R. J., T. Hoshi, and A. K. Kashyap. "Zombie Lending and Depressed Restructuring in Japan," *American Economic Review*, 98/5, 2008.

Chikava, L. "Demographic development in the South Caucasian countries: current trends and future prospects." *The Caucasus & Globalization*. 1 (2), 2007.

Chubin, Shahram. *Iran's Nuclear Ambitions*. Washington, DC: Carnegie Endowment for International Peace, 2006).

Clem, R. "The New Central Asia: Prospects for Development." M. Bradshaw (ed.). *Geography and Transition in the Post-Soviet Republics*. New York: John Wiley and Sons, 1997.

Coates, D. *Models of Capitalism: Growth and Stagnation in the Modern Era*. Cambridge, UK: Polity Press, 2000.

Cockburn, Patrick. *Muqtada al-Sadr, the Shia Revival, and the Struggle for Iraq*. New York: Simon and Schuster, 2008.

Cornell, S. E. *Small Nations and Great Powers. A Study of Ethnopolitical Conflict in the Caucasus*. Surrey: Curzon Press, 2001; Herzig, E., ibid.

Cornell, S. E., and S. F. Starr, eds. *The Guns of August 2008: Russia's War in Georgia*. Armonk: M.E. Sharpe, 2009.

Cornell, Svante E. and S. Frederick Starr. *The Caucasus: A Challenge for Europe*. Upsala. Central Asia & Caucasus Institute. Sweden, 2006.

Curtis, G. E., ed. "Armenia, Azerbaijan, and Georgia: country Studies." Washington, D.C.: Federal Research Division Library of Congress, 1995.

Dahms, H. F., ed. *Transformations of Capitalism: Economy, Society and the State in Modern Times*. Hampshire, UK: MacMillian Press, 2000; Gwynne, R.N., T. Klak and D.J.B. Shaw.

Daly, John C. K., "Growing Azeri Defense Budget Buildup—In Earnest or for Show?" *Eurasia Daily Monitor*, Vol. 5, Issue 209, October 31, 2008,

Dedeyev, Bilal. *Daglik Karabagh Sorununun Tarihi Arkaplanina Bakishm Karabagh Savashi*, Baku, Kafkasya Arashtirmalari Enstitusu, 2008.

Elma, Fikret. "The Problems of Democracy, Security and Cooperation in Globalisation Process in South Caucasia," *The Journal of International Social Research*, Volume 2/6 Winter 2009.

Erhan, C. "ABD'nin Orta Asya Politikalari ve 11 Eylul Sonrasi Acilimlari" [US Policy towards Central Asia and Changes since September 11].

Erikson, E. *Identity: Youth and Crisis*. N.Y.: Norton & Company, 1968.

Freedman and Karsh, "The Gulf Conflict 1990-1991: Diplomacy and War in the New World Order."

Freedman, Lawrence and Efraim Karsh. *The Gulf Conflict, 1990-1991: Diplomacy and War in the New World Order*. Princeton, NJ: Princeton University Press, 1993.

Friedman, Thomas L. *The Lexus and the Olive Tree*. Farrar, Straus and Giroux, 1999.

Gachechiladze, R. G., M. A. Nadzhafaliyev and A. D. Rondeli. "The Regional Development Problems of Transcaucasia." *Geoforum*, 15/1, 1984. Nauka Publishers, 1973.

Gajiev, K. S. *Geopolitika Kavkaza (Geopolitics of the Caucasus)*, Moscow: Mezhdunarodnye otnoshenia Publishers, 2003.

Gause III, F. Gregory. "The Illogic of Dual Containment," *Foreign Affairs* 73 (1994).

Gerges, Fawaz A. *The Far Enemy: Why Jihad Went Global*. New York, NY: Cambridge University Press, 2005.

Gültekin, Bç *Die islamischen Staaten und ihr Verhältnis zur westlichenWelt*. München 2000.

Gurtov, Melvin. *Superpower on Crusade: The Bush Doctrine in US Foreign Policy*. Boulder, CO: Lynne Rienner Publishers, 2006.

Herzig, E. *The New Caucasus: Armenia, Azerbaijan and Georgia*. London, UK: Royal Institute of International Affairs, 1999.

Hübner, G., and M. Jainzik. "Splendid Isolation? Azerbaijan's Economy Between Crisis Resistance and Debased Performance," *Caucasus Analytical Digest*: The Caucasus in the Global Financial Crisis, No. 6, May 21, 2009.

Ian S. Lustick, *Trapped in the War on Terror*. Philadelphia, PA: University of Pennsylvania Press, 2006.

Iskandaryan, Alexander. "NATO and Armenia: A Long Game of Complementarism," *Caucasus Analytical Digest*, no.4, 16 April 2009.

Ismailov, E., and V. Papava. "A New Concept for the Caucasus," *Southeast European and Black Sea Studies*, 8/3, 2008.

Ismailov, E., and V. Papava. *The Central Caucasus: Problems of Geopolitical Economy*. New York: Nova Science Publishers, 2008.

Ismailov, Eldar. "Finansovo-kreditnıy mexanizm ekonomiçeskoy integratsii Kavkaza." *Central and East European Studies: Abstracts*. 2000, Tampere, Finland.

Jones, Toby Craig. "Religious Revivalism and Its Challenge to the Saudi Regime." in *Religion and Politics in Saudi Arabia: Wahhabism and the State*. 109-120 vols, ed. Mohammed Ayoob and Hasan Kosebalaban. Boulder, CO: Lynne Rienner, 2009.

Karaosmanoglu, A, *Crossroads and Conflict: Security and Foreign Policy in the Caucasus and Central Asia*. New York/London, 2000.

Kaye, Dalia Dassa and Frederic M. Wehrey. "A Nuclear Iran: The Reactions of Neighbours." *Survival* 49 (2), 2007.

Kelly, J. B. *Arabia, the Gulf, and the West*. London: Weidenfeld and Nicolson, 1980.

Kerr, Malcolm H. *The Arab Cold War: Gamal Abd al-Nasir and His Rivals, 1958-1970*. 3rd ed. London, New York: Oxford University Press, 1971.

Kimball, Jeffrey. "The Nixon Doctrine: A Saga of Misunderstanding," *Presidential Studies Quarterly* 36 (1), 2006.

King, Charles. "The Five-Day War," *Foreing Affairs*, V. 87, Nunber 6, November-December 2008.

Kinzer, Stephen. *All the Shah's Men : an American Coup and the Roots of Middle East Terror*. 2nd ed. Hoboken, N.J.: John Wiley & Sons, 2008.

Kotchikian, Asbed, "Secular Nationalism Versus Political Islam in Azerbaijan." *Terrorism Monitor*, Vol. 3, Issue 3. Jamestown Foundation. February 9, 2005.

Kuniholm, Bruce Robellet. *The Origins of the Cold War in the Near East: Great Power Conflict and Diplomacy in Iran, Turkey, and Greece.* Princeton, N.J.: Princeton University Press, 1980.

Lake, Anthony. "Confronting Backlash states." *Foreign Affairs* 73 (2), 1994.

Lawrence, Albert Bressand and Takatoshi Ito. "A Vision for the World Economy: Openness, Diversity, and Cohesion." Brookings Institution. Integrating National Economies Project. Washington DC, 1996.

Lindsey, B. *Against the Dead Hand: The Uncertain Struggle for Global Capitalism.* New York: John Wiley & Sons, 2002.

Lustick, Ian S. *Trapped in the War on Terror.* Philadelphia, PA: University of Pennsylvania Press, 2006.

Makiya, Kanan. "Is Iraq Viable?" *Middle East Brief* No. 30. Crown Center for Middle East Studies, Brandeis University, 2008.

Maloney, Suzanne. *Iran's Long Reach: Iran as a Pivotal State in the Muslim World.* Washington, DC: United States Institute of Peace Press, 2008.

Mamdani, Mahmood. *Good Muslim, Bad Muslim: America, the Cold War, and the Roots of Terror.* New York: Pantheon Books, 2004.

Mammadyarov, Elmar. "Walking a Tightrope: Azerbaijan's foreign Policy Strategy in a Changing Environment," *Azerbaijan Focus*, Volume 1 (1), June-August 2009.

Mansoor A. and B. Quillin. *Migration and Remittances: Eastern Europe and the Former Soviet Union.* World Bank. Europe and Central Asia Region, 2006.

Markedonov, Sergei. "The Paradoxes of Russia's Georgia Policy." *Russia in Global Affairs*, vol.5, no.2, April-June 2007.

Matosyan, Tigran. "Europe: A Model of Replication or a Threat to Identity? The Case of Armenia." *Dynamics of National Identity and Transnational Identities in the Process of European Integration.* Elena Marushiakova (ed.). Newcastle: Cambridge Scholars Publishing, 2008.

McDermott, Roger. "Azerbaijan Deepens Military Cooperation with US and NATO." *Eurasia Daily Monitor*, vol.5, issue 173. 22 Sep 2009.

Mehdiyev, Ramiz. "Onsoz." *Azerbaijan Focus*, No: 1 (1), 2009.

Memmedyarov, Elmar and Kendir Uzerinde Yerish, "Deyishen Muhitte Azerbaycanin Harici Siyaset Strategiyasi," *Azerbaijan Focus*, No: 1 (1), 2009.

Minasyan, Sergey and Grigor Hakobyan. "Balance of Power in South Caucasus and the Probability for Resumption of War in Nagorno Karabakh." Armenian News Network, Groong. 11 Apr 2006.

Mitchell, Jeanene. "EU Neighborhood Initiatives and Prospects for Improved Energy Governance in the broader Black Sea-South Caucasus Region," *Azerbaijan Focus*, Volume 1 (2), September-November 2009.

Mkrtchyan, Tigran and Tabib Huseynov, Kakha Gogolashvili. "The European Union and the South Caucasus. Three Perspectives on the Future of the European Project from the Caucasus." *Europe in Dialogue* 2009/ 01. Bertelsmann Stifung. Gütersloh 2009.

Murinson, Alexander. "The secessions of Abkhazia and Nagorny Karabagh. The roots and patterns of development of post-Soviet micro-secessions in Transcaucasia," *Central Asian Survey* (March, 2004) 23 (1).

Nakash, Yitzhak. *Reaching for Power: The Shi'a in the Modern Arab World.* Princeton, NJ: Princeton University Press, 2006.

Nasr, Vali, and Ray Takeyh. "Costs of Containing Iran: Washington's Misguided New Middle East Policy." *Foreign Affairs* 87 (1), 2008.

Nasr, Vali. *The Shia Revival: How Conflicts within Islam will Shape the Future.* New York: W. W. Norton 2006.

Nelson, R., and S. G. Winter. *An Evolutionary Theory of Economic Change.* Cambridge: The Belknap Press of Harvard University press, 1982.

Nuriyev, E. *The South Caucasus at the Crossroads: Conflicts, Caspian Oil and Great Power Politics.* Berlin: Lit, 2007.

Oran, B. (ed.), *Turk Dis Politikasi, Kurtulus Savasindan Bugune Olgular, Belgeler, Yorumlar* [*Turkish Foreign Policy, Facts, Documents and Comments since the War of Independence*]. Istanbul: Iletisim, 2002.

Ozcan, G. and S. Kut (eds.). *En Uzun Onyil, Turkiye'nin Ulusal Guvenlik ve Dis Politika Gundeminde Doksanli Yillar* [*The Longest Decade; 1990s in Turkey's National Security and Foreign Policy Agenda*], Istanbul, Buke, 2000.

Papava, V. "Necroeconomics—the Theory of Post-Communist Transformation of an Economy." *International Journal of Social Economics*, 29 Sep 10.

Papava, V. G., and T. A. Beridze. *Ocherki politicheskoi ekonomii postkommunisticheskogo kapitalizma (opyt Gruzii)* (*Essays on the Political Economy of Post-Communist Capitalism (the Georgian Experience)*). Moscow: Delo i servis Publishers, 2005.

Papava, V. *Necroeconomics: The Political Economy of Post-Communist Capitalism.* New York: Universe, 2005.

Papava, V., and M. Tokmazishvili. "Necroeconomic Foundations and the Development of Extraordinary European Council." Brussels, 1 Sep, 2008, 12594/08. Presidency Conclusions. Brussels: Council of the European Union, 2008.

Petro, Nikolai. "The legal Case for Russian Intervention in Georgia." *Fordham International Law Journal*, vol. 32, Issue 5 (May 2009).

Pollack, Kenneth and Ray Takeyh. "Taking on Tehran." *Foreign Affairs* 84 (2), 2005.

Priego, Alberto: "NATO cooperation towards South Caucasus," in: *Caucasian Review of Internation Affairs*, Baku, 1/2008.

Rashid, Ahmed. *Descent into Chaos: The US and the Failure of Nation Building in Pakistan, Afghanistan, and Central Asia.* New York: Viking, 2008.

Ritter, Scott. *Target Iran: The Truth about the White House's Plans for Regime Change.* New York: Nation Books, 2006.

Robert Mabro, "The Oil Weapon: Can It Be Used Today?" *Harvard International Review* 29 (2007).

Ross, Dennis. "Considering Soviet Threats to the Persian Gulf." International Security 6 (2), 1981.

Rubin, "Turkey and the Newly Independent States of Central Asia and the Transcaucasus."

Rumer, B. Z. "The Potential for Political Instability and Regional Conflicts", A. Banuazizi & M. Weiner (ed.), *The New Geopolitics of Central Asia and Its Borderlands*, London, I. B. Tauris, 1994.

Rummel, R. J. "Democracies Don't Fight Democracies." *Peace Magazine.* May-June 1999, (October 27, 2009).

Rywkin, Michael. "The Great Game Revisited: The Larger Geopolitical, American Foreign Policy Interests." 2004, No: 26.

Sahakyan, V. and A. Atanesyan. "Democratization in Armenia: Some Trends of Political Culture and Behavior." *Demokratizatsiya: The Journal of Post-Soviet Democratization.* Vol.14, No. 3, Summer 2006.

Samedzade, Z. *Etapy bol'shogo puti. Ekonomika Azerbaidzhana za polveka, ee osnovnye realii i perspektivy (Stages in a Long Journey. The Economy of Azerbaijan over Fifty Years, Its Main Realities and Prospects).* Baku: Nurlar Publishers, 2004.

Sánchez-Andrés, A., and J. M. March-Poquet. "The Construction of Market Institutions in Russia: A view from the Institutionalism of Polanyi." *Journal of Economic Issues.* XXXVI/3, 2002.

Schaffer, Brenda. "Iran's Role in the South Caucasus and Caspian Region: Diverging Views of the US and Europe." *Iran and Its Neighbors: Diverging Views on a Strategic Region.* Eugene Whitlock (Ed.), Stiftung Wissenschaft und Politik/German Institute for International and Security Affairs, Berlin, July 2003.

Schofield, C. & M. Pratt, "Claims to the Caspian Sea." *Jane's Intelligence Review,* February 1996.

Smith, D. C. "Loans to Japanese borrowers" *Japanese International Economies,* 17/3, 2003.

Soysal, I. (Hg.). *The Security of the Caspian Sea Region.* Oxford, 2001.

Starr, S. F. "The Investment Climate in Central Asia and the Caucasus." *Russian-Eurasian Renaissance? US Trade and Investment in Russia and Eurasia*. J. H. Kalicki and E. K. Lawson, (eds.). Washington, D.C.: Woodrow Wilson Center Press, 2003.

Stern, Jonathan. "Soviet and Russian Gas" in *Gas to Europe: The Strategies of four Major Suppliers*. Robert Mabro and Ian Wybrew-Bond, editors, Oxford University Press, 1999.

Sullivan, Robert R. "Saudi Arabia in International Politics." *The Review of Politics* 32 (4), 1970.

Takeyh, Ray. *Hidden Iran: Paradox and Power in the Islamic Republic*. New York: Times Book, 2006.

Takeyh, Ray. *The Origins of the Eisenhower Doctrine: the US, Britain, and Nasser's Egypt, 1953-57*. New York: St. Martin's Press, 2000.

Telhami, Shibley. "The Ties That Bind: Americans, Arabs, and Israelis After September 11." *Foreign Affairs* 83 (2), 2004.

Torbakov, Igor. "Abashidze Falls, Power Shifts In The South Caucasus," Eurasia Daily Monitor, Volume: 1 Issue: 5. <http://www.jamestown.org/articles-by-author/?no_cache=1&tx_cablanttnewsstaffrelation_pi1%5Bauthor%5D=163>.

Trenin, Dmitri. "Toward A New Euro-Atlantic 'Hard' Security Agenda: Prospects for Trilateral US-EU-Russia Cooperation."

Winrow, G. *Turkish Views on Eurasia*. Istanbul 2001.

Yapıcı, Merve İrem. "Kafkasyanın Sorunlu Bölgesi: Güney Osetya," *QAKA*, C. II, 2007.

Yastrzhembsky, Sergey. "Trust, not double standards: What Russia expects from the EU."

Yetiv, Steve R. *The Absence of Grand Strategy: The United States in the Persian Gulf, 1972-2005*. Baltimore, MD: Johns Hopkins University Press, 2008.

Yilmaz, Bagimsizlik Sonrasi. *Ermeni-Rusya Iliskileri, Rusya Çalışmaları Stratejik Arastirmalar II*. Ankara: TASAM Yayınları, 2009.

Yilmaz, Uluslararasi. "Terorism ve Ermeni Terorunun Analizi." *Journal of Qafqaz University*, Number 18, 2006.

Zverev, Alexei. "Ethnic Conflicts in the Caucasus 1988-1994."

Андреева Г. М. Психология социального познания. М.: Аспент Пресс, 2000.

Арутюнян Л.А. Новые тенденции миграции в Армении. В сб.: Миграционная ситуация в странах СНГ. М.: Комплекс-Прогресс, 1999.

Бадурашвили И.Н., Гугушвили Т. Вынужденная миграция в Грузии.. В сб.: Миграционная ситуация в странах СНГ. М.: Комплекс-Прогресс, 1999.

Бергер П. Л. Культурная динамика глобализации / Многоликая глобализация / Под ред. П. Бергера и С. Хантингтона; пер. с англ. М.: Аспект Пресс, 2004.

Исмаилов Э. Новый регионализм на Кавказе: концептуальный подход // Кавказ и глобализация. Том 1 (1), 2006.

Лом Х. Джавахети после Революции роз: Прогресс и регресс в поисках национального единства в Грузии. Рабочий доклад Европейского центра по делам меньшинств №38 (апрель 2006).

Лункин Р. Протестантизм и глобализация на просторах Евразии / Религия и глобализация на просторах Евразии / Под ред. А. Малашенко и С. Филатова; Моск. Центр Карнеги. М.: Неостром, 2005.

Малашенко, А. и С. Филатова. М.: Российская политическая энциклопедия, 2007.

Мурадов Ш.М., Гезалова А.К., Эфендиев Р. Дж. Глобализация, демографическое развитие и трудовая активность населения в Азербайджане. Баку: Элм, 2007.

Погосян А.,Хоецян А., Манасян М. Особенности миграции населения Республики Армения. Центр миграционных исследований проблемы миграции и опыт ее регулирования в полиэтничном Кавказском регионе. Тезисы международной научной конференции. / Под общей редакцией Ж. Зайончковской и В. Белозерова. Ставропольский госуниверситет. Центр изучения проблем вынужденной миграции в СНГ. М., 2001.

Сванидзе Г., Кокоев К. Эмиграция из Грузии и ее причины. Центральная Азия и Кавказ, 4 (22), 2002.

Силантьев Р. Религиозный фактор во внешнеполитических конфликтах на Кавказе / Религия и конфликт.

Харатян Г. Армения: Религия // Центральная Евразия — 2008. Аналитический ежегодник. Швеция, 2009.

# CONTRIBUTOR BIOGRAPHIES

**Oksana Antonenko**

Oksana Antonenko is a Senior Fellow and the Program Director for Russia and Eurasia at the International Institute for Strategic Studies. Ms. Antonenko oversees the IISS's work on Russia, Central Asia, other CIS countries and the South Caucasus. Ms. Antonenko contributes to IISS publications, provides briefings for IISS members worldwide, presents papers and reports at international conferences, and comments on developments in Eurasia for international press and media. She frequently travels to the region and provides expert advice to policymakers there, as well as in Europe and the US, on conflict resolution.

**Mustafa Aydın**

Professor Mustafa Aydın is Rector at Kadir Has University in Turkey since February 2010. He graduated from the Department of International Relations, Ankara University in 1988. He obtained his M.A. in International Relations and Strategic Studies (1991) and his Ph.D. in Political Sciences and International Relations (1994) from Lancaster University, UK. He later joined Ankara University's Faculty of Political Sciences in 1995 as assistant professor, becoming associate professor in 1999 and full professor in 2005. He was the founding head of the Global and Regional Studies Program. Between 2005 and 2009, he worked for the University of Economics and Technology as the Head of the Department of International Relations. He was also member of the same University's Senate and Governing Board Member of both Faculty of Administrative and Economic Sciences and the Graduate School.

Dr. Mustafa Aydın is a member of the Planning and Evaluation Board of the Turkish General Staff's Strategic Research and Study Centre (SAREM), the Advisory Board of the Centre for Strategic Research (SAM) of the

Ministry of Foreign Affairs and the Governing Board of the World Council for Middle Eastern Studies (WOCMES). He is also the President of the International Relations Council of Turkey, Director of the International Policy Research Institute (IPRI) and the Co-Coordinator for the International Commission on the Black Sea. He is a referee for the EU INTAS Young Scientists Fellowship Program, the Social Sciences and Humanities Research Council (Canada), and the Social Sciences Research Committee of the Scientific and Technological Research Council of Turkey (TUBITAK-SOBAG). Dr. Aydın serves as an advisor for the International Centre for Black Sea Studies (ICBSS) and the Hellenic Center for European Studies (EKEM).

## Albert Bressand

Albert Bressand is Director at the Center for Energy, Marine Transportation and Public Policy at Columbia University. He is also a member of the faculty of the World Economic Forum, and has chaired a number of sessions at the Davos Annual Meetings. He serves on the Board of the New York Energy Forum, on the Steering Committee of the Sovereign Wealth Funds initiative of Chaire du Développement Durable at Université Paris-Dauphine and on the Advisory Council of the Lenfest Center for Sustainable Energy at Columbia. Bressand formerly led the Global Business Environment department at Royal Dutch Shell's global headquarters in London from 2003-2006. Bressand has also been appointed Special Adviser to the EU Commissioner for Energy in Brussels. Previously, Bressand was managing director and cofounder of Promethée, a nonprofit, Paris-based think tank specializing in the emerging global networked economy and its implications for corporate strategies, capital markets and international economic relations. Bressand also served as Economic Advisor to the Minister of Foreign Affairs of France and held key positions with the French Institute for International Relations and the World Bank.

Bressand holds advanced degrees from École Polytechnique in Paris, École Nationale des Ponts et Chaussées and Paris-Sorbonne, as well as an MPA and a Ph.D. from the Kennedy School of Government at Harvard University. He has published notably in *Foreign Affairs, International*

*Affairs*, *Futuribles*, *Politique Internationale*, *Revue d'Economie Financiére*, and *Le Monde*.


## Ariel Cohen

Dr. Ariel Cohen is a Senior Research Fellow at The Heritage Foundation, having joined Heritage in 1992. Dr. Cohen brings firsthand knowledge of the former Soviet Union and the Middle East through a wide range of studies, covering issues such as economic development and political reform in the former Soviet republics, US energy security, the global War on Terrorism and the continuing conflict in the Middle East. He earned his doctorate at the Fletcher School of Law and Diplomacy at Tufts University in Massachusetts. He has served as a consultant to both the Executive Branch and the private sector on policy toward Russia, Eastern and Central Europe, the Caucasus, and Central Asia. He participated in a long-term study known as Russia 2025 conducted by the World Economic Forum and in the Multilateral Deterrence Study for the Office of the Secretary of Defense (OSD), as well as in other projects. He is often called upon to testify on Russian and Eurasian politics, economics, and law before the US Congress, and regularly provides commentary on Russian, Eurasian and Middle Eastern affairs for ABC, BBC, CNN, FOX and all three national TV channels in Russia. He was a weekly contributor to the Voice of America radio and TV programs for eight years.


## Robert M. Cutler

Dr. Robert M. Cutler is Senior Research Fellow at the Institute of European, Russian & Eurasian Studies at Carleton University, Ottawa. He is also Research Fellow at the Institute for the Study of Coherence and Emergence (Boston), and Non-Resident Scholar at the Institute for Near East and Gulf Military Analysis (Dubai). He was educated at the Massachusetts Institute of Technology (B.Sc.), Geneva Graduate Institute of International Studies (Gallatin Fellow) and The University of Michigan (Ph.D.), and has held research and teaching appointments at major universities in the United States, Canada, France, Switzerland and Russia. He then expanded into policy analysis and consulting, foremost as an Energy Security and Geo-economics Specialist now covering the whole of Eurasia with a special focus on Central, South and Southwest Asia, with a secondary focus on Europe, Russia and China. He consults for international institutions, think tanks, governments and the private sector, with experience over the entire range of skills involving negotiation and strategy, planning and execution, design and implementation, and evaluation and instruction; and on topics from international energy security and geo-economics to Caspian Sea region investment advice to human and minority rights (including immigration/asylum applications to the US and Canada) to the organizational design of international institutions. Dr. Cutler has won numerous competitive research grants and fellowships, serving also on a half-dozen academic-journal and policy-review editorial boards, in addition to executive committees of professional scholarly and policy research organizations.

### Kevin DeCorla-Souza

Kevin DeCorla-Souza has worked as a Senior Associate at IFC International since September 2011. Previously, he was an energy analyst at the Science Applications International Corporation. Mr. DeCorla-Souza conducts expert economic, technical, and policy analyses of energy projects and systems for public and private sector clients. Through more than 5 years experience in energy consulting, Mr. DeCorla-Souza has developed an in-depth understanding of US and international oil, gas, and electricity markets and infrastructure, including subject matter expertise in liquefied natural gas (LNG). Mr. DeCorla-Souza has advanced economic and financial modeling skills, including experience estimating capital expenditures for large infrastructure projects, forecasting energy prices, and building discounted cash flow and project finance models. Mr. DeCorla-Souza has a background in journalism, and has experience presenting research to clients and before expert panels. A passionate energy professional, Mr. DeCorla-Souza, in his free time, writes freelance articles on international energy security with Dr. Ariel Cohen of the Heritage Foundation.

## Rauf Garagozov

Dr. Rauf Garagozov is a leading research fellow at the Center for Strategic Studies (Baku, Azerbaijan). Prior to his current position, he also served as a member of the Editorial Board of *The Caucasus and Globalization* journal. He has authored over eighty articles, several book chapters and books, and was a Fulbright Professor at Washington University in St. Louis in 2002-2003. Dr. Garagozov holds a Ph.D. in Psychology from Moscow State University.

## Elmir Guliyev

Elmir Guliyev is Director of the Department of Geoculture at the Institute of Strategic Studies of the Caucasus. He has nine fundamental works and over 50 articles and translations to his name, all of them dealing with the history and philosophy of Islam, Muslim law and the dialogue between the cultures. In 2002, he completed a translation of the meanings of the Holy Quran into Russian and later commented on it. Cultural security in Central Eurasia is one of his current interests.

## Uwe Halbach

Dr. Uwe Halbach is a Senior Associate of the German Institute for International and Security Affairs. His areas of expertise are the Caucasus, Central Asia and the southern regions of Russia/non-Russian regions of the Federation.

## Glen Howard

Glen Howard is the President of The Jamestown Foundation. Mr. Howard is fluent in Russian and proficient in Azerbaijani and Arabic, and is a regional expert on the Caucasus and Central Asia. He was formerly an Analyst at the Science Applications International Corporation (SAIC) Strategic Assessment Center. His articles have appeared in *The Wall Street Journal*, the *Central Asia-Caucasus Analyst* and *Jane's Defense Weekly*. Mr.

Howard has served as a consultant to private sector and governmental agencies, including the US Department of Defense, the National Intelligence Council and major oil companies operating in Central Asia and the Middle East.

### Fariz Ismailzade

Mr. Fariz Ismailzade is Executive Vice Rector at the Azerbaijan Diplomatic Academy. Prior to joining ADA, Mr. Ismailzade has worked 10 years in NGO sector in Azerbaijan. Most recently he was Director of Political Programs at the International Republican Institute. Mr. Ismailzade has done research at the Center for Strategic and International Studies in Washington, DC. His research interests include political affairs in the Caucasus and Central Asia, energy security, and development.

Mr. Ismailzade has regularly published with *EurasiaNet, Transitions Online, Eurasia Daily Monitor, Central Asia-Caucasus Analyst, Institute for War and Peace Report*, East-West Institute, *Analysis of Current Events*, Freedom House and *Caucasus Context*. In 2009, he co-edited the book, *Azerbaijan in Global Politics: Crafting Foreign Policy*. Mr. Ismailzade holds a Masters Degree in Social and Economic Development from Washington University in St. Louis, and a B.A. in Political Science from Western University in Baku with one-year interim studies at Wesleyan University in Connecticut.

### Ramiz Mehdiyev

Dr. Ramiz Mehdiyev is the Chief-of-Staff of the Azerbaijani Presidential Administration. State Adviser and academician, Dr. Mehdiyev is a member of the Azerbaijan National Academy of Sciences and president of the Azerbaijan Association of Philosophical and Social-Political Sciences. Ramiz Mehdiyev has authored approximately 200 scholarly articles, 20 books – including several monographs – and research works on current problems in relations between nations, globalization, democratic transformations, national elite and national identity issues. His published works include: "On the Path Towards Democracy: Thinking About Heritage," "Azerbaijan: Challenges of Globalization," "Democracy in

Transitional Societies" and "Defining the Strategy of Tomorrow: Course Towards Modernization."

## Vladimer Papava

Vladimer Papava is a Senior Fellow at the Georgian Foundation for Strategic and International Studies. He is the author of more than 200 works devoted to the problems of economic theory, macroeconomics and economic/mathematical modeling, most notably, his study of economic transformation in post-Communist countries. His research is complemented by unique practical experience. In 1994-2000, serving as Minister of Economy of the Republic of Georgia, he was actively involved in fiscal reform, complete liberalization of the wheat market, institutional reforms and so on. As a member of the Georgian government, he was one of the leading participants in negotiations with the IMF and World Bank. Dr. Papava is a Member of the Parliament of Georgia and a member of the Georgian Academy of Sciences.

## John Roberts

Mr. John Roberts is Energy Security Specialist with Platts, the world's leading independent source of energy information. He has been asked to testify before several UK parliamentary committees on Turkish, Russian, Caspian and Mideast energy security issues. He has written extensively on the security of oil and gas supplies, energy diversification, European energy security, Caspian and Caucasian pipeline politics, the Southern Energy Corridor, as well as European and Eurasian energy markets. His latest book, *Pipeline Politics: The Caspian and Global Energy Security,* is due to be published shortly by Platts and the Royal Institute of International Affairs, London (the US publisher is the Brookings Institution). In 1996, Mr. Roberts also authored the book, *Caspian Pipelines.*

## Barry Rubin

Professor Barry Rubin is director of the Global Research for International Affairs (GLORIA) Center and a professor at the Interdisciplinary Center in Herzliya, Israel. He is editor of *the Middle East Review of International Affairs (MERIA) Journal* and of the *Turkish Studies* journal. He writes the Middle East column for the *Jerusalem Post*. His latest books are *The Truth About Syria* (Palgrave-MacMillan, April 2007) and *The Future of the Middle East* (Sharpe, in press). His recent edited works include *Iraq After Saddam* (Sharpe, in press), Global Survey of Islamism (Sharpe, in press), the three-volume collection *Political Islam* (Routledge) and an eight-volume introductory book series to the Middle East (Sharpe, in press).

## S. Frederick Starr

Dr. S. Frederick Starr is Chairman of the Central Asia-Caucasus Institute and Silk Road Studies Program. He is a Research Professor at the Paul H. Nitze School of Advanced International Studies, Johns Hopkins University. Dr. Starr for several years served as Rector Pro Tem of the University of Central Asia, and is a Trustee of the Eurasia Foundation. Prior to founding the Central Asia-Caucasus Institute, he served as founding Director of the Kennan Institute for Advanced Russian Studies 1974-79; as Vice-President for Academic Affairs at Tulane University in 1979-1982; as Scholar-in-Residence of the Historical New Orleans Foundation in 1982-83. He was appointed President of Oberlin College in 1983, a position he held for eleven years. In 1994-96, he served as President of the Aspen Institute. Dr. Starr served as an advisor on Soviet Affairs to President Reagan in 1985-86 and to President George H.W. Bush in 1990-92. Starr holds a Ph.D. in History from Princeton University, an M.A. from King's College, Cambridge University, and a BA from Yale University.

## Udo Steinbach

Dr. Udo Steinbach is a Middle East specialist who teaches at the Centre of Near and Middle East Studies at Philipps University in Marburg, Germany and is professor of International Politics at the University of Hamburg. He was Director of the German Institute for Middle East Studies, a research institute dealing with the contemporary Middle East, North Africa and Central Asia from 1976 to January 2007, before becoming Director of GIGA Institute of Middle East Studies (IMES) from February to December, 2007.

Dr. Steinbach was awarded a Ph.D. in Arabic and Islamic Studies in Freiburg and Basel and has written numerous books and publications on political and social developments in the Middle East. He is an adviser and expert for various public and private institutions. His main areas of research are political and social change in the Arab countries and Turkey, Iran, Afghanistan and Pakistan; the manifestations of political Islam; and the Middle East in the international system.


## Dmitri Trenin

Dmitri Trenin, Director of the Carnegie Moscow Center, has been with the Center since its inception. He also chairs the Research Council and the Foreign and Security Policy Program. From 1993-1997, Trenin held a post as a Senior Research Fellow at the Institute of Europe in Moscow, and in 1993, he was a Senior Research Fellow at the NATO Defense College in Rome. He served in the Soviet and Russian armed forces from 1972 to 1993, including experience working as a liaison officer in the External Relations Branch of the Group of Soviet Forces (stationed in Potsdam) and as a staff member of the delegation to the US-Soviet nuclear arms talks in Geneva from 1985 to 1991. He also taught at the war studies department of the Military Institute from 1986 to 1993. Dr. Trenin retired from the Russian Army in 1993. He received his Ph.D. from the Institute of the USA and Canada in 1984.